THE MU

THE MURIEL RUKEYSER ERA

SELECTED PROSE

MURIEL RUKEYSER

EDITED BY ERIC KEENAGHAN
AND ROWENA KENNEDY-EPSTEIN

CORNELL UNIVERSITY PRESS
Ithaca and London

All material by Muriel Rukeyser © Muriel Rukeyser.
Reprinted by permission of the Estate of Muriel
Rukeyser and ICM Partners.

Editors' Introduction copyright © 2023 by Rowena
Kennedy-Epstein and Eric Keenaghan.

Volume copyright © 2023 by Cornell University.

Full bibliographic information for texts by Muriel
Rukeyser appears in the Appendix.

All other authors' permissions appear in the
Acknowledgments and Permissions.

All rights reserved. Except for brief quotations in
a review, this book, or parts thereof, must not be
reproduced in any form without permission in
writing from the publisher. For information, address
Cornell University Press, Sage House, 512 East State
Street, Ithaca, New York 14850. Visit our website
at cornellpress.cornell.edu.

First published 2023 by Cornell University Press.

Library of Congress Cataloging-in-Publication Data
Names: Rukeyser, Muriel, 1913–1980, author. |
   Keenaghan, Eric, editor. | Kennedy-Epstein, Rowena,
   editor.
Title: The Muriel Rukeyser era : selected prose / Muriel
   Rukeyser; edited by Eric Keenaghan and Rowena
   Kennedy-Epstein.
Description: Ithaca [New York] : Cornell University Press,
   2023. | Includes bibliographical references and index.
Identifiers: LCCN 2023011174 (print) | LCCN
   2023011175 (ebook) | ISBN 9781501771743
   (hardcover) | ISBN 9781501771750 (paperback) |
   ISBN 9781501771774 (epub)
Subjects: LCSH: Rukeyser, Muriel, 1913–1980—Criticism
   and interpretation. | LCGFT: Creative nonfiction.
Classification: LCC PS3535.U4 M87 2023 (print) |
   LCC PS3535.U4 (ebook) | DDC 818/.5208—dc23/
   eng/20230515
LC record available at https://lccn.loc.gov/2023011174
LC ebook record available at https://lccn.loc.gov/
   2023011175

*New York formed me and bore me, Spain made me,
California tore me apart, my child and my wilderness,
Gave me a ship to be my vision of life*

—Muriel Rukeyser, note on a draft table of contents for her *Selected Poems*, c. 1950–1951

Contents

Acknowledgments and Permissions   xi
List of Abbreviations   xv
Note on This Textual Edition   xvii

Editors' Introduction   1

All You Have to Do Is Challenge Them:
The Muriel Rukeyser Era, Eric Keenaghan
and Rowena Kennedy-Epstein

Author's Introduction   30

Biographical Statement for "Under
Forty: A Symposium on American
Literature and the Younger
Generation of American Jews"
(1944), Muriel Rukeyser

Part I. The Usable Truth: Five Talks on Communication and Poetry

1. "The Fear of Poetry" (1940, 1941)   39
2. "The Speed of the Image" (1940)   57
3. "Belief and Poetry" (1940)   67
4. "Poetry and Peace" (1940)   77
5. "Communication and Poetry" (1940)   90

CONTENTS

PART II. TWENTIETH-CENTURY RADICALISM: ON POLITICS, SOCIETY, AND CULTURE

6. "The Flown Arrow: The Aftermath of the Sacco-Vanzetti Case" (1932) — 103
7. "From Scottsboro to Decatur" (1933) — 113
8. "Women and Scottsboro" (1933) — 123
9. "Barcelona on the Barricades" (1936) — 127
10. "Barcelona, 1936" (1936) — 134
11. "Words and Images" (1943) — 145
12. "War and Poetry" (1945) — 150
13. "A Pane of Glass" (1953) — 152
14. "She Came to Us" (1958) — 159
15. "The Killing of the Children" (1973) — 167
16. "The Uses of Fear" (1978) — 172

PART III. MEDIA AND DEMOCRATIC EDUCATION: A PHOTO-TEXT AND RADIO SCRIPTS

17. "So Easy to See" (1946), Photography-and-Text Collaboration with Berenice Abbott — 179
18. From *Sunday at Nine* (1949), Scripts for Two Radio Broadcasts — 184

    Series Introduction
    Episode One: Emily Dickinson — 186
    Episode Four: The Blues — 195

PART IV. MODERNIST INTERVENTIONS: ON GENDER, POETRY, AND POETICS

19. "Modern Trends: American Poetry" (1932) — 203

CONTENTS

20. "Long Step Ahead Taken by Gregory in New Epic Poem" (1935), review of Horace Gregory's *Chorus for Survival* — 208

21. "In a Speaking Voice" (1939), review of Robert Frost's *Collected Poems* — 211

22. "The Classic Ground" (1941), review of Marya Zaturenska's *The Listening Landscape* — 216

23. "Nearer to the Well-Spring" (1943), review of Rainer Maria Rilke's *Sonnets to Orpheus* — 220

24. "A Simple Theme" (1949), review of Charlotte Marletto's *Jewel of Our Longing* — 224

25. "A Lorca Evening" (1951) — 229

26. "Many Keys" (1957), on women's poetry — 232

27. "Lyrical 'Rage'" (1957), review of Kenneth Rexroth's *In Defense of the Earth* — 242

28. "A Crystal for the Metaphysical" (1966), review of Marianne Moore's *Tell Me, Tell Me: Granite, Steel, and Other Topics* — 246

29. "Poetry and the Unverifiable Fact" (1968) — 252

30. "The Music of Translation" (1971) — 267

31. "Thoreau and Poetry" (1972) — 277

32. "Glitter and Wounds, Several Wildnesses" (1973), review of Anne Sexton's *The Book of Folly* — 290

33. "The Life to Which I Belong" (1974), review of Franz Kafka's *Letters to Felice* — 298

34. "Women of Words: A Prefatory Note" (1974)   304

Appendix: Bibliographic and Archival Information for Selections by Muriel Rukeyser   309

Notes on Contributors   315

Selected Bibliography   317

Index   329

Acknowledgments and Permissions

We wish to begin by thanking Bill and Rebecca Rukeyser, Muriel's son and granddaughter, whose support of this project from its inception has been vital. They gave us their blessing and the estate's permission to publish or reprint all the materials by Rukeyser appearing in this volume. Our editor at Cornell University Press, Mahinder Kingra, finally gave this collection a home. A community of Rukeyser scholars—including Elisabeth Däumer, Catherine Gander, Stefania Heim, Vivian Pollak, Jan Heller Levi, and Jan Freeman—supported our efforts with this and other Rukeyser-related endeavors. Tamara Kawar and Tina Dubois at ICM Partners provided timely assistance and coordination with the Muriel Rukeyser Estate. The keen eyes and guidance of Cornell University Press's Jennifer Savran Kelly and Lori Rider, our production editor and copyeditor, respectively, helped bring the manuscript through the final editing and production processes. Lisa DeBoer assembled the index.

Eric began this undertaking many years ago. He would like to thank Rowena for joining him when the project was stalled. Her assistance in paring back the selections, giving the volume shape, and bringing the work to completion has been invaluable. Through the Faculty Research Award Program, the University at Albany (SUNY) and the SUNY Research Foundation funded three archival trips to the Library of Congress. Staff members at New York Public Library's Berg Collection and the Library of Congress's Manuscript Division provided much assistance during and following these trips. Barbara Bair, the Manuscript Division's specialist in literature, culture, and arts, especially, has been a proactive supporter. Many thanks also to Rob Casper, the head of the Library of Congress's Poetry and Literature Center, for enthusiastically putting us into contact with her. Two of Eric's former research assistants, James Searle and Farhana Islam, helped transcribe some of this volume's materials. Cassandra Laity welcomed Eric's first edited version of Rukeyser's lost essay "Many Keys" for the inaugural issue of

Feminist Modernist Studies. Many other colleagues and friends—in and outside the worlds of academia and poetry—urged the project's completion. Eric is especially grateful for the support and interest of Rachel Blau DuPlessis, Lynne Tillman, Katharine Umsted, and his husband, Jeffrey Lependorf.

After being immersed in this archival material for many years while working on other books, Rowena was excited to join Eric on this project and make the material available to a wider audience. She would like to thank him for being such a generous and knowledgeable collaborator, and for the truly enormous effort he has put into transcribing and editing these texts. This has been a labor of love, evidenced in his attention to detail and care for Rukeyser's work. The research for this work has been supported by the University of Bristol Faculty Research Fund, which has sponsored trips to Rukeyser's archives at the New York Public Library and the Library of Congress. As always, Rowena is so grateful for the support and love of her partner, Casey, and her children, Augie and Perry.

All material by Muriel Rukeyser is copyright Muriel Rukeyser, and reprinted by permission of the Estate of Muriel Rukeyser and ICM Partners. Some selections originally appeared in *American Poetry Review*, *Contemporary Jewish Record*, *Daily Worker*, *Decision*, *Discovery*, *Henry David Thoreau: Studies and Commentaries*, *Housatonic*, *Kenyon Review*, *Life and Letters To-day*, *New Masses*, *New Republic*, *New Statesman* (UK), *New York Times*, *Parnassus*, *Poetry*, *Saturday Review*, *Scripps College Bulletin*, *Vassar Miscellany News*, *The War Poets*, *The World of Translation*, and *The World Split Open*. The following previously unpublished texts are archived in the Papers of Muriel Rukeyser, Manuscript Division, Library of Congress, Washington, DC: *The Four Fears* (cover image), *The Usable Truth: Five Talks on Communication and Poetry*, "So Easy to See," *Sunday at Nine*, "Many Keys," "She Came to Us" (unpublished version), "The Killing of the Children," and "The Uses of Fear" (unpublished version). "Women and Scottsboro" is previously unpublished and archived at the Muriel Rukeyser Collection of Papers, Henry W. and Albert A. Berg Collection of English and American Literature, New York Public Library, Astor, Lenox, and Tilden Foundations, New York, New York. Full bibliographic information about all the selected texts by Muriel Rukeyser appears in the appendix.

Some editorial notes for "Many Keys" are derived in part from "'There Is No Glass Woman': Muriel Rukeyser's Lost Essay 'Many Keys,'" an article by Eric Keenaghan published in *Feminist Modernist Studies*, 2018,

ACKNOWLEDGMENTS AND PERMISSIONS

copyright Taylor and Francis, available online: http://www.tandfonline.com/10.1080/24692921.2017.1368883. Editorial notes for "Barcelona, 1936" are derived in part from *"Barcelona, 1936" and Selections from the Spanish Civil War Archive*, edited by Rowena Kennedy-Epstein, Lost and Found: The CUNY Poetic Document Initiative, series 2, no. 6, 2011, copyright Ammiel Alcalay and Lost and Found.

Permission to reprint quoted material in Rukeyser's selections has been granted by Patrick Gregory, on behalf of the Horace Gregory and Marya Zaturenska literary estate, and Bradford Morrow, on behalf of the Kenneth Rexroth literary estate. All materials by Anne Sexton reprinted by permission of SLL/Sterling Lord Literistic, Inc. Copyright by Anne Sexton, % Linda Sexton, Literary Executor. All other authors' materials cited by Rukeyser or by the editors are in the public domain, are fair use, or have been edited down by the editors to comply with fair use standards.

Our work on this project was motivated by the enthusiasm of the graduate and undergraduate students who, over the years, have been excited by their first encounters with Muriel Rukeyser and her work. Their energy and new interpretations have revitalized our own relationships to Rukeyser's career as an author and activist. We dedicate this volume to our students, past and present, and to the next generations of readers who will carry on our work to illuminate that the twentieth century was, indeed, the Muriel Rukeyser Era.

Abbreviations

CP *The Collected Poems of Muriel Rukeyser*, edited by Janet Kaufman and Anne E. Herzog with Jan Heller Levi
ct copytext
fc fair copy
holo. holograph document or notes
LC Draft archived at the Muriel Rukeyser Papers, Manuscript Division, Library of Congress, Washington, D.C. Followed by series and container number.
ts typescript draft or correspondence

Note on This Textual Edition

For each selection, either the version Muriel Rukeyser published during her lifetime or the fair copy she prepared for publication serves as this edition's copytext. For the political essays "She Came to Us" and "The Uses of Fear" (originally published as "The Fear"), the editors have chosen to restore the fullest versions based, respectively, on Rukeyser's typescript drafts and fair copy. Likely cut for space, these two articles' abridged published versions are less persuasive than Rukeyser's original ones. Minor editorial changes in the first published versions create tonal shifts contributing to the obfuscation, if not erasure, of Rukeyser's activist and aesthetic vision.

For previously unpublished work, the copytext is either the latest dated surviving draft, the undated draft judged by the editors as the latest surviving version, or the fair copy incorporating the most edits. Only significant differences in earlier versions and unincorporated annotations are documented in this edition's notes. The editors have opted to limit bibliographic notes to render Rukeyser's prose more accessible to students and general readers. Recovering her lost and forgotten work is this volume's chief aim. Future scholars will be free to provide a full bibliographic accounting about all these texts.

All selections have been quietly edited to correct errors, including of foreign words, as well as to introduce consistency in Rukeyser's spelling and punctuation. The editors have maintained her idiosyncratic approach to the latter, except when regularizing serial commas for consistency. As other scholars recovering her work have noted, Rukeyser, frustrated by editorial "corrections" during her lifetime, affixed her custom-made stamp "Please Believe the Punctuation" to every submitted manuscript. Bill, her son, has provided us with an image of that stamp, reproduced here. To the best of our ability, albeit sometimes testing our patience, we have observed Rukeyser's wishes. Her idiosyncratic or questionable word choices also remain untouched, and notes about them have been added when appropriate. The editors have modernized

xvii

her hyphenation of certain compound nouns, and they have corrected her hyphenation of adverbial phrases. Now-outdated spellings of some words (like *theatre* for *theater*) are preserved, and the possessive form of all singular proper nouns (such as *Jeffers's*) has been regularized for consistency.

During her lectures and radio broadcast scripts, Rukeyser often improvised sections, working from fragmentary notes. Most improvisation notes from her lectures' and scripts' fair copies are relegated to annotations, but the editors have included a few improvisation notes in the main body of *The Usable Truth* lectures because Rukeyser references that material directly thereafter in her talks' fully scripted portions. For those exceptions, the editors' annotations explain and interpret Rukeyser's fragments to assist readers. Other editorial notes avoid interpretative glosses of Rukeyser's ideas, instead offering only contextualizing information.

Notes are provided to specific editions, monthlies, pamphlets, and private correspondence Rukeyser referenced when those materials have been located. Most of her references to daily periodicals are not annotated. To conform with fair use standards, the editors have reduced Rukeyser's outsized quotations from other writers' works that are not in the public domain. Such instances are signaled in the notes. If material has been excised from those passages, the location of cut lines is indicated by a bracketed ellipsis. Lengthier quotations meriting full reproduction have been permitted by the respective authors' literary estates or copyright holders, as noted in this volume's acknowledgments. The editors have abridged only "A Crystal for the Metaphysical," Rukeyser's review of Marianne Moore, to render a clearer treatment of her subject with reduced citation. With a few exceptions, recorded in the annotations, the editors have quietly corrected Rukeyser's misquotations of her sources.

In keeping with the *Chicago Manual of Style*, 17th edition, the editors' annotations do not specify source texts for classic works that are in the public domain or available in multiple editions. Full citations are provided for canonical authors' paraliterary published essays, journals, and letters, as well as for specific editions used and cited by Rukeyser herself. Bibliographic information about recordings played during the selected episodes of *Sunday at Nine*, as identified by surviving engineering notes, appear in the annotations.

PLEASE BELIEVE THE
PUNCTUATION

Editors' Introduction
All You Have to Do Is Challenge Them:
The Muriel Rukeyser Era

ERIC KEENAGHAN AND ROWENA KENNEDY-EPSTEIN

In autumn 1947, two important events happened in the life of Muriel Rukeyser (1913–1980). She gave birth to her only child, choosing motherhood as a queer, single woman when doing so was deemed not merely unconventional but scandalous. She also submitted to Doubleday *The Green Wave* (1948), a collection later considered for the prestigious Bollingen Prize for Poetry. These major milestones coincided with her struggle to implement revisions to an unrealized off-Broadway production of her antifascist feminist verse-play *The Middle of the Air*, as well as her adapting *The Usable Truth*, a 1940 lecture series on the uses of poetry in times of crisis, for workshops offered to union members and veterans at San Francisco's California Labor School. The postwar national political climate was inhospitable to such a mode of living and writing as Rukeyser's, though. That November, the House Un-American Activities Committee (HUAC) had become increasingly active, holding hearings on alleged communist activities in Hollywood and initiating a period of intensifying political repression and blacklisting that eventually caught up Rukeyser and many of her friends. When it was formed in 1938, HUAC was interested in Rukeyser because of her political publications since her return from the first days of the Spanish Civil War. After she applied for a government position in the Office of War Information in 1942, she was officially placed under surveillance by the FBI.[1]

The Green Wave is a response to this moment of anti-leftist hysteria. In its poems, Rukeyser wrestles with the ominous postwar climate's authoritarian politics. The volume opens with "Water Night," a poem preoccupied with isolation and surveillance. "The farthest shore" seems "darker" than when "I go to sleep," Rukeyser writes in its opening lines.[2] The next poem's very title, "Eyes of Night-Time," ominously tracks her sense of being watched.[3] Throughout the collection, she depicts her surveilled body and interior sense of self as made grotesque in the shadow of war, nuclear disaster, and failed personal connections.

But *The Green Wave* does not just dwell on its author's sense of her negative and limiting circumstances. Its poems also turn away from what Rukeyser would later call this period's "dark beginnings," as she moved toward a vision of transnational anti-fascist feminism.[4] Even amid an ominous sociopolitical environment, Rukeyser lays claim to possibility and hope. "My dark around me let shine one ray," she writes in "Eyes of Night-Time," thus indicating her consciousness of how "in this almost total dark" there is "the one broad fact of light."[5] Her first translations of Mexican poet Octavio Paz and of Mao Tatua's Raris, or Native chants from the Marquesas Islands, appear here as well, signaling her deepening commitment to theories of translation as a form of transcultural, human connection. Decades later, she would put it the following way: translators end up betraying one world order, and to realize a more democratic one, they "must dive far underneath into a place where we share experience."[6] *The Green Wave* ends with three astonishing long poems about the radical possibilities of women's writing: "Easter Eve, 1945," "Elegy in Joy," and "Nine Poems for the Unborn Child." These poems lyricize Rukeyser's developing ideas about the intersections of anti-fascism, poetic process, birth, and feminism. In *The Usable Truth* lectures, she had already begun to develop

---

1. Federal Bureau of Investigation, Muriel Rukeyser, file no. 77-27812, n.d. [1942–1978], FBI Records: The Vault, accessed September 30, 2022, https://vault.fbi.gov/Muriel%20Rukeyser.
2. Muriel Rukeyser, "Water Night," in *Collected Poems*, ed. Janet E. Kaufman and Anne F. Herzog with Jan Heller Levi (Pittsburgh: University of Pittsburgh Press, 2005), 253, hereafter cited as *CP*.
3. Muriel Rukeyser, "Eyes of Night-time," in *CP*, 253–254.
4. Muriel Rukeyser, "A Birth," from *Body of Waking*, in *CP*, 335.
5. Muriel Rukeyser, "Eyes of Night-Time," in *CP*, 253.
6. Muriel Rukeyser, "The Music of Translation," in this volume.

these themes, which became more central to her prose writing over the rest of her career, as is reflected in many of the essays collected here in *The Muriel Rukeyser Era*.

The Green Wave is a tour de force, and so it is unsurprising it was nominated for the Library of Congress's inaugural Bollingen Prize, along with three other volumes published in 1948: Ezra Pound's *Pisan Cantos*, William Carlos Williams's *Paterson (Book Two)*, and Randall Jarrell's *Losses*. Pound received the award, despite his book's fascist content and his broadcasting of anti-American propaganda on Italian state radio during the Second World War. Tried for treason, in lieu of prison or execution he was committed in 1946 to St. Elizabeth's Hospital for the Criminally Insane, outside Washington, DC. His receipt of the award provoked a contentious debate among the anti-communist literary left and more mainstream liberal readers.[7] Should form and aesthetic achievement be considered apart from politics? Or, as the *Partisan Review* put the question, "How far is it possible, in a lyric poem, to transform viscious and ugly matter into beautiful poetry?"[8] Many, though not all, on the Left felt such a separation impossible, but that was not the sentiment of the selection committee, which consisted of the Library of Congress's Fellows in American Letters and was chaired by T. S. Eliot. The committee's official award announcement read, in part, "To permit other considerations than that of poetic achievement would destroy the significance of the award and would in principle deny the validity of that objective perception of value on which civilized society must rest." Anti-communist leftist Dwight MacDonald cited this passage, calling the announcement "the best political statement made in this country for some time" and believing the determination of the award "the brightest political act in a dark period."[9] The jury of twelve considered it an apolitical decision, though. Aesthetically, art supposedly provided an "objective perception of value" affirming the basis for "civilized society," regardless of how antidemocratic—or, indeed, fascist—the poetic content or the author's views.

---

7. For an overview of the debate, see Robert A. Corrigan, "Ezra Pound and the Bollingen Prize Controversy," *Midcontinent American Studies Journal* 8, no. 2 (Fall 1967): 43–57, https://www.jstor.org/stable/40640705.

8. William Barrett, "A Prize for Ezra Pound," *Partisan Review*, April 1949, 347.

9. Dwight MacDonald, "Homage to Twelve Judges: An Editorial," *politics* 6 (Winter 1949): 1. MacDonald quotes from the Bollingen Prize Award Committee's announcement on March 4, 1948.

Such sentiment was shared by poets and critics like Richard Eberhart (incidentally, a friend of Rukeyser's), who asserted, "Fifty years will remove the politics and leave the poetry. *The Cantos* can be read disinterestedly, which is only to pay them their due as art."[10] That is, form can be extricated from meaning. For former anti-fascists and radicals who had become conservative anti-communist liberals during and after the war, to implicitly censor a poet for holding repugnant ideological views would be as bad as Stalin himself. In that same moment, HUAC's activities demonstrated the opposite argument to that of those determining the Bollingen Prize. The federal committee asserted that leftist politics—including those we would associate with Rukeyser's anti-fascism, feminism, sex positivity, anti-racism, and anti-imperialism—were intrinsic to the aesthetic forms implemented by creators who held those beliefs.[11] These contradictory ideas about the relationship between aesthetic form and political commitment concretized the postwar period's ideological crisis, with which Rukeyser's prose would assertively engage and which often was the reason for the suppression of her writings.

Except for Rukeyser, the sole woman, the other nominees for the Bollingen Prize have received their biographies, single-author monographs, critical editions, selected editions, and annotated editions. Consequently, their works have formed our understanding of poetics, history, and modernism. Pound has been privileged above the others. Even the title of Hugh Kenner's field-defining and canon-forming book *The Pound Era* (1971), which originated in a much earlier project that helped rehabilitate Pound's literary career, gave a nearly unshakable impression of that centrality.[12] Rukeyser's work has not received as much attention, and her career was impacted by the Bollingen decision.

---

10. Richard Eberhart, "Pound's New Cantos," *Quarterly Review of Literature* 5 (1949): 174.

11. In October 1947, HUAC conducted the infamous "Hollywood 10" hearings about alleged "communist subversion" in the film industry. Studios responded by refusing to employ alleged communists and unapologetic fellow travelers, the beginning of the blacklist period. The Hollywood blacklisting soon affected New York literary culture too. For instance, editor Angus Cameron was forced out at Little, Brown; by 1953, all his authors, including Rukeyser, lost their contracts. Rukeyser's close friend Ella Winter writes about the "Hollywood 10" hearings in *And Not to Yield: An Autobiography* (New York: Harcourt, Brace, 1963). For an overview of the period, see Thomas Doherty, *Show Trial: Hollywood, HUAC, and the Birth of the Blacklist* (New York: Columbia University Press, 2019).

12. Hugh Kenner, *The Pound Era* (Berkeley: University of California Press, 1971). Kenner's first book, *The Poetry of Ezra Pound* (Norfolk, CT: New Directions, 1951), emerged from his 1948 visit to Pound at St. Elizabeth's.

After *The Green Wave*, she would not publish another collection of new poetry for nearly a decade.[13] Her only poetics volume published during her lifetime, *The Life of Poetry* (1949), fell out of print after its first run, much to Rukeyser's disappointment. During the postwar period, she developed and planned several other major projects, including a biography about and the selected letters and writings of Franz Boas and a Herman Melville anthology, among others. Such unpublished and often unfinished work "did not linger in obscurity for lack of authorial energy or talent, or editorial stubbornness," but instead was the product of "an often hostile and sexist readership" who targeted her because of her gender, radicalism, and queerness.[14] Although these projects remained unrealized, she continued to write and publish short-form prose.

Today, there are several in-print editions of her selected poems, stand-alone republications of her key poetic works *Elegies* (1949, republished 2013) and *The Book of the Dead* (1938, republished 2018), and an authorized critical volume of collected poems. Her only prose work that has remained in print throughout most of its publication history is *Willard Gibbs* (1942), a biography of the first theoretical physicist and chemist. Several other major life-writing projects—including *One Life* (1957), a biography in verse and documents of politician Wendell Willkie, and *The Traces of Thomas Hariot* (1971), about the eponymous Renaissance polymath and discoverer—as well as all her children's books, quickly fell out of print and remain in that status. The turn of the millennium saw a recovery by the independent publisher Paris Press of two out-of-print prose books—*The Orgy* (1965, republished 1997) and *The Life of Poetry* (1949, republished 1996)—as well as one play, *Houdini: A Musical* (previously unpublished, 2002). In 2013, the lost novel *Savage Coast* was published with the Feminist Press, receiving substantial attention and bringing new readers to Rukeyser. Barring the inclusion of a few isolated essays in other recovery projects, most of her nonfiction short-form prose has not been republished or rediscovered.[15] While a volume

---

13. Muriel Rukeyser's two full collections following *The Green Wave*—*Elegies* (Norfolk, CT: New Directions, 1949) and *Selected Poems* (Norfolk, CT: New Directions, 1951)—included poems previously appearing in earlier volumes. Her only new collection of poems during this decade was the short chapbook *Orpheus* (San Francisco: Centaur Press, 1949).

14. Rowena Kennedy-Epstein, *Unfinished Spirit: Muriel Rukeyser's Twentieth Century* (Ithaca, NY: Cornell University Press, 2022), 6, 7.

15. Three previously recovered short prose works by Rukeyser are not included in this volume: "The Education of a Poet," rpt. in Muriel Rukeyser, *A Muriel Rukeyser Reader*, ed.

of selected critical essays about her work and influence appeared at the end of the twentieth century and a lightly biographical study of her career publications appeared months after her death, only during the last decade have a handful of critical monographs about Rukeyser begun to appear, along with two special issues of academic journals dedicated to her work.[16] Most other criticism is consigned to isolated journal articles or single chapters in period-ranging books on modernism. Only one website is devoted to her legacy and teaching her work to new generations of readers, and, at the time of this writing, she has no author society.[17] The imbalance is clear. Authors like Pound have been given an institutional path through history, and so they have come to define the critical field and their literary periods and even the periods that followed; and then there are writers like Rukeyser whose histories have been left fragmented and incomplete, with major works and key texts detailing their social and poetic vision left uncollected, not even selected.

What would have happened if Rukeyser had won the Bollingen Prize? What would it have meant if modernism were epitomized by a collection that moves from depictions of a gendered body stifled by war and crisis toward a body that is expansive and parturient? What would have happened if a Jewish, radical, bisexual, single mother had been the defining voice of postwar American poetry? What if it had been the Rukeyser Era? Posing these questions is more than just a thought experiment. We ask them as a provocation, to reorient our position to hierarchies of literary and cultural influence and to teach and read a more expansive version of the twentieth century in our present.

Jan Heller Levi (New York: W. W. Norton, 1994), 277–285; "We Came for Games," rpt. in Muriel Rukeyser, *Savage Coast*, ed. Rowena Kennedy-Epstein (New York: Feminist Press, 2013), 281–298; and *Darwin and the Writers*, ed. Stefania Heim (New York: Lost & Found, 2003). "Barcelona, 1936," in this volume, previously appeared in Muriel Rukeyser, *"Barcelona, 1936" and Selections from the Spanish Civil War Archive*, ed. Rowena Kennedy-Epstein (New York: Lost & Found, 2011), 9–22.

16. See Anne F. Herzog and Janet E. Kaufman, eds., *"How Shall We Tell Each Other of the Poet?": The Life and Writing of Muriel Rukeyser* (New York: Palgrave Macmillan, 1999); Elisabeth Däumer, ed., "Muriel Rukeyser Centenary Issue," *Journal of Narrative Theory* 43, no. 3 (Fall 2013): 287–425, https://www.jstor.org/stable/i24482959; Catherine Gander, ed., "Muriel Rukeyser's *The Life of Poetry*," *Textual Practice* 32, no. 7 (September 2018): 1095–1253; Louise Kertesz, *The Poetic Vision of Muriel Rukeyser* (Baton Rouge: Louisiana State University Press, 1980); Catherine Gander, *Muriel Rukeyser and Documentary: The Poetics of Connection* (Edinburgh: Edinburgh University Press, 2013); and Kennedy-Epstein, *Unfinished Spirit* (2022).

17. See Elisabeth Däumer and Bill Rukeyser, *Muriel Rukeyser: A Living Archive*, Eastern Michigan University, Department of English, 2022, http://murielrukeyser.emuenglish.org/.

As the Bollingen Prize anecdote encapsulates, our recovery effort with this volume is about more than making sure one author's writings get fuller exposure via academic journals, in classrooms, or even among general audiences. Through Rukeyser's unpublished and out-of-print prose, we can better comprehend the conditions that would suppress her and her contemporaries' vision of transnational, liberatory inclusiveness to elevate racism, antisemitism, misogyny, homophobia, and antidemocratism, generally.

Although she is now known primarily for her poetry, Rukeyser also produced an extensive body of prose. A deeply committed thinker interested in the processes, conflicts, lineages, and possibilities of twentieth-century thought, in her accessible but philosophically complex work she addresses issues related to racial, gender, and class justice, war and war crimes, the prison-industrial complex, Jewish culture and diaspora, and many other facets of American history, politics, and culture. Throughout her varied career, she produced biographies, film scripts and teleplays, stage plays, children's books, short stories, novels, essays, radio shows, and public lectures, as well as an extensive portfolio of journalism and nonfiction essays on the arts, social justice, and politics. During a period when few women were allowed to position themselves as public intellectuals—much less as equal citizens—most of this writing by Rukeyser has been forgotten, not reprinted since its first appearance if it was published at all, buried by editors and publishers because of conservative mid-century gender and political orthodoxies. By bringing forth a selection of Rukeyser's political, social, and aesthetic writings for the first time, this volume introduces a new generation of readers to a writer who was trying to think her way through a period as dangerous, promising, and painful as our own. This is the Rukeyser Era, long delayed, but just in time.

Our archival encounters with Rukeyser's prose writing have made us aware of just how narrowly constructed our understanding of American literary and political history has been. Through her prose we have found new orientations, not just for understanding Rukeyser and her work but also for finding new artistic networks and political affiliations. Her traditions are anti-fascist and anti-imperialist, feminist and queer. As a journalist, she turned her gaze toward those who were not seen fully, and she also theorizes the very idea of seeing. As an activist and writer shaped by the political and social unrest of the 1930s, her commitments originated in that decade's anti-fascism and remained a central preoccupation throughout her life. Consequently, anti-fascism is a key point of departure for this recovery project and its reassessment of Rukeyser's career. The term *anti-fascist* ought to be understood expansively, as encompassing more than a negating or oppositional political force. Anti-fascists "tend to fight not only *against* fascism, but also *for* racial justice, for socialist (or anarchist) transformation, and for gender equality."[18] That is to say, anti-fascism is, at its core, a creative and future-oriented sociopolitical vision—rooted in a belief or, as Rukeyser herself often called it, a wish for intersectional manifestations of social justice and democracy. There is no better way to characterize her career-long personal and political commitments, which run throughout her poetry and most of her other literary and paraliterary writings. Through our selections, we have tried to bring to the fore Rukeyser's continuity of thinking and making, her constellations of political and aesthetic concerns, so clearly traced from her earliest work through the end of her life.

Rukeyser recognized early on how politics and aesthetics were inextricably connected in her worldview. During the Second World War, she provided an autobiographical statement for a special issue of the *Contemporary Jewish Record*, which we have selected as the author's introduction to this volume. There, Rukeyser characterizes two forces as her primary influences: "poetry and fire," the poetry of the Bible and her apocryphal maternal genealogy stemming from the "fire" of second-century Israeli revolutionary Rabbi Akiva ben Josef.[19] She writes:

> To live as a poet, woman, American, and Jew—this chalks in my position. If the four come together in one person, each strengthens the others. Red-baiting, undercuts at the position of women, anti-intellectual and anti-imaginative drives such as Congress has recently been conducting—these are on the same level as the growing storm of anti-Semitism.[20]

Gender consciousness, her sense of her national culture's responsibility to fight for democracy, her expressed opposition to HUAC's forerunner, the Dies Committee—all are interwoven forces motivating Rukeyser's work as a poet. For her to mark them as bearing the same level of

---

18. Bill V. Mullen and Christopher Vials, "Introduction: Anti/Fascism and the United States," in *The U.S. Antifascism Reader* (New York: Verso, 2020), 13. Original emphases.
19. Muriel Rukeyser, "Biographical Statement for 'Under Forty': A Symposium on American Literature and the Younger Generation of American Jews," in this volume.
20. Rukeyser, "Biographical Statement."

intensity as the moment's antisemitism, at home and abroad, amid the Holocaust, is a remarkable and prescient rebuke of the marginalization of her voice in later years, a marginalization precipitated in part when the Bollingen committee overlooked her and instead gave accolades to a fascist.

Rukeyser began her career as a journalist and reviewer in 1932, while an undergraduate at Vassar College. She served as contributing editor for the *Vassar Miscellany News*, researching and writing pieces on topics ranging from modern poetry to strip-mining. She cofounded with classmates Eleanor and Eunice Clark the magazine *Housatonic*, which focused on New England's culture, political history, and literature. She also cofounded the avant-garde magazine *Con Spirito* with Mary McCarthy, Elizabeth Bishop, and the Clarks. As happened with many of her peers, Rukeyser's radical political sensibilities were activated during this time. According to historian Robert Cohen, her generation of student activists "viewed the Depression as the great radicalizing force of their time."[21] After attending workers' talks sponsored by the Student League for Industrial Democracy during the spring of her sophomore year, Rukeyser was so moved that she drove to Pennsylvania to investigate labor conditions for herself and then reported on them to her classmates.[22] That experience predated by four years her 1936 trip to Gauley Bridge, West Virginia, which informed *The Book of the Dead* (1938), her now-celebrated documentarian poem about silica mining and industrial illness. Because of her family's Depression-related financial straits, Rukeyser's parents pulled her out of Vassar before the start of the next semester. Through the Communist Party–allied National Student League, she continued to work with student organizers in New York City. For that group's periodical, *Student Review*, she covered the first, now largely forgotten, free speech movement, a response to the City College of New York's firing of communist professor Oakley Johnson.[23] More famously, in 1933, Rukeyser also wrote a probing *Student Review* editorial on the infamous trial of the so-called Scottsboro Boys, nine African American youths wrongfully accused of rape by two white women. She intended to write a follow-up

---

21. Robert Cohen, *When the Old Left Was Young: Student Radicals and America's First Mass Student Movement, 1929–1941* (New York: Oxford University Press, 1993), 258.

22. See Muriel Rukeyser, "The Color of Coal Is Black," *Vassar Miscellany News*, March 12, 1932.

23. See Muriel Rukeyser, "Students Fight for Free Speech at City College," *Vassar Miscellany News*, November 5, 1932.

piece on the trial's gender dynamics, but that essay, though completed, was left unpublished, until now.

In the years that followed, she continued to work with leftist organizations, as a dance and theater reviewer for the communist magazine *New Theatre*, as a freelance agent for the New Theatre League, and as an editor at Frontier Films. Rukeyser's early experiences as a student activist and in the leftist Cultural Front shaped the anti-racist, anti-patriarchal, and pro-labor views that characterized her entire career. The single most defining experience of her political life, though, occurred in July 1936. She had been invited by the British progressive cultural monthly *Life and Letters To-day* to cover the People's Olympiad, or the Anti-fascist Olympics, in Barcelona. En route to the games, she witnessed the outbreak of the Spanish Civil War. Read alongside *Savage Coast* (2013), Rukeyser's posthumously published novel about her experiences in Spain, her editorials in *Life and Letters To-day*, the mainstream *New York Herald Tribune*, and the communist magazine *New Masses* provide crucial understandings of the conflict.[24] What she witnessed informed her steadfast anti-fascism, a radically democratic vision she upheld for the rest of her life. As Rukeyser's typed header on a handwritten table of contents for her *Selected Poems* (1951) states, "Spain made me."[25]

Throughout the 1940s and 1950s, in addition to writing biographies and plays, Rukeyser continued to work as a journalist, an editor of both film and print, a scriptwriter for film and then television, and an essayist. Her prose writing on politics illustrates the development of her leftist radical thought in the 1930s into anti-war activism and feminism in the 1970s. She wrote on topics as varied as film and images, and she wrote the narratives for photo-essays featured in glossy magazines like *Coronet* and *Life*.[26] She often used her book and theater reviews to highlight the work of women who had been or would be written out of the emerging chauvinist modernist canon.[27] These crucial

---

24. See Muriel Rukeyser, "Barcelona, 1936," in this volume; Muriel Rukeyser, "Barcelona on the Barricades," in this volume; Muriel Rukeyser, "Start of Strife in Spain Is Told by Eyewitness," *New York Herald Tribune*, July 29, 1936.

25. Muriel Rukeyser, Table of contents for Selected Poems, n.d. [c. 1950-1951], 1 holo. p. with ts. epigraph, Box I:35, Muriel Rukeyser Papers, Manuscript Division, Library of Congress, Washington, DC, hereafter cited as LC and followed by series and container number.

26. See Muriel Rukeyser, "Adventures of Children," *Coronet*, September 1939, 23-38; Muriel Rukeyser, "Worlds Alongside," *Coronet*, October 1939, 83-98. She also is the uncredited author of "The Telephone Company," *Life*, July 17, 1939, 56-63.

27. For example, see Muriel Rukeyser, "The Classic Ground," on Marya Zaturenska; Muriel Rukeyser, "A Simple Theme," on Charlotte Marletto; and Muriel Rukeyser, "A Crystal for the Metaphysical," on Marianne Moore, all in this volume. For a review of proletarian

pieces develop feminist theories of gender and literary production, and through them, Rukeyser cultivates a public voice on gender equity and motherhood that offers rich nuance about mid-century women's lives and the intersections of political and aesthetic forms in women's writing. Her educational commitments to racial justice in the 1950s can be seen through a documentary short she scripted about redlining and housing discrimination.[28] They also can be read in her lost articles and fictionalized stories about the effects of racial integration on American schools and neighborhoods that originally appeared in such magazines as *New Statesman* (UK) and *Discovery*. Later, during the Vietnam conflict, Rukeyser became a public face for anti-war activism. During a nonviolent protest at the US Capitol Building in 1972, she and others were arrested for participating in the direct action. Rukeyser opted to serve a brief prison sentence, despite her ill health, rather than pay a court-ordered fine. This experience marked the beginning of her late human rights activism targeting the prison-industrial complex's injustices and its connections to the white supremacist and imperialist war state. Between her trial and self-surrender to the authorities, Rukeyser went on an unofficial ambassadorial peace mission to Hanoi with fellow poet-activist Denise Levertov and Jane Hart, a US senator's spouse. The trip reinforced her conviction that literary translation, especially of poetry, could be used by the peace movement as a protest tool.

As a standard-bearer for social, gender, and sexual justice who wove her activist commitments into her creative work, Rukeyser was, out of necessity, a fighter. In an extended Vietnam-era meditation on Henry David Thoreau's theory of civil disobedience, she concludes:

> I know it is only the violent person who understands nonviolence—who has to wake up every morning and be nonviolent for one more day. It is only the person who knows what it is to be irritating, to be hostile, who knows what the long physical battle is to put down—not put down, but to deal with hostility in oneself, to use all the parts of it which are usable, because there *are* ways to use war in oneself.

---

choreographer Trudi Schoop, see Muriel Rukeyser, "Trudi on the Road," *New Theatre* 3, no. 2 (1936): 6.

28. See Muriel Rukeyser, *All the Way Home*, dir. Lee R. Bobker, Dynamic Films, 1957, YouTube, 2018, film, 29:45, https://www.youtube.com/watch?v=S9e7zXKNNwg.

> One man can make art of this. This is one of the ways of art, to use the warlike, to use the ways of active struggle. It can be shown; it can be given to other people; it can be given in art.[29]

In this passage culminates much of Rukeyser's theorizing over several decades about a radical American tradition—about the uses of the imagination in a country defined by settler colonialism, slavery, war, expansion, and immigration, and about citizens' and residents' personal embodiments of that history. She is also describing something we grapple with today in our current political climate: How do we become conscious of the violence and repression that have shaped our bodies and identities? How might we transform such recognition into the generative, connecting, and radiant possibilities of artistic making and political solidarity?

These are some of the questions the texts included in *The Muriel Rukeyser Era* try to answer. Rukeyser was a prolific and energetic writer, working across mediums and genres. Just as the themes in her poetry are recurrent, so too are themes that thread through her prose. In making our selections, we have sought to bring a diverse range of her work together that demonstrates her political and aesthetic vision as it developed over the course of her life. Some of this work has never been published before, and we have left the breaks and lacunae of the drafts visible. In other cases, originally published versions were substantially edited from her archived fair copies, so we have noted how publishing pressures might have altered her more radical message. These texts, and their cultural erasure, tell stories about the places and communities Rukeyser was working in—the Depression years' radical Cultural Front, Hollywood and Broadway in the 1930s and 1940s, the Office of War Information during the Second World War, the New York City juvenile court system, Manhattan's downtown and uptown literary scenes, the San Francisco Renaissance, second-wave feminism and other arms of the New Left, anti-war and anti-nuclear organizations, prisoner and refugee rights, and other human rights movements. These selections also show Rukeyser as trying to elucidate her own times by writing and thinking at the forefront of them, thus giving them shape. We could not include all the unpublished or uncollected prose items she authored—essays, book reviews, dance and theater reviews, film scripts, stories—too many to name. Future scholarly and editorial efforts surely will bring out of the archives some of what we have omitted. What we

---

29. Muriel Rukeyser, "Thoreau and Poetry," in this volume.

have chosen to present here, though, is representative of how Rukeyser's prose reflects her dual investment in aesthetic theorization and sociopolitical commitment. Through this representative selection, we set out to tell a cohesive story about a literary and activist visionary whose name, rather than a fascist's, should characterize an era of American poetry and literature.

Part I. *The Usable Truth: Five Talks on Communication and Poetry*

In August 1940, anthologist and critic Louis Untermeyer published a feature on Muriel Rukeyser's poetry in the widely circulating *Saturday Review of Literature*. His opening line praises her as "the most inventive and challenging poet of the generation which has not yet reached thirty."[30] Just twenty-six years old, she had already published three poetry collections: *Theory of Flight* (1935), *U.S. 1* (1938), and *A Turning Wind* (1939). Within a week of the appearance of Untermeyer's article, Henry MacCracken, the president of Rukeyser's alma mater, Vassar College, invited her to come speak at the school.[31] The resulting lecture series, *The Usable Truth: Five Talks on Communication and Poetry*, would inform *The Life of Poetry* (1949), her best-known prose work, an artful meditation on mid-century poetics that opens with a reminiscence of her flight from the outbreak of civil war in Spain.[32] We open this volume with Rukeyser's previously unpublished lectures because they bring together in new ways her thinking about war, poetry, and gender politics, anchored in an immediate, explicit response to historical contingencies. Her responses to the day's crises intersect with questions of artistic forms and traditions, thus providing the basis for so much of her theoretical and poetic thinking.

In subsequent years, Rukeyser retooled her original talks, giving them the socialist-sounding title "Poetry and the People" while refashioning them into poetry workshops for workers and activists at San Francisco's California Labor School, offered in 1945 and 1948. She also taught a ten-week course with the same title at Columbia University's

---

30. Louis Untermeyer, "The Language of Muriel Rukeyser," *Saturday Review of Literature* 22, no. 16 (August 10, 1940): 11.

31. Henry Noble MacCracken, letter to Muriel Rukeyser, August 16, 1940, 1 ts p., LC I:5.

32. On *The Life of Poetry*'s origins in various workshops and lecture series, see Eric Keenaghan, "The Life of Politics: The Compositional History of *The Life of Poetry* and Muriel Rukeyser's Changing Appraisal of Emotion and Belief," *Textual Practice* 32, no. 7 (2018): 1103–1126, doi:10.1080/0950236X.2018.1477109.

extension school in 1946. Only a handful of fragmented talks and notes from these courses and workshops survive, but, thankfully, all the original Vassar talks have been archived in their entirety. Without access to these initial lectures, many readers might be inclined to believe, erroneously, that *The Usable Truth* merely offers an undeveloped version of *The Life of Poetry*. The similarity of certain anecdotes in the lectures and the book, such as the opening story about leaving war-torn Barcelona as well as Rukeyser's ideas about poetry's affective and imaginative nature, are unsurprising. She was an iterative writer, returning to and repeating certain themes, stories, and ideas, though always with changes.[33] But the Vassar talks crucially underscore how Rukeyser's formalist and at times ontological claims in the postwar *Life of Poetry* sprung from historically grounded responses to her immediate, prewar political and cultural circumstances.

From their inception, Rukeyser wrote the lectures with an eye toward composing a new book to speak to her historical moment. Unlike many of the talks she gave later in her career, *The Usable Truth* is fully written out and neatly typed on paginated, looseleaf pages that contain relatively few emendations or notes for improvisation. Despite her intentions to publish her lectures as a book, only the first, "The Fear of Poetry," would be printed in full, appearing in the art and politics journal *Twice a Year*. A revised brief extract from the series' final talk, "Communication and Poetry," appeared in *Poetry: A Magazine of Verse*.[34] Rukeyser crafted the talks during the "Plague Summer" of 1940, as her acquaintance Kenneth Patchen referred to the season when the US Congress debated legislation mandating the first "peacetime" draft.[35] In the first lecture, given shortly after the controversial conscription law went into effect, she self-consciously signals how she and most of her audience at the all-women's college would not be affected by the war in the same ways as their male counterparts. Throughout the series, Rukeyser references other current events—from Japan's recent attacks on China to the European refugee crisis—as well as cultural and literary magazines' debates about the war's significance. She was intent upon

---

33. On Rukeyser's use of repetition in her writings on Spain, see Rowena Kennedy-Epstein, "Part 1: Novel Proliferations," in *Unfinished Spirit*, 25–87.

34. See Muriel Rukeyser, "The Fear of Poetry," *Twice a Year*, Fall/Winter 1941, 15–33; Muriel Rukeyser, "The Usable Truth," *Poetry: A Magazine of Verse*, July 1941, 206–209, https//www.jstor.org/stable/20582634.

35. Kenneth Patchen, *The Journal of Albion Moonlight* (New York: New Directions, 1961), 1.

using her poet's eye and imagination to imbue the destruction and chaos with new meaning, to move toward a humanistic and democratically inclusive age of peace.

Rukeyser casts her net wide to accomplish this end. She sought to synthesize new meaning out of major box office releases by Alfred Hitchcock, recent translations of Soviet filmmakers on cinema's political power, and refugees' reports about a German poet and doctor who practiced a form of resistance others misread as collaborationism. She returns, repeatedly, to the philosophy of Søren Kierkegaard, a touchstone uncommon in her other work and prescient of Jean-Paul Sartre and Simone de Beauvoir's existentialism, born of their own experiences of the Nazi occupation. She also discusses at length Herman Melville's April 1851 letter to Nathaniel Hawthorne. That letter's theorization of "visible truth"—erroneously transcribed by scholars as "usable truth"—lent Rukeyser's series its title. Much of the material in *The Usable Truth* and its timely contextual references invaluably fill out our sense of how Rukeyser and other anti-fascists and activist-writers struggled with the prospect of the United States entering what was, before the bombing of Pearl Harbor over a year later, an unpopular foreign war.

Rukeyser tried to bring *The Usable Truth* into print soon after her Vassar visit. However, major publishing houses rejected her proposal because, as one editor put it, her approach to her material was too politically current, so her book would quickly become dated.[36] But as late as October 1945, after the Second World War's end, her literary agent was hopeful a major house would buy it.[37] Over the next several years, following her teaching at Columbia and the California Labor School, and as she developed various poetic, dramatic, and film projects, her revisions of her ideas gave them more transhistorical viability. *The Life of Poetry* is both exciting and challenging, but with Rukeyser's revisions something integral to her thinking, to what made that book possible, was lost. *The Usable Truth*'s explicitly political and timely contents reveal how Rukeyser, in the shadow of the war-state, eventually suppressed certain historical and political material to bring into print a potentially paradigm-shifting argument about poetry's resistant potential. Not only do the talks give us a glimpse of Rukeyser's own public

---

36. Quincy Howe (Simon and Schuster, Inc.), letter to Muriel Rukeyser, March 28, 1941, 1 ts p., LC I:7.

37. Naomi Burton (Curtis Brown, Ltd.), letter to Muriel Rukeyser, November 28, 1945, 1 ts p., LC II:5.

intellectualism in action, but they also provide a clearer sense of how a form of later modernist poetics sprung explicitly from its author's weaving together of aesthetic theorization and an anti-fascist feminist engagement with national and global political crises.

Part II. Twentieth-Century Radicalism: On Politics, Society, and Culture

The second section of this volume charts Muriel Rukeyser's development as an activist and public intellectual from her college days until the years shortly before her death. Her student writing reflects how her political consciousness was shaped by the first wave of radicalization on American college campuses. For *Housatonic*, a magazine she cofounded and coedited with two classmates in 1932, Rukeyser wrote "The Flown Arrow," on the repercussions of the execution five years earlier of Nicola Sacco and Bartolomeo Vanzetti, Italian immigrants and anarchists sentenced to death without due process. This early piece signals how Rukeyser's journalism, throughout her career, tracked the way legal and political injustices often driven by anti-leftist hysteria are justified by, and extended through, cultural and aesthetic norms that police race, ethnicity, gender, labor, and their intersections. On the execution, she writes that "the arrow has flown. It has lodged in our flesh, and we feel, deep in this body of our strength, the split wound that the deaths of men like Sacco and Vanzetti enlarge in America." She then moves from fatalism toward possibility by reminding the reader that "while the struggle for balance lasts, the arrow has not flown."[38] Decades later, she continued this thread in "The Uses of Fear," a revised version of which the *New York Times* published in 1978, that looks back at the lasting consequences of another politicized state execution—that of Julius and Ethel Rosenberg in 1953—which encapsulated the Cold War's paranoia and terror. In this essay, too, she invites readers to face the fears and terrors of our past. Rukeyser also subjected the present to similar scrutiny, as her previously unpublished Vietnam-era essay, "The Killing of the Children" from 1973, demonstrates. There, following the author's movements from an anti-war protest at the US Capitol Building to Hanoi and then to jail, where she meets a young Black girl incarcerated for killing her child, Rukeyser shows the interconnected

---

38. Muriel Rukeyser, "The Flown Arrow," in this volume.

crises of America. War making occurs both abroad and at home, in the forms of carceral capitalism, racism, and sexism.

Rukeyser's early career as a journalist and activist prepared her for such undertakings in writing about social and political issues. After leaving Vassar, she took anthropology classes at Columbia University, where she became the publicity chair for the "Conference on Negro Student Problems." Through that committee, Rukeyser met and worked alongside established radical intellectuals and artists, including Franz Boas, Alain Locke, Augusta Savage, and Zora Neale Hurston. It was partially in this role that she, with two communist organizer friends, traveled to Alabama in 1933 to report for the *Student Review* on the trial of the Scottsboro Nine. Her published article "From Scottsboro to Decatur" and her unpublished follow-up essay "Women and Scottsboro" depict the contexts of a trial central to anti-racist organizing and solidarity in the 1930s. Rukeyser documents how the local police's ominous exertion of segregation laws stymied her ability to report, even leading to her detention overnight on framed-up charges of distributing inflammatory propaganda. Both articles mix first-person narrative with journalistic techniques, focusing on the intersections of race, gender, and place.

Developing what would become her signature hybridization of lyrical prose and documentary evidence, Rukeyser's journalism about the first days of the Spanish Civil War, "Barcelona on the Barricades" and "Barcelona, 1936," mix modernist collage techniques with anti-fascist politics. She traveled in July 1936 from London to Barcelona on a last-minute assignment for the British magazine *Life and Letters To-day* to report on the People's Olympiad, an alternative to Hitler's Berlin games. Instead of reporting on the games, she witnessed the outbreak of civil war. Her experience was transformational. She would write about it for the rest of her life, including pieces memorializing her lover Otto Boch, a German exile and long-distance runner who had died fighting Franco's fascist advance on the Zaragoza front.[39] When evacuated by boat from Barcelona, Rukeyser was famously asked, "And poetry—among all this—where is there a place for poetry?"[40] She made her career out of

---

39. In addition to *Savage Coast* and the two essays in this volume, see Muriel Rukeyser, *The Life of Poetry* (Ashfield, MA: Paris Press, 1996), 1-3; Rukeyser, "Mediterranean," in *CP*, 144–151; Rukeyser, "We Came for Games."

40. Rukeyser, *Life of Poetry*, 3.

continually responding to this question, theorizing the relationship between politics and aesthetics.

Rukeyser's thinking on perception, especially during moments of political crisis like wartime, is especially illuminated in two essays presented here. The first, "Words and Images," was written in response to her resignation in 1943 from the Office of War Information, a federal propaganda agency. Exploring the relationship between the photographic image, its caption, and state propaganda, Rukeyser outlines a compelling, politicized poetics for multimodal practice. "The point is not in the *naming* of a picture," she writes, "but in a reinforcement which is mutual, so that the words and the picture attack the same theme from slightly different approaches."[41] Such reciprocity between word and image infuses meaning into wartime atrocities, which would otherwise remain meaningless. As she writes in the second essay, "War and Poetry," from 1945: "War enters all our lives, but even that horror is only a beginning. The war is in our poetry only so far as it is in our imaginations, as a meaning, as a relationship, or simply as a fact."[42] These pieces develop Rukeyser's ongoing thinking through a documentary poetics of witness, which have become invaluable for later generations of writers, including Susan Sontag, Carolyn Forché, C. D. Wright, Claudia Rankine, Ada Limón, and Solmaz Sharif.

Rukeyser is especially interested in how a crucial political event causes laws and norms to change or when a political crisis comes to a climax. But in her essays about social transformation, she tells more complicated stories about such moments and traces longer, less triumphant histories. She studies moments when a culture shifts subtly, moments like the volta in a sonnet when there is a "turn" in thought or shift in tone. Rukeyser then follows the repercussions that unfold. Her essays take us beyond the historically recognizable moment and into generative and surprising places, where the stories' subjects or their descendants reassert their voices, thus keeping the narrative open. Exemplifying this dynamic is "She Came to Us," an article written in 1958 for the *New Statesman*, a British newspaper. Here, Rukeyser's subject is Minnijean Brown, one of the Little Rock Nine, the group of Black adolescents who pioneered the federally mandated educational desegregation by enrolling in Arkansas's formerly all-white Little Rock

---

41. Muriel Rukeyser, "Words and Images," in this volume. Original emphasis.
42. Muriel Rukeyser, "War and Poetry," in this volume.

Central High School. The essay depicts Minnijean's arrival in her new school in Manhattan. She had been wrongfully expelled from her home institution in the Jim Crow South for resisting her white classmates' violent racist backlash. Rukeyser closes with a scene of Minnijean analyzing a Shakespeare sonnet in English class, which very well could read as the author's own assertion of her theory not just about poetry but also about social life: "She talks about the music and the rhyme. You cannot separate out any of these elements, she says, and hope to keep the beauty. The beauty is the entire thing, she says."[43]

Many of the pieces included in this section model how Rukeyser's short-form stories about sociopolitical issues anticipate, and fall somewhere between, the experimentalism of Norman Mailer's New Journalism and later New Narrative and autofiction by queer writers like Robert Glück, Eileen Myles, and Maggie Nelson. Rukeyser, for instance, imagined her 1953 short story "A Pane of Glass," after its initial publication, as part of a cycle blurring the boundaries of fiction, theory, and autobiographical essay.[44] The story opens during a snowy New Year's Day on the Upper West Side, the writer and her five-year-old son walking home together from sledding in Central Park. They encounter a group of teenage boys—"men, really"—who are ominous in their self-protective powers of whiteness and masculinity.[45] The young men take up the entire street, throw snowballs indiscriminately, and break the pane of glass in her building's front door. She takes her son and goes down the block to confront the group, but she realizes she has no recourse. They challenge her, laughing. Her son says they "have no shame."[46] Later, she learns that while she was getting ready to go out for a holiday party, a teenage girl had given birth alone in the building and, from the frozen roof, threw the newborn down the air shaft. Certain people are allowed to move freely, with no thought for the consequences of their actions, no matter how destructive, while others live always in forms of legal and social dispossession from their

---

43. Muriel Rukeyser, "She Came to Us," in this volume.
44. Rukeyser planned to collect four previously published stories into a cycle of what is now called autofiction: "We Came for Games" (*Esquire*, October 1974, 192-194, 368-370), "A Pane of Glass" (*Discovery*, October 1953, 29-37, and in this volume), "Little" (*Ladies' Home Journal*, February 1965, 82-85, 88-89), and "The Club" (*Ellery Queen's Mystery Magazine*, August 1960, 112-121). See Muriel Rukeyser, We Came for Games [Outline for ts short story cycle], n.d. [c. 1973-1974], LC I:16.
45. Muriel Rukeyser, "A Pane of Glass," in this volume.
46. Rukeyser, "Pane of Glass."

own bodies, in shame, no matter how much potential and power they hold. For Rukeyser, these contradictions, magnified in New York City's racial, gender, and class disparities, constitute the crisis of America.

"A Pane of Glass" ends with the writer searching for the girl at her arraignment downtown, in New York City's juvenile courts. Rukeyser became personally familiar with this legal setting over the next several years. In 1955, she worked with—and planned a book about—educator Helen Parkhurst's advocacy of so-called "delinquent" youth.[47] Later, around 1958, after being targeted and essentially blacklisted by anticommunist organizations, Rukeyser was recruited to work with a mayoral commission to write a report, for which she ultimately was uncredited, on New York City's juvenile court system. Her intimate, sympathetic accounts of the lives of children in these systems, especially of teenage girls like those in "A Pane of Glass" and "The Killing of the Children," speak to Rukeyser's career-long awareness of how the law is unevenly exerted in America. Toward the end of "A Pane of Glass," standing in the halls of a courthouse, she reflects on her own choice to become a mother, wondering who she can call to help the young girl. But her thinking about the different outcomes of pregnancy before legal abortion is interrupted by a surprise reencounter with Steve, a travel companion from the train to Barcelona and on the ship with evacuees out of that city almost a decade and a half earlier.[48] His presence compels her to recall the old question posed to her as they left Barcelona: "Here, in the soft-shining marble, we might still have been on the deck of that far ship, just evacuated from the city at peace, the great city so soon to fall. We had looked across the shore-waves to the city, and then at each other. He turned just such a look on me, and then the printer from Paris had said, 'And where, in all this, is the place for poetry?'"[49] Now Steve is an attorney, and he fills her in on the girl's case and its history. "That's a different story, isn't it?" he asks. Though she momentarily believes it is, she realizes nothing has changed—about the girl's situation or even her own. "Yes, I did; for a moment I did change

---

47. See Muriel Rukeyser, Parkhurst Notebook, 1955, LC I:30. For a proposal and projected table of contents for the Parkhurst book, see Muriel Rukeyser, The Voice of the Child—Outline, n.d. [c. 1955], 4 ts pp., LC II:13. For two extant completed chapters, see Muriel Rukeyser, A Dark Night, A Perfect Night, n.d. [c. 1955], 17 ts (carbon) pp., LC I:16; and Muriel Rukeyser, I Could Have Kissed Him, n.d. [c. 1955], 10 ts (carbon) pp., LC I:16.

48. "Steve" is a pseudonym for Ernest Tischter, who also appears as Peter in Rukeyser's novel *Savage Coast*.

49. Rukeyser, "Pane of Glass."

my mind. But how do I dare? This will open, and open, and all be the same story."[50] With such repetitions of the same story, the same fight, social justice activists find new opportunities to connect, in solidarity, and open outward.

Part III. Media and Democratic Education: A Photo-Text and Radio Scripts

During the interwar years, Muriel Rukeyser sought to popularize radical modernism's formal possibilities to counter the predominant, conservative vision of American literature and intellectual thought. Her interest in bringing together word and image informed her early photo-essays for glossy magazines as well as the long poem *The Book of the Dead* (1938), initially intended to be an ekphrastic project featuring photographs by Nancy Naumburg and then planned for a film adaptation.[51] After the war, Rukeyser further developed her thinking about and her practice of multimodality as a form of democratic education through several projects meant to make complex aesthetic and political ideas accessible to general audiences. Two such projects are featured in *The Muriel Rukeyser Era*: *Sunday at Nine* (1949), a radio series on poetry and music developed for KDFC, San Francisco's first classical music radio station, and *So Easy to See* (1946), an unrealized scientific photo-text collaboration with photographer and inventor Berenice Abbott. Rukeyser's exciting choices of formal and material hybridity remake our understanding of political and aesthetic intersections, while also modeling new formal modes for writing a queer vision of the democratic imagination.

Rukeyser met Berenice Abbott in Greenwich Village at the end of the 1930s, and they worked as collaborators and friends for the next three decades. From the early 1940s through the 1960s, when the sciences were elevated over the arts in the United States, they shared a similar goal: to develop new methods for demonstrating the uses of and relationships between the two fields of knowledge. Abbott had already established herself as a preeminent modernist portrait photographer

---

50. Rukeyser, "Pane of Glass."
51. Nancy Naumburg's three surviving photographs from the ekphrastic project are reproduced in Muriel Rukeyser, *The Book of the Dead* (Morgantown: West Virginia University Press, 2018), 5, 22, 25. For excerpts from the planned film adaptation, see Muriel Rukeyser, "Gauley Bridge: Four Episodes from a Scenario," *Films: A Quarterly Discussion and Analysis* 1, no. 3 (Summer 1940): 51–64.

in 1920s Paris. Through the 1930s, she had been working on another photo-text collaboration with her partner, Elizabeth McCausland, the groundbreaking Works Progress Administration photo series *Changing New York* (1935–1939), from which a fraction of the photos were published with McCausland's captions as a city guidebook.[52] But it was with Rukeyser that Abbott became especially interested in harnessing the democratizing potential of photography, and their collaboration resulted in an extraordinary though unrealized project.[53]

From the archive's traces of their collaboration, we have selected Rukeyser's introduction to what would have been her book with Abbott, *So Easy to See*. If finished, their project would have continued the endeavor Rukeyser began a few years earlier with her biography of mathematical physicist Willard Gibbs, the work of making visible complex theoretical and ontological forms of knowledge. Abbott, using a Supersight camera she had invented, took photographs of everyday objects—an apple, a leaf, a fish head, Rukeyser's eye and hand. *So Easy to See* would have paired those images with Rukeyser's poetic-theoretical discussions of "seeing." Her text moves the reader through a series of what the poet calls correspondences centered around Abbott's "Apple" photograph. Rukeyser takes us from the halved apple's correlation to the vulva and lesbian desire, to the split atom and the atomic bomb, making us think of all the connections between the apple and women's relationship to knowledge. Their project was repeatedly rejected by male editors and curators, who demeaned and undervalued its innovative nature. Working against accepted gendered and disciplinary boundaries to reveal "a meeting-place for art and science" as sources of imaginative possibility and social progress, their project engenders questions about what kinds of collaborative and artistic practices are sanctioned, about the ontology of things and the everyday, about materialist philosophy, and about the radical possibilities of interdisciplinarity.[54]

Just as photography appealed to Rukeyser as a means of democratically recasting modernist art, she also recognized the democratic

---

52. The full photo series, plus variant images and planning drawings, is included in Berenice Abbott, *Changing New York*, ed. Bonnie Yochelson (New York: New Press, 2008).

53. On Abbott and Rukeyser, see Julia Van Haaften, *Berenice Abbott: A Life in Photography* (New York: W. W. Norton, 2018), esp. 262–266; Rowena Kennedy-Epstein, "So Easy to See: The Unfinished Collaboration with Berenice Abbott," in *Unfinished Spirit*, 114–134.

54. Muriel Rukeyser, "So Easy to See," in this volume.

potential of another modern technology: radio. Until the ascendancy of television in the 1950s, radio was the dominant form of broadcast communications, with tens of millions of sets in American homes. Rukeyser decided to try her hand at producing her own broadcast. The result was *Sunday at Nine*, a four-part educational series juxtaposing poetry and music. Rukeyser proposed her series to the new, small San Francisco company KDFC, the Bay Area's first classical music station, founded in 1948.[55] In her proposal's extant draft, Rukeyser explains she was inspired by similar broadcast poetry programs produced by the British Broadcast Company and the Mexican National Lottery, though they did not feature music as hers would; she also believed the Library of Congress would be interested in sponsoring *Sunday at Nine*.[56] The introduction she recorded for the series informs her audience that she wished to take advantage of the popularity of music broadcasts to foreground poetry's ability to move audiences and bring them together, a power stemming from poems' roots in music. In *The Life of Poetry*, she would put it this way: "And the songs and poems, used on radio, throw away the gift of the isolated voice. Radio poetry could now make its leap, could enter a level in which the single voice, or a very few voices, might invite an opening-up of consciousness undefined by the other senses."[57] Over the course of *Sunday at Nine*'s four sixty-minute episodes, Rukeyser introduced listeners to a wide range of poetry.[58] She read full poems fitting each episode's theme or focus, and she interspersed those readings with musical recordings carefully curated for how they speak to the episode's poetic themes and content. The only exception to this format was the final episode, wherein the music *was* the poetry.

The first episode focuses on Emily Dickinson. Shortly following the publication of a selection of Dickinson's poems and her first biography, Rukeyser set out to recover for popular audiences this then largely ignored predecessor. As such, this episode is a key project of postwar feminism. Furthermore, amid the early Cold War's climate of homosexual panic, she uses coded language, which we have flagged for readers in our notes, to signal the queerness of Dickinson's work and life. The second

---

55. For the station's history, see KDFC, "The Story of Classical KDFC," Classical California KDFC, accessed September 30, 2022, kdfc.com/culture/story-classical-kdfc/.

56. Rukeyser, Notes for a Poetry and Music Series of FM Programs for KDFC Saus[alito], December 2, 1948, 1 holo. p., LC II:15.

57. Rukeyser, *Life of Poetry*, 118.

58. The archive contains all four episodes' scripts, extant as a mix of holo. and ts drafts. See Muriel Rukeyser, Sunday at Nine: First Four Programs, n.d. [1949], LC II:14.

episode of *Sunday at Nine* focuses on the work of American regionalist Robert Frost, about whom Rukeyser had written a trenchant review a decade earlier.[59] As in that earlier piece, she explores how Frost provides an opportunity for readers to wrestle with the question of localist senses of place and national identity. The series' third installment foregrounds the poetry of war and peace, represented by writers ranging from her friend Richard Eberhart to her publisher James Laughlin, the British conscientious objector Alex Comfort, and a translated poem by Greek author George Seferis. Using such "more general" themes as points of departure from popular lyricists like Dylan Thomas, Rukeyser believed she could highlight how "modern poetry" provides "moments [. . .] in which one recognizes oneself" and one's "fantasies," exteriorized in the public and political worlds.[60] The series' final episode redefines American poetry and modernist poetics in an anti-racist manner by expanding the definition of poetry to include the blues.

Indeed, this fourth installment reveals much about Rukeyser's motivation to develop a radio program and about why this effort should be regarded as both a mode of democratic education and the establishment of a modernist countertradition. As noted earlier, Ezra Pound's legal troubles stemmed from his anti-American broadcasts on Italian state radio, and the Bollingen Prize controversy of 1948 and 1949 largely focused on the political and ethical content of those fascistic, racist, and antisemitic programs. Exactly when those debates about modernist aesthetics and fascist politics were circulating, Rukeyser decided to appropriate the Poundian ideological broadcast and use it to amplify her own democratic messaging, an objective especially clear in her focus on the blues in *Sunday at Nine*'s fourth episode. Rukeyser uses that cultural form to construct an anti-racist and anti-fascist poetic and musical tradition that recasts modernist poetics, including her own, as stemming from Black aesthetic forms and history. In her broadcast, she explicitly poses the blues as the alternate musical basis of the pre-Renaissance Provençal troubadours, whom Pound had long championed as forerunners of Euro-American modernism.[61] As

---

59. See Muriel Rukeyser, "In a Speaking Voice," in this volume.
60. Rukeyser, Episode 3, in Sunday at Nine: First Four Programs, n.d. [1949], III-4, LC II:14.
61. See Ezra Pound, *The Spirit of Romance* (New York: New Directions, 2005); Ezra Pound, *Pound's Cavalcanti: An Edition of the Translations, Notes, and Essays*, ed. David Anderson (Princeton, NJ: Princeton University Press, 1983).

a white Jewish American, Rukeyser implicitly continues a line of radical modernist blues poetries running from Harlem Renaissance writers like Sterling Brown and Langston Hughes to blues performer Josh White, a friend she features on her program. Ultimately, this episode anticipates the revolutionary music history of poet LeRoi Jones/Amiri Baraka's *Blues People: Negro Music in White America* (1963) and *Black Music* (1967).

Rukeyser and her producers attempted to syndicate *Sunday at Nine* through other radio stations, and they also sought to sell it for educational use in "universities, museums, schools, and related institutions."[62] The four realized episodes were just the first in a projected total of thirteen—which were to include "evenings of the Elizabethans, the Pacific Islanders, poets of other times and places, of many religions, and of myth."[63] Those other episodes were neither written nor broadcast. If they had been, we would have been gifted with the multimodal version of *The Life of Poetry*! Only the first episode's engineering cues exist, and Rukeyser's son, William, has located the recording of her readings and commentary for only the second episode, on Frost.[64] The full scripts for all four produced and broadcast installments survive, though. We have selected to present here the first and the last episodes because they provide important insights into Rukeyser's queer feminism and her anti-racism, key facets of her anti-fascist poetics and activist commitments. Print cannot duplicate the full multimodal experience of listening to Rukeyser's readings or the accompanying musical recordings, but we have used the surviving engineering notes to annotate, in most cases, the exact versions of classical compositions she had curated for her episode on Dickinson. And we have identified versions of the blues songs Rukeyser either indicated or is likely to have been thinking of for her final episode. Many of these recordings are available online or through streaming services. Adventurous readers can reconstruct the musical interludes while reading Rukeyser's scripts, thus bringing to life these key popular texts of her anti-fascist and anti-racist feminist pedagogy.

---

62. E. G. K. Deverill (KDFC/Sundial Broadcasting Corporation), sales form letter for *Sunday at Nine*, n.d. [1949], 2 ts pp., LC II:14.

63. Deverill, sales form letter.

64. Rukeyser prerecorded roughly fifteen minutes for each episode. The music was engineered afterward for the live broadcast. KDFC's sales letter to educational and cultural institutions instructed buyers to supply their own music. See Deverill, sales form letter.

Part IV. Modernist Interventions: On Gender, Poetry, and Poetics

Muriel Rukeyser's unrecovered and uncollected short-form prose includes considerable writing about the aesthetics and poetics of twentieth-century poetry. As is evident in the sole student essay about poetry selected for this volume, "Modern Trends: American Poetry" (1932), originally published in the *Vassar Miscellany News*, she was an astute poetry reader from the earliest point in her career. With its insightful introduction of its student audience to three modernist writers—T. S. Eliot, Archibald MacLeish, and Robinson Jeffers—the piece exemplifies her early and unwavering sense of American modernism as spanning formalist experimentation (Eliot), social commitment (MacLeish), and visionary lyricism (Jeffers). She would combine those tendencies, to different extents, in her own poetry. In other selections, such as her reviews of American regionalist Robert Frost ("In a Speaking Voice," 1939) and of translations of Rainer Maria Rilke ("Nearer to the Well-Spring," 1943) and her presentation at a celebration of recent translations of Federico García Lorca's poetry and plays ("A Lorca Evening," 1951), we find Rukeyser similarly testing the staying power of major predecessors and contemporaries, all with implications for her own evolution of modernist lyric.

Three major essays included here—"Poetry and the Unverifiable Fact" (1968), "The Music of Translation" (1971), and "Thoreau and Poetry" (1972)—provide further indications of how Rukeyser envisioned poetry, as well as literary translation, as bridging the gap between personal expression and social transformation. These texts are indispensable for extending understandings of Rukeyser's vision for the culturally transformative work performed through poetry. These major pieces originated as talks at either academic or professional conferences, thus highlighting her position as a public intellectual and situating her critical and theoretical work in their historical contexts. As in her early *Usable Truth* lectures, Rukeyser produces some of her most potent and durable ideas in these essays by working out of, and responding to, her present moment in public forums.

These short-form writings also provide fascinating insights into her evolving poetics and sociopolitical vision. Take, for instance, her early review of the now-forgotten epic *Chorus for Survival* (1935), by the socialist poet-activist Horace Gregory. The essay, which appeared in the Communist Party newspaper the *Daily Worker*, is a deft, autotelic performance with which Rukeyser creates herself as poet-critic through her rereading of a friend and mentor. She highlights how the formal innovation of Gregory's project translates high-modernist precedents into the register of what was called revolutionary poetics. Rukeyser notices the formal similarities between Gregory's long poem and Eliot's *The Waste Land* (1922) and Hart Crane's *The Bridge* (1930), how each fashions a loosely cohering narrative out of multiple-voiced lyrics. Without explicitly arguing it, Rukeyser makes the case through her reading of Gregory's use of a poetics of fragmentation and polyvocality to theorize the foundation for a new, more politically engaged American modernist long poem. She soon went on to implement those ideas in her own long poem *The Book of the Dead* (1938), the epitome of Popular Front poetics in its fusion of documentarian objectivity and more personal lyric forms.

In "Lyrical 'Rage'" (1957), a review of her friend Kenneth Rexroth, Rukeyser theorizes this fusion as giving poetry the power to transform "rage, in the speaking man," into a more controlled "sharp willingness to condemn," like what one finds in "the committed man."[65] Women writers, especially, tackle the connections between political commitment and poetic form. Selections explicitly about gender that we have chosen include a review of the third collection by Rukeyser's friend and Gregory's wife, Marya Zaturenska ("The Classic Ground," 1941); a review of the forgotten poet Charlotte Marletto's sole collection, about childbirth and motherhood ("A Simple Theme," 1949); a review essay on Marianne Moore ("A Crystal for the Metaphysical," 1966); a late review of Anne Sexton ("Glitter and Wounds, Several Wildnesses," 1973); a meditation on the love letters between Franz Kafka and his fiancée ("The Life to Which I Belong," 1974); and a preface for the first second-wave anthology of women's poetry ("Women of Words," 1974). Each piece provides a deeper understanding of Rukeyser's sense of how gendered personal experience and intimacies inform political commitment and literary expression. Her example influenced a generation of feminist and bisexual and lesbian poet-activists—ranging from Sexton to June Jordan, Adrienne Rich, Audre Lorde, Diane di Prima, Alice Walker, and Judy Grahn. As the editor of the feminist anthology *The World Split Open* (1974) remarks in the headnote for Rukeyser's contribution, "Historically, she is one of this country's most important poets and one of the first and most persistent women to possess the

---

65. Muriel Rukeyser, "Lyrical 'Rage,'" in this volume.

consciousness that shapes this collection."[66] Rukeyser's poem "Käthe Kollwitz" (1968) even had lent the anthology its title: "What would happen if one woman told the truth about her life? / The world would split open."[67]

"Many Keys" (1957), a suppressed article commissioned and then rejected by *The Nation*, exemplifies Rukeyser's politicized and gendered poetics. This lost essay charts the precariousness faced by American women writers. In it, Rukeyser deftly illuminates how the sexist marginalization of women and their writing owes to the patriarchal denigration of women's experience, domestic labor, and motherhood. "There is waste in nature, waste in art, and plenty of waste in the lives of women," she asserts. "Waste is an influence, and the making of poetry works against waste."[68] Giving value to such "waste" necessitates a gendered poetics of open form, "to make the forms so that experience is seen to include the world, so that all things of daily life are seen in their essential and full vitality."[69] Her ideas provide a hitherto little-known feminist complement to the field poetics of such contemporaries as Charles Olson, Robert Duncan, and Denise Levertov, and she anticipates the theorization of motherhood and creative life so central to feminist thought.

Recovering Rukeyser's prose on gender and poetry begs another question about canon making: what if Rukeyser's feminist theorization of open-form writing emanating from dailiness and waste, rather than from Olson's male-centered projective verse, were put at the center of the so-called New American Poetry?[70] If it had been, generations of female and queer writers could have been clued in earlier to how poetry is a testing ground for what queer feminist Sara Ahmed calls *sweaty concepts*, experiential and embodied struggles toward self-liberation, feminist community building, and institutional transformation.[71] If these writings had not been lost, overlooked, or wasted, then perhaps Rukeyser would have sooner helped generations of scholars and writers reconcile

---

66. Louise Berkinow, headnote for Muriel Rukeyser, in Berkinow, ed., *The World Split Open: Four Centuries of Women Poets in England and America, 1552–1950* (New York: Vintage, 1974), 330.
67. Muriel Rukeyser, "Käthe Kollwitz," in *CP*, 463.
68. Muriel Rukeyser, "Many Keys," in this volume.
69. Rukeyser, "Many Keys."
70. On projective verse, see Charles Olson, "Projective Verse and Letter to Elaine Feinstein," in *Selected Writings*, ed. Robert Creeley (New York: New Directions, 1967), 15–30.
71. See Sara Ahmed, *Living a Feminist Life* (Durham, NC: Duke University Press, 2017), esp. 12–14.

themselves to the fact that cultural work and the dailiness of women's and queer persons' lives can be the origin points for raising consciousness and motivating activism.

As we strive toward a conceptual vocabulary better serving the activist and creative work demanded of us and the social transformation our world desperately requires, Rukeyser's texts can help us find this language, fill in historical and theoretical gaps, and ask new questions about poetry's role and artistic practice, more broadly. Such questioning is crucial to facing down an oppressive power culture and overcoming the fears propping it up. "That is the enemy, the form and content of fear, to be driven against us," Rukeyser writes in *The Usable Truth*. "And if you come with your lives to meet what is here, you are the heroes of the poems, for there is the meeting-place. And that defines the form and content of the poetry I tell you. Facing and communicating, that will be our life, in the world and poetry."[72] Her prose provides another meeting place where readers can communicate with and learn from her, a first step in staging our own resistance. Rukeyser's caption to her gouache painting *The Four Fears* (1955), which supplies this volume's cover image, encourages herself, and us, to do just that: "*All you have to do is challenge them.*"[73] A tiny woman resembling the poet, dark-haired and dressed in blue, stands at the bottom of the frame. Her back is turned to us, as she faces head on the titular fears, personified as giant figures, ominously clad in black robes before an infernal red backdrop. The prose found here, in *The Muriel Rukeyser Era*, equips us to make our own stand, to face the complex challenges and oppressions of our time, as Rukeyser did throughout her career.

---

72. Muriel Rukeyser, "The Fear of Poetry," from *The Usable Truth*, in this volume.
73. Muriel Rukeyser, *The Four Fears*, 1955, gouache painting, 8.5" x 11", LC II:20.

Author's Introduction
Biographical Statement for "Under Forty: A Symposium on American Literature and the Younger Generation of American Jews" (1944)
MURIEL RUKEYSER

I was born in New York, and I always loved the city. I remember an association test in school; the name "New York" was given, and the others responded "stone," "big," "crowds," "high." I thought "home." But home did not mean ease and a cottage. It meant clash and growth. My father is a businessman—a salesman really, the member of a group that shifts in society according to the period—and during my childhood and adolescence he was in the building business, sharing responsibility in the fierce skyscrapers whose stone climbed up the frames of steel, where short fire was flung and caught by the riveters—sharing excitement in the implacable cranes that dug sand, in the roads leaping out from the city, even in the horrible real estate developments whose jerry-built walls would lean before a strong wind. I thought of my father as a builder. He was helping to make New York. Even the sidewalk I played on, in front of an apartment house like a huge trunk, was partly made by him.

It is true that we have to reckon the generations of the Jews according to their wanderings. Most of the younger Jewish writers in America are the children of immigrants, and I am not representative of that generation. It has the qualities which Margaret Mead points out as "second-generation"—split with the parent culture, leaning over backward to be

"American" at its most acceptable.¹ My father's cousin recently stood up at a Town Hall meeting and said, needlessly, "*I am an American.*"

My parents did not migrate from Europe, but from America. My father came to New York from Wisconsin, where his grandfather had gone in 1848. He was brought up among the Western stories—Hill putting the railroads through, Juneau who went to Alaska.² His mother had gone to a parochial school before there were any secular schools. His family was large, with many cousins as well as brothers and sisters, and he made most of his friends inside the family, but left as soon as he could. My mother came from Yonkers, which was then a rather English town on the Hudson, and had not yet become an industrial offshoot of New York. Her sisters and brothers, and she herself, were going through an anti-religious reaction against their studious and improvident father. The young man my father and the young woman my mother had no cultural resources to strengthen them. There was not a trace of Jewish culture that I could feel—no stories, no songs, no special food—but then there was not *any* cultural background that could make itself felt. My father had reacted even further from religion after an early tragedy, and art seemed not to mean anything to him. *Julius Caesar* was the only written work he ever mentioned. His friends were of several religions, and so were his business associates. His partner in business was an Italian, an enthusiastic pioneer for fascism here and in Italy.³

There was no mark of Judaism in my childhood home except for a silver ceremonial goblet, handed down from a great-grandfather who had been a cantor, and a legend that my mother's family was directly descended from Akiba.⁴

I went to religious school automatically. Once there, I was excited, not by the digests and easy versions of Jewish history or by the smattering of prayer book Hebrew, but by the Bible itself in English. And

---

1. See Margaret Mead, *And Keep Your Powder Dry: An Anthropologist Looks at America* (New York: Berghahn Books, 2000), esp. 17–33.
2. Great Northern Railway executive officer James Hill and French Canadian prospector Joe Juneau.
3. Generoso Pope, business partner of Rukeyser's father and a media magnate whose Italian-language newspapers supported Benito Mussolini before the United States entered the Second World War.
4. Rabbi Akiva ben Josef, a second-century BCE Jewish scholar and Midrash contributor. The Romans executed him for participating in the anti-imperialist Bar Kokhba revolt and for teaching the outlawed Torah. Rukeyser celebrates him in her 1968 poem "Akiba," in *CP*, 454–460.

all this time, I had no idea of what a Christian was. I knew that our maids were Christian, and all the governesses my sister and I ever had were Christian. I did not know what a Jew was, nor that the term could be used in contempt. Once it had been shouted, but to a bunch of us who were ringing doorbells and running, and we knew we could expect scolding if we were caught at that. I was told never to say the name "Jesus"; I knew that there was something about Christians that had color and tenderness and a child in it, and that suffering of some sort was bound up with all of that. But what I knew of my religion was confined to the trip on Sunday morning across the Park to where the Temple stood, its pale green copper dome rising over the little round lake where other children sailed boats, and where the trees flowered pink in Spring.[5]

Then, suddenly, out of a need or sadness of her own, my mother turned to religion. She cannot be said to have turned back, for she had never known anything like this impulse and response. There was a sudden new insistence, and its force was sharply felt in my family. I began to go to Temple with my mother, instead of to the Museum, and I went every Saturday for seven years. They were years in which I was learning through hostility. I was having a "sheltered" childhood, and the fact that I played with street-gangs and knew about the prostitutes on the Drive and the house across the street and the chauffeur's private life were breaches which escaped my parents.[6] There were a few sets of books at home, but after I had gone through these, I read whatever the maids recommended. This was the sheltered life, this was a life of comfort. All I knew was that it was not comfortable for me. I was beginning to care about a set of values which poetry was giving me. School could back up some of this; but there was nothing at home or in the Temple to answer me.

I think that many people brought up in reformed Judaism must go starving for two phases of religion: poetry and politics. The sermons I heard were pale and mechanically balanced talks. I grew up among a group of Jews who wished, more than anything else, I think, to be invisible. They were playing possum. They shrank away from the occasional anger of the rabbi, and said that such a man ought not be in that pulpit; they were the people who read Sokolsky's column at breakfast,

---

5. Central Park.
6. During the Great Depression, along the Upper West Side's Riverside Drive and in its adjacent park, Manhattan's sex trade thrived.

and agreed with him every time he said that Jews should be quiet and polite, and should never protest; they were the people who felt that Hitler would be all right if he would only leave the Jews alone; they were, later, the people who told van Paassen he was crazy to worry about the Jews in Germany and Poland.[7] They supported big charities. They gave generously of their money. Some of the women even gave their time. But they wanted a religion of reassurance; they listened to the muted organ, and refused to be involved in suffering that demanded resistance, and refused to acknowledge evil. If they had a mission as a responsible and inspired people, they did not want it. It was enough to be Jewish. Charity was about the most they could give; not struggle; they would neither approach the source nor make the connections.

There was one place where this was done, for me; and that was in the Bible. I sat under the shadowy dome during the drone of the watered-down sermon and the watered-down liturgical music, and I read the Bible. Its clash and poetry and nakedness, its fiery vision of conflict resolved only in God, were true to me, no matter what I was coming to believe about the reality of the world or power or divinity or death or love. The Bible was closer to the city than anything that was going on or could possibly go on in the Temple.

Now it is much later, and I am being asked questions about my heritage and my writing. But it is not late enough; it is more than ten years since that time, and I have begun to come a little closer to the source and the connections. But just begun. I have moved around this country some, South a few times, west to California, north into Canada. I have lived in the Middle West and Mexico, and once I went to Europe. I have seen Scottsboro and Gauley Bridge, had good years at College, and looked for my first jobs in the middle of the depression. I crossed the frontier into Spain on the first day of the war, and stayed long enough to see Catalonia win its own war and make peace, a peace that could not be held. I have had a government job in wartime, with a division that was undermined from the beginning, making war posters for American

---

7. George Sokolsky was an anti-communist columnist for the *New York Herald Tribune* and the *New York Sun*. Dutch-born Pierre van Paassen was a foreign correspondent for the *New York Evening World* and the *Toronto Globe*. He had been imprisoned for nine days at an unidentified concentration camp in 1933. After escaping, he provided early warnings about the Nazi death camps and Italian and Spanish fascism.

distribution. And all the time I have been writing poems, and after each trip I have come back to New York.

I do not know how far I am representative of any group in Jewish life. I was brought up without any reason to be proud of being Jewish, and then was told to be proud; without any reason for shame, and then saw that people were ashamed. I was a fat child, and hated that condition until I grew up and grew into my skin. I saw people feeling toward their Jewishness as I felt toward my size. But I never had that. I saw my religion sharply divided into three divisions: there was the dogma, the ethic, with which I wrestled; there was the poetry and fire, a deepening source of power to me; and there was the organized church, which I saw as torpid and conservative, and which I repudiated. The chief pressures against me, and against what was coming to be my work and belief, came from torpor and conservatism—or from fear, from active reaction, as in the person, again, of my father's cousin, who began to want me to change my name, so that it would not so much resemble his own.[8] But these people were narrow, on the side of narrowness; whatever grew from the fact that I was Jewish, I would have to live, I knew, for the other side.

My themes and the use I have made of them have depended on my life as a poet, as a woman, as an American, and as a Jew. I do not know what part of that is Jewish; I know I have tried to integrate these four aspects, and to solve my work and my personality in terms of all four. I feel that I am at the beginning of that attempt, too. Jewish references have come into some of my poems—the strong cry of the *Shema*, the raw, primitive blast of the *Shofar*, the Friday candles, the tragic migrations, modern tortures and the Warsaw ghetto, Joel and Ezekiel (in terms of John Brown), images started in me by the poetry of the prophets in the English Bible. I have always accepted the fact that the treatment of minorities is a good test of democracy, or any other system; I do not believe that is a particularly Jewish idea. I have wanted Jews, and everyone else, to have social equality anywhere in the world. On the way out of adolescence, I searched, as others do, for ancestors. I felt, then and now, that if one is free, freedom can extend to a certain degree into the past, and one may choose one's ancestors, to go on with their wishes and their fight. But I do not think that Jews are any more responsive to

---

8. Rukeyser's second cousin was financial columnist and popular author Merryle Stanley Rukeyser.

any of these ideas than are Christians. I am not afraid of allies in anything I may undertake, and I would work for my few beliefs with anyone who is willing to work for them.

To live as a poet, woman, American, and Jew—this chalks in my position. If the four come together in one person, each strengthens the others. Red-baiting, undercuts at the position of women, anti-intellectual and anti-imaginative drives such as Congress has recently been conducting—these are on the same level as the growing storm of anti-Semitism.

One questions oneself when all these attacks arrive; and one looks at the Jews. The Jews I knew as a child, the Jewish professionals who were able to get out of Europe and come here as refugees, the Jews who could put up with fascism as long as it left them alone, the Jews who objected to a poster against discrimination because it mentioned Jews and Negroes together. The Jews that so many Christians, fighting fascism and its implications, look sideward at. And then one thinks of the men and women in the Warsaw ghetto, standing as the Loyalists stood in Spain, weaponless against what must have seemed like the thunder and steel of the whole world; one thinks of the men and women, Jews moving freely in Russia; one thinks of the men and women, planting Palestine and taking a fierce oath never to put down their arms.

To me, the value of my Jewish heritage, in life and in writing, is its value as a guarantee. Once one's responsibility as a Jew is really assumed, one is guaranteed, not only against fascism, but against many kinds of temptation to close the spirit. It is a strong force in oneself against many kinds of hardness which may arrive in the war—the idea that when you throw off insight, you travel light and are equipped for fighting; the idea that it is impractical to plan and create, and that concrete construction and invention are the only practical things, apart from killing. Organized religion has not been able to take a strong stand about these things, any more than it has been able to stand with the Jews in Warsaw, or against the disguised Fascists at home.

But the conflict enlarges and grows, with one's own life and writing swept up in it. And the imagination moves, the spirit opens, one knows again what it is to be Jewish; and what it will always be at its best in one's life and one's writing: memory and fire and poetry and the wandering spirit that never changes in its love of man.

(*Contemporary Jewish Record*, 1944)

Part I

The Usable Truth

Five Talks on
Communication and Poetry

CHAPTER 1

The Fear of Poetry (1940, 1941)

                              There is, under all the surface shouting of the year, a silence in the country now.[1] We feel it in the contemplation of the facts, too large, too violent to accept with reason; we know this silencing in its symptoms, the turn of the arts, the glossing over of the Presidential election, all the omissions of the deep conflict which we feel this year. I wish to speak of this silence, the fear which has fathered it, the communication which may break it, making it possible to meet the world with all the resources we have, the fund of faith, the generous instruments of imagination and knowledge. I wish to speak to you of poetry as the sum of such equipment, as an image of a kind of weapon that can best meet these enemies, the outer cloud, the stealthy inner silence of fear. Now we invoke memory, we search all the days we had forgotten for a tradition

---

    1. Muriel Rukeyser's note inside the cover page of the fc to *The Usable Truth*: "Note: These lectures are prepared for reading, with gaps at some of the more important places, and before and after all the illustrations. In delivering them, I read them as they stand here, ad libbing where omissions are indicated. It will be a simple matter to revise them for publication. I hope the material here will indicate the fullness of the papers as they were presented.—M. R." This first lecture was delivered at Vassar College on Tuesday, October 29, 1940, at 8:20 p.m. It is the only published talk from the series, appearing in 1941 in *Twice a Year*, Dorothy Norman's magazine of politics and culture. Except for a few variances drawn from the fc, as noted below, the published article, which is close to the original lecture, provides this edition's copytext.

that can support our arms in this moment; we invoke a rigorous positive that will enable us to make our choices; we invoke poetry as the attitude that can clear us and make whole the spirit to face its life.

There are great gashes in our world that we have built up and that we love with so much pain. Deep gashes from which we all must suffer, the ones who foresee the effects, and the ones who never foresee any effect, but live through them only once, when they occur. Gashes are inflicted on awareness very early, and we recognize them when we look at children, or receive news of primitive people in their religion, their poetry, their ability to make dances to help them understand their foreboding. Much of that has been taken away from us; we need it now; this is the moment when we must recognize what we need, a moment in the world when whole peoples open their consciousness to their lack, and try to store up quickly whatever is most valuable, to prepare and defend and grow; and in this context enters poetry, and the fear of poetry.

There was, for a time, what appeared to be an Age of Tourists. The years of exploration, on the surface of this world, in education, or sightseeing, actually sailing seas and visiting strange cities with the stare of innocence, the quick brightness of youth abroad, or the easy aging cynicism of the perennial diplomat. That faded; we entered the Age of Fear.

When we were tourists, we were children; these were the legends and fairy stories that could be put away before we slept. Some of us were lucky; we saw these legends come to life at home; actually at home, in the day-by-day process of family and early learning. Or, later, in our own countryside, very much loved, very much trusted, but showing in glimpses the same landscapes, the same struggles, the same trials and failures. There was time to go to school with every hero. Here was a conqueror, Roman and still in his poise, who had kept notebooks of conquest that we might learn grammar; here was a statesman to provide us a parable; here was a playwright through whose faded grace, as through the curtains of his stage, we might perceive our language. There were these communications. We were told there was a sequence, there were mounting curves of incident to follow, whose heights curved up into dramatic relief. But, in our lives, shock followed shock. The symptoms of works of art became more than efforts at speech; it was clear that there was a breakdown of communication, that the arts were not as they had been, that they were lining themselves up and shouting angrily, half-heard across the distance; but during this breakdown—"breakdown of standards, breakdown of communication"—it was apparent that the myths they told were taking shape in the world, that certain cloudy struggles were actually defined and enlarging. Then the newspapers were full of it; then, at last, it could not be kept out of conversation, then it filled the world as war again, with fear its weapon.

I think now of a boat on which I sailed away from Spain. I saw very little of Spain, very little of the war. The situation that I was in was of a different nature. I had come in on the morning that the war began, on a train crowded with unprepared people from every country in Europe, and America, thrown abruptly together in the midst of crisis, and falling—and this is almost incredible, even now—into opinions which were indeed shadows cast by that future glare of wild skies full of fire, shadows cast backward into a small Spanish valley, with its sashed and sandaled men running among the trees. It was clear then, at that outbreak, which was on a small and primitive scale compared to what was to follow, that there was an arch of belief, cracked and badly sprung, but standing.[2] That shape remained, through the small first battle in Catalonia, until those of us who did not go at once into the army were evacuated, and this was a ship sailing, overcrowded, its decks full, the pattern of many refugee ships to come, sailing through the dark water of the Mediterranean. On deck that night, people talked quietly about what they had just seen and what it might mean to the world. There were long pauses between these broken sentences, spoken in language after language. Suddenly, a printer, a man who had already been several times a refugee and was then publishing in Paris, said: "And poetry—among all this—where is there a place for poetry?"

That question. There it is, asked out loud.

And the pause that follows, and the force behind it! Taking one high above that ship in a black sea at the beginning of a war. High, staring down, high enough to see all Europe night-dark beneath. High, as time passes. Higher, as the years go. Until the edge sinks, and the Atlantic lies there, and higher, until the ship has disappeared completely, and Europe and America are far as maps, and the years go, and the world is visible this year. That question.

"Is there a place for poetry?"

When I say Yes, there is—when I say, I believe in poetry as the clew—I speak only very closely and for purposes of definition of the lines themselves.[3] I disregard the physical reaction that defines a poem for you,

---

2. On fc, "arch of belief" reads "arch of opinion."
3. The editors preserve Rukeyser's spelling *clew* on the fc, rather than *clue* in the published article version. The archaism signifies a ball of thread or yarn like what Greek mythic

what happens to the top of your head, or what crawlings go along your skin. I speak of an expressed attitude.[4]

Our education has made its gifts to us with an admonition: Use! All we tell you, say the schools, is to be absorbed in your lives. Every attitude is from now on your tradition. This is your equipment, with this we send you to your wars, wherever they may be. Whatever they mean. There is just this one learning, this one branch of your heritage. It is very precious, it is to be preserved; it preserves *us*, entire ages are given us by its grace alone—but, although it is to be memorized and stored, it is not to be used. This, of course, is poetry. In an otherwise utilitarian culture, this one knowledge is to be taught us as being Not For Use. What place has it? What is its use, indeed?[5]

I speak against the fear that shapes that question. And against the fear that rules out poetry, with all the other work in pure imagination, abstract art, abstract science. If communication has broken down, it is time to tap the roots of communication. Poetry is written from those depths, a source speaking to another source. And it is deep at that level that it has been stopped. The question comes up again at this moment of shock, when no kind of speech seems powerful and pure enough to carry above catastrophe. The fear that cuts it off is as deep. It plunges us deep in childhood.

---

hero Theseus uses to escape the Minotaur's labyrinth, which Rukeyser references later. *Clew* also means "a round bunch or cluster of things." *Oxford English Dictionary*, 2nd ed. (1989), s.v. "Clew" 3a and 1b. Rukeyser later theorized that poems communicate emotions through images that "move like a cluster" and form "a constellation." Muriel Rukeyser, *The Life of Poetry* (Ashfield, MA: Paris Press, 1996), 19.

4. Last sentence not on fc. Instead, there is a self-edited and fragmentary note: "Sensations are there, ~~as much as for wind or alcohol or anger or music~~; they are the body of poetry; out . . . etc. etc." Rukeyser alludes to Emily Dickinson's August 16, 1870, letter to Thomas Wentworth Higginson: "If I read a book and it makes my whole body so cold no fire can warm me I know *that* is poetry. If I feel physically as if the top of my head were taken off, I know *that* is poetry." Emily Dickinson, *The Letters of Emily Dickinson*, vol. 2, ed. Thomas H. Johnson and Theodora Ward (Cambridge, MA: Belknap Press of Harvard University Press, 1958), 473–474. Original emphases.

5. This paragraph, appearing only in the published article, reworks the first half of an insert on fc's facing page. The second half was unused by Rukeyser: "It seems to me that now, in this moment when we are called upon to face what is admittedly the most complicated situation the world has yet known, that it is high time to inquire into this attitude. Now, when it is hard to hold in the head for more than a moment the giant cluster of any front-page situation, it is time to remember this other kind of knowledge, which has forever been a way of learning complexes of emotion and situation, the attitude that perhaps might be our equipment to face the world now—the attitude of poetry."

Remembering that childhood, we remember the beginnings of that malignant process. The first breaks in expression follow soon; you may visit classrooms and see it happen before you, too often—the question cut off, the meanings of books undercut by explanations and parsings which in themselves need not destroy, but take that effect when they are turned loose on the very young. You may overhear it in libraries, when high school students ask each other offhand, in contempt or embarrassment, "Do you read poetry?" and wait for the headshake that means No. Or see it in adults who put all such expression far behind them. But not naturally, as a child's toy; they put it away with a certain painful shocked awareness that here is something not for them, something that does not belong, that has no social acceptability.

And this is for the direct call, this is for the knowledge that the world is in many ways unbegun, that its beginnings, that its good and evil and all its praise is in our own hands, that as long as there is passion and agony and love and promise, the world is still to be made! That knowledge, in its full directness and under its firmest control, is the base. It is that which is met with fear.

The history of the self-control of nations is the history of civilization—their self-control and objectivity, and the products of these. The lives of those to whom we turn back are stories of the self-control of power. It is that control that gives us our traditions. And poetry is communication self-controlled, turning its powers according to the laws of the spirit. That is form, in poetry.

The quality itself has suddenly stood up alive for us once more, in the British behavior that has carried those islanders through the torture of waiting with the wave poised over them, through the torture under the wave of attack as it fell. This bracing, this silence, this critical faith and equilibrium under fire, common to any people with a sense of unity, is one of the qualities which is a source of courage to us. I speak of it here because it has, in the English, often been identified with the gesture of denial of passion and meaning which I most deeply attack: the fear itself; and it is not that. I must speak in these terms, they are the terms in which we think now. We are living in a long time of decision; many of our battles are being fought abroad; there is a fatality which brings us closer every day to those battles.[6] I am glad now that I am speaking to you, and not to men of our own age; this is not anything that I would

---

6. On fc, "fatality" is "fatalism."

care to say to men in the months in which they are facing conscription.[7] But once that machine has been switched on, there is little time to balance point against point. We recognize, among ourselves, the existence of good and evil and the wide middle country between those fearful ranges where common life is lived, that Middle West of daily life's production, common sense, and conflict. But it is from the central conflict that the works of invention and imagination rise; to face the conflict itself requires courage and imagination. The refusal to face the conflict is the fear of poetry. The strength of poetry is the fact that it is an index to this tearing human web, to our own vivid lives. Before any of our guns begin, this is our strength, this is our equipment.

The equipment of the other side is fear. And we know that fear. The other side is as much ourselves as any external threat. The external threat cannot be met with these qualities. When war begins, qualitative differences are in armaments, not in virtues. All of these barriers are down the minute the shooting starts and the speculative thought ends for the duration; exceptions to the rule becoming rare. Many fears end at that moment, many fears are absorbed physically into the body as a meal is absorbed, so that under fire or in the stress of a night raid the only thing that can be said of stone-faced crowds in shelters, or the stony humor that develops, is that here are people undergoing fear. But what we know now, what we have in this great moment of influence, when all the forces are already at work but we are not fighting, is the old fear—the fear we had at home, and in the classroom and toward our early emotion. The fear of meaning. The fear of intensity—that curtain, allowing us to blank out, allowing us in shock to ward off meanings that turn our own lives. Often the object is too immense and harrowing. We have heard them say, Who can imagine the Chinese people, flooded and starved and broken by earthquake and bombing? Who can imagine the people of France, refugees at home, going mad on the roads, starving and betrayed and lost in their own countryside? Who can see the long stone of the Great Wall, flowing over the old mountains, and dream that it ever meant protection? Or the pillboxes of the obscenely

---

7. On fc, Rukeyser inked over the "d" in *I dare*, changing it to *I care*. This edit to her script at the time of her lectures reflects her immediate awareness of the gendered dynamics of the first peacetime draft, instituted with the passage of the Selective Training and Service Act on September 16, 1940. Males ages twenty-one to thirty-six, exempting disabled persons and conscientious objectors belonging to historic peace churches, were legally required to register for a draft lottery. Weeks later, Rukeyser gave this lecture to a predominantly female audience at Vassar, then a women's college.

inappropriate Maginot Line, and imagine peace? Who can face these meanings now, so soon? But this is the moment to face them. This is the only time we have. We need equipment, we need all the time and all the equipment in the world. And as it is true that everyone in the world has the same amount of time, it is also true that we are almost the only ones left who can be using that time. The others are foraging for food, looking for a place to stay the night, are out fighting fires.[8] Not busy with meanings. The time for that has passed, and has not yet come again. Another deadlier tradition has been invoked.

We have our own tradition to retrace. So many times, when our scholars have talked of tradition, they have been thinking, "Repeat! Repeat!" mourning some Golden Age to whose special knowledge they had felt admitted. But tradition is not repetition, that is blasphemy against tradition. Tradition is, rather, the search for the clew—to know oneself in one's own labyrinth, and be suddenly aware that by a thread, a subtle thread, by a thread only, could the center be reached. As it was, as it has been! But as it will not be again, except for indirection. Sheridan caught the phrase there; he warns us not to "anticipate the past."[9] Kierkegaard speaks of the foreboding eye which looks behind so that it may see, by indirection, what lies ahead.[10] But at this crisis we stand at a height—a great height over the world, your truly objective visionary, with the world fighting its battles laid out as on a map far under us, with a little boat on the sea and a question asked in dread, "Where is the place for poetry?" and with the entire past from which

---

8. For the published article version, Rukeyser added the phrase "are out fighting fires," absent from the fc.

9. In Richard Brinsley Sheridan's play *The Rivals: A Comedy* (1775), Mrs. Malaprop notes sardonically that, to forgive the elopement of her charge, Lydia, "we will not anticipate the past"; instead, "our retrospection will be all to the future."

10. Philosopher Søren Kierkegaard argued that most communication is indirect. Thus, even philosophy cannot reveal the truth of existence, whose essence is spiritual and immediate. Using pseudonyms and devices such as parables and retrospective narratives, he deployed what he termed indirect communication to unsettle his own authority and to cause readers to "reach a true mutual understanding [with him] in inwardness," thus compelling their responsibility for belief. Søren Kierkegaard, *Concluding Unscientific Postscript to the Philosophical Crumbs*, ed. and trans. Alastair Hannay (New York: Cambridge University Press, 2009), 232. *Fear and Trembling* (1843), which Rukeyser mentions here and discusses in depth later (see Muriel Rukeyser, "Belief and Poetry," in this volume), exemplifies this method. There, Kierkegaard characterizes the poet as "the hero's better nature" and "the genius of recollection, [who] can do nothing except call to mind what has been done, do nothing but admire what has been done" by heroes. The poet's song of the past creates a "transfigured" memory for the future. Kierkegaard, *Fear and Trembling and The Sickness unto Death*, trans. Walter Lowrie (1941; reis., Princeton, NJ: Princeton University Press, 2013), 46.

to choose. For it is given to human beings to choose their tradition, when they have come to this point. Very early, before the ignorant tree of Good and Evil, and at the late point, with that dream of peace and freedom as common as rain and impossible to conjure out of a cloud of battle-smoke, and still with a choice of tradition! I have been living in New Haven, a town that has set up a memorial to its choice in a curious way that shocked me when I first realized what it meant. On the New Haven Green, itself a hub of tradition, there is a church which is old and respected and well-proportioned and serene. Its cornerstones are the monuments of two of the Regicides, the judges who condemned King Charles to death and escaped to America as refugees after the Restoration.[11] A church founded on the stones of king-killers, on the breaking of the most extreme taboo! D. H. Lawrence speaks of the verbal shock of a first reading of *Lady Chatterley's Lover*, a shock that is over as soon as the meanings themselves come across in their honesty, and this is another shock of the same order.[12] But that is our gesture, the violent axiom-breaking gesture of the imagination that takes its sides, chooses its own tradition, and gets to work, facing what it must face. Our religion is that, in this country, religions built on the stones of regicides. Our poetry is that. Founded on the breaking of axioms; and our sciences, our inventions. It is a tradition of the audacious spirit, of the imagination that asserts itself against the world, life and death and all the dead wars. Our poetry is the clew to much of this—it is the most naked emblem of the double image, the murder and the new church. It is a question for the psychiatrists how much the sense of guilt involved in one made for the immediate necessity of the other. But we can be sure of this, that the sense of guilt has its furious power here, it is the deepest ambition, the strongest point, perhaps indeed the Archimedean point from which the earth may be moved at will.

But all this must be used in strength. It is fatal now to hold back from any of it. Even this war that is over the world. This is a war imagination

---

11. To escape execution, three regicides who had sentenced King Charles I to death were sheltered in New Haven, in colonial Connecticut. Three intersecting streets bearing their names—Whalley, Goffe, and Dixon—now converge on New Haven Green.

12. After the US Customs Office banned his novel *Lady Chatterley's Lover* (1928) on grounds of obscenity, British modernist D. H. Lawrence tied this state action to reactionary "mob-meaning." He instead privileged "individual meaning," which draws on experience, imagination, memory, and cultural history. See D. H. Lawrence, "Pornography and Obscenity," in *Late Essays and Articles*, ed. James T. Boulton (New York: Cambridge University Press, 2004), 236–253.

made; we saw it coming, and those a little before us saw it; and our imaginations must be strong enough to create a peace. First, to create an image of that peace, and then to bring it about. And, in the meantime, we need the audacity always to cry for more freedom, more imagination, more poetry with all its meanings.

As we approach a condition of war we will find ourselves more and more in a condition of slavery; the mock-peace of waste, pre-war conscription, and then the final constraints of war. More and more we shall need to be free in our own beliefs, since it is clear that once we accept this long momentum of rules and constraints, we shall slowly be losing many of our chances to act in freedom. And then it is too late to look at our leaders. If they represent us, indeed, they represent our weaknesses, too; in democracy, we know what we have, we elect ourselves, and our eccentric will and hesitation are reflected statistically. We shall not be wrong, I think, at any point during the rest of our lives if we call always for more freedom, more honesty. Social, personal, aesthetic beliefs need to be shaken loose; all the moulds are broken; our opinions of war and sex and tomorrow's headlines need to be faced, recast. The last audacity will be this call: to demand that people bring their lives, their mature wishes, to this effort. Many people will be calling for the gifts of death. It is not their death, in wars or poverty, but their life. More Life, we say.

Poetry has failed us here. It has not been good enough. We want this voice now, we want voices to speak to us *as we move, directly*, insisting on full consciousness and a wish to move and come to life. And there is little enough to which anyone can point and say, "That poem speaks for me." But we know that is the place. Even the advertisements know it; they cover full pages of the magazines, announcing the Oxford Book of English Verse as *all that is imperishable of England*—including Walt Whitman, as an English imperishable.[13] And it is true, although it is not possible to prove. There will be very little of what I say that is possible to prove, or even to find tolerable examples for. The meaning is here, but few of the words have reached it. Many of the dead ones are shabby, some have shaken off the grave and stand shining and alive, but looking away, in another direction. It is not quite what we mean. They have not been saying quite what we wanted to hear. Well, we shall be saying our own words to each other; and part of our job will never be done.

---

13. Two weeks before Rukeyser's lectures, the Book-of-the-Month Club ran a full-page ad for the *Oxford Book of English Verse* with this banner. See *Life*, October 14, 1940, 5.

It is necessary that the twenty-fifth century be able to discard our work, to reject our time. Our poems will have failed if our readers are not brought by them beyond them. "What we once admired as poetry has long since come to be a sound of tin pans; and many of our later books we have outgrown. Perhaps Homer and Milton will be tin pans yet. Better not to be easily pleased. The poet should rejoice if he has taught us to despise his song; if he has so moved us as to lift us,—to open the eye of the intellect to see farther and better."[14] That is Emerson saying "tin pans." But Emerson is speaking in a very different voice from the voices we recently have heard. The war has been a Cadmus's stone, thrown among us to turn us on what we know best; statesman has turned on statesman, shouting treason; labor has turned on labor, business on business, in fury of self-hatred and confession. The French, I am led to believe, hate the British bitterly, as the Spaniards did after their war, but most of all they hate their own surrendering leaders.[15] Something as bad as that, and close to the main symptom, has happened here already, among our intellectuals, who have turned on one another, dealing out blame for the attitudes of whole generations, calling for the destruction of attitudes—at many places the attack amounts to calling for the burning of books. All through the year, which has been a crisis of evaluation and loneliness, one heard of person after person renouncing the standards of the spirit and the critical mind which had been built up through the grueling years of waste, and turn against the one face of life which was best known, ready to smash out in a gesture of rage which can best be explained as an obscure gesture of self-destruction, a gesture of impotence and failure at home. But that gesture is completely negative, very different in its nature from the anger that comes of the wish to be reached, the wish for fuller expression. Emerson makes the last demands with the greatest tolerance. He says, "Newton may be permitted to call Terence a playbook, and to wonder at the frivolous taste for rhymers: he only predicts, one would say, a grander poetry: he only shows that he is not yet reached; that the poetry which satisfies more youthful souls is not such to a mind like his, accustomed to grander harmonies;—this being a child's whistle to his ear; that the music must rise to a loftier strain, up to Handel, up to

---

14. Ralph Waldo Emerson, "Poetry and Imagination" (1872).
15. On fc, holo. note opposite page verso: "The Civil War in Europe started with the split that showed in Spain; moved on to divide France and England in a division of one unit like that of our own Civil War."

Beethoven, up to the thorough-base of the sea-shore, up to the largeness of astronomy. . . ."[16] That is insistence very far removed from the carping which we have been hearing.

It is that demand which is to be put on our poetry. Make it grow. Make it assume all the questions we are asked. Make it live our life; ask us and answer us. It is our own wish that needs more strength, not alone the poetry that is feeble. It is reflecting life.

It is reflecting your lives.

Art and nature are imitations, not of each other, but of the same third thing—both images of the real, the spectral and vivid reality. Reality employs all means. If we fear it in art, we fear it in nature, and our fear brings its object upon us, in that compulsive manner of fear, unleashing force upon the world we love. There are reasons for terror now. The middle pitch of life is not where we are going to live. The moment of great height, of infinite depth, is here. There is a famous passage in the works of the great imaginative scientist, Clerk Maxwell, in which he draws attention to the implications of what are termed in mathematics "singular points." A stone poised on another stone, a ball rolling in perfect motion on a perfect wedge, a supersaturated solution, are examples, and the equations for their systems break down at these extraordinary moments in their history. Maxwell believed that the science of the future would be deeply concerned with these breakdowns in "systems of high rank."[17] We may be said to be living in a system which has reached such a point. Science, unfortunately, has not yet caught up with this breakdown—except insofar as it has warned us and implemented us; that is, sociology and economics made the footnotes to their foresight, for anyone to read; and we are provided with dive-bombers. But there is no exact historic science; there is no poetic science. There is history, and there is poetry, and both are going to have to reach "the largeness of astronomy" for this crisis.[18]

---

16. Emerson, "Poetry and Imagination."

17. Rukeyser is extrapolating an idea of, rather than directly citing from, Scottish physicist James Clerk Maxwell, the first theorist of electromagnetism: "Every existence above a certain rank has its singular points: the higher the rank, the more of them." He concludes, "All great results produced by human endeavor depend on taking advantage of these singular states when they occur." James Clerk Maxwell, "Science and Free Will," in *The Life of James Clerk Maxwell with a Selection from His Correspondence and Occasional Writings*, by Lewis Campbell and William Garnett (London: Macmillan, 1882), 443.

18. Emerson, "Poetry and Imagination."

But we live in it. It is our ritual moment, our moment of proof, and we need all our implements, all the equipment tradition and invention offer.

It would be easy to be swamped by material. There is an entire theology of the Constitution. Whitman, we say, Whitman, Melville. There are clews. Melville has given us a challenge which could stand as the core of a tradition—the phrase, "the usable truth." It is *that* we plunge for, *that* we try for again and again, burying ourselves deep in death so that we may emerge alive with it, risking whatever we are given to risk for it. He speaks of it in a moving and potent letter to Hawthorne.[19] But it is this; and not the usable past, that is the kernel.[20] This is capable of much life; it has not to do with time's dimension, but with the two other dimensions in which meaning lives: function and relation. Truth in its function, truth in its relations to us, it is that that is behind my wish for poetry, and my insistence that if we face the meanings here, we have our equipment well begun. Truth, write of truth and your sentences will read like love-letters; it is something to haunt us, and we in turn may hunt it and never speak a word.

The usable truth! That is Yankee enough to satisfy the most practical person shopping for common sense. Hard-headed and durable, and serving its own purpose, and calling for its own poetry, and not countenancing any kind of fear. It makes its own demands. It sets its own standards.

What faces does it take? How shall we come by it? What color? What form? What content? Question: scan the first twenty lines of usable truth. No, but it is not so ridiculous as what is often done to poetry; because we have two criteria here. It must be there for use, immediate use; and it must be true. Nothing said about beauty, you will note. Not all this time. Not mentioned once.[21] *Nothing* said about beauty, only

---

19. Herman Melville, April 1851 letter to Nathaniel Hawthorne. Melville actually wrote "visable [sic] truth," which was erroneously transcribed by Hawthorne's family as "usable truth." See Harrison Hayford, "Usable or Visible Truth," *Modern Language Notes* 74, no. 8 (1959): 702–705, http://www.jstor.org/stable/3040391; Herman Melville, *Correspondence*, ed. Lynn Horth (Evanston, IL: Northwestern University Press, 1991), 184–187.

20. Van Wyck Brooks coined the term "the usable past" to describe how the American professoriate could develop a national culture by renarrating history and using literature to map a "spiritual past." Van Wyck Brooks, "On Creating a Usable Past," *Dial*, April 11, 1918, 338.

21. Holo. improvisation notes on opposite page verso: "Ivory tower and birdcage—*no* ivory tower, always an outside, verdict term. / space-saver, time-saver—what do you have to save? Energy, sensation? / Life will forgive you, you know, if you ask for forgiveness, You will be told

facing things, and be ready, and poetry as nourishment for that, and usable truth. What has happened to all the standards? It is simple: the standards have broken down; but that, too, has nothing to do with beauty. That was before the breakdown, when "standards" and "beauty" were the same. I have not mentioned many delights, I have not spoken of the happiness we all know daily, nor of the clews we have been given, in childhood and in school and here. There are many things—but as a basis we have the fact that we are all alive in this room at the same time, and one or two wishes. A wish for immediacy, for speech. If they will only say what we want to hear! If the poems will say what we have meant all along! I think they come closest of any form to that. That is why I have my belief. I need them to be immediate, to reach my life. First of all. To make that quick acute communication, to make contact, clearing the distance between people until the real meaning lies between them, and only meaning. There are barriers, there are the deafening lonelinesses. But here is the immediacy and the voice.

People want it. They need it. The fear of poetry is a complicated and civilized expression of that need. It is not a fear of children, or of primitives, or of deeply religious people. But the great hesitation and defeat is an expression of complex need, the need for a single gesture that will cut through doubt with one dramatizing stroke. John Brown is the actor of such a gesture, who in one fanatic campaign lit up the imagination of a whole people.[22] In the nature of things, Lincoln was forced to call him a crazy reckless old man, and condemn the gesture. But that gesture was able to fit into the tradition of many people, recognizably, as an active clew.

I have recently heard the story of a poet in Germany.[23] He is there now, one of the few poets left, and I was told the story by one who, understanding his motives, was trying to explain the phenomenon of a poet, a man of good will, who stays in Germany and has never attempted to leave. This poet is a very generous and mild man whose writings have consisted of delicate and rather exquisite lyrics, fine but

---

you were unimportant, that any person is unimportant, you will be told to go to sleep, it is all right; but that is not quite true."

22. Rukeyser discusses white abolitionist John Brown, who was executed after fomenting a slave rebellion, only in the published article. On fc, a holo. improvisation note appears: "John Brown's act." Before her Vassar lectures, Rukeyser mythologized the historical figure in "The Soul and Body of John Brown," in *CP*, 247–250. First published in *Poetry* in 1940, the long poem was reprinted as a private edition featuring lithographs by Rudolph von Ripper.

23. Hans Carossa, German doctor and poet.

frail, in a frail voice, and his novels and journals. He earns his living as a doctor. He has stayed on in his old house, watching one after another of his friends leave the country. His wife is quite old now, as he is, and his son is an invalid. He was asked at one time to accept the presidency of the Academy, and his name was printed on the stationary before his refusal was made public.[24] He did refuse, but the announcements were out, and there was a certain resentment among the refugees about all of this. There has been a lot of bitterness about his staying on without a gesture, and particularly about his acceptance of invitations to come and read his poems at meetings of the Hitler Youth. He does accept; he does go and read, to packed meetings in uniform; and he defends himself by saying, "I cannot withhold my gentle voice."[25]

The meaning of that gesture is a marginal meaning whose strength has not yet been tried. Here is a man living with the framework, answering without feeling himself and his work compromised. He answers them. With what? This is one of the poems he reads to the Hitler Youth; this is a poem for which *the refugees* resent him.[26]

> To keep and conceal may be, in times of crisis,
> a godly service. No one's too weak for this.
> I have heard often about our ancestress,
> who was a stupid child, learning her lessons
> slowly. In time the village turned
> the cattle over to her, and she loved her labor.
> Until, in a darkened spring, the war-ghost came.
> The arrogant strange leader rushed with his army
> across our country and over the frontier.
> One evening they heard distant insistent drums.
> The farmers ran and stared at each other in the road.
> The girl was silent; but her still spirit planned
> the act which reaches our village now as legend.

---

24. In 1933, Carossa rejected a post in the Prussian Academy of Arts after its literature division signed a loyalty oath to the Third Reich. See Jan-Pieter Barbian, *The Politics of Literature in Nazi Germany: Books in the Media Dictatorship*, trans. Kate Sturge (New York: Bloomsbury, 2013), 13–16.

25. There is no evidence Carossa said this.

26. Fc of this passage is substantially different: "Here is a man who has been criticized for staying in Nazi Germany; an old man, who cannot withhold his voice—as he says, his gentle voice—from the Hitler Youth organization. It is, in a way, a mild and subtle way indeed, but there—an answer to them. A weapon against them. But they ask for it. They seem to want it very much. They invite it and he cannot withhold it from them."

She stole by night from farm to farm unchaining
in every stable the finest and most perfect beasts
and led them from that village, chained in dreams.
Not a dog barked; animals knew the girl.
She drove the herd through towns and off the highway
past fragrant reaches to the mountain pastures'
deep meadows; and she talked to her animals;
they were quieted by the voice of the wise child.
A bellow would have betrayed their hiding-place;
they were never betrayed to the terrible enemy
ransacking their village. And for a long time
she lived in this way, on milk and bitter berries.
At home they listed her among the missing,
lost in the meadows of the underworld.

One day the last of the soldiers left the land,
the soft land lay, green in the light of peace.
And then she gathered her leaves and flowers, and singing
led the wreathed marvellous herd down from the forests;
and the new-born calves leapt along in the field.
The girl had grown tall and lovely in that time.
She walked behind them, tall and garlanded.
She sang; she sang. And the young and old ran out.
And all the cattle streamed back to their farms.
The shouts of the children. The weeping of the old.

To whom do I speak today? Who shall tell us
that you are alive again? Who shall tell us today
that you will eat the bread of the earthly fields?
Ah, this star we live on is burning full in danger.
All we know is this: across existence
and across its lapse passes something unknown.
We name it love. And, love, we pray to you.
—It takes only a second to walk around a man.
Whoever wishes to circle the soul of a lover
needs longer than his pilgrimage of years.[27]

---

27. Muriel Rukeyser, "From 'To the Unborn Child,'" in *CP*, 229-230. Originally titled "A Translation, from To the Unborn Child by Hans Carossa" and credited to Elizabeth Mayer and Rukeyser. See Muriel Rukeyser, *Beast in View* (New York: Doubleday, Doran, 1944), 38-39.

CHAPTER 1

Carossa the poet provides an answer to one sort of harshness, opens himself to give graciousness of word to anyone asking it. It is his way of facing the tradition and its demand. There are many things that are not faced, and it is possible that the encounter that poetry provides is the equipment with which we will be able to face today. And there are the great strokes which we know are not yet absorbed. There are more of these daily now than can be borne. We cannot yet think about France. I do not know many people who can think about France, a nation of refugees at home, for more than a moment before they glance off of that sight.[28] Or of what conscription means to us now, of what is conscripted, of that Maginot army that any conscripted army may well be.[29] These shells of defense, a shell like Chicago's lakefront before the great dark city, like the ancient ruinous Great Wall of China, like the crust of the Maginot Line, like the fear that devastates us when we shrink before the sense of destiny that fascism has turned loose, or before the deep realization offered by the meanings of poetry.

Strength is *behind* such shells, or it is nowhere found. And it goes deep, there will be no more level pitch of moderate and smug enthusiasm, or tourist eyesight. Faith is found here, not in a destiny that raids its earth, but in a people who, person by person, believes itself. Do you believe yourselves? When you speak, do you believe what you say? When you act, do you believe what you are doing? It comes down to that. Profound and ironic honesty, that tests itself, that stays alert and sensitive. Only let us believe ourselves and stay aware, and we are safe. For we want to be safe, the last ten years have said that with every hour. And we can be safe only by asking for more—there is a deep safety in calling, for the rest of our lives, for more liberty, more rebellion, more belief. There are many things to be fought, and these fight them. And poetry fights them, and we are safe in holding that in our lives, so that wherever we live, there is a place for poetry, and the planting of the meanings.

These faiths are possible in this country—wide faiths in a full, wide country, a promise in a land whose meanings are growing. The possible

---

28. From late May 1940 until March 1941, as Nazis invaded and the collaborationist Vichy regime was established, millions of residents of Paris and surrounding areas became internal refugees, moving outside the occupied zone.

29. A conscripted "Maginot army" would provide a weak defense and false sense of security. In the 1930s, to deter German invasion France began to build along its eastern border concrete fortifications housing artillery and anti-tank guns. This Maginot Line remained incomplete from Belgium to the English Channel. The Germans exploited that weakness, resulting in France's fall.

becomes very dear these days—the possible becomes *the most necessary*. Many acts must be effective, and quickly—to rectify, to plan, to imagine. If we can imagine the poems for this time. If we can imagine the peace for the time to come. The form and content of peace!

In poetry, form and content, relation and function, become the prey of the grammar book and the notating pencil, and these fail. The form and content of belief so reach and merge, light, penumbra, and dark unknown. The content of faith, for us, is not the opposite of another faith—it is not like the whirlpools which, north of the Equator, circle in one direction, and, southward, drive eternally opposite. It is the form that distinguishes. War or construction. Fear or imagination. I place those opposite. What threats does fear bring to your belief? What threats arrive to your imagination? How deeply are you cut off? Is your pride so frail that it can be broken by struggle? Can your privacy be threatened?

I speak of the long ranges before us, of the scenes yet to be awakened, the cities to be built, the poems written. The seas we know, the summer fields, the mountains, the dark perspectives of the choices ahead. We know, too, the shattered world coming closer to us daily—a burning ship sailing this ocean, these years—the caverns of this war, the faces of refugees pared down to nerve and bone, the sudden flaring courage and the witless death.

And the fear that is touched in all of us, that we all must learn to face and use. Know and use, and we must know and use poetry. For so long, it has been our skill that we have not used, our skill at reaching. And we must reach now. It is for us to reach each other now. Poets and their subjects, their heroes, must be meeting. We cannot allow division; most of all, we cannot allow the division of the heart. That is the enemy. The form and content of fear, to be driven against us, and we begin to know what forms it may take.

And if you come with your lives to meet what is here, you are the heroes of the poems, for there is the meeting-place. And that defines the form and content of the poetry I tell you. Facing and communicating, that will be our life, in the world and in poetry. Are we to teach this to people? All we can show them is themselves; show them what passion they possess, and we all will have learned the poetry. This is the knowledge of communication, and it is the fear of this that we have known, and that has held our hand. There are many fears that we must kill, and this is not the least of them. The uses of our knowledge are very wide, the uses of our ignorance fatal. Our lives, in a curious way, may rest on this; and our lives are our only metaphor.

The printer asked, as many may ask, Where is the place for poetry?

And shot his question over the boat, over the warlike sea, over the world at war.

You, my heroes, meet that cry with your lives! More imagination, more audacity, more poetry! It has to do with the peace to come; it has to do with personal love; it has to do with facing our hopes, deep as the bone, as surely deep in us as the living bone. Katherine Anne Porter in a letter writes, "As for facing things, we will face them as best we can; that will be our history."[30]

The full collection of our lives, brought to the event, with all the grace, all the imagination and poetry we contain, will make such meeting possible.[31]

(Twice a Year, 1941)

---

30. Katherine Anne Porter, American fiction writer. Katherine Anne Porter, letter to Muriel Rukeyser, August 30, 1940, 2 ts pp., Muriel Rukeyser Collection of Papers, Incoming Correspondence: Porter, Katherine Anne, Henry W. and Albert A. Berg Collection of American Literature, New York Public Library, Astor, Lenox, and Tilden Foundation, New York, New York.

31. Fc indicates Rukeyser closed her talk by reading an excerpt from "Mediterranean," in *CP*, 144–151; "Reading Time: 1 Minute, 26 Seconds," in *CP*, 155; and "The Soul and Body of John Brown," in *CP*, 247–250. The published lecture included the first two poems.

Chapter 2

The Speed of the Image (1940)

It is a curious way to begin on a theme by approaching the resistances to it, the obstacles which prevent all the lost people, the great populations of the world, the faces which fall away on every page of the history books, from ever reaching the state of communication of which I speak, and which is in itself only a means to higher states which may find their existence only in secret and in silence.[1] It was necessary and human, as it is in the description of anything possible and desirable, but not *here*, to begin by telling with grief of the main force which restrains us from that state. It would seem to be the most desirable and difficult step in the world, to meet each moment with a full focus, bringing one's history to each moment, giving each word of life a rich attention and the laughter and imagination and graveness it requires. But we must always begin by saying: It is not so. It is another way. And we must know that fear prevents us, even from the processes which lead us to the state of full meeting, full communication.

In speech, we mediate and deny to a certain extent because of the apparatus itself. Poetry, and the arts it approaches, have attempted to

---

1. Muriel Rukeyser delivered this second lecture from *The Usable Truth* at Vassar College on Wednesday, October 30, 1940, at 10:40 a.m.

do away with the counterfeit in expression, at the most complicated level; and, as life has become more complicated—as the population, to put it on the most ordinary level, has increased, and the complications have become available to more people—the search for a clarity which can assume any complication has become of terrifying importance. There has been a frenzied casting-about for forms, with every now and then, in times of urgency and crisis, a calm and tragic knowledge that memory will serve us, that tradition is not far away, that the distances remind us only that the past cannot be repeated, not that it cannot be carried ahead.

In any communicative act, the hope is not for an identical attitude, because that would destroy the need for communication. And communication is the social pleasure of shared relationship towards the same object. I spoke of the link between art and nature, not a link of imitation of each other, but rather of imitation of some third phase, the object. The connection between them is of the nature of communication, in which speaker and audience are fixed on an object which turns and is expounded and clarified. Full communication, in that definition, would be reached when the full consciousness of both members is turned on the object.

But the description, the illumination under which the object can be shown in its meaning, the processes of that act, the grammar of communication itself, is the formal interest of poetry. And as other arts have emerged, the possibilities have increased.

I know that what I am saying presupposes more than anyone is meant to do. But I wish to presuppose, I wish to take for granted. There are too many preliminary steps to the subject, and they can be made anywhere. They must be taken for granted when one approaches the end. It is the beast in view at the end of the chase, and one cannot go through the preparation for the hunt whenever the beast is the concern.[2] There is an experience of life and an experience of criticism

---

2. The phrase "beast in view," also the title of Rukeyser's 1944 poetry collection, comes from John Dryden's last poem, "The Secular Masque" (1700), which stages an encounter between Mars, Venus, Janus, and other Roman gods at the dawn of a new era. The final chorus reads:

Thy Chase had a Beast in View;
Thy Wars brought nothing about;
Thy Lovers were all untrue.
'Tis well an Old Age is out,
And time to begin a New.

which need to be absorbed, really assimilated into oneself, to focus on the belief in poetry at this time—to focus on the belief in communication at any time, people being what they are. But the preparation does need to be absorbed as completely as your dinner, and there is no good throwing out facts and references. There are many excellently clumsy books of criticism, and they hold the material, if you read them with all your antagonism up; and in them the flashes of insight are something to be grateful for, and they are rare. I know it has been quite clear to you from the beginning that I am not speaking critically, and do not mean to, at any of these times; I am speaking of possibility and hope. As far as I myself am concerned, little enough of what I need to hear is being talked and written about, and the one positive application of our time of war to this is that everything else is now to be pared away. Let us have what we want to hear more than anything else. As for the rest—as for amusement, that is, it is quite simple, and Hollywood has been quick to recognize the fact and gives us as much tap-dancing and detective thriller entertainment as it can, shelving all other pursuits, all straight projected movies. It's perfectly possible to know what a movie will be like for the next months; during its course you will laugh a lot, and at the end you will know that the one important thing is to defend the shores of this country. That is the stock pattern; and the movies which get past that point will say, as I say now, that the people are to be defended, not alone the shores. The tradition at this point is to hand out guns; and it is a very good idea, too, that every family has a gun to defend democracy. But it is not going very far to do that; it is a little like being at a picnic at which paper napkins are handed out. All you can be sure of at that moment, if your people are reasonably hungry, is that everyone is waiting for food. And if we think for a moment of the values involved in this crisis of the world, we can be very sure that there are meanings for which everyone is starving.[3]

Not very many of those meanings have reached us through art, which may be one of the reasons that Isaac Newton complained so bitterly about the lack of poetry; and much meaning has always been encumbered by an exorbitant interest in *devices*. Part of this, surely, is due to the curiosity which keeps the race alive; part to the wish that we turn against ourselves and that hinders us in everything we do from honesty

---

3. Holo. improvisation note on opposite page verso: "enlarge / entertainment, wartime."

and sensitivity that should add up to truth; and part a wish of the imagination to conquer our shortcomings and double-dealings. But in the end, we learn our tools. The sharp elusive images are revealed, the cutting edge of the world presents itself in its excitement, one more degree is added to the ways in which people may reach each other, and there is something new in the world.

Hollywood, in all its suburban tropical display, is full of clews.[4] It is one of the few places in the world where cheapness—the shabby spirit walking around the streets—has anything but a savage and tragic appearance. The irony is so terrible, the laugh is so dark. The town has in its one trade, its one obsession, carried deeply American (and that is an absurdity, for the appeal is not restricted)—carried a *possession* over the boundary. It is an obsessive-compulsive town, and the making of films takes the place of manual therapy in a madhouse; but one of the forces which haunts it is a wish for communication, and several valuable clews have emerged.

The cutting of films is a parable in the ethics of communication. I say "ethics" because of the values and needs involved, and the obligations. The scene itself is familiar: the cameras set up in the great hangars of studios, the players spotlit in a little corner of the darkness loaded with painted flats and ropes and girders; the signal to shoot, the hush as the cameras mark an exchange lasting, say, two minutes; the ending; the repeat; the countless repeats—until spools and spools of repetition turn up in a laboratory, waiting for the selective shears. The business of such selection is a business of *preparation*. Anything can be said in art, if it is prepared; as with Mozart, as with Kafka, as with Chaplin, all can be accepted, it has been indicated. The single image, which arrives to us with incredible speed, takes its place in a sequence which reinforces the image itself.[5]

This happens most recognizably in films and in poetry. If you isolate certain moments in Hitchcock films, you have the illustration of the reinforced image that is used in poetry constantly. There was a point in *The 39 Steps* at which a landlady opened the door of an apartment, walked in and saw the corpse of a woman flung across the bed, with a

---

4. On the word *clew*, see Muriel Rukeyser, "The Fear of Poetry," in this volume, note 3.
5. Holo. improvisation note on opposite page verso: "Explain, here, about preparation." Rukeyser was speaking from her experience in the mid- to late 1930s as an editor at Frontier Films.

knife handle rising fiercely from the dead back.[6] The landlady turned to you, and opened her mouth with a scream of horror which was much more pure horror than scream; hard to place; and not identified until a moment later, when you saw the image of the train hurling out of a black tunnel, and knew the train had screamed, and it was that blast that served the moment before.

Again, in *The Woman Alone*, there is a moment at the aquarium, when looking into a fish tank with two conspirators who have met in this safe and shadowy public place, you see the water troubled by the swimming motion, until a distortion is produced which makes the little structures of the tank shudder and seem to lean; and suddenly it is clear, not only that the bomb that these conspirators have plotted has gone off, and that this fish tank is Piccadilly Circus, and the buildings are falling down; but also a comment on the nature of an explosion.[7] An explosion, says the image in the fish tank, is distorting, is maximum derangement, is a warping of reality that becomes more unbearable as you see it more clearly; in this case, as you see it more slowly. That comment is the reinforcement, the *additional* note which happens when an image is well-placed in a work of art. In a Russian film, *Life Is Beautiful*, the ending of war is shown as earlier shots in reverse; great explosions of earth are gathered back into the ground as you watch, with a moving and ironic gesture of wishful thinking.[8] In another Hitchcock film, *Foreign Correspondent*, one of the most exciting and melodramatic sequences ever made, the airplane crash in mid-ocean, is made with a minimum of reference, and marked in with the speed and economy that is to be found in the most laconic poetry.[9] If you have seen the film, you will remember that the only continuity is the screaming of the plane's engines in the fall. What we see is broken and maneuvered, and although I do not know the circumstances of the scene's shooting, very easy to reconstruct. The plane has been established in the beginning of the sequence. The first shot was one of the plane itself from outside,

---

6. Alfred Hitchcock, dir., *The 39 Steps* (1935).
7. *The Woman Alone* (1936), directed by Alfred Hitchcock, adapted Joseph Conrad's *The Secret Agent* (1907), about an anarchist plot to bomb the Greenwich Observatory. The film later was renamed *Sabotage* to distinguish it from a British drama titled *A Woman Alone*, released the same year.
8. *Life Is Beautiful* (1930), a Soviet silent film codirected by Vsevolod Pudovkin and Mikhail Doller.
9. Hitchcock's classic *Foreign Correspondent* (1940), nominated for six Oscars, was released three months before Rukeyser's Vassar lectures.

and the camera drew closer and closer to the fuselage, and finally went through one of the windows. From then on, we were inside the plane, and stayed there as it fell. It would have destroyed the fear of the fall to see the plane falling from the outside. No; we were all trapped in that fall. What we saw were fragmentary impressions of disaster; an end of the wing ripped; an expression of fear stamped on a face seen for a second; the posture of bodies braced for the fall; the end of the wing breaking; the tense stubborn attitudes of the pilot and radio operator, remaining at the dangerous nose of the ship; the rush of the passengers toward the tail of the plane; the stump of wing; the water hurling into the cabin as the plane crashed in the sea. But these were all fragments arbitrarily—and ethically—assembled. One may speculate about how much of the breaking-wing image our ancestors would have felt, or play with a rearrangement of the pieces. But the process was this: one constant, in this case the constant of sound—threaded on that, a group of related but broken images, which add up to an experience so convincing and satisfactory and melodramatic that it is completely successful within its own definition.

The examples all have their parallels in poetry. They are all instances of reinforced sensation or understanding, and in at least one of them, the explosion-aquarium analogy, a comment on the situation itself which leads to a revaluation.

This kind of engineering is inherent in movie making as we know it, and has been accepted instantly, as far back as the shots of pounding horses' hooves in *The Birth of a Nation*.[10] The scientific material we have to go on is the material of the psychologists who have measured some of these responses, and that of the engineers in every field, who have taught the kind of preparation that is useful. Not really taught, but made a tradition—that is, gone on with the intuitions that the earlier artists have given us, in their work.

In this kind of communication, which is territory in which poetry and the films share, there is not to be found the distinction between direct and indirect communication. What the artist is presenting is a development in which timing is one of the most important factors. The

---

10. *The Birth of a Nation* (1915), silent film classic directed by D. W. Griffith. On fc, Rukeyser struck: "In sound movies, as in the plays of Shakespeare, there is additional support. The soundtrack in *Foreign Correspondent* acts as a skin, if you will, on the rest, presenting its shape. The plotlines of Shakespeare increase the internal juxtaposition."

sequence is, in its own nature, dramatic; and speed and timing become of the greatest importance. Most of the difficulty with recent poetry can be traced to this; references are introduced as they are in *Foreign Correspondent*—a face, a braced back, a breaking wing, another face, until the effect is built up. The place of the soundtrack, with its increasing scream of the chute, must be taken by the curve of emotion in the poem, or the curve of belief, if you will. We look for that, we wish it, it is the unity we hope for in emotion.

As for the structural unity, there are two categories in which it can be analyzed. The two sides have been defended expertly in a discussion between two eminent film artists—Eisenstein and Dovzhenko.[11] They are the two processes themselves—linkage and collision, the two kinds of relationship that mean growth, the processes of birth and love. The distinction there is the distinction between evolution and revolution, that is falsified again and again when one term is used to exclude the other. Seen over short periods of time, or in short works of art, they may appear singly. But, in a work of art of any size, or over years, they appear together as process. As history.

In art, the use of linkage predominantly produces the beautiful, even, and sure effects of work we have come to regard as traditional. The use of collision produces the beautiful, uneven, and sure effects of the dramatic, the fantastic and mordant other line which has risen into recent work as art founded on the knowledge of the subconscious, in the best of the anti-poetic writers—and I use their term, which I feel was false but useful from the beginning—and at its most romantic level, of the surrealists. In any extended work of art, the effects fuse. *The Waste Land* is a masterpiece of collision, and yet at its climaxes and at its close, the cry for belief and the cry of despair that whatever belief arrives will have arrived too late is clear, and the reader realizes that these cries have provided a constant as pronounced as the soundtrack

---

11. Soviet directors Sergei Eisenstein and Alexander Dovzhenko (misidentified on fc as "Dostchko") theorized and practiced film montage. Eisenstein used montage in stories about political revolution in films like *Battleship Potemkin* (1925) and *October: Ten Days That Shook the World* (1928). In *Earth* (1930), Dovzhenko incorporated more lyrical montages of nature and folk culture from his native Ukraine. The "discussion" to which Rukeyser refers has not been identified. Later, in 1944, Eisenstein did criticize Dovzhenko's close-ups of a nude female peasant in *Earth* as too surrealistic. See Sergei Eisenstein, "Dickens, Griffith, and the Film Today," in *Film Form: Essays in Film Theory*, ed. and trans. Jay Leyda (New York: Harcourt Brace Jovanovich, 1949), 195-255.

in *Foreign Correspondent*'s airplane sequence.[12] On the other hand, most of the work of MacLeish has been built on the links of a fluid emotion which could play on fluid images that moved under the attention without break.[13] Blake, I should say, builds the importance of his meaning on impact, on collision, as does Coleridge; Wordsworth and Tennyson work link by link.[14]

There has been a great deal of hesitation before contemporary poetry, and much explanation of its difficulties. I think one of the fairest and simplest avenues to sympathy with its advances may be made through an understanding of the method of collision. The work, laid on, as it were, stroke by stroke, emphasizes placing and timing, the relations between the parts. What we need to know is first, the connection that allows for collision, the line of emotion that sets a center to all this activity, and the relation of the parts to it.[15]

I think it is best sometimes to begin at the bottom. There is no reason to approach a process with respect for itself, and it is my feeling that a lot of the uneasiness about art—a lot of the fear of poetry—is taught to people when they first find their teachers treating the mechanics of art with a fiendish reverence. I should feel that a good beginning was in sight if I knew that nobody would ever parse a line of verse in high school, or learn to read poems by memorizing rules of form. Anyone who is interested in the formal aspect of any art will know it soon enough by himself, and ask to learn. I should like to begin in rage and mouthings at the misuses, and I think it is possible to do that here; if we can work up to an understanding, we shall really have found communication, and I propose to begin with Joyce Kilmer's world-famous production, "Trees," which is incomparable of its kind—it is difficult to

---

12. T. S. Eliot, *The Waste Land* (1922).

13. For her reading of Archibald MacLeish's early poetry, see Muriel Rukeyser, "Modern Trends: American Poetry," in this volume. MacLeish was appointed librarian of Congress in 1939 and later became the ex-officio head of the Office of Facts and Figures, which propagandized national defense. In autumn 1942, he recruited Rukeyser to work for the Office of War Information's Graphics Workshop.

14. Four nineteenth-century British poets: the Romantics William Blake, Samuel Taylor Coleridge, and William Wordsworth, as well as the Victorian Alfred Tennyson. Of them, Coleridge most influenced Rukeyser, lending her Wendell Willkie biography its title (*One Life*, 1957) and appearing as a character in her late unpublished and unproduced play *Arabian Nights: An American Comedy* (1975).

15. Holo. improvisation note on opposite page verso: "Instantaneous apprehension of all forms / recognize that they possess aspects transcending their elements / transposablity [*sic*] // traces of forms left in the mind."

think of comparisons in other fields.[16] I think of the Albert Memorial in London, and the Bahá'í Temple in Winnetka.[17]

But the object of all of this, the beast in view, for there is a beast at the end of the hunt, and all this speed is not only for the pleasure of speed, is a deep wish for structure. Unity is a hope of all human beings; and the "devouring unity" that Emerson knew is the unity of form, poetry is in love with that.[18] As a matter of fact, unity is the hero of the formalists. Every poet is in love with some hero, there is praise involved somewhere, and praise of unity is general in the world's welter of complexity. All devices such as rhyme are unifying devices, although they seem to speak variety. When we leave them and go to the naked unity of emotion, many readers feel balked. They wanted to recognize more than that. You remember when every movie had a theme song. It came back whenever the heroine smiled, not once, as a rhyme does. That is something which has baffled me for a long while—what deep satisfaction could have been found in rhyming, in the pairing of lines, what deep and staying satisfaction strong enough to keep writers from going ahead. Refrain and the parallelism of the Bible, in which whole circuits of thought and phrase are repeated, seemed to me more whole and healing, than this single recurrent sound that vanished. There was a reflection as if a tree had been seen in water once, and passed by, on a ride that rode past once and for all. There is other pleasure, that pleasure of parallels I mentioned, the pleasure we take in looking at skyscrapers,

---

16. After the next sentence, the fc provides extended ts improvisation notes wherein Rukeyser proceeds to contrast Joyce Kilmer's popular poem "Trees" (1913) with several modernist poems: the "logic of association" in Hart Crane's modernist sequence "Voyages" (1926), the poetics of "collision" in Arthur Rimbaud's *Le bateau ivre* ("The Drunken Boat," 1871), and poetics of "linkage" in an unspecified poem by W. B. Yeats (which, according to other archived notes, could have been either "Hound Voice" [1933] or "Byzantium" [1930]). She then discusses "[t]he gap here between what has been absorbed, and our own generation," as modeled in the recent socialist poetry of Horace Gregory, W. H. Auden, and Kenneth Fearing. "The speed of their images" was anticipated by turn-of-the-century thinker and novelist Henry Adams. She identifies "the critical obligation" to abate an "intellectual lag," and she finds promise to do so in American communist Stuart Chase's economic theory, I. A. Richards's practical criticism, and American linguist Alfred Korzybski's theory of general semantics. Finally, she connected these theories to "[t]he use of the document. The slowing-up that its incomplete incorporation has meant," as exemplified by William Carlos Williams's cultural history *In the American Grain* (1926), Ezra Pound's epic *The Cantos* (1915-1962), and "the greatest of all 'documentary' writings," Herman Melville's novel *Moby Dick* (1851).

17. The Albert Memorial (1861-1872), Queen Victoria's Gothic Revival memorial to Prince Albert in Kensington Gardens, and the Bahá'í Temple (1912-1953) in Wilmette, Illinois.

18. Ralph Waldo Emerson, "Poetry and Imagination" (1872).

whose tall lines fly upward past many windows—whose windows race upward in rows of repetition, no two quite alike because of spacing and relationship, like the repeated phrases in Gertrude Stein. The charm of that repetition is in the difference of place and the ensuing difference of relationship to the other parts and to the whole itself.

As for myself, I was never quite satisfied with one echo of anything in a poem; and I would like to read two poems to you now.[19]

This, again, is a wish for unity, a wish for reinforcement, a hope for a form that will reinforce the images and carry them more quickly and mortally to the reader. We receive these images in a flash of welcome, once we are open to the process; and all this talk of kinds and devices must be carried on in hope and in a wish to share an attitude toward the material, toward poetry and its material, which is indeed as various and infinite as the named and suggested world.[20]

(Unpublished, 1940)

---

19. As examples of her interest in repeating rhymes, Rukeyser reads her poem "The Minotaur," in *CP*, 223–224; and "Leg in a Plastic Cast," in *CP*, 230–231. Followed by ts improvisation note: "Explanation of held rhyme."

20. Ts improvisation note: "If there is time here, take apart those films in which poetry has been used: *Night Mail, China Strikes Back, The Two of Us*. Realism and antirealism in films; *Romeo and Juliet, Blind Alley*. Fusions. Form as a symptom of unity, the line along which variation can be made and argued . . . leading to belief." Holo. note on opposite page verso: "The freeing of the soundtrack: possibilities."

Chapter 3

Belief and Poetry (1940)

But what I wish is to come away from these dissections with you, for you to see why I am so angry at all the lack, all the hesitation and loss.[1] It is again the spectacle of the history books, and at every page the countless faces of the anonymous going down; the search through country after country for greatness, for great women—to take an example—when one may be sure that, as far as women are concerned, the great ones are all anonymous; the drives in art that have pushed through to set the great ones at the top, great rush of energy and spirit, laughter, darkness, and the marvelous knowledge; and so many wishes gone down in hesitation and despair and decoration. It will never be *form* that connects people or works of art; it will not be schools; you may be sure of that. The schools will be blasted to pieces; there will be nothing but a corkscrew of twisted steel where they thought the structure was. No school, no effort of the will, is going to keep anything alive; an effort of the will is not enough. The insistence there is like the insistence of those starved and rigorous people who go around calling for honesty, saying, "All I ask is honesty." That is like asking that nobody die of starvation in the midst of plenty. It is all right

---

1. Muriel Rukeyser delivered this third lecture from *The Usable Truth* at Vassar College on Wednesday, October 30, 1940, at 11:40 a.m.

to ask that out loud once in your life, and then to keep it handy in your mind; but it is nothing to repeat, it is not a stopping-place or even a place where you may rest for a moment.

The ones who cry for honesty are selling out. That is not the price; and yet it is a terrible thing how much crying for that there must be, how little there is. I remember when I was an oblivious child, and had no hint that there was an outside world; there was a track between home and school, and there were newspapers, until one day I read in the newspaper that a man had been found dead of starvation. He had been the nightwatchman of a storage warehouse. The warehouse was full of food, and he had died outside the door. It is one of the deaths of our time. One of those deaths is died when people cry for honesty. Let them go ahead and take their honesty; there is enough for all.

Belief is another such—a price, almost, a compromise if you call for it. Just as it is, belief. Honesty toward what? Belief toward what? These forces do not live in emptiness. They will not live in the dry test tube. It is the laboratory problem. You can isolate, you can make slides, but this is not living tissue you see, you are not examining mortal substance, there is not the shimmer, you have lost a clew.[2]

You are given the dead and rattling vines. When I speak of process, all I can show you is the vine. You will be right to tear it away at all of this; what is behind the linkage, what is behind the collision? Linkage of what; collision of what?

What can possibly make for flow? What will produce impact? How can we reach an end that can be shared? It is very well to talk about communication. But by what grace is the gift given?

Belief becomes a clew to form. It is along this line that linkage grows; or against it that the impact of images shocks. The acute immediate mind, glad to find a track set or waiting for the shock. Those two structures, those two forms, depend on awareness and belief. They depend on the mind in what might be defined as aggressive and receptive states; supply the involved but easily traceable flow of images that may be followed, actively pursued; or the fixed point of departure, after which the world of that poem is brought in color by color and shock by shock to play upon the receptive and waiting imagination. And then the higher type, the more complicated activity, when the burden is shared, when variety becomes so potent and attractive that the motion itself becomes

---

2. On the word *clew*, see Muriel Rukeyser, "The Fear of Poetry," in this volume, note 3.

a conversation, and the reader enters it, assuming the play of mind of the voices in the poem, meeting and following and breaking, being urged along, and flashing upon its meanings.

There is a real pursuit, and the hunt itself is in the name of belief. But it is treacherous, even when all the rules are accepted, a legendary hunt.

As if an archaic huntsman left in the morning, gay and confident and well-equipped, and followed all the heroic day until he was torn and exhausted and hoped only for the beast to be as tired, and for the beast to turn and wait; and forgot what beast there was, but begged in the growing darkness for one thing only, that the beast be brought to bay and turn and wait; until finally all he could remember was his own ache and hard breathing and the darkness, and it was *then* that he looked up and saw the beast turned indeed and waiting, but with all the morning ferocity and wildness not to be caught that could be feared.

But it is a mythic and savage beast if we do not say its name. Or, to come closer to ourselves, it is that underground river that has recently been searched for by a blind inventor.[3] There is, in Ohio, a river that suddenly dives and is lost. Scientists have poured dyes into the water where it comes to the surface, and hoped to see the color at a distant surface, and they have thrown instruments into the river. A little while ago, a blind inventor—who would certainly be the most fit to trace the path of an underground river—set afloat in it a ball containing radio equipment, and followed it above ground with a radio divining-rod, going farther along its course than anyone had before.

That is the change, from simple to complex. From the hunt, the traditional activity that can be understood by child and primitive man, by city-liver and farmhand—to this deliberate tracing by an invented instrument of a subterranean devious course. And, if we carry the analogy into art, even the descriptions change. For what we have here is the passage from unity to multiplicity, from a simple faith into a complicated belief in possibility. The passage from the map to the symbol. And all we can say of both of them is that the structure, in each case, is to remind us of another structure. It is a different emphasis, also, in a change from form to belief—as if we traced a poem through in one way after another—as if we traced *Moby Dick*'s line of development through

---

3. Rukeyser reprises this anecdote in "Letter to the Front," in *CP*, 239: "Women and poets believe and resist forever: / The blind inventor finds the underground river."

twice, once as the hunt for the whale, plotting the ship's route on a globe, explaining all the terms, all the failures and successes and the final climax, and then went through the book once more to trace the deep storm in Ahab, the conflict in him for which the white whale was an outer image, a reminder that suddenly took a fierce and unanswerable shape. The difference is simple enough in the story of the inventor and the river. In the one case, we have the map of the river as far as we know it, and then possibly an arrow for the unknown course. On the other hand, we have the face with its blind eyes.

What we are looking for in poetry, however, is not the opinion or pompousness of dogma, although it is always easy enough to find. Always: we *always* will have models to parallel "I think that I shall never see / A poem lovely as a tree."[4] The distinction must be a question of taste here, I think; it must be arbitrary to that extent. And it has nothing to do with the importance of poems, trees, or the more priggish standards, but the more subtle shades of what each one of us finds important. What are we looking for? What are we waiting to hear? What ranges elude us? Pavlov's dogs were trained to associate food with the darker of two shades of gray, the more intensely black. When they went to that sample, they would be given food; and they humbled a good many people by distinguishing differences that the human eye could not perceive. They could classify fifty different shades of darkness at the end of the experiment. And the darker of the two took on a bias, a "significant aspect" based on the first association.[5]

D. L. Watson, in his illuminating book, *Scientists Are Human*, speaks of all experience, all classification, as "biased abstraction," and I think there is an index in that term to the kind of belief that is most effective in poetry, that is deepest in the definitions of poetic perception.[6] And thinking of the term—the conjunction of terms—raised to the most creative level, I think we may find here the double process that is to be hoped for and that the wish for any single virtue—honesty, for example—

---

4. Joyce Kilmer, "Trees" (1913). See Rukeyser's discussion in her second *Usable Truth* lecture, "The Speed of the Image."

5. On the grayscale experiments with dogs, see Ivan Petrovich Pavlov, *Conditioned Reflexes*, trans. G. V. Anrep (New York: Oxford University Press, 1927), 110–151. Pavlov does not use the phrase Rukeyser attributes to him.

6. David Lindsay Watson, *Scientists Are Human* (London: Watts, 1938), 197. Watson speculates that scientists' individual personalities, informed by politics and ideology, affect their objectivity. His book was prefaced by John Dewey and explicitly draws on Alfred North Whitehead's process philosophy, two of Rukeyser's influences.

does not meet. "Biased abstraction" combines two kinds of selection: the belief and selection according to belief that offers the "bias," and the ability to classify and apply and *create* according to a *structure* that provides "abstraction."

That definition is at rock-bottom for the creative process. As Watson uses it, it is a formula for all experience—all recognition. You look at a shape moving down the path toward you, and place it as a friend; you see a furry and smooth-lined creature of a breed you do not know, and place it immediately as *cat*; or Rilke speaks of constellations and we figure the sky with them as he wills, although these stars were never seen.[7] The term "biased abstraction" carries a double warning, even for simple recognition—you are advised that it is you who are intruding with the whole load of your life to reach whatever bias you will. You are advised that it is you who are jumping to a conclusion, that the abstraction is *your own*. And if you carry that process and warning all down the line, you see what you are doing, and with what warnings, when you reach a belief, or paint a picture.

From the map, with the same warnings, to the symbol itself, the process of recognition goes, and should stagger under its threats. But even when it is burdened with models and comparisons, its speed is very great. And models, if they are thrown away in time, are of the first order of usefulness, in poetry as in science. If one takes up a model to use toward an end, and becomes fascinated by the object itself, the whole experiment—of whatever nature—will be corrupted. Physicists have been thrown off the track again and again by having a concrete example—and image—before them, and trusting it. Lord Kelvin, who would not allow himself to be convinced by anything unless he could make a model of it, was one of the authoritative voices raised to say that airplanes were impossible—that nothing heavier than air could fly.[8] But the model is a stinging reality, and the most effective ally when there is

---

7. Ts note in middle of sentence after mention of Rainer Maria Rilke's constellations: "here quote *Duino Elegies*." Rilke's collection, translated in 1939 by J. B. Leishman and Stephen Spender, influenced Rukeyser's *Elegies*, in *CP,* 297–330. In Rilke's "Tenth Elegy," a male youth is shown by Lament, a female figure, new constellations formed by "Stars of the Land of Pain." Rainer Maria Rilke, *Duino Elegies*, trans. J. B. Leishman and Stephen Spender, 4th ed. (1939; reis., London: Chatto & Windus, 1963), 97.

8. Irish-born British mathematician and physicist William Thomson, the first Baron Kelvin, whose work informed the first and second laws of thermodynamics. Rukeyser's biography *Willard Gibbs*, which she was researching when preparing her Vassar lectures, represents Kelvin as a man of limited imagination and little faith in scientific progress. See Muriel Rukeyser, *Willard Gibbs* (Garden City, NY: Doubleday, Doran, 1942), 325, 405.

need for concrete "fact." The art is to know when to throw your model away. What is necessary is an imagery appropriate to a line of emotion or belief. When the line is involved, the point-by-point development is much clearer if the points are marked. To carry your example all the way to the end is a little like following a road and gathering the signposts to take along as you go. That is not an argument against signposts.

Two kinds of models have their uses as signposts. Each is, in its way, an index to belief; one, the document, the more concrete and rigid, to supply reinforcement along the way, to prove and argue; the other and more flexible and inclusive, the myth, lies as a point of reference at the beginning, to cut through complexities and impose its unity. These two instruments of conviction are powerful weapons in the hands of masters. The distinction at the end is likely to be that between unity and complexity; the myth, the parable, setting the form and level at the very beginning and forcing the new material back to its outline from time to time; the document adding complexity, fresh material, opinion and color and variety, at every turn.[9] To accept either of these forms is to acknowledge a central faith, and to declare oneself and one's central position, as well as a choice for complexity or unity. Recent examples are Ezra Pound's *Cantos*, with their heavily documented scenes, and Kafka's novels, *The Trial* and *The Castle*, both based on parable, a simple motion, which refers back at each new development, until the meaning of the original motion is revealed in its full moment. It would be possible to draw an analogy between the use of the two processes: linkage and collision—and the two indicators: myth and document.[10]

Two extremely interesting examples of modern belief in art, and the methods under discussion, are Eliot's *Waste Land*, in which lack of faith is objectified and described as the characteristic of our time, by a series of dramatic and tortured scenes; and Kierkegaard's *Fear and Trembling*, in which a myth of perfect faith is told and analyzed and woven into a confession of lack of faith that is one of the most perfect and searching treatments of the nostalgia for faith, the wish for it and sense of loss without it, that has ever been written.[11] The power of this material—and

---

9. In a 1968 lecture, Rukeyser characterizes this pairing of myth and document as unverifiable fact and documentary poetics, respectively. See Muriel Rukeyser, "Poetry and the Unverifiable Fact," in this volume.

10. Holo. note on opposite page verso: "Dante combined myth & document."

11. Ts reading and improvisation notes: "Read some of *The Waste Land*. Take it apart. / Tell a little about Kierkegaard, and *Fear & Trembling*. / Read 'In Praise of Abraham.'" Rukeyser

"BELIEF AND POETRY" 73

I think in the case of "In Praise of Abraham" its poetic power must be referred to immediately—is not a more simple result than the effect of *The Waste Land*, although at first glance the components seem simpler.[12] There are the same elements: the nostalgia for faith, the illustration, the subjective generalization.

(Infinitely different nervous reaction—tone—net effect.

Threat to the compartmented mind each of these is. Threat that belief is. Threat that poetry is. Attacks of this year. Dollard's attack.)[13]

One answer is the answer of Carossa, about whom I spoke last night, and whom I see constantly, on a platform, very quiet, very gentle, reading his poems to a great uniformed crowd of the Hitler Youth.[14] His is an oblique answer. What he is saying is, "I am alive. There is something in the world besides what you have been taught." That is all that he is saying, the rest is muffled, completely muffled. It is the first embryonic gesture, before protest, before conclusive faith, before any kind of organized emotion. It is to protest what John Brown is to civil war, the first premonition. But it is impossible, in either case, I believe, that the generalization should fail to follow.

One of the functions of poetry is to take a stand at that point. It is likely to be an untenable point; that is a good enough reason why poetry belongs there. It is playing angel on a pinpoint, at the most priggish and self-conscious; if you add optimism, Emerson has the words.

---

introduces Søren Kierkegaard's *Fear and Trembling* (1843) in her first lecture. See Muriel Rukeyser, "The Fear of Poetry," in this volume.

12. *Fear and Trembling* begins with a proverb usually translated as "Speech in Praise of Abraham" or "A Panegyric upon Abraham," an account of an unlearned man's innate understanding of the biblical story of God's ordering Abraham to sacrifice his son Isaac. See Søren Kierkegaard, *Fear and Trembling and The Sickness unto Death*, trans. Walter Lowrie (1941; reis., Princeton, NJ: Princeton University Press, 2013), 37-58.

13. Fc leaves these sentences incomplete; Rukeyser intended to improvise an argument about recent controversies. "Dollard's attack" refers to cultural anthropologist John Dollard's critique of monolithic value systems in *Children of Bondage: Caste and Class in a Southern Town* (1940), coauthored with Allison Davis and later republished, retitled and credited only to Dollard. One chapter, "Defensive Beliefs of the White Caste," explains the evolution of working classes' white supremacist beliefs as a culturally conservative defense mechanism to appear to conform with dominant ideologies. See John Dollard, *Caste and Class in a Southern Town* (Madison: University of Wisconsin Press, 1988), 364-389.

14. For her earlier discussion of the German poet Hans Carossa, see Muriel Rukeyser, "The Fear of Poetry," in this volume.

"For poetry is faith. To the poet the world is virgin soil; all is practicable; the men are ready for virtue; it is always time to do right."[15]

The hope is for communication on a level of belief. Carossa, in the story, is not making that communication. He is gesturing towards it; there is a shadowy indication; at the most, he says it exists. There is abject humility in the situation; the choice is death or exile, or that almost colorless and passive indication that is the highest expression possible of the whole world that stands against what power, in his case, signifies. All he can hope to do is say: Look at me. There is another world.

It is very different with us. We are in that other world, and we have our sovereignty there. We breathe the air of possibility, we find it necessary to believe in possibility—actually, what I have been pointing out as a duty all through this is just that: our obligation at this point is to hold fast, with all the faith and imagination we have, to possibility, and to whatever tradition we learn there is for us. But all the keenness and pride and incision are for us, all the chances of communication and liberty, actual creation, are there, and the traditions are strong. They have to do with the churches built on stones put up to regicides, with the fierce and contradictory migrations, in one spirit after another, from Europe to the Atlantic shore, from the shore across the country, accompanied by religion and slavery and poetry and hardheaded oppression and blasphemous laughter—the breaking of tradition, and the search for a native tradition that is seen in this letter of courage and genius:

> Herman Melville to Nathaniel Hawthorne—Pittsfield, March 1851
> (Dealing with *The House of the Seven Gables*)
> ... There is a certain tragic phase of humanity which, in our opinion, was never more powerfully embodied than by Hawthorne. We mean the tragedies of human thought in its own unbiassed, native, and profounder workings. We think that into no recorded mind has the intense feeling of the usable truth ever entered more deeply than into this man's. By usable truth, we mean the apprehension of the absolute condition of present things as they strike the eye of the man who fears them not, though they do their worst to him,—the man who, like Russia or the British Empire, declares himself a sovereign nature (in himself) amid the powers of heaven, hell, and earth. He may perish; but so long as he exists

---

15. Ralph Waldo Emerson, "Poetry and Imagination" (1872).

he insists upon treating with all Powers upon an equal basis. If any of those other Powers choose to withhold certain secrets, let them; that does not impair my sovereignty in myself; that does not make me tributary. And perhaps, after all, there is *no* secret. We incline to think that the Problem of the Universe is like the Freemason's mighty secret, so terrible to all children. It turns out, at last, to consist in a triangle, a mallet, and an apron—nothing more! We incline to think that God cannot explain His own secrets, and that He would like a little information upon certain points Himself. We mortals astonish Him as much as He us. But it is this *Being* of the matter; there lies the knot with which we choke ourselves. As soon as you say *Me*, a *God*, a *Nature*, so soon you jump off from your stool and hang from the beam. Yes, that word is the hangman. Take God out of the dictionary, and you would have Him in the street . . .[16]

That kind of pride is deep in our meaning. That is tradition, too. And there is fundamental communication here—no need to *learn* meaning, no need to consult references when God is in the street.

That form of belief is the belief of a free man, who seems to have achieved faith, to be moving securely within it, and is interested only in practicalities. Once in that territory, as Kierkegaard points out, that is where his concerns lie. And there is a startling difference between that, and Eliot, and Kierkegaard. They are talking about the same thing, and that is even more startling than the differences between them.

Belief has its structures, and its symbols change, its tradition changes, all the relationships within the structures are interdependent. We look at the symbols, we hope to read them, we hope for communication. Sometimes it is there at once, we find it before the words arrive, as in the communication of great actors, whose gesture and attitude tell us before their speech elaborates; sometimes it is as fanciful as skywriting, and there we do care about the technique first. Tremendous acrobatics over cities, and hardly anything said, and all our interest in the process itself. All these rhythms in space, motion in the air, in the body, motion communicating motion, belief communicating belief, until the thing is printed on us bodily, until a poem becomes a fossil of perception, a belief becomes an image recognized in the blood, the image of a pattern. . . .

---

16. Rukeyser's ellipses and errors preserved. On her misreading of this letter, see Rukeyser, "The Fear of Poetry," in this volume, note 19.

But not so set, not that kind of rigidity there. There is too much inequality still. That is why the Melville lets fresh air into the room. The poet does live the life of his people: in times of great perversity, sometimes it is the life inverted; but on the level of belief, we still have it, the life of the tribe. In subjugated peoples, you will find the poet as witch doctor, as politician, as an evasive voice. I think of the Indian tribes of California, who after their last subjugation in 1870, turned to dream-singing, sang their hopes that the ghosts of the warriors would return and fight the battles again and have the victory; and soon lost that, and dreamed and sang of how they would rise and fight; and, losing that, dreamed and sang and fused their wishful dreams into their religion.[17] I think of Carossa and his gentle voice; of all these wishes for a faith and wholeness; and of that strong voice speaking of the present, its absolute conditions, and the usable truth. That is our tradition; it is there; and "usable" sets the obligation on us; it *is* there to be used; and deep among our truth is the symbol of it in poetry.

(Unpublished, 1940)

---

17. In 1889, Northern Paiute shaman Wovoka, a.k.a. Jack Wilson, founded the indigenous anti-settler spiritual movement known as the Ghost Dance. Rukeyser analogizes dream-singing and poets' responses to the Second World War in "Seventh Elegy: Dream-Singing Elegy," in *CP*, 318–321.

Chapter 4

Poetry and Peace (1940)

In the great periods of the past which we have grown used to calling times of peace, there were always the millions of faces falling, the long processions of those whose farmlands were overrun, whose villages were burned, who moved away from home and always instinctively took the bedding along.[1] If there was room, they would take remembrances, so that life might be resumed somewhere else according to a tradition. The great world was kept to a rigid framework of force, if there were times of peace; there was some overlord with his rule that promised death, or a chieftain who had whipped other chieftains and did not allow them to snarl; or an empire that could stretch a firm rule even over the seas. God knows it is a wretched thing to be cut down by a sword one day when the weather is fine for fighting for a piece of land in the name of an animal-god; and things have moved along since then. But, to go back to the processes I have been talking about—the two processes of linkage and collision—all invention, all history moves along their tracks, and I daresay linkage has the say for a good part of the time. It is when one flies above a neighborhood one knows, and sees the cities laid out in tilted irregular

---

1. Muriel Rukeyser delivered this fourth lecture from *The Usable Truth* at Vassar College on Thursday, October 31, 1940, at 2:40 p.m.

color, and the crossroads growth of life around a filling-station or a store, and the roads themselves, that one sees their history plainly, and knows one of the very good reasons why planes did not come into our life before they did. It seems quite clear, flying above those roads, that people were working on their improvement a good many years—from animal-track in a field, to mud-ruts and thank-you-ma'ams, to leveling off and asphalt and concrete six-lane highway complete with cloverleaves. When people are working on their roads, you get the long and steady line of development that finally produces engines that may be—by a stroke of imagination—lifted off the road and put into a plane. But if they had not been thinking about their roads!

In the history of our wars and states, it is that, too. Tribal hatred, a barrier broken and crossed, the dead, the stack of tribute and gold cups, and a larger tribe with its work of assimilation and conquest still to do. Conquest of ploughland, conquest of forest, conquest of roads, of desert, of cities and mines—frontiers set and fought for and set again, thrown down like a smokescreen to conceal the surge of ambition of each tribe behind a boundary. The tribal wars, the tribal gains, imposts and tribute and corruption of language. Until the sea, the indivisible, is fought for and divided, and its code is drawn up, so that now we reverence Mahan, who taught us sixty years ago that sea power was the key to world dominion.[2] Until we may look forward from tribal war to tribal war to the time when the air itself is partitioned to give power and empire, and we live on an ocean floor of maneuvering navies of planes belonging only to the master-nation.

Our lives have been partitioned as the process went on. There was never quite enough foresight to give up the main tradition—to give up the "road" and think in an entirely new set of terms. It is always much easier to fall in agreement, or to see the long period of strain coming on, as it came over the last years to England, and fail to make the effort that the English are now making to keep humor and commonplace and endurance.[3] There is a ritual impatience that seizes us—the impatience

---

2. American Civil War naval officer and historian Alfred Thayer Mahan theorized seafaring's and naval forces' centrality to Western empire and nationhood. See Captain A. T. Mahan, *The Influence of Sea Power upon History, 1660–1783* (Boston: Little, Brown, 1890).

3. This comment obliquely continues Rukeyser's central concern in this lecture with aerial warfare. In 1937, the United Kingdom began preparing for Nazi air attacks by establishing the Air Raid Wardens Service and the Women's Voluntary Service and by constructing air raid shelters. Blackouts began in September 1939, when Great Britain declared war against Germany. The Battle of Britain, between the Royal Air Force and Luftwaffe, occurred between July

of the body for the crisis—once the crisis is foretold. And at times when calculation and reserve are necessary, that quality of ritual impatience may be ranked with the seven deadly sins. It is the obsession with foresight that paralyzes action.[4]

This quality is to be found, on every level, in poetry that deals with the present in the implications, with possibilities for the future—and most of all, in the poetry that, seeking for a hero in the midst of loss and confusion, has found the victims of social process, of machine insanity or tribal war or class ambition. The search at its most honest has been an attempt to understand the human victims of process; both the victims who were crushed without understanding either the weapons or their defense against them, and those other victims who used the power in their hands and were brutalized through it. The recent efforts toward a conscious social poetry have been full of images of war and waste, darkened by the recurrence of war that has been clearly visible for the last decade, at least, and in direct revolt against the decorativeness of the movement immediately preceding it. It was never a true movement. There was never a formal "school." But there was a small structure that developed its own rules and rulers much too soon. There have been advances made in consciousness and vocabulary, at least. There has, indeed, been an offering made.[5] There is, at this moment, a group of poets who stand in a relationship to society that is vastly different from that of the group of poets who emerged during the 1914 war. And if this is, as I believe it must be seen to be, a second movement in a war that is to be dated—arbitrarily—from 1914, it is in place to review the movements in poetry since then. Very briefly, as may be done if we summarize movements and not the work of the first-rate poets outside of any groups, who have—not of themselves, but through the nature of their work—refused to be allied with *any* other people—first-rate and original imaginations such as those of Robinson Jeffers and Wallace Stevens.[6] Both of these men are implemented to deal with major crisis and catastrophe, Stevens because of his eye for the fantastic, for

---

and October 1940, when Rukeyser was preparing and delivering these lectures. The Blitzkrieg began with the bombing of London in September 1940 and lasted until May 1941.

4. Ts improvisation note: "Expand this: illustrate in strategy, Russia, Cassandra. John Brown."

5. By striking a sentence on fc ("Poetry is a different relationship."), Rukeyser avoids generalization and instead stresses differences between her generation and earlier modernists.

6. Rukeyser rarely discusses modernist poet Wallace Stevens, but she had been writing about Robinson Jeffers since her college days. See Muriel Rukeyser, "Modern Trends," in this volume.

the painted quality of life, the wrenched forms in everyday occurrence that merely become heightened, and Jeffers since he has seen all history as a headlong plunge towards catastrophe echoed in all the forms of nature and love and death—a catastrophe which he needs very much, since he wishes so desperately for perfection—a catastrophe which must have a cleaning effect. He has said over and over that anything that may happen will be to the good if there can be more distance between people. Fewer people. And he must feel horribly confirmed and relieved at last. There is a certain tragic relief which the actual breaking of war may bring—the prophet's relief, the impression that one would get in a movie-house if a jammed reel had shown a train advancing and advancing again and coming to the same point over and over, until at last the film flowed again and the train passed. Or, more physically close, if it were a real train that were doing that.[7]

When the Imagists first began to publish, the same point had been reached.[8] It was a revulsion away from suspense, a very civilized wish not to give in to ritual impatience, not to be carried away and broken down by the horror and pity and self-pity that the press and writing in general collapse into in years like 1917 and 1940 that, as much as anything, led to the wish to define in emotional terms—to make clear—to select a point and make it live. In a season of chaos, there are motions that the mind may make, but the important thing is the choice. And to choose becomes a self-conscious act; to throw oneself into a boiling stream of emotionalism, and from time to time reach the surface with an article or a poem for one of the Sunday magazine supplements; or to bandage oneself in a formal device—these are the extremes of choice. But it is like that for those who are identified with a *group in art* at such a time; and even for the artist of deepest integrity, the choice becomes the peak of concentration. The identification is often false. In one of the most moving statements I know, a personal and simple story, the purest of the Imagists, H. D., has broken through the question and exposed it. This is her own note on her poems, one of the notes that each living contributor to *The Oxford Book of American Literature* was asked to add to the work itself:

---

7. Ts improvisation note: "go on from here."
8. Imagism was a London-based poetic avant-garde launched by Ezra Pound, active between 1912 and 1916. Without consent, Pound gave American expatriate Hilda Doolittle, discussed below, the pen name "H. D., *Imagiste*"; she resisted the title as too narrow. Rukeyser had met H. D. in London while en route to Barcelona in 1936.

I let my pencil run riot in those early days of my apprenticeship, in an old-fashioned copybook—when I could get one. Then I would select from many pages of automatic or pseudo-automatic writing the few lines that satisfied me. [. . .] I cannot give actual dates to these early finished fragments, but they would be just pre-war and at latest, early-war period. Finished fragments? Yes, I suppose they are that—stylistic slashings, definitely self-conscious, though, as I say, impelled by some inner conflict.[9]

That bridges the gap, I think, and it is beyond any school.[10]

The idea of schools and movements in art is one of the happiest and, I suspect, most fanciful of Utopian schemes. The term "school of poetry" presupposes a level of civilization, a centralization of forces, a benevolence of rule, and an expansion of the state in which it occurs, that rarely happen. The material of, say, six people ready with their ideas, just short of their creative height of power, and drawn together by some community of belief or passion, active enough so that they will be stimulated and reinforced by the contact, and not have their energies drawn off into conversation, comes very close to the Olympian standard. But, more important than the gearing of personalities, the climate of belief necessary to a group stand takes first place. And perhaps I come closer here to a definition of belief in the way I have been using it than at any other time. You know that I am not advancing a dogma; I am trying to

---

9. H. D., "A Note on Poetry," in *Oxford Anthology of American Literature*, ed. William Rose Benét and Norman Holmes Pearson (New York: Oxford University Press, 1938), 1288. Fc does not provide the quote; Rukeyser only notes to herself to read a passage from "halfway" in the piece. Rukeyser later repeats H. D.'s word *self-conscious* from this passage, and she also narrates, as this excerpt does, how H. D. wrote her Imagist poems out of personal experience rather than a movement's prescriptions.

10. Ts improvisation note: "Go on to talk about the lyric, Wylie-Millay tradition—the anti-lyric Sandburg, etc.—the social group and how it got into the *New Yorker*; regionalists: Frost, the agrarians; patchwork scholasticism." Rukeyser contrasts 1910s socially committed female lyricists Elinor Wylie and Edna St. Vincent Millay with the masculinism of anti-lyrical contemporaries like Charles Sandburg. These two gendered forms of leftist poetics were grouped together in the literary marketplace, as seen in the *New Yorker*'s review of *Proletarian Literature in the United States*, a collection featuring Horace Gregory, Genevieve Taggard, and other renowned social poets (i.e., "the social group"), who championed the working class. The reviewer called it "one of the most useful books of the year, if only because it will help to settle a lot of windy conversation and café-table nonsense" about what constitutes proletarian literature. Clifton Fadiman, review of *Proletarian Literature in the United States: An Anthology*, ed. Granville Hicks et al., *New Yorker*, October 12, 1935, 90–91. Rukeyser separates Robert Frost and other regionalists from the social poets. Southern Agrarians and Fugitive poets like Allen Tate and John Crowe Ransom epitomized regionalist conservatism. Their "scholasticism" as New Critics promoted closed poetic forms, impersonal lyric, ahistoricism, and apoliticism.

work this foundation of all that I have been saying into a communicable necessity without turning it into bald statement or leaving you with nothing but a halo of evangelical half-light around something in very soft focus indeed. But, at the beginning, my attempt was to delimit this question by speaking of its lack. The fear of poetry and all that it means in our personal lives, all that it does to our attitude and conduct, is the acid reverse, the destructive lack of this quality. In everything I have claimed, the system that becomes what I have called poetry—the system that is common to all of us, accessible to all of us, whether it finds formal expression or not—is definite and has an existence of its own. But the threat is just as real, and has many more allies in a threatening world, one of whose chief and most deadly weapons is this threat, this fear. And there can be no real stability of effort—not in community—in that atmosphere. What you may find is the extreme and heightened effort of exiles or conspirators who design and maneuver and skillfully contrive to achieve a known end. That happens in politics; it happens in art. But it is conspiracy to a *known* end; and I think the point will illuminate more than anything that I can say that the belief toward which everything I have said is pointed is an *unknown* and *undefined* belief. This may be a weakness. I do not think it is, but I know the times call for incisive definition and immediate action, and I feel very diffident in standing before you with anything more general. Except that candor is best; formulas will not do; what I must say to you is that there are possibilities, and it is those which must be worked out.

    The history of poetic movements provides excellent models, the best models of all, I think, better than any in the history of religion or statecraft or any other exploration. I think of Amy Lowell with her capacity for arranging and provoking and organizing, and I do not believe that she had a movement with her; or of some of the recent efforts to build up groups in an atmosphere of pressures and frictions and constraints.[11] There are two periods in English history when the motion was made freely, full tide, in gestures that had no object—no label—that permitted the imagination to exercise its range, and provided a climate of belief. One was the Elizabethan period, when at a flash, or so it seems at this distance, many people saw human capacities that had not until then been guessed at in their richness; the other was the time of that

---

    11. American poet Amy Lowell began publishing Imagist anthologies in 1915. Ezra Pound, dubbing her takeover "Amygism," derided her collections as opportunistic, weak free verse.

group which revolved around Coleridge and Wordsworth and their further intuition about the capacity of the human spirit. The parallel in this country is that time which has been rightly seen as flowering and springtime and frontier, which gave us the Concord group.[12] And these artists had liberated themselves from formula, they guessed, they guessed continually in an expanding age, their guesses turned on greatness, and they moved in an air of unboundaried belief.

The wish for belief of this sort is a subtle and terrible thing. And the belief itself, because it is based on no dogma at all, but on a suspicion of great capacity, is likely to break down during great wars, great horror, when not only belief but everything else is killed. So much death in the world; the weight of so much death; and the only solidarity the frightful solidarity of guilt, and the knowledge that we are all implicated in this crime. The belief breaks down; your token is *The Waste Land*, its symbols of impotence and drought, and the sure consciousness that even if the rain arrives this moment, it arrives too late. People wish for it most of all in despair and madness and war; the wish breeds insanity. I have heard of a Frenchman in this country who went mad last spring, as Paris fell.[13] His madness took this form: he went about and asked the people he met to give him orders. He begged for it, only give him orders, any orders, and he would carry them out. One wonders what new forms of madness are taking shape in France.

I have just had the good luck to be offered a chance to read the most revealing document I have ever seen. It is the first of its kind, although it would seem that the science of which it is a part would have a main obligation to assemble material like this for years and years, until there was a base that would be available to all those working in the field.

(Tell about the SCHIZ manuscript; compare Joyce; tell suffering; tell wish; read parts about freedom and belief and passion.)[14]

---

12. Rukeyser's friend F. O. Matthiessen connected Ralph Waldo Emerson and Henry David Thoreau ("the Concord group") to the British Romantics (Coleridge and Wordsworth). See F. O. Matthiessen, *American Renaissance: Art and Expression in the Age of Emerson and Whitman* (New York: Oxford University Press, 1941).

13. Paris fell to invading German forces on June 14, 1940, thus beginning a four-year period of Nazi occupation with the Vichy government administering the occupied zone.

14. Parenthetical passage consists of ts improvisation notes. Rukeyser refers to James Joyce's *Finnegans Wake* (1939) and one of several 1940 studies on schizophrenia and social isolation, later quoted in "Communication and Poetry," in this volume.

CHAPTER 4

Now that is the statement of a madman; and its imagery is that of madness. But it is also the deep wish of a person who is preoccupied with his trouble, and the shocking thing about it is that he comes so close, he is absorbed in his suffering and thinking about it and he recognizes his need. The moment he does recognize his own need, he hits on the one healing principle. He is quite right; if he can find one belief, one axis of reality, he can be cured. The point is that he is right. And until he finds that axis, all that he can express is catastrophe.

If you dilute that suffering—and the only dilution is that of reason—and generalize, and multiply it by the population of a country, I think you will have an approximation of England, or Germany, or any country faced by war today, and split to its heart. England is not, I think, murderously divided against itself, any more than this sick boy is; but we have seen a real *civil* war between France and England, as real as our own Civil War; and I think the shock of that cleavage has had a lot to do with England's spiritual resurgence. Again, the only answer in the face of sickness is a set towards belief, and, again here, not a formal belief, but rather a belief in capacity that must grow with action, and feed as it grows, and be elusive, not in its nature, but in the elusive and promising movement of its boundaries.

The answer in this country is very often rigid, much more rigid than one would expect. It is in terms of censorship and hush-editorials; the war is upon us, give up all of this, for the time being at least, talk of nothing but our health, our buoyancy, the splendid vigor of our forces, the necessity of everything as it is accomplished . . . at least until the crisis is past. I know there is a widespread feeling that an unspoken censorship has already arrived, and that a real censorship must follow soon. I should like to read you a comment that has come out of bombed London, emerged in a voice so human and clear, so against all the hysteria that can make straitjackets and gags out of the flags of countries, so deeply civilized that it offers real civilization to the reader:

> "The general feeling," I read [in a letter from an American reader], "is that we are on your side. As pro-British as Roosevelt, but no more." To be on our side, the side which is against Hitler-steria, against nazi-ness, is to be—"pro-British."
>
> [. . .]
>
> There were many nations, not necessarily pro-German, who saw no need to be pro-British. [. . .] They could not see that to be against Hitler was to be *for* something shared by all civilization,

something far bigger than can be contained by any word of only national denomination.

[...]

We—the Englishmen, Scots, Welsh, Irish, French, Norwegians, Czechs, Poles, Canadians, New Zealanders, Australians, now making our stand in this island—know that we have looked into our souls, and what we have not liked that we have seen there, has borne the imprint of Satan, an imprint we recognize; we are determined to do away, at last, with this split personality, having seen what a split the darker side can so wantonly make when it gets the upper hand. We know it is not a war between countries, nor as some would have us believe among classes, but each man's war for his soul.[15]

The slap in the face is a good one; it is the treatment for hysteria, and it works.[16]

This audacity is very much alive, not the mouthfuls of election talk we have been having, or the overstimulated glandular variety of despair. It is close to the spirit of the Melville letter I read yesterday.[17] Its material is the usable truth, and it has no need to be pompous or bloodshot about anything, least of all itself. One looks around for writing like this, for talk like this. I have spoken about immediate emotion, and the need to face meanings, but I do not forget how badly we all want freshness and pleasure and relaxation and delight. A musical comedy can do that, a mystery thriller or a day in the country or going dancing or any number of delightful and irrelevant pastimes can do it, and not wipe out the main fact, but rather add to the effect of not facing, of playing and behaving surreptitiously and behind the back of the world. The editorial and the note about planes crossing over the Channel take the general and very effective horror and put it on a human level again. We need that very deeply. We need it in our day-to-day affairs, in our talk,

---

15. Fc here only notes: "(Read Herring's editorial in L & L)." The editors have supplied extracts from that piece. Robert Herring, "Editorial," *Life and Letters To-day*, September 1940, 197–200. In July 1936, Herring hired Rukeyser to cover the Popular Olympiad in Barcelona. See Muriel Rukeyser, "Barcelona, 1936," in this volume.

16. Ts improvisation notes: "(Go on with L & L attitude, news notes, etc.)." Following his editorial, Herring supplied news items, recounted from his first-person eyewitness perspective, about everyday life in wartime London. See Robert Herring, "News Reel," *Life and Letters To-day*, September 1940, 201–214.

17. See Muriel Rukeyser, "Belief and Poetry," in this volume.

in our poetry.[18] It is at that point that poetry will inevitably not satisfy us at the moment. It will not be able quite so quickly to absorb not the war itself, but the change of world that must include the conditions of war. We'll have ballads, and songs, and the official verse of laureates and newspaper columnists. There was a horrifying statement reprinted in the newspapers last spring, to the effect that Mr. MacNeice had said that the war was not very interesting yet and there would be no war poetry, in his estimate, until it improved.[19] If that statement had been true, it could not have been topped for cold horror and cynicism. But it seemed to be at bottom a statement about catastrophe and expression during catastrophe. If the shock is great and general enough, it is the leveler of expression, and you will have your queens and scrubwomen making identical statements of absolute nobility or absolute banality, but—and you may rely on this—extremely simple and direct. Statement during shock is always likely to be extreme understatement of an almost formal quality. Hemingway is master of it; he has taken his characters through entire books, and kept them talking as if they had not yet got over the shock which started them off.[20] The point is, of course, that they never will. It is a quality that hardly comes off on the stage, and which makes the most searing and expressive photography. If you have followed *Life* during its record of France and England this year, you will have been struck by face after face caught in declarative horror, sometimes making a joke of it, or fitting it into the life of that day, but always struck by it and expressing just that.[21] That is what happens, and it does not fit into an art-form. It is certainly not ruled out—I cannot see any exclusion possible, of any subject or any attitude, once that subject or attitude has been absorbed; but very few have gone through the process of absorption. And, as the editorial in *Life and Letters To-day* points out, it is always a surprise to see America using the worn-out phrases;

---

18. Holo. note on opposite page verso: "reading people do now—short time poetry." Rukeyser preferred longer poems that took time for the complexity of war and other social issues to unfold.

19. Irish poet Louis MacNeice told Buffalo's *Courier-Express*: "The world is not very likely to see much war poetry coming out of the present war between Germany, England, and France. Prospects may improve if and when the war speeds up a little, but right now there is too much boredom about the whole thing to encourage either poets or poetry." Associated Press, "Expects Little War Poetry," *New York Times*, February 25, 1940.

20. Ernest Hemingway, American modernist novelist.

21. *Life*, popular photojournalism magazine published by Henry Luce. Rukeyser was the unattributed author of a recent photo-essay published there. See [Muriel Rukeyser], "The Telephone Company," *Life*, July 19, 1939.

it is a surprise to see the attitudes revert. One magazine, for example, printed a war issue in the same month that this issue of *Life and Letters To-day* appeared.[22] It was an anti-war issue, but without the sharpness of *Life and Letters To-day*, and without a twist of the humor that can arrive under fire, but which is almost impossible in the moments before that, while there is still time. It spoke of the mistakes made in considering "writers'" problems in the face of war, of the refugees, of the gold buried at Fort Knox, of the new generation to be drafted.[23] The issue was in many ways an occasional issue, and showed up in the weaknesses of the "social poets," for the social poets had become the occasional versemakers; from drawing-room poets, they had become headline poets, and were corrupted with the disease that struck so many writers in the month of September 1939, and has not ceased to strike; the need to be absolutely right about the headlines twelve hours after they appeared, at the very latest.[24]

The worst thing that would happen to our poetry at this point, except to neglect it altogether, would be for it to become an occasional poetry of war. A good deal of the repugnance to social poetry was caused, I think, because there were so many degrees of blood-savagery in it, ranging all the way from self-pity, naked or identified with one victim after another, to actual bloodlust and display of wounds, a rotten sort of literary begging for attention and sympathy and charity that did not persuade anybody and did not take in very many. We need the emphasis that the last ten years have given to our poetry. Actually, what the so-called social poets have insisted on has been a tradition in art—one of the few traditions that goes beyond a formal shell to an organic structure which we can in conscience claim and use.[25]

---

22. First page of this lecture's fc specifies the periodical as *Poetry: A Magazine of Verse*, September 1940. The special issue, featuring minor writers, was titled "Poets on War."

23. Kenneth Fearing, "U.S. Writers in War," *Poetry: A Magazine of Verse*, September 1940, 318–323, https://www.jstor.org/stable/20582262. Fearing criticizes how, when wars arise, readers distance themselves by adopting the "very pleasant" "fashion" of asking, "What do you as a writer think about it [i.e., war], and what ought you as a writer to do about it?" The better question, he posits, is: "What is it going to do to us?"

24. Holo. improvisation note on opposite page verso: "Complain of inability—even here / all the writers who were *able* a year ago to be right about the headlines in time for the weeklies."

25. Holo. improvisation note: "Portraits against background of *circumstances of life*—on the stage demanded—*Of Human Bondage*." It is unknown if Rukeyser means W. Somerset Maugham's novel *Of Human Bondage* (1915) or its film adaptation (1936), directed by John Cromwell.

88   CHAPTER 4

To keep our validity now, however, we must go beyond the war. Actually, some of us have been writing of nothing else for the last four or five years.[26] This has nothing to do with minorities, although it deals with victims. It is the true historic reversal; the line of war the great example of minority rule; the driven people trapped in shock and without expression; the forms of expression, cornered and paralyzed until, a moment later, the gag itself is slipped in place.

They say, and we know to go on from there: We must plan the future as if it extended forever, and work according to that plan. But compromise may be the rule tomorrow.[27] And even if it is, we must see over that rule. It is time for the most brilliant and mature imagination, for we must look to the peace that may emerge from this war, to an end of the flights of refugees, to a decentralization of ruined countries, and a building up from the ground of ruin. The lonely ruined countries, of whom we are the last, and in this moment, intact still but with all commitments made! Lonely Ethiopia, lonely Spain, all western Europe, China fantastically ragged and enduring in the east, England swept down-on and alone. Conference tables will not make peace here, and the shrewd hidden reasons of statesmen will not make very much happen. There will need to be live acts, heroic acts of the imagination in the torn countries. (Not just *believing*. I haven't talked about what I believe in or what you believe in any more than I've talked about what you're doing or I'm doing—because we have to find our terms and they must be somewhere between. I am just saying your own belief is the measure of yourself, and is the line to hang method on.)[28] And in this country, it will mean the reckless premature gestures that we live on in America. That we start our processes with. Like John Brown, that meteor, a crazy murderous old man whom Lincoln had to condemn, but whose act was responsible, was the precipitating stroke that was necessary and right according to its own laws and the laws of action.

It is strokes like that that we need, in poetry as well as in action. Firm rebellious strokes based on belief, and not narrowed by a rigid

---

26. Holo. improvisation note: "talk about Ken and Al and Davy and Auden's travels and me." Rukeyser refers to English transplant W. H. Auden, her friend Kenneth Fearing, British poet and novelist Alfred Hayes, and Jewish Scottish poet David Daiches, the latter two of whom lived in the United States in the late 1930s. Daiches and Fearing provided commentary in *Poetry*'s "Poets on War" special issue. See notes 22 and 23 above.

27. On fc, Rukeyser crossed out "the gag" and substituted, in holo., "compromise."

28. Preceding two sentences in holo. on opposite page verso. Reworked and inserted by editors.

framework. Since this is not the end of belief, but the beginning, and the rules are not yet laid. There will be a lot of fighting before the peace can be seen. As for rules, you will be able to recognize the peace this way: if it is a false peace, there will be a great many rules; if it is peace, there will not be many. Because then there will be a science to begin, the building-up; and there will be a poetry to suit that growth.

That is the poetry we may begin now. The age *has* cracked open; our lives *have* cracked open. It had been coming for a long time; it is our main promise, the sign of a beginning; and if it seems now to cut us off and choke off all speech, we have reminders of what it is we are to imagine, and with what powers we must answer. Dryden has the final lines:

> All, all of a piece throughout!
> Thy Chase had a Beast in View;
> Thy Wars brought nothing about;
> Thy Lovers were all untrue.
> 'Tis well an Old Age is out,
> And time to begin a New.[29]

That is the only young world left, the one that has not yet been clearly imagined. That is the poetry ahead of us.[30]

(Unpublished, 1940)

---

29. John Dryden, "The Secular Masque" (1700). Also see Muriel Rukeyser, "The Speed of the Image," in this volume, note 2.

30. Fc indicates that an hour-long discussion was scheduled to follow this lecture.

CHAPTER 5

Communication and Poetry (1940)

The two figures of communication that I have had before me as I thought about communication in relation to poetry and our time have been those of John Brown and Carossa.[1] They are as I see them highly dramatic figures, and each of them in their great moments tells us more about reaching each other than can be said in words. In one, we have the extreme and pathological moment, the boiling over at Harpers Ferry, that had been led up to, prepared for dramatically in the same way that the crisis in a play or a great poem is prepared for. We have a small band of soldiers, in one desperate raid, throwing such passion into their cause that it must lead to

---

1. Muriel Rukeyser gave this fifth and final lecture from *The Usable Truth* at Vassar College on Friday, November 1, 1940, at 9:15 a.m. She had discussed abolitionist John Brown and contemporary German poet Han Carossa in the first and third lectures of *The Usable Truth*, "The Fear of Poetry" and "Belief and Poetry," both in this volume. Two ts notes on opposite page verso of the lecture's first page: "Introduction here adequate to explain believing not the end of belief; likeness of individual action (Brown and Carossa) to poem in providing the communication to many people who can fit the action (poem) into a tradition which is found to be theirs, in which climate they easily can move and take to be their usable truth. Movement of groups, of masses, after that recognition." Followed by: "1860-1900-1940 / Emergence of Henry Adams into twentieth century most conscious entrance, possibly, in history. Nearer year 1 or 1900 question." Clues to this cryptic note can be extrapolated from the discussion of Henry Adams as a historian in Muriel Rukeyser, *Willard Gibbs* (Garden City, NY: Doubleday, Doran, 1942), 404–416.

an incalculable enlargement of the struggle itself. That execution and martyrdom should come out of such a move is terribly logical; that Civil War should break in another year and a half is part of that pattern. Carossa the poet is passive compared with the figure of Brown, a furious prophetic old man; Carossa is on the other side, finds himself surrounded by violence and the education of violence, and is unable to *refuse* to oppose it by withholding what he himself calls "his gentle voice."[2] But the gesture is part of the same pattern as Brown's, no matter how far removed it is in kind. It is the same kind of communication they are trying for. It is the communication that is not prophecy at all, for it is concerned with the present and the past, too, as much as it is concerned with the possible future; it is the attempt at a gesture of revelation, to rip away circumstance and show at one stroke the immediate and powerful moment in its implications. That is the gesture of poetry. It is questioned continually; it is called unimportant—what if it fails? what if it does not communicate? what if it becomes one in a long series of ineffectual gestures? what if it becomes merely statistical? And the old twisted complaint, that if you tell them the truth, they will say you speak in symbols. Brown did not fail; Brown communicated. As for Carossa, we do not yet know. But there is the gesture. And it has been pointed out that the homerun makes more unity in the grandstand than in the batting average. We come of a generation that has been brought up to deal with figures of statistical magnitude, and the index can be made to shift bewilderingly, and the relations of these statistics to each other contain their own bias, are indeed another example of biased abstraction.[3] The gestures of Brown and Carossa can be broken down, as any number can be; there are motives to find, cross-currents, delicate balances of outside forces to account for; but what is important in each instance is that here was a whole gesture, with the vitality of a whole life behind it, made in the Harpers Ferry raid with reckless insistence and trust and hopelessness, and in the scene on the platform before the Hitler Youth, with the quiet unemphasized calm that summarizes a lifetime of steady belief. Both of these gestures reach us immediately; they stamp themselves on us without a word.

Scholars, in speaking of the audience to whom Shakespeare directed his plays, have repeated with a wry and jealous smile the fact that the action had to be played to an illiterate audience; and when we deal with

---

2. See Muriel Rukeyser, "The Fear of Poetry," in this volume, note 25.
3. On biased abstraction, see Muriel Rukeyser, "Belief and Poetry," in this volume, note 6.

any of these problems of communication, it is a good standard to keep in mind. If we in our plays directed the action to the illiterate, the words could be as complicated as you like, the communication would be made on the other level primarily. The incisive gesture would be made in an atmosphere of silence. And that significant gesture made in silence is the communication that is universal.

But take it off the stage. Think of it in poetry, whose nature must be *against* silence. Poetry cannot even require rests. On the stage, in the films, long pauses between speeches and between actions may supply the most important effects of all. In music, the rest contributes relief and renewal. In poetry, no rest is possible; no breathing-space longer than a full stop, or, at the very most, a blank line which you can never be sure that your reader will observe. Writers like Cummings can juggle all the combinations, but they can never do more than slow down the action of their words; they cannot stop the flow at will.[4]

The time-material you deal with in writing a poem—and this is true of any kind of writing to a lesser extent, since prose has more time at its disposal, as a rule, and the long poem faces the same hazards of treatment by the reader that prose does—the material of a poem is its length of time, and the hope that it is written in is the hope that it may find that time a receptive period. Its obligation is to *make* it receptive; but, of its nature, it is fluid, and all its preparation must be made as it goes past in its full intensity.

But to talk in terms of significant action, or of this flow, as if one were snatching at a river, is not as close as I wish to come to the central problem: the problem of communication. Does it reach you? Does it reach your life? Is there a "moment of proof" at which your life meets the work of art? That is the only test.

There has been a breakdown in communication, it is true. It comes through clearly in the specialized jargon of the professions, in the unmanageable multiplicity of terms and half-meanings and shadows of meanings that we use. It comes through very clearly in the word-slinging of a presidential election campaign, with contradiction and evasion and contradiction, until we drown in words.[5] And the breakdown has nothing to do with unintelligibility, although this seems a paradox.

---

    4. American writer and painter E. E. Cummings bridged the gap between popular poetry and modernist experimentation in humorous poems that play with words and typography while addressing accessible subjects like love and popular culture.

    5. Rukeyser delivered *The Usable Truth* lectures near the end of the 1940 US presidential contest between Democratic incumbent Franklin Delano Roosevelt and Republican

It is not the experimenters, the ones who are always called unintelligible for a few years at least, who have the guilt. They are working in communication, they are doing the lab work, and you may be reasonably sure of their honesty and conviction, although often they lack the clews that will force them to be communicable, and without which they can talk and analyze and invent to wit's end, and still be unheard and choked.[6] But it is the debasers who break meaning down; they stand in the same relation to meaning that the ward heelers do to the principles they twist to their own ends to keep their jobs, or get new ones. Debasers of values, of meanings, of words, those who dilute and soften and corrupt, the majority in the field, the ward heelers, the magazine versifiers, the soft of will who pick up an instrument and use it in such a way that not only the job is botched, but the subtle instrument is blunted and the corruption goes on.[7] The thing is alive, as any disease might be. It grows at its own rate, and thrives—and grows faster than its own nature, because of the culture it lives in; a culture that grows more complicated, and fosters more complicated organisms of all sorts, good and malevolent.

If art fails at this level, it fails in a thorough and complicated way. There is no good in talking about an illiterate audience; it is not an illiterate audience that one has to deal with, but the audience not only literate but sophisticated in comparisons. This audience has seen many worlds, and heard many comments on them. The newspapers and the movies and the radio have seen to that. It is an audience that is sophisticated in a mechanical way, that is sophisticated not through any particular choice of its own, but because these worlds have been poured in on it, and there was not much reason to set up resistance, or even a healthy antagonism.

During the long analysis of the schizophrenia case, from the transcript of which I read some sections yesterday, the mad boy asked a question that I thought struck home tragically.[8] In speaking about his own indifference, the key characteristic of his disease, the fact that he feels himself standing still, not planning and living, not having any future, he breaks in with the question, "Just one thing . . . Is there any psychological term at all that is the meaning of a person that just lives right in the present, a person that hasn't any ideas of his own, that is

---

challenger Wendell Willkie. She later wrote a biography about Willkie. See Muriel Rukeyser, *One Life* (New York: Simon & Schuster, 1957).
    6. On the word *clew*, see Muriel Rukeyser, "The Fear of Poetry," in this volume, note 3.
    7. A ward heeler canvasses for a political party.
    8. See Muriel Rukeyser, "Poetry and Peace," in this volume.

all ideas he's collected from other people, learned a great many things from books and from understanding and from talking and experience, but he hasn't any of his own that he has figured out? Is that a certain type of person or isn't it?" The analyst tells him that everyone does that to a certain extent, and the boy goes on, "That's the way I imagine myself. I can't think of myself any other way because I can't see where I figured out myself about these things. I've taken ideas from other people and they've proved true and I accepted them as they came along, but I haven't fought for ideas of my own . . . That's what I—I thought there was probably some word for it—some term that'd tell about it—explain it, but I guess there isn't . . ." The analyst tells him that he doesn't know of any word for that kind of person. There should be a word. The boy has here come very close to his own suffering. It is this fact of living in the moment without the feeling of ever having worked for an idea—a definition that many people might give offhandedly of enjoyment, of a pleasant condition—that really means being cut off—and that is much more dangerous to a group as a whole than the so-called unintelligibility of the experimental artist. That is the insanity of the audience, and we are all in that audience, no matter to what degree we are producing.

And in a culture of technically "high rank"—using that in the sense that Maxwell spoke of organizations of high rank—we have communication of high rank, although that moves much more slowly, and the kind of communication has not developed as the means for communication have.[9] Shakespeare and his candle-lit wooden stage! But it would be naïve to look at the radio in proportional horror. At least we can in conscience devote ourselves to poetry if we want to. We have all the devices.

What the devices have done is to filter poetry down, to get it to its audience in the only way that poetry ever can reach its audience; in a gradual process by which from the poets and that small audience that actually reads poetry, it arrives to the prose writers and is incorporated, and finds form after form which may be touched by it and reminded, until those who are going to be referred back to the poems themselves reach the books, and the others are touched in lesser ways by the changed forms. It is an absurdity to complain about smallness of audience. Of course the audience is small, has always been. The entire audience that saw the performances of all of Shakespeare's plays during his

---

9. On physicist James Clerk Maxwell, see Rukeyser, "The Fear of Poetry," in this volume.

lifetime—the whole Elizabethan audience of all the plays of that period, if you prefer—is lost among the number of people going to the movies in any one day in America. I suppose the audience that heard either of MacLeish's radio plays is larger than Shakespeare's audience.[10]

The poetic drama is as good a test as any for poetry trying to make itself heard.[11] The reasonable solution for the play, it seems to me, has not yet been naturally developed—and that would be the prose play, whose climaxes and heightened situations are thrown into the diction they require, the diction of poetry. The poetic drama of today is either bogged down in Elizabethan mannerisms and hangovers, or is openly experimental and produced only within a narrow range. Jeffers's *Tower Beyond Tragedy*, which contains the finest poetry of any American verse play written to date, is written along the lines of Greek blind tragedy—brought sharply and naturally to the present in the magnificent prophecy which Cassandra makes, a prophecy which leaps three thousand years. That play is almost unplayable, except as pageantry and recitation; it has been done by a university group in California.[12] Eliot's *Sweeney Agonistes* has been done here; Auden has been done here, and at Yale, and, very badly, by the Federal Theatre; Eliot's *Murder in the Cathedral* was given a performance by the Federal Theatre which was uneven theatre, but which sent the poetry into the air and shook the audience with it; Maxwell Anderson is performed by professional groups all over the country; and MacLeish's one play, *Panic*, was given a brief and stylized performance and was ripped to pieces afterwards in one of the weirdest symposiums I ever attended, in which MacLeish was actually martyred.[13] The high spot of that evening—the high point

---

10. Archibald MacLeish's verse plays about the Spanish Civil War, *The Fall of the City* (1937) and *Air Raid* (1938), were broadcast by CBS's Columbia Workshop and starred Orson Welles.

11. Holo. note on opposite page verso: "Committee to Find an Audience for Poetry." In 1935, while working for the New Theatre League, Rukeyser traveled on the East Coast with poets Horace Gregory, Alfred Hayes, and Sol Funaroff to advocate for using new poetic forms in progressive and proletarian theater.

12. A stage adaptation of Robinson Jeffers's "The Tower Beyond Tragedy" (1925) was produced by the University of California at Berkeley's Mortar Board Dramatic Group in 1932.

13. At Vassar, Hallie Flanagan, who later directed Rukeyser's verse play *The Middle of the Air* (1945), premiered T. S. Eliot's *Sweeney Agonistes* (1926-1927; produced 1933) and Ernst Toller's *No More Peace* (lyrics by W. H. Auden; published and produced 1937). From 1935 to 1938, Flanagan headed the Works Progress Administration's Federal Theatre Project. She mounted productions of Eliot's *Murder in the Cathedral* (1935; produced 1936) and Auden's *The Dance of Death* (1933; produced 1936). The Broadway production of Maxwell Anderson's verse play *Winterset* (1935) received accolades. Archibald MacLeish's *Panic* (1935), about the banking crisis, was produced by John Houseman, choreographed by Martha Graham, and

of all discussions of poetic drama, it seems to me—arrived when one particularly frightening partisan critic objected to the play's political attitude, because, he said, the author's political bias was shown by the fact that his hero, the banker, was given a five-foot line while the chorus, the masses who should be in possession, were permitted only three feet to the line! This has been the recent development of poetry on the stage in this country. We have yet to see the broken and electric play that will combine vivid and native speech with the brilliant action that the medium deserves. Radio may do it, television may do it. The failure so far was accented the week following the broadcast of MacLeish's *Air Raid*, when Orson Welles's nightmare adventure proved not only that the premises of MacLeish's work were false—he was saying, you will remember, that people would not believe a raid—but also proved what the state of receptivity of this country was, what "audience response" really was when it was laid bare.[14]

The difficulty with recent poetic drama has been its extreme lack of action. Action has been interpreted to mean sweeping and athletic gestures, rather than the smaller and significant detail of movement which will suddenly illuminate a relationship. Another great hindrance, and this has been true of all poetry and not alone the poetry of the theatre, has been its inconclusive search for a tradition.[15] The only possible tradition that would seem valid would be that in which all axiom is cut away at the beginning, and a stand is taken with that line of people who may be said to belong to a "non-axiomatic tradition." For in itself that forms a line, a tradition in the healthiest sense, since repetition is not possible, not permissible within its definition.

And there would be a fortifying, a sense of the past and a continuous present that would defy the paralysis which is seizing so many here, and

---

starred Orson Welles. The production was panned at a symposium organized by the New Theatre League and *New Masses*. A holo. note on opposite page verso—"Gertrude Stein: Four Saints. The static. 'A saint is enough.'"—indicates Rukeyser's intention to add material about Stein's opera *Four Saints in Three Acts* (1927), which premiered in Connecticut in 1934 and then moved to Broadway. The avant-garde production featured a score by Virgil Thomson (1928), sets by Florine Stettheimer, and an all-Black cast.

14. Orson Welles's hoax *The War of the Worlds* (1938). See note 10 above.

15. Here, there is a ts improvisation note to reprise elements from *The Usable Truth* series' first lecture, "The Fear of Poetry": "(Traditionalism here—the church and the regicides—Eliot and Pound—Gibbs and Melville and Dickinson—Auden and the refugees)." On opposite page verso, there also is a holo. improvisation note about cultural affairs in Britain: "directions across the Atlantic changed in 20 yrs. for those in search of a tradition in which they could live."

which must have been creeping across Europe in an epidemic before the war itself broke; the paralysis of anticipation which is likely to prey on the creative mind. At any moment, the balance may be set which will influence all the possibilities of survival—at any moment at all, not this one more or less than any other—and it is with the business of survival and its attendant destructions that tradition itself is concerned. The hope is for a quick glimpse of possibility; but these glimpses are given at the end of long preparation; the hope is for a flash of communication which will reach with the validity of a miracle witnessed; but these miracles are ordered. We must remember continually out of what material the communication must come; on what scene the miracle must be played. For a great part of the world, whatever reaches will be in the nature of dream-singing, a dream-singing in defeat.[16] And as we search for a tradition, and for the dreams themselves that will help us to reach one another, we search for the myths of our existence. Read Kafka, and you will feel that search throughout. Kierkegaard and his work stand behind that effort, but almost a hundred years away, and while Kierkegaard felt free to move in the air of the Biblical myth, Kafka could not, and must find his own.[17] Kierkegaard saw in Abraham a father, a father of faith, and a father of myth. Kafka accepted a web of complexity, and his images were the endless trial—the networks of courts and laws and questions and answers and deceptions and legalities—or the errand, the smoky detective story that is close to all our hearts of half-known clues, half-known messages, and tricks and fumbling effort and undiscovered reasonings.[18] It is as if there were to be some tremendous structure of a story built on, say, the process of an examination, whose form is very close to the Kafka equation, as if you faced unknown questions on which your life hung, and for which there was no preparation possible and no appeal from which could possibly be imagined. It is myth like that, images like that, that have come to express the horror and mystery of the human heart before a complicated and murderous civilization. And, although the process becomes fantastic very soon, cloudy and fantastic, it escapes at least the cynicism which any realistic treatment falls

---

16. Ts improvisation cue: "(Tell about the prophet-dances, the religions of 1870 . . .)." On dream-singing, see Rukeyser, "Belief and Poetry," in this volume, note 17.

17. Rukeyser here reprises her earlier discussion about Franz Kafka's fiction and Søren Kierkegaard's parable "In Praise of Abraham." See Rukeyser, "Belief and Poetry," in this volume.

18. Unlike in the rest of *The Usable Truth*, Rukeyser here uses the conventional spelling for *clue*, rather than the archaic *clew*.

into. Cynicism which is apparent, for example, in most bottom-dog novels, in the course of which it is clear that most of the characters, and certainly the writer himself, has reached a toleration of the hell he describes. The Kafka framework is never one of acceptance, although always the characters fit into the framework; but the very cloudiness breeds questioning.

The myth and the immediacy are found together in poetry, which gives many voices to the questions, and many scenes to the immediacy. Poetry comes the closest of all the communications, I feel, and it is this that brings the vivid discomfort that so many people feel when their barrier, their fear, is threatened. It *is* uncomfortable, as any approach to naked consciousness is. It is as if you came into a theatre, and sat in your seat to feel the familiar warmth of excitement and leaving yourself as the house darkened and the curtain went up; but as if the curtain went up on a character who stepped forward to make a curtain speech, saying, "This is a play we have come to watch, and it is true that we will be watching throughout, I shall be standing in the wings and you will be sitting in your seats. But what it concerns is your life, and more than that; not only your life but your relation in life to the people who are sitting on either side of you; not only the friend you came with who is sitting at one side, but the stranger who is sitting at the other side; for at this moment, the one thing that we have in common is that we are all alive in a room together—" and all the house lights went on full, and everyone looked at his neighbor. There would be a self-consciousness at that moment, and a place-consciousness, and time-consciousness, that might make *that* the moment of climax and destroy any possibility that the play itself would get across; but that state would be the acute moment that comes within the range of poetry; the cover would be off; and whatever was possible would be possible at that moment, in all its rawness and shock.

There is a danger of emphasizing shock and rawness. It is like the danger of emphasizing honesty.[19] What is hoped for is perception, and the crude bases of that perception are not desirable one by one. A bombardment is *not* what is meant at all, and the crudity of that curtain speech, for example, would probably be disastrous. The finest poetry is shaded most finely and to prepare a person to wear fine clothes and love fine textures does not require that she be flayed alive. It would be

---

19. On the insufficiency of honesty, see Rukeyser, "Belief and Poetry," in this volume.

a desperate simplification to call for any violence in preparation, and it would be the same kind of desperate simplification that has called for violence, and nothing but more violence, and more brutality, in poetry. What we hope for is communication of greater complexity to more highly organized readers, people who are sensitive along a constantly increasing range. What poetry can do is to communicate a wide range of expression along a firm and living axis of reality. The forms are limitless, the material itself limitless, and this is true of poetry as much as it is true of any other channel of the human imagination. But what poetry can do that many of the other forms cannot, or can do less directly, is to focus on that complexity—to throw it into an order, to lead its traced developments as subtly as the developments of music, and explicitly—and, in showing us focus after focus of complexity, strengthen that area of attention that so urgently needs to be strengthened now.[20]

We need sophistication in this, the ability to face clusters, to face a complicated ensemble, and there is everything to suggest that we will need more and more of this sophistication, and that what will best communicate this knowledge will serve us best. We have classified many other kinds of knowledge, and know many uses for them; we are largely utilitarian, and the tendency is to throw out poetry as not falling in with our utilitarian needs. But that in itself is an act against our civilization, which can convert peanut shells into silk, and vegetables into plane fuselages. It is this kind of knowledge that has not been used; and it is against all of our best directions to throw it away as we have. Many barriers have broken down; many countries of the world are split across by the issues now before them; these split peoples need communication more urgently than ever before; and we need desperately to reach ourselves—each other.[21] We need communication and insight, and the alertness of perception that is based on those two, and that reaches its concentration in poetry and the attitude that poetry supposes in the world. We very badly need the tradition in which this knowledge may move freely and be at home, that air of acceptance which Melville indicated when he spoke of the usable truth.[22]

---

20. Ts improvisation note: "(Henry Adams on unity and multiplicity, science and the rush of phase)." Also holo. note opposite page verso: "H. Adams's conscious entrance into the XXth cent." On Henry Adams, see note 1 above; also see Muriel Rukeyser, "The Speed of the Image," in this volume, note 16.

21. Fc originally read "split tribes," but Rukeyser changed it, in holo., to "split peoples."

22. Ts cue here: "(Re-read part of the letter). " See Rukeyser, "The Fear of Poetry," in this volume, note 19; and Rukeyser, "Belief and Poetry," in this volume.

That, I think, is a tradition we may freely choose. The use of truth is its communication. It is a tradition that has to be fought for with whatever insight and power and poetry we can summon in ourselves.[23] But there is not only that base of tradition; there are the possibilities involved. Our lives are the nearest of those possibilities; for, very closely, our lives are all implicated, and the next years will cut through many layers of refusal and hesitation, until the choice is made which will have to do for us, for we will have to live according to it.[24] But if we can catch the resonance between ourselves, if we can respond to these facts which cluster into their systems and confront us now—with insight, and keep open what communications there are, the communication itself may mean discovery. The age does fall away and change, the poetries do issue, there will be vast destructions before anything is whole and able to stand, but there is a world to emerge, and the hope for poetry is a hope for a world and a peace in which poetry may live, as people may live—a world in which the life of poetry will be the life of people.[25]

(Unpublished, 1940)

---

23. Holo. note on opposite page: "Individual action only communicates a tradition that a *group* can accept & convert into mass action."

24. At the time, the United States was officially a neutral nation and the prospect of entering the European war was unpopular, thus Americans' "refusal and hesitation."

25. Fc contains several holo. changes, which affect this sentence's meaning: "will be vast destructions" originally read "may be vast destructions"; "there is a world to emerge" originally read "there will be a world to imagine"; and "the life of people" originally read "the life of the people."

PART II

Twentieth-Century Radicalism

On Politics, Society, and Culture

CHAPTER 6

The Flown Arrow: The Aftermath of the Sacco-Vanzetti Case (1932)

Five years ago this month, Nicola Sacco and Bartolomeo Vanzetti were killed in the electric chair in Massachusetts.[1] The case had taken seven years; it has become public property, so that no one in the country was free of it; it had been argued and pled in so many different ways, and so widespread an activity had become concentrated on the case that the burden belonged to the world. There were those who believed during the seven years of trial and imprisonment that the accused were innocent. There were others who were convinced when the court records, the testimony of psychologists, the letters of Sacco and Vanzetti themselves were made public. But some were never convinced; and among these were their judge, Webster Thayer, President Lowell of Harvard and his investigation committee, Governor Fuller of Massachusetts, President Coolidge, and the laws of Massachusetts and the United States.

---

1. In April 1920, Italian immigrants Nicola Sacco and Bartolomeo Vanzetti were charged with armed robbery and a guard's murder at two shops south of Boston, Massachusetts. All evidence pointed to their innocence. Known anarchists during a xenophobic and anti-radical period, they were held without due process, found guilty, and, after failed appeals, executed seven years later.

CHAPTER 6

Sacco and Vanzetti were murdered; a few days after, the *Boston Herald* said, editorially: "We have an idea that the case will soon be over, and that the public here and abroad, of every shade of opinion, will accept the result, and forget about it. The whole affair will then pass into history, not again to be heard from . . . The arrow is flown." All of the conservative publications were hoping for some quiet after the protest. There was in New England an idea that the execution was the end. The *Boston Evening Transcript* reprinted a cartoon showing an oil-skinned, rugged sailor standing squarely on a wharf, holding a great volume of "The LAW of Mass." under his arm, haloed with black clouds that darkened the background and were split only by a set of sprawling capitals, that informed the reader that they were the "Storm of Anarchistic Propaganda and Intimidation." The title of the cartoon was "Weathered." Massachusetts stood bravely on the shore, back turned to the sort of propaganda that made Vanzetti say to the court: "Not only am I innocent of these two crimes, not only in all my life I have never stole, never killed, never spilled blood, but I have struggled all my life, since I began to reason, to eliminate crime from the earth."[2]

They were condemned, virtually, on charges that claimed that, whether the witnesses were perjured or not, the men seemed conscious of their guilt when they were arrested. At that time, they were living the way they always had been; they had not received the money it was claimed they had stolen at Bridgewater and Braintree; but they did not seem to enjoy being forcibly arrested on a charge of murder. During the seven years spent in jail, Sacco and Vanzetti prepared themselves for a death that would immediately mark them as signal victims of prejudice and fear. Their death on August 23, 1927, began their career in history.

The execution set loose a volley of condemning comment that riddled the pride of Massachusetts. It is true that a few of the old guard were left to set up headlines; papers like the *New York Times* with its streaming "Parade of 150 Sympathizers," "Four Final Legal Pleas Made to the Governor that Failed to Delay Execution of Death Sentence," showing its feeling through a split veil of conservatism, were typical. The *Evening Transcript* continued its policy of toadying to tradition by telling of how a magistrate sentenced a man to two months in the workhouse

---

2. Bartolomeo Vanzetti, final sentencing statement, April 9, 1927, in Robert P. Weeks, ed., *Commonwealth vs. Sacco and Vanzetti* (Englewood Cliffs, NJ: Prentice-Hall, 1958), 221.

for distributing Sacco-Vanzetti literature, but even here a touch of irony may be found in the story of the sentencing by Judge Thayer of brothers who had admitted thirteen burglaries to thirteen years in jail. Sacco and Vanzetti, with widespread denial of their guilt, received death.

Immediately after the execution, Arthur Garfield Hays, the well-known labor defense lawyer, took test cases of six arrests to the Supreme Court.[3] The arrests had been made during the processions in front of the Charlestown jail, and among the victims were John Howard Lawton, the playwright, Professor Ellen Hayes, of Wellesley, and Edna St. Vincent Millay. They were representative of the group of radicals and intellectuals who had come to Boston from all over New England, and from the eastern and middle-western states to add their demonstrations in protest. This publicity was capitalized by hostile critics. George A. Bacon of Springfield, Massachusetts, said in a speech that day that "well-meaning but dangerous intellectuals caused hysteria." The *Impero* of Rome blamed the anarchists and revolutionaries for the death of the two men, as did the German communists.[4] These European sympathizers had hoped during the imprisonment that the two men would be freed by intercession, by the Governor, the President, or the Supreme Court, but Coolidge was silent, Governor Fuller was silent, the Justices Holmes, Taft, and Brandeis, who might have spoken then, were silent.

Silence was more effective, perhaps, than speech, immediately after the execution, but it was impossible in the face of such an outrage. The American Legion was planning to march through Paris, and expected lines of French citizens, eager and proud along the roadways. *L'Humanité* printed this statement before they arrived: "Do the Fascists of the American Legion want to be welcomed in Paris as the assassins of Sacco and Vanzetti?"[5] No capital between Bern and Mexico City was allowed to go without extra police protection. Men do not do this sort of thing for murderers, with no conviction of their heroism.

There were other reverberations immediately after the fact. In the *American Year Book* for 1927, the statement was made that "in the opinion of many besides the Socialists, Sacco and Vanzetti had not been proved guilty of the crime for which they were sentenced, but were

---

3. Arthur Garfield Hays, an American Civil Liberties Union lawyer, was on Sacco and Vanzetti's defense team.

4. The neocolonial Italian Fascist state dubbed itself *Il Impero*, or the Empire.

5. *L'Humanité*, founded in 1904, is a still-operating newspaper of the French Communist Party.

being victimized for their activity as labor radicals." The *Harvard Progressive* covered the front page of their first issue, in 1929, with an article entitled "President Lowell Should Explain." Magazines that were voices for the country spoke: *Current History, The Living Age, The Nation, The Outlook, The New Republic* all protested. Dr. Meiklejohn wrote an article, "In Memoriam."[6] Edna St. Vincent Millay wrote "Fear."[7] There was an anthology of poems for Sacco and Vanzetti compiled, which included the opinions of the strongest of living poets in a volume called *America Arraigned!*[8] The Sacco-Vanzetti Defense Committee had published regularly broadsides and defenses, and mourned the crime that must fall on the country.[9] Upton Sinclair wrote the novel *Boston* that commemorates them.[10] The play *Gods of the Lightning* followed, by Maxwell Anderson and Harold Hickerson.[11] John Dos Passos's book *Facing the Chair*, written before the execution, was given wider circulation.[12]

But Governor Fuller said, "Thank God it is all over!"[13]

.... the executioner threw the switch
and set them free into the wind
they are free of dreams now
free of greasy prison denim
their voices blow back in a thousand lingoes singing one song

---

6. Alexander Meiklejohn, "In Memoriam," *New Republic*, September 5, 1928, 69–71. In 1927, Meiklejohn, a free speech and university reform advocate, helped found the University of Wisconsin Experimental College, a short-lived hub of the 1930s radical student movement.

7. Edna St. Vincent Millay, "Fear," *Outlook*, November 9, 1927, 293–295, 310. The essay by Millay, a famed bohemian leftist poet, protests against the anti-leftist and anti-immigrant rhetoric in media coverage about the Sacco-Vanzetti case.

8. Lucia Trent and Ralph Cheyney, eds., *America Arraigned!* (New York: Dean, 1928).

9. From 1920 until 1927, authors Lola Ridge, Edna St. Vincent Millay, Upton Sinclair, John Dos Passos, and Dorothy Parker worked with the Sacco-Vanzetti Defense Committee to raise money for the accused men's defense, to spearhead publicity campaigns, and to organize protests. Physicist Albert Einstein and British authors H. G. Wells and George Bernard Shaw were signatories of the committee's open letters.

10. Upton Sinclair, *Boston: A Novel*, 2 vols. (New York: Alfred and Charles Boni, 1928). Sinclair's novel innovated documentarian fiction, a leftist form influencing Rukeyser's activist long poem *The Book of the Dead*, in *CP*, 73–111.

11. Maxwell Anderson and Harold Hickerson, *Gods of the Lightning* (New York: Longmans, Green, 1928). The play ran on Broadway in October and November 1928.

12. John Dos Passos, *Facing the Chair: Story of the Americanization of Two Foreign-Born Workmen* (Boston: Sacco-Vanzetti Defense Committee, 1927). The novelist's documentarian plea was privately published immediately after Sacco and Vanzetti's final sentencing.

13. Following Sacco and Vanzetti's execution, this possibly apocryphal statement appeared as a pull quote in the *Sacco-Vanzetti Defense Committee Bulletin* 1, no. 18, (n.d. [September 1927]).

to burst the eardrums of Massachusetts.
Make a poem of that if you dare![14]

And why should we, now—why should we five years after the deed, care, or stop in the year of 1932, pausing to inquire after these two men? They are dead, and wise men do not harbor rancor against the killers of the quiet dead. They are dead, and there are better and more pleasant things to do than mourn. . . . and we have our own dead to bury, and it is hard enough to face the beautiful without being reminded of death. And why do we stop in what we are doing to remember these, and prophesy?

Two days before the electric current was switched through the strapped legs, they said, for a world that might or might not listen, "Only two of us will die."[15] Vanzetti wrote to Sacco's son, in the English that he had learned so masterfully in jail, "If we will be executed after seven years, four months, and seventeen days of unspeakable tortures and wrong, it is for what I have already told you; because we were for the poor and against the exploitation and oppression of the man by the man."[16]

People do not forget, we, in our optimism, say. John Haynes Holmes, in the introduction to *America Arraigned!* said, "'Massachusetts, there she stands!'—triumphant, scornful, contented, bloody . . . But deeds like this live on . . . A work of violence and horror, like that achieved upon Sacco and Vanzetti, disrupts the cosmic order . . . There are millions of men who will never forget, until Sacco and Vanzetti are justified . . . So will the story become a legend through all future time—the names Sacco and Vanzetti, the perpetual symbols of victorious martyrdom."[17]

That is not quite true, patently. Our cosmic order, we say, has been disrupted by more important things: the price of wheat, the fall of stocks, sickness and death closer to us than these deaths. We want no martyrs, we

---

14. John Dos Passos, "They Are Dead Now," *New Masses*, October 1927, 7. Reprinted in Trent and Cheyney, *America Arraigned!*, 82-83. Rukeyser italicized the final line. Also see Rukeyser's poem about the jurors' decision, "The Committee-Room," from "The Lynchings of Jesus," in *CP*, 26-28.

15. From Sacco and Vanzetti's final public letter, published in the *Sacco-Vanzetti Defense Committee Bulletin*. Reprinted in Weeks, *Commonwealth v. Sacco and Vanzetti*, 235-236.

16. Bartolomeo Vanzetti, letter to Dante Vanzetti, August 21, 1927, in Nicola Sacco and Bartolomeo Vanzetti, *The Letters of Sacco and Vanzetti*, ed. Marian Denman Frankfurter and Gardner Jackson (New York: Penguin, 2007), 233.

17. John Haynes Holmes, introduction to Trent and Cheyney, *America Arraigned!*, 18-19.

CHAPTER 6

want no legends. The law decided and the law is as fair as any of us could be. And anyway, time passes, people forget.

People forget editorials like the one in the *Evening Transcript* that was called "The Only Possible End," and tried to justify the verdict liberally, seeing the force of public opinion, seeing the questions raised, and saying that nothing else could have been done. "It would have been lynch law..." and then, suddenly, explaining all their rationalizations away with one stroke, adding, "We could not do less without trampling on all our traditions." That explains the Sacco-Vanzetti case, and has explained it ever since the court records were published: six volumes of searching questions and answers that showed inadequacy, stupidity, confusion.

Edna St. Vincent Millay wrote for *The Outlook* an article called "Fear," a week after the execution. She was wise. She did not mention the names of the murdered. She said that Massachusetts and New England and America would not be anxious to mention two certain names, that the fear of death was lodged a little deeper in our hearts after two certain deaths had been accomplished. She said that there would be quiet now for a little time as America considered what had been done, that the children of the generation would be more anxious to inquire than the generation itself of the executioners. She said that there was a dull external quiet, now, and no word spoken of two dead: "And the tumult is in the mind; the shouting and rioting are in the thinking mind."[18]

Five years are gone since the month they lived in the death-house, and the days drew in. The headlines of their death notices were, with clumsy irony, placed next to 1927 advertisements of evening dresses that proclaimed that those styles were "sponsoring black for evening." Today's headlines are different. The Boston paper has, in that same place, "Guard White House as Radicals March."[19] Maybe the two were prophets, those mad Italians, who allowed themselves to be drawn into the web of American freedom!

The State capitol has a government building with a gold dome which is bright over the city.[20] And there is a library in which information may

---

18. Millay, "Fear," 293-294.
19. On July 28, 1932, the Bonus Army—a demonstration of unemployed and unhoused veterans who had nonviolently occupied the nation's capital since the spring—was violently cleared by Washington, DC police and the US Army, on President Herbert Hoover's orders.
20. With its distinctive golden dome, the Massachusetts State House, in downtown Boston's Beacon Hill, is the commonwealth's capitol building.

be found, in which there are books kept that record even this thing.[21] And people walk in the streets, and are no busier than other people in other streets this year, and may be stopped and asked whether they remember this far-gone incident of the lives of the two foreign-born who were called criminals and killed. There was one who worked in the library, a young man who surrounded himself with legal documents, and ran up and down among the records, who remembered the case. He thought that it happened a long, long time ago. He said, "Oh, I don't know—I can't tell—yes, I know about it, but I don't want to have anything to do with it." There was an old man who sat in the sun in front of the library doors, and slowly tamped the tobacco down into his pipe with a thumb, and put up his face to the sun. He said, "I don't remember it," and when it was called to his memory, he said, "I don't like to form opinions. Yes, now I remember it, but I don't think anything about it. What should I think about it?" There is a back section of town, with churches that have rawly painted figures on their walls, and restaurants, and fruit stores. An Italian in a fruit store remembered Sacco and Vanzetti, but what could one do? he asked—the government kill them, it is awful, it is no right, but what to do? Yes, what to do. There are Greeks serving in restaurants who never heard of this case, who know only Greeks, who like their own business. In front of the Capitol is a park that is cool and green and absorbent of the sun, and people rest, protected by the State.[22] A worker reads a book, covered with a newspaper dust cover, and, from the fineness of the type, on law or economics or philosophy. There are two children playing at his feet, and he looks a little bit like Vanzetti, the same deep eyes, the droop of the mustache. But he looks up, and you recognize him for a central European, from some Slavic country, and you know before he answers that he will not remember. A woman, neat-boned, pale with native paleness, walks across the cement. She remembers, but it was a long time ago, there was mention in the papers, but people did not talk about it much, she cannot see how it should affect anyone now. Five years is a long time. You turn away. A dark, intent young man with a briefcase comes up the road. He is an English student, a friend of Ralph Cheyney's and Lucia Trent's, who compiled the anthology *America Arraigned!*, so that he will be prejudiced, he says, but he thinks the trial was terribly, terribly

---

21. Established in 1848, the Boston Public Library was the first American public circulating library. The library's downtown building, completed in 1895, was commonly called "the palace for the people."
22. Boston Common, the nation's oldest public park.

biased. But then, he says, he is English and a friend of Ralph Cheyney's, and how can he say, fairly? There is a postman who grins and thinks he ought to be interested, for he was born not ten miles away from the scene in Massachusetts, but, to tell the truth, he ran away from school to join the Service, and he was in the Service during the trial, so how could he know anything about it? He got his job as postman from the points he had from the Service, and he's pretty glad he did run away, after all, but he doesn't know. Strikes? Oh, yes, there's a big theatre and moving picture strike going on now—a little disturbance—one bomb thrown—some smoke-bombs—nothing serious—yes, the bomb-throwing is bad, but it's those foreign reds again . . .[23] People in gas stations remember the names. Some people think that the case was used as a means to glorify two who never deserved any glorification.

But in a book review published this month, a review of modern poetry, the reviewer says, "As far as I can make out, much of this stuff seems to trace back to one Bartolomeo Vanzetti, who appears to have lived and written, in 1927 or thereabouts, some major poetry."[24]

The arrow has flown. It has lodged in our flesh, and we feel, deep in this body of our strength, the split wound that the deaths of men like Sacco and Vanzetti enlarge in America.

The case never meant the death of two men. That does not signify in a country whose president remarked that "men are cheaper than timber."[25] The deaths of Sacco and Vanzetti mean continuance of the existence of class against class, country against country, brain against brain. Their case is the symbol of the "vs." sign. And the old form, which so many would have it is the best, used to substitute U for V.

Not that these men were ever against the country, were ever unpatriotic, in any broad sense of the term. They always were disappointed that they hoped too high for America, expected too much of a land that promised freedom. They were for something that was a generalization of American principles, basically American idealism. But their beliefs do not enter into any discussion of the merits of their case. The upholders of the two were

---

23. In the early 1930s, a nationwide rash of movie theater bombings resulted in local and state investigations of motion pictures operators' labor unions.
24. Unidentified source. Vanzetti often is likened to a poet and inspired many poems, but he himself did not write poetry.
25. In the early twentieth century, labor organizers commonly attributed this phrase to mine owners and other industrialists, not American presidents.

not anarchists, but other philosophers, writers, preachers, radicals. Their death convinced many people that the country was ploughed under too deep in tradition. The *Baltimore Sun*, a respectable newspaper, said, "Every man whose name stands out today in American history as a power in the land began as a radical." (And then goes on to cite the honored examples of Lincoln, Jackson, Wilson.)[26] ". . . True, Czolgosz and Guiteau also were radicals as well as assassins. But their intellectual feebleness, not their radicalism, made them criminals. What this country needs is not exclusion of radicalism, but bigger and better radicals."[27]

The passion and death of Sacco and Vanzetti are continued in this country. The slightest evidence of foreign prejudice, prejudice against color, race, creed, will regenerate such hatred. In crises like the Manchurian situation, the imperialist war hysteria will rise and overflow, wrecking our judgment.[28] Fear of propaganda that might rock the stability of our conditions—however shaky they might be of their own accord—will motivate action as murderous as this. There are cases to parallel the Sacco and Vanzetti case today. Mooney and Billings age in prison in California for no crime upheld by clear witnesses other than their own avowed freedom of thought and speech.[29] Nine Negro boys are condemned to be killed in Alabama on a charge of assault which is obviously false in the eyes of very many, enough to raise serious doubt in any free community.[30] Vanzetti said that the Mooney-Billings case and his own were no more different than two drops of water.[31] And five years have passed since Sacco and Vanzetti died.

---

26. Former US presidents Abraham Lincoln, Andrew Jackson, and Woodrow Wilson.

27. Anarchist Leon Czolgosz assassinated President William McKinley in 1901. Writer and lawyer Charles Guiteau assassinated President James Garfield in 1881.

28. Japan invaded Manchuria, a northeastern Chinese province, in September 1931 and established the puppet state of Manchukuo there in February 1932. Rukeyser was the uncredited scriptwriter of the anti-imperialist documentary film *Stop Japan!*, dir. Joris Ivens (New York: Garrison Films, 1936).

29. Labor organizer Warren K. Billings and Socialist Party candidate Tom Mooney were falsely accused and convicted of the 1916 Preparedness Day Bombing in San Francisco. They were released from prison in 1939.

30. The so-called Scottsboro Boys were nine African American youths wrongly accused and convicted in 1931 of raping two white women on an Alabama-bound train. In May 1932, before this essay appeared, the US Supreme Court announced it would hear the case's appeal. In September, it ordered a retrial. In spring 1933, Rukeyser attended and reported on those proceedings for *Student Review*. See Muriel Rukeyser, "From Scottsboro to Decatur" and "Women and Scottsboro," both in this volume.

31. "[. . .] [T]he State will bury us alive in Charlestown, as the State of California did with Mooney whose case is like ours as two drops of water are alike. That case is a terrible precedent and it must be stricken off from the judiciary record by those who have the right and

CHAPTER 6

The strikes in New England, the Lawrence disturbances, the theatre strikes, have not changed fundamentally from the uprisings of five years ago.[32] Differences of thought are blamed now as much as ever before on differences in birth. No matter how many books are written about the influx of foreigners in New England, there will always be letters such as the one in the *Hartford Times* claiming that, since the writer's ancestors were born in Ireland and came here two generations ago, marrying Irish stock, that he should be recognized as "Irish, but an American citizen." Race vanity persists; false pride in birth persists strangely in a place that is having all sorts of barriers broken down continually. And five years have passed since Sacco and Vanzetti died.

While these feelings are handed down; while boundaries of birth and thought, mountains and rivers, divide us from each other; while Sacco and Vanzetti die, Mooney and Billings grow old, races are excluded, the Scottsboro boys are killed; while the struggle for balance lasts, the arrow has not flown.[33] Not that there should be no charity, no mercy. But that we should see the blindness and stupidity, and set these broken things apart, and rectify. This is the breakdown of justice, that these things should not be accomplished. And five years have passed since Sacco and Vanzetti died.

(*Housatonic*, 1932)

---

the might to do it—and the duty." Bartolomeo Vanzetti, letter to Gertrude Winslow, June 10, 1927, in *Letters of Sacco and Vanzetti*, 204.

32. Lawrence, Massachusetts, an industrial city north of Boston, was the site of the 1912 Bread and Roses Strike, organized by the anarcho-syndicalist Industrial Workers of the World.

33. Though initially sentenced to death, none of the Scottsboro Nine was executed. One, Ozzie Powell, was murdered by a sheriff while attempting a prison break in 1936.

CHAPTER 7

From Scottsboro to Decatur (1933)

We borrowed a car—a car a bit too conspicuous, perhaps, and a car with the prime error of having New York license plates—and left for Decatur. They were being tried; we wanted to see that trial.[1] It was not to be read in newspapers, we thought, but something to be seen. There was no assurance that we would get in the courtroom, since our credentials could not compare in assurance with those of the *New York Times*. But there would be other people like ourselves down there, reporting, and anxious above all things that the Scottsboro boys be free, and the issues that had grown to immensity out of their unique case be won. However, the car we rode in had New York license plates.

---

1. In March 1933, Rukeyser went to Alabama to observe the US Supreme Court–ordered retrial of nine African American youths—Charley Weems, Ozzie Powell, Clarence Norris, Andy and Roy Wright, Olen Montgomery, Willie Roberson, Haywood Patterson, and Eugene Williams—who had been falsely accused and found guilty of raping two white women, Ruby Bates and Victoria Price. Rukeyser traveled with two other students, Edward Sagarin and her then-boyfriend Hank Fuller. In 1931, the latter had reported on the first trial. On student activism and the Scottsboro case, see Britt Haas, "The Scottsboro Boys: Demands for Equality from the Deep South to New York City," in *Fighting Authoritarianism: American Youth Activism in the 1930s* (New York: Fordham University Press, 2017), 61–81.

CHAPTER 7

The road to Decatur is lined with wide fields, with billboards, hitch-hikers, and stretches of mountains and farms. In Baltimore, at five in the morning, the streets are asleep. In Washington, morning comes on the city swiftly—papers are sold on corners, decrying the move to have Negroes on the Scottsboro jury. Just south of the bridge, we come to the first railroad station marked in one corner "White Entrance" and in the other "Negro."

From raw March in New York City, we enter the warmer South. In the back of our minds we remember the slogans: "There is terror in Alabama," "Free the Scottsboro boys."

Virginia is long and green, and peaceful with Spring. The fields look moist and fertile; horses stand quietly in the pastures; pale cows stretch their throats for the rich grass. It seems impossible that the stories we have heard of fear and hatred are not exaggerated. This is, for two of us, our first trip South. The other grins a bit when we go pastoral. We drive very fast and steadily, eager to reach Decatur and the trial.

The second night was long. The country seemed to rush into greenness by morning, as we crossed Tennessee into Alabama. The roads wriggled steeply down the sides of the mountain-chain, and we looked over the first plainlands of north Alabama. Wooden houses stood tentatively on posts; little dark children sat on the porches, still half-asleep. We drove down the highway into Scottsboro. Farmers were up, and deputy sheriffs. The town is built around a large square, the dark houses face the Jackson County courtroom. A soft, finely wooded hill leans over the town. It still seems hard to believe that this place is the town that has been so bitter with the trial. That Fair Day two years ago seems very far away from us. Two stony-looking tall men turn and stare after the car. One of us had been threatened with lynching three weeks ago in Scottsboro, for being in town to do newspaper work; and our car has a New York license.

Scottsboro, Huntsville, Paint Rock, are names which have become legends in the Scottsboro case. We go through, following the railroad tracks part of the way, wondering just where the fight on the train took place, just where the white boys jumped off.[2] We lurch over the tracks

---

2. The crisis resulted from a confrontation between two white men and the Black men, all of whom had illegally boarded a Memphis-bound freight train. Bates and Price falsely accused the Black youths of rape to deflect from their own arrests for vagrancy and prostitution. For a classic history of the case, see Dan T. Carter, *Scottsboro: A Tragedy of the American South*, rev. ed. (Baton Rouge: Louisiana State University Press, 2007).

at Paint Rock, where the train was stopped. A bus passes us, crowded with white children on their way to school. Some little Negro children, just the same age, turn and watch the bus, and continue walking in the other direction to their school. We go on. Farmers crowd herds of cows out of our way. An old man flicks his whip at a mule. Some Negroes, walking at the roadside, do not turn, as the white boys do, to ask us for a lift. They have been taught better. In the South, Negroes walk. We had taken a student at the University of Virginia down the road a way. He had not heard of the case; he said he supposed the Negroes had problems. He was a junior in a university. A homeless boy we had given a lift knew. People were talking in Chattanooga.[3] He knew about Negro problems. He had had a fight with a Negro boy a while back, and had been given ten days in jail. He had been drunk. The Negro was given six weeks. We told both of these boys what we knew about Scottsboro. To the University boy we gave a copy of the "Call to Action" for the Conference on Negro Student Problems.[4]

But that was all different. That was in the North. We would not give copies of the "Call" to people in Decatur. We were there to report.

The signs pointing to Decatur and Scottsboro were strange to see on a roadside, after having seen the names in newsprint for so long. We had a feeling that we were entering strange land, but the fields were very peaceful. The Negro houses looked like some of the houses in the Central Park Hooverville, but they were surrounded with wet fields instead of the rubble of New York City.[5] We thought that the Hooverville people might envy these, the Negroes too, who could have country and air and fishing, even when they were poor. This was our first trip South.

Decatur is approached over a concrete bridge. It is built along two streets, Bank Street, which has cafeterias and grocery stores, the post office, and a small block lined with empty stores, with a gas station on

---

3. The train originated in Chattanooga, Tennessee.
4. In March 1933, when Rukeyser left for Alabama, *Student Review* published an unsigned call for delegates to a public "Conference on Negro Student Problems," to be held in New York City in April. Rukeyser was the publicity chairperson and probably authored the manifesto-like call. She and other student-age activists were signatories, as were philosophers Alain Locke and Reinhold Niebuhr, anthropologist Franz Boas (about whom Rukeyser later developed an unrealized biography), artists Augusta Savage and Aaron Douglass, and poet Countee Cullen. See [Muriel Rukeyser et al.], "A Call to Action," *Student Review*, March 1933, 6–7.
5. During the Depression, unhoused persons erected tent cities called "Hoovervilles," named after President Herbert Hoover, whom many believed responsible for the economic crisis. One of the largest was in Manhattan's Central Park, not far from Rukeyser's family home.

one corner and a drugstore across the street—a Negro drugstore. On the other street is the courthouse of Morgan County, which stands next to the jail, an undertaker's establishment, more cafeterias, a picture-house—the usual array. The rest of the town includes private houses, a bungalow-model library, a few soft drink bottling factories, the building that has been recently converted into National Guard quarters, and a candy-stand slapped up across the street from the courthouse. Decatur is doing good business on the trial. We found that out soon, and completely.

The judge had called a recess that day. We looked for the newspapermen, stopping in a small colony on the outskirts of the residential district. We went across the bridge again, and were told we could find more reporters in the Magnolia Drug Store. The car had New York license plates. That was our big mistake. Standing in front of the Magnolia Drug Store, which is across the street from the filling-station, we noticed a blue roadster which approached the street corner, turned in a wide arc, and retired down the street. We drove out that afternoon to the red-and-tawny cliffs behind the town. We had not slept since we left New York, and the cliffs were sunny. The South, we thought, is very peaceful. Decatur will be quiet during the rest of the trial. We were glad of that. Disturbance would not help the Scottsboro boys at all. If the town stayed quiet, they would be surer, certainly, of a fair trial. That night we went back to the drugstore, and one of us went in, while the other two waited. A roadster came to the corner, turned its headlights on us, swung in a wide arc, and disappeared. Various cars came, separately and at intervals, trailing a bright path of light over our car, and pulled down the block.

Court opened early the next morning. National Guardsmen stood, dapper and khaki, leaning on their bayoneted guns at the head of the stairs. More Guardsmen surrounded the entrance and the path from the jail to the courthouse. We went to the jail to get press passes from the sheriff. Sheriff Bud Davis is a huge man, and looked twice as large in the confinement of the jail room. The building itself is rickety, with holes where bricks have fallen loose, and a chewed-up wall. The Sheriff's pass took us beyond the bayonets and into the courtroom. Morgan County has come out in full force for the Scottsboro trial, but the court seats only four hundred and fifty. We approached the trial with the seriousness that most history books have failed to evoke. It was the gravest thing that had happened in a long time. Here we were to see at last Leibowitz, who had been defending the boys with skill and courage; and

Attorney General Knight, a little man, darting questions; and Haywood Patterson, who was up first for trial, a tall, quiet, dark boy, sitting over in the corner, forcing himself to listen through the tedium of most of the technical work, sometimes genuinely excited by the proceedings.[6] Here the history of the American Negroes was being made: the fight for jury service, for equalization of rights, and for his life, and the lives of those others.

I was down there to report the trial. I shall not report it here. You will have known about it already from the news accounts. I felt that no news articles could have reached the value of those few days I spent in Decatur. But the story developed into something different for me, and from being the article of an individual who went down to Decatur, this becomes the protest of a student, interested in student problems, and involved in Decatur because of that.

The two days at court went naturally for us. We sat in at the sessions all day every day. Sometimes we went back to the drugstore, which was a Negro drugstore, down the street, and the cars would come, and swing long headlights across us. We had a feeling we were being trailed. But then, we had New York licenses. Some of the New York people had had the sense and the money to change to Alabama tags. We had not. There was talk of a meeting in Decatur, like the one recently held in Birmingham, that broke the Jim Crow rulings to protest in favor of the Scottsboro boys. The Jim Crow laws had become a very real thing to us since we crossed the Mason-Dixon line. But nothing was done about that meeting. In court we talked to William Jones, the editor of the *Afro-American*, about the Conference, but we distributed none of the "Calls."[7] There is a fine white school in Decatur, but we saw no Negro high schools or colleges that could have sent delegates. Decatur believes in "keeping the niggers in their place." But we had seen no terror, and it looked as though the Scottsboro boys would not have to fear the dreaded lynching that so many people had prophesied.

---

6. On behalf of the International Labor Defense, the legal advocacy arm of the Communist Party USA, Samuel Leibowitz worked pro bono on the Scottsboro Nine's appeal and three of their retrials. Haywood Patterson's case was the first Leibowitz defended. He lost. Thomas Knight, Alabama's attorney general, headed the prosecution.

7. Founded in 1892, the *Afro-American* is a still-operating Black diasporic newspaper based in Baltimore, Maryland.

CHAPTER 7

On Friday night, we sat in the car in front of the drugstore. The town was very quiet. One of us went into the store, and the other two, who were tired and had nothing to do but wait—Decatur retires at eight—gradually fell asleep. We were awakened by voices around us, very loud, very gruff and authoritative. "All right," we were told, "you're the people we're looking for. Go on—drive on down to the station." I asked where the station was, and drove the man down. It was hard to see him, in the dark of the car, and just waked from sleep. Another car, full of police, followed us.

We reached the police station, and went into the large, brown hall filled with chairs. A dais with a judge's bench was lit by a hanging light at the far end, and we were told to sit down. "Will you open your bags?" they demanded. We wanted to know on what charge we were there. "Never mind," they said. They were very sure of their position. Decatur is a small town, and does not have the chance to show its authority often. "Open them—if you want, we can get a search warrant." The man was pale and fleshy, and his flat cap made him look a bit ridiculous. He was one of about six. We opened the bag. It was my bag, and there was nothing in it but clothes, and some copy paper, and about thirty "Calls" to a Negro Student Conference, to be held at MacMillan Theatre, Columbia University, New York City.[8] They looked relieved. This was what they wanted. This was *proof*. We were in the station all that night, waiting for the "chief," waiting for them to make some charge against us.[9] A few men came up to me, one by one, and I explained what the "Calls" were. They listened. "Weren't times hard for the white students?" Of course they were, they said, one by one—anybody would admit that. "And if white students couldn't get employment, what was going to happen to the Negroes?" Well, whatever happened, no white woman had any right being seen in Niggertown, no, or even being in a car in those streets. Interested in niggers—what nationality was I? American! he repeated blankly, incredulous. Was this my first trip down South? Well, if that was so, I'd find out how much things were different. I'd find out that niggers weren't to be talked to—why, he continued, he'd just as soon slap a nigger in the face as call him mister. Yes, he said, you'd better not

---

8. A Decatur police officer told the *New York Times* that Rukeyser was carrying letters about the trial and propaganda promoting the National Student League, the Communist Party affiliate that published *Student Review*. See F. Raymond Daniell, "Bailiffs Isolate Scottsboro Jury," *New York Times*, April 2, 1933.

9. Two unnamed Black men from Birmingham were arrested alongside Rukeyser.

go into Georgia. Down there they're giving folks like you eighteen to twenty years. He turned from me. "Nigger!" he shouted, and grabbed the sleeping boy by the collar. "Nigger!" he said, "what were you doing with these?" There had been some Workers Ex-Servicemen League cards found in a suitcase.[10] "And you . . ." to another Negro—"Trying to stir up more trouble . . . You'll be trying to make laws for yourself, some of these days." "No, sir," said the man, very quietly, "No, sir."

"Well," the officer said, "now look here. We're honest, law-abiding citizens, and we didn't want this trial anyway. The fair name of Morgan County's not going to be spoiled by no nigger-trial held here, and none of you thieves are going to come into Decatur and raise hell by talking to the niggers. Don't you know better, you white folks, than to talk to niggers? You just stay out—what do you care anyhow, what happens to a lot of nigger-boys?" He was being very honest, very sincere in his feeling. He really wanted to know, behind all his feeling as a police officer that here were prisoners to be "handled properly."

We were in the station until about four-thirty. The police were getting in touch with the Attorney General, to find out what was to be done with us—with the "chief," to find a good charge to place against us. We asked what we were charged with. "Contempt of court," they told us. "You're cited for contempt." We had been arrested for associating with Negro reporters, and for the fact that I carried in my suitcase "Calls" to a student conference to be held at Columbia University.

We left the station house and got in the car.[11] Gas was running low— among the disabilities of the car was its gluttony for gas—and we didn't want to be stuck. We drew to the curb. One of the ubiquitous police cars passed, and someone shouted, "Go on, get out of there." It was like Decatur to catch us for a framed-up traffic violation at the end of this evening. We pulled out, and drove slowly through the town. Birmingham would be the place to go, we thought. Birmingham would be

---

10. The Workers Ex-Servicemen League, a faction of the Bonus Army, was a radicalized veterans' group organized by the Communist Party. See Muriel Rukeyser, "The Flown Arrow," in this volume, note 19.

11. Rukeyser, Sagarin, and Fuller left town immediately after their release. The National Student League belatedly wired the Decatur chief of police to demand Rukeyser's release. See F. Raymond Daniell, "'Observers' Leave Scottsboro Trial," *New York Times*, April 3, 1933. Sagarin and Rukeyser contested the *Times*'s assertion that Leibowitz encouraged them to leave out of fear of bad publicity about communists attending the trial. They also argued that they did not disseminate "A Call to Action" anywhere in the South: "We did not go to Decatur to agitate, but to report." Edward Sagarin and Muriel Rukeyser, letter to the editor, *New York Times*, April 7, 1933.

CHAPTER 7

civilized and decent—and we might be able to get legal advice about our "contempt of court" charge.

But they were out for us. We drove very slowly—someone had warned us that the mobs were around. And Decatur had been restless and explosive enough during the last few days to be ready for anything. One of us had been run out of Scottsboro at a gun's end; Decatur knows its precedents.[12] Morgan County was not going to have its fair name tarnished. We stopped before a small knot of men to ask whether it was all right to park in the town, and to inquire of an officer the way to the Birmingham highway. The sky was turning peacock-green at the edges. Everything seemed quite peaceful. But we knew better, after that night in police court.

The one who had left us to ask the law came back. He grinned. "We're under arrest," he said. Twice in the evening. Southern hospitality. There had been hundreds of flies dead in the globe of the court-lamp, clustered blackly around the bottom. The story went that in Cullman County there were six Negroes left—the rest had been killed.[13] That, of course, was a story. There is another one that Decatur stands third in the United States homicide list.[14] This may be unfounded, but at five in the morning, arrested fifteen minutes after our first release, it appears very near truth. A thick man turned a flashlight in our faces, and asked about our credentials, and the ownership of the car. Another came. We could smell the whisky almost before he opened the car door. "You know what I think," he said hoarsely, "I think this is all so much rot—where's the other guy?" He was coming out of the court. The man went up to meet him. Together they returned to the car.

"Well," he said, "this man is a plainclothes man who says he wants to help us." "Yes," said the man, and the whisky fumes leaped on the air,

---

12. The three New Yorkers, covering the trial for a Communist Party–affiliated publication, had reason to fear lynching. Hank Fuller had already been "run out of Scottsboro" when reporting on the original trial in 1931. See Daniell, "Bailiffs." Additionally, Rukeyser and Sagarin were Jewish, and it was verboten for Rukeyser, as a woman, to socialize with Black men in the Jim Crow South.

13. Cullman, the seat of Cullman County, was a reputed "sundown town," where Black persons discovered after dark within city limits risked lynching. In ct, corrected above, Rukeyser misidentifies it as "Cullen County."

14. The US Census Bureau identified Birmingham, not Decatur, as having the nation's third highest homicide rate, following Memphis, Tennessee, and Jacksonville, Florida. The statistics for all three cities were explained as due to "the large numbers of deaths among the colored population." US Department of Commerce and Bureau of the Census, *Mortality Statistics: 1932* (Washington, DC, 1935), 47.

"I'm sick of all this chasing around, and talking about red literature.[15] What have they got on you? Nothing at all. And that whole gang, ready to beat you up, ready maybe to string you up. Lookyere, I'm sick of it." Well, we wanted to know, would he put us on the road to Birmingham? Sure he would, and he'd send us to a gas station down the road where they'd give us gas on credit, in his name. Here, he said, turn here. We turned, and he got out. The sky was almost grey at the edges.

The road to Birmingham stopped at a crossroad. To left and right was highway. How could we know this was not a trap, after the night's events? How could we know what the plainclothes man wanted? A lynch gang could be posted outside the town with no danger at all to the fair name of Morgan County. And they *had* threatened violence. We turned in the road, and headed back for town. Decatur was not inviting, just then. But they had made mistakes all night—telling us we had registered at the hotel under false names, accusing us of having been in Scottsboro two years ago, putting us on the wrong road to Birmingham. We headed for the place where the reporters were staying. Cars turned corners. They had wanted to beat us up, we had been told—for carrying "Calls," for talking to Negroes on the streets and in the shops of Decatur. There were a bad five minutes before we got to the hotel, before we left our typewriter as security for a safe night's lodging—the sky was quite light then, and the streets empty.

By morning, the story of our arrest had got around. We were advised that the best thing to do would be not to appear to face our charges, so that the issue might have less publicity, and not interfere with the process of the case. It was true that publicity given to us might have influenced opinion about the case—but to remember that we had been held for nothing, that we were innocent of any misdemeanor, and wanted more than all things to see the Scottsboro boys freed!

The court had kept the "Calls." They are not going to be circulated in Decatur. Decatur is a town of contented cows, and men with faces burned the color of the bright cliffs, whose foreheads are innocently white where their caps have rested, and who hate anyone, white or black, who makes the slightest move to help the Negro, to assure him protection or relief or friendliness. Decatur's students will not have representatives at the Conference on Negro Student Problems.

---

15. "Red literature" refers to communist or other leftist and anti-racist propaganda or publications, such as the "Call to Action" carried by Rukeyser and her companions.

CHAPTER 7

We found the clear highway leading to Birmingham, which is civilized, which would mean flight from the barbarian country of green fields and wide farms. A truck followed us, suspiciously close, trailing us doggedly. Soon it passed us and seemed to lead the way. We kept it in sight. At the next town it slowed down. They might have phoned after us, we thought. We drove on, quite steadily, keeping the truck in sight. The only things we had left in Decatur were some copy paper and some "Calls." We had taken a lot away, things we will not forget, resentments that will not heal.

The truck finally turned off into a sideroad. The drivers might have been farmers, going home. It was Farmers' Day in Decatur. We remembered Fair Day in Scottsboro. But the truck was gone. The road ahead of us lay clear to Birmingham.

(*Student Review*, 1933)

CHAPTER 8

Women and Scottsboro (1933)

The women who have played important parts in the Scottsboro case are spectacular contrasts.[1] There are the two pairs: on the one side, the mothers who have been most prominent, Ada Wright and Janie Patterson, who have seen the slow sacrifice of their sons to a deepening class struggle; and, on the other, the two women who have led the boys to conviction, Ruby Bates and Victoria Price. Behind one pair stand the other mothers, and all conscious women workers—behind the other are grouped the ignorance and vulgarity of the bourgeoisie and the prejudice of the group that used to be referred to delicately as "the flower of Southern womanhood."

The mothers have become symbols to us of the working woman lifted by catastrophe into the knowledge of her position. Mrs. Wright's tour of Europe with J. Louis Engdahl has become a historic fact.[2] A year before she started on that tour, she did not care or know about the issues that were to face her, the forces which she would have to fight to save a son. She started, with no background, and no assurance, on an international tour that was part of the wide appeal for the Scotts-

---

1. On fc, in holo. under Rukeyser's byline: "An Eye-witness."
2. In 1932, Ada Wright traveled through Europe with J. Louis Engdahl, the International Labor Defense's national secretary, stationed in Moscow, to draw attention to her son's trial.

boro boys. She has been educated to recognize the struggle behind the case, and to enter into her part in it, by her own close and personal experience. Mrs. Patterson is rapidly repeating her career.[3]

But on the witness stand, the star witnesses for the prosecution repeat flimsy charges, and indict the nine boys. The two prostitutes are, unfortunately, more typical of the South than are Mrs. Wright or Mrs. Patterson.[4] They repeat "rape" to a bigoted jury, and Haywood Patterson is again convicted.[5]

These are the two main parts played in the trial by women. There was also Carol Weiss King, one of the four I.L.D. lawyers who assisted in the final preparation of the defense, and spoke and worked for the boys' release.[6]

But these women have immediate and personal interests in the case. To know what the woman thrown by accident in contact with the Scottsboro case must feel, we may turn to Decatur itself, a town with a recent and artificial concern in the trial.

The courtroom tells our story. During the court proceedings, there were three other white women regularly present: Joseph Brodsky's sister, who sat near the lawyer on the official side of the barrier and who took a studious interest in the process of the case, Mary Heaton Vorse, of the *New Republic*, and another student.[7] There were one or two stenographers, one or two town girls who came, dressed in starched new clothes, to talk and be seen and to see who was there. There were no women representatives of the industrial workers, nor of any workers' organization or press. There were Negro workingwomen of the town, some quite young, some older, who brought their children with them. The women made up almost one third of the Negro court attendance, in a Jim Crow courtroom whose bailiff had forbidden the presence of

---

3. After their sons' convictions, Janie Patterson and Ada Wright regularly spoke at rallies sponsored by the International Labor Defense and the National Association for the Advancement of Colored People.
4. Price allegedly supplemented her income through sex work. Bates had been married three times and was not a sex worker. On fc, Rukeyser struck a judgmental sentence here: "Completely cheap, completely tough, ready to be used for anything."
5. Patterson and the other defendants, tried and found guilty in Scottsboro, were retried in Decatur following the US Supreme Court's ruling, in *Powell v. Alabama* (1932), that the initial proceedings violated due process.
6. The International Labor Defense (ILD), the Communist Party USA's legal defense arm, headed the Scottsboro Nine's appeals to the Alabama and US Supreme Courts and later assisted defense lawyers with the retrials.
7. Joseph Brodsky, a member of the defense team; Mary Heaton Vorse, a writer and social justice activist reporting for liberal and leftist outlets.

Negroes. The white women were conspicuous because they were so few. And, during the testimony of Victoria Price and Ruby Bates, when the court was ordered cleared of women, there were no visitors.

The townswomen of Decatur are divided in feeling. Most of them, the crisp leisure class, the office workers, waitresses, are indifferent. When they do express an opinion, it is ingrained with prejudice. I talked to one woman who believed the boys should be free if they are innocent. But her reason was based on the fact that she ran a filling-station, and had seen hundreds of Ruby Bateses, of Haywood Pattersons, of homeless families, take to the roads, hitching aimlessly or in search of jobs, from town to town in Alabama.[8] As we stood talking, she pointed down the highway. "There's one, now," she said. Far down the road walked a man carrying his coat, and a woman leading a small child. A Model T Ford sputtered around a bend. They hailed it. The man driving slowed down, stopped, let them in. They drove past the filling-station. "They come like that every day past here, sometimes one, sometimes two, sometimes with children," she said. "They've been more than ever these last three, four years. And my husband says how freights are ten times worse." But she was pushing the prostitutes' testimony away, and excusing their position, justifying it, not accepting the innocence of the boys.

The Negro women of the town appear in numbers in and around the courtroom, and these numbers are an index of their strength. The working woman's strength is an important factor in the case, since so many of its issues depend on women's problems.

Indeed, the fundamental issues of the Scottsboro case are more clearly tied up with the problems of the woman worker than has been pointed out. The fact that the boys were dependent on their mothers in Atlanta and Chattanooga when they were sent by freight to look for jobs; the fact that prostitution has played so large a part, socially and in the case (here we can remember the State's star witnesses in the Sacco-Vanzetti case, the Mooney case, and now the Scottsboro case, have all been prostitutes); all these should bring the case home to the woman worker.[9]

---

8. The Scottsboro Nine and their accusers did not hitchhike or drive to look for employment. Like many others during the Great Depression, they migrated instead by "riding the rails." They had illegally boarded a freight train from Chattanooga, Tennessee.

9. Nicola Sacco, Bartolomeo Vanzetti, and Tom Mooney, leftist organizers falsely accused of, and imprisoned for, violent crimes. See Muriel Rukeyser, "The Flown Arrow," in this volume.

Our problem in the remainder of the battle is one of organizing and educating. In the North, we can rally, protest, be our classes' voice. In the South, there is even more to do: the century-long prejudices must be fought even harder, the old cry of "Rape! Rape!" whenever a Negro is to be persecuted must be drowned out, the whole problem of employment for women must be examined, the facts of prostitution made clear.

These are less immediate than the day-to-day cooperation which must be given to the I.L.D. in the defense of the Scottsboro Boys. The case has long ago become the property of the working class. The woman worker must accept its problems and devote her energies to further the fight to free the Scottsboro boys, and to save the problems which have led to their condemnation.

(Unpublished, 1933)

CHAPTER 9

Barcelona on the Barricades (1936)

When the Paris express changed at the frontier into a Spanish train which stopped at even the smallest stations, and later, when the military guard on the train and the workers' guard on the Moncada station covered the train with their guns, nobody, of all the tourists and visitors and athletes going to the Barcelona Workers' Olympiad, knew what was happening.

I had been sent to cover the first People's Olympiad in Barcelona by the London magazine *Life and Letters To-Day*.[1] It was to be the great anti-Nazi celebration of the workers' sports clubs of Europe and America, the retort to Hitler Olympics, a week of united front games, theater, festival. The games were to start that evening, with a torchlight procession through Barcelona.

The guidebook says, "There is nothing in Moncada that need detain the tourist, who would do well to proceed to the capital, Barcelona." Some of us got out and looked at the town. The Catalonians had settled down to bread and sausages, wine and peaches and almonds. The tourists were noticeably flustered: an express train that stops for two hours at an insignificant way station!

---

1. Also see Muriel Rukeyser, "Barcelona, 1936," in this volume; and Muriel Rukeyser, *Savage Coast*, ed. Rowena Kennedy-Epstein (New York: Feminist Press, 2013).

CHAPTER 9

In the town, a *camión* of young boys, most of them no more than seventeen years old, was leaving for Barcelona.[2] We heard that there had been a tremendous battle, starting that morning with an attack on the telephone building, and continuing through the day. The generals, the priests, the wealth of the country, had risen against the people and a people's left-wing government, uniting with the Carlists in a savage attempt to make a fascist, if not a monarchist, Spain.[3]

The *camión* went off. The boys stood quite still as it left the town. They had said they were Anarchists.[4] One of the athletes clenched his fist in greeting. One of the mothers screamed, begging her son not to go. No two of their guns matched: old firearms, hunting rifles, revolvers. The *camión* went down the road to Barcelona, its radio playing Beethoven's Fifth Symphony.

During the afternoon, rumors ran through the train, the beginning of days of contradictory news: the army would put this down by nightfall, it was an Anarchist uprising. Two thousand had been killed at Barcelona, the tracks were torn up, it was a Communist uprising, the government could put it down immediately, the train would move during the evening, the train would move at seven o'clock.

Only these things became certain: the wires were down, no communication was possible; the train lying dead in the station, with the town promenading on the platform and the little children climbing trees to look in the windows, was the one neutral place in town.

At dinnertime, men came walking back from the battle in Barcelona, fifteen miles away. A bus driver walked in with his wounded brother and their families, carrying stories of the tremendous battle; now we could hear the role of the artillery fire growing ever louder in the hills. The hill-pocket around Moncada is on the direct line to the frontier—the direct line of retreat for the fascists, who were broken after the day's fierce fighting, scattered and driven into hiding in the city or the hills.

---

2. *Camión*, Spanish for "truck."

3. Carlism, the Spanish right-wing monarchist and Catholic nationalist movement begun in the nineteenth century.

4. From 1936 to 1939, anarchism was a major force in Spain's Popular Front government, primarily represented by the anarcho-syndicalist party the Confederación Nacional del Trabajo (National Confederation of Labor). Rukeyser never self-identified as an anarchist, but her idiosyncratic blend of Marxist class politics and pragmatist individualism resembles the philosophical anarchism of such peers as poets Kenneth Rexroth and Robert Duncan and polymaths Paul Goodman and Herbert Read.

In the evening, the Americans set up a train committee to take a message of sympathy and thanks for the town's courtesy and a small collection to the Mayor. The town had been very kind; the only search made was for cameras and photographs of armed civilians, and that had frightened only a few people on their way to the bullfights; those who did not agree with the sympathies of the message said cheerfully that it was politic and would ensure them a quiet night. The chorus of six platinum blondes who were to have opened in Barcelona that night was heartbroken but soothed. The professor from Madrid translated our message into Spanish, and we took it into the town.

Moncada is usually quiet, I suppose, but during these nights the radio, the sign that the government was still in power, roared from the cafés; war news, bulletins, the death of General Sanjurjo, the broadcast forced on the fascist general, after his capture.[5] We took the note to the mayor, who refused it. He said it was too important for him; to take it to the secretariat. The committee received it in a hot, bright room with the picture of Lluís Companys, president of Catalonia, looking down. We were not then allowed to express sympathies; we were foreign nationals, and it was correct that we keep out of revolutionary situations. We went back to sleep on the seats of the Madrid-Saragossa-Alicante line.

Waking at 4:45 next morning to the brief sharp sounds of rifle-fire crackling in the hills, we were out on the platform in time for the deep detonation that meant the church had been bombed. Five fascist officers had been executed that morning; some said they had died cravenly, others that they had died bravely.

Other rumors flew about. But all the reports tallied to one sum: the fascists were retreating through the hills.

Trucks loaded with guns and ammunition hurried through the town, carrying the painted initials of their trade-union organizations, or of the Anarchists. A machine-gun rolled through after the milk-wagon. A Red funeral was held. The train was given an hour and a half to buy provisions, and was ordered to shut itself in—the fascists were expected.

All day there was shooting and chase in the hills. A shot smacked against the tile roof of a peasant's house; almost before I could turn, the inhabitants were inside, piling furniture against the doors and

---

5. General José Sanjurjo y Sacanell, one of four Spanish generals who led the Nationalist coup d'état. He was killed in a plane crash on a flight to Spain from Portugal.

CHAPTER 9

windows. "There has been fighting before," they said, walled into the little house, "but never like this."

That evening the first plane passed overhead as we all stood watching before the schoolhouse, which had been allotted to us. It came from over the hills, where short men with sandals and black sashes and rifles were hunting fascists; it was impossible to tell whether the plane was friend or fascist, scout or bomber. After a terrible, long minute it passed harmlessly overhead.

And that night the *Guardia Civil* was stationed to protect the train while machine-gun fire clattered in the town.[6]

Moncada, being just outside Barcelona, is afflicted with absentee landlordship, and a row of imposing houses facing the station are owned by fascist sympathizers who live in the capital. A small group of armed citizens entered these houses, forcing the locks or going in by the windows, to collect weapons. There was not a sign of thievery or the looting that has been reported. One little boy about six years old ran down the street with three towels under his arm. His mother caught him halfway down, spanked him soundly, and came back with the towels and a noisy scolding for the leader who had permitted it.

Watching uneasily from the windows of the stifling train, the tourists felt it was time to be going. The English started to organize an international group to walk through the gun-filled hills to Barcelona.

But that afternoon order began to appear in the restless sensitized town. The clenched fist was seen for the first time everywhere, in the streets and thrust from the armored cars. The Party cars arrived, and all those connected with the Workers' Olympics were taken in open trucks with one armed guard in the truck and one with the driver.[7] Our suitcases were piled up for fortification; we were told to duck when shot at. The Party man from Barcelona spoke on the necessity for discipline and Party order, instructing the guards not to shoot until it was necessary. There were barricades all along the road—the walls of the farms were piled with bales of hay along the top. People were hiding behind

---

6. Spain's Guardia Civil (Civil Guard) was a nonpartisan national police force. During the Civil War's first years, most of its officers supported the fascist rebels.

7. Partido Comunista de España (PCE, Spanish Communist Party), the primary force in the leftist Popular Front government. *New Masses*, where this article appeared, was affiliated with the Communist Party USA. The anti-fascist games were alternately called the Popular Olympiad, the People's Olympics, or the Workers' Olympics.

wagons turned over on their sides. They greeted us with clenched fists; so did the traffic cops and the gypsies.

As we got nearer the city we saw them tearing up paving stones for barricades. There were houses flying white flags. In the city itself there were barricades almost every hundred yards, and the cars were stopped so that people could be identified. There were machine-gun nests behind many of the barricades. The government service had organized food provision. Everything was shut down except for the apothecary shops, which were ordered ready for emergencies; the hospitals were open.

Coming into Barcelona we saw shooting along the streets. The driver took the long way around the city to the Hotel Olympic on the Plaza España, which had been requisitioned for people connected with the Workers' Olympiad. Mattresses were put down on the floor for the two thousand athletes. The Hotel was converted into a refuge for foreigners. One Frenchman had lost his team at the border. I could never find the man who was managing the publicity for the Olympics because he was always out on the street fighting with the People's Front. We were taken to dinner that night in an automobile spangled with bullet holes, the upholstery stained with blood; the officials apologized for the condition of the car, explaining that there had been fighting that day.

That night all teams held meetings to decide whether to stay in Spain or not. All had great majorities in favor of staying. However, the French had orders that they were to go back. We felt that it was right for them to go, that the Popular Front in France and Spain must be preserved at all costs.

The next morning everybody who could was asked to leave the Hotel Olympic and make any arrangements possible in town. I went to look for the American and English teams who had rooms in hotels. On the way over, I stopped at the American consulate, and learned that the consul, Drew Franklin, had been approached by Lluís Companys, who told him he could not be responsible for any foreigners' lives. At the consulate, they were willing to give us safe conduct to the border, but safe conduct meant nothing, as they would not supply boats and it would have been suicide to attempt to leave in cars. The three Hollywood people from the train, two newsreel men and an executive, got away, issuing pro-fascist statements along the road. We got no recognition from the consulate because the team was not backed by an athletic association in this country; neither did we get any recognition as citizens.[8] On the American team were eleven boys, mostly baseball players, all from New York, except for one boxer from Pittsburgh. Henson and Chamberlain were the heads of the team.[9]

The people in Barcelona felt that everything would be all right if other countries would not interfere. Then German and Italian gunboats began to come around. The lineup among the nationalities became clear: the French, Russian, and Spanish on one side, and the English, German, and Italian on the other.

The French team left on Wednesday afternoon. One of their athletes had been killed. The two French boats slowly pulled away down the harbor, alive with singing as the thousands on the boats raised clenched fists to sing the "Internationale" along with the hundreds on shore.[10] To a great cry of *"Les Soviets partout!"* the French left.[11]

And all during that night and the days after, the dark, unprotected armies left for Saragossa, the heaviest fascist stronghold; two Hungarians, a Belgian, and at least ten anti-fascist Germans joined that workers' army, and I have heard from them since then: they write to say, outside Saragossa, their morale is strong, and the People's Front they defend is invincible.[12]

On Thursday, the athletes and the groups with them marched halfway through Barcelona in a tremendous demonstration with the people's army, all wearing strips of black for that week's dead. As the army passed, team after team sang the "Internationale": Norwegian, Dutch, English, Belgian, German, Italian, Hungarian, American. Later, knowing that Italian money and guns were behind the fascists in Spain, and that a machine-gun had sprayed the street in front of the Italian

---

8. The conservative American Athletic Association censured US athletes who participated in the Popular Olympiad. The American embassy refused to recognize travelers who were not athletes because they were allied with leftist causes and news outlets.

9. Francis Henson and William Chamberlain, the treasurer and general secretary, respectively, for the American Committee for Fair Play in Sports. Rukeyser later worked with Henson to raise money for medical aid for the Loyalists. See James Stout, *The Popular Front and the Barcelona 1936 Popular Olympics: Playing as If the World Was Watching* (New York: Palgrave Macmillan, 2020), 106. Also see Ray Physick, "The *Olimpiada Popular*: Barcelona 1936, Sport, and Politics in an Age of War, Dictatorship, and Revolution," *Sport in History* 37, no. 1 (2017): 51–75, doi.10.1080/17460263.2016.1246380.

10. At the time, the "Internationale" was the official Communist Party anthem.

11. Translation from French: "Soviets everywhere," a French communist slogan of the 1930s and 1940s.

12. Rukeyser's correspondents included Otto Boch, a German communist runner with whom she had a brief but life-changing affair en route to Barcelona. She fictionalizes their relationship in *Savage Coast*.

consulate before it was burned, an Italian boy shouted to the people: "The Italian people are with you, watching your victory—and when we get our chance—!" The rest was drowned in a burst of *vivas* and cheering.

But at the second demonstration we were given our responsibility as foreign nationals when Martín, the organizer of the games, said, "You came to see games, and have remained to witness the triumph of our People's Front. Now your task is clear; you will go back to your countries and spread through the world the news of what you have seen in Spain."[13]

In Sète, where we arrived en route to France, Sunday is fête-day; and the feudal games are held. A red-and-white boat, with its piper and drummer, its team in white on a ladder topped by the jouster, wooden lance and shield ready, advances down the canal, to the old music, to tilt at a blue-and-white boatload.

And, as they meet in the medieval joust, in the rain or sunlight, with the antique music, they raise their clenched fists in a new salute.

(New Masses, 1936)

---

13. Andrés Martín, the head of the Federación Cultural Deportiva Obrera (Sports Workers' Cultural Federation).

Chapter 10

Barcelona, 1936 (1936)

> The author left London alone on July 18th. She was in the last train to enter Spain after fighting began and arrived back in London on July 27th. This was her first visit to Europe.—Editors[1]

> *Torchlight Procession through the City of Barcelona. Finish of the International Relay-Courses.*
>
> Program, People's Olympiad, First Day[2]

As the train began to wake up, Cerbère was reached, the last town in France, and the old water, the Mediterranean. Very quickly, the terraces became mountains, covered with cactus and olive, the Pyrenees produced their little pale villages, stonemasonry and plaster and stucco became prominent as we crossed the Spanish border.

The big shed of the customs building burst into noise as the train drew in. Everyone lined up; they were taking down the names. One or two of the Olympic teams, traveling on collective passports, had some

---

1. Robert Herring and Petrie Townshend's original editorial note. Rukeyser was visiting London when Herring, the editor for *Life and Letters To-day*, asked her to fill in for him and cover the People's Olympiad.

2. The People's Olympiad, held from July 19 to 26, 1936, was planned as an anti-fascist protest of the official Summer Olympics in Nazi Berlin. Twenty-two countries sent athletes, primarily via their labor unions.

difficulty, and the change from the smart, green metal of the French express to the wooden compartments of the Spanish third-class cars, plus heat, plus a first strange cataract of Spanish spoken, pushed the passengers into confusion.

The train started into Spain, very slowly, its noise wiped out by a tremendous conversation. Seven Catalonian peasant women discussing Spanish politics will wipe out any noise, any scene, fill a compartment to henhouse madness, fill the head with "communista," "monarchista," "facisti," "republica," until the next town is reached, they all descend, and peace and slowness return.[3] The train stands in this station an extraordinarily long time. More Spanish families get in; the Olympic teams, hurrying to Barcelona from Paris, Switzerland, all over France, begin to make friends. The train stops at every little station, rests, moves as if exhausted when it does move. Two Spanish soldiers, in comic-opera olive uniforms with natty yellow leather straps, patent leather hats slapped down on top, grin over English cigarettes and the conversation of the Spaniards, deep in political discussions with the Olympic athletes. Catalonians answer, "No," with a swipe of the hand to all questions about the army, "Some on one side, some on the other . . . Not good to talk." They are pointing out olive trees, castles, churches. There is time to point out any amount of landscape. At the little stations, the soldiers stick their guns out of the windows, and armed workers patrol the platforms. This impresses the foreigners. The Spaniards gossip about a change in government last midnight.[4] The train stops at a not very important station. The town begins to circulate around it, dead in its tracks, getting hotter and deader, stopped twelve kilometers from Barcelona. An old Frenchwoman, who has lived in Spain for forty-eight years, says like a Sibyl, "This train won't go, not anymore."

> *Moncada is a little town between Gerona and Barcelona, on the inland route. There is nothing in it that need detain the tourist, who will do well to proceed to the capital immediately.*
>
> Guidebook of N. Spain

---

3. Rukeyser's faulty Catalan preserved, as she heard it: "communist" (*comunista*), "monarchist" (*monàrquic*), "fascist" (*feixista*), and "republican" (*republicà*).

4. The Spanish Civil War began with a military coup, led by General Francisco Franco and supported by Nazi Germany and Fascist Italy, launched on July 17, 1936. The Nationalist rebels had overthrown Spain's Second Republic by April 1, 1939.

CHAPTER 10

A wildfire of rumors goes through the train from that moment on. The Catalonians, who have been fighting, leave the train, buy bread and sausages and wine, and begin lunch on the benches; the foreigners begin to meet each other after two hours of waiting. Word goes through, the news of a general strike.[5]

This, a slogan at the end of a pamphlet, the last words of a poem. Suddenly, the guns come through the train, following a girl who demands all photographs. The soldiers have disappeared. The tourists, inconvenienced and frightened, sit down, whispering. The lady from Peapack, New Jersey, who cannot wait to see a bullfight, lets her face go white and older. General Strike! The train will not move. The mayor, grave, with a black stripe of mourning in his lapel, speaks to the professor from Madrid, a man who will act as go-between from the train to the village. There is fighting in Barcelona. The government has moved farther left, the Popular Front has hardened to a battlefront. The army is insurgent, in the north, perhaps all over Spain. Rumors fly down the train. The lines are down. The soldiers who were on the train. Where are they?

> *Official Welcome to assembled Sportsmen. Boxing. Wrestling. Gymnastics. Addresses. Theatrical Performances.*
>
> Program, People's Olympiad

The station begins to take on the appearance of a fête-day. Couples walk down the platform, looking with curiosity at the travelers. Small boys climb the little blossoming trees, hooting and whistling. The short, compact men, sandaled, with rifles over their shoulders, patrol, search, guard. The teams go into the main street of Moncada, where a *camión* is about to depart from Barcelona with nine armed volunteers. A Hungarian makes the clenched fist, saluting them, but they glare and make a clawing sign. "But who are you? Aren't you communists?" "Communists? No. We're anarchists." "Well, what does it mean? What do you want?" What do they want? That's different, perhaps . . . why, they don't want law, they don't want money, they don't want government. The radio in the truck produces, startlingly, Beethoven's Fifth. One of the mothers screams at the boys, but the truck starts off to Barcelona.

---

5. On July 18, 1936, a work stoppage was ordered, and all workers were called upon to take up arms in defense of the Republic.

The rumors persist. There'll be a battle in the village tonight, we're right on the line of retreat to the border, the cables are closed, the lines are down, they'll bomb Barcelona, the consulates won't *permit* anything like that, the train will move in an hour, at the most . . . The tourists begin to make themselves at home. The handsome young English couple, on their way to Mallorca, have it in for the man at Cook's, who should have told them there was to be a revolution.[6] The chorus of six platinumed Rodney Hudson Young Ladies must go on to Barcelona, where they are to open in the evening.[7] They fascinate the town, they are so blonde. The Olympic teams begin to round up everyone connected with the Games. The town has promised to feed everyone going to the Olimpiada.

Night shuts down. Two families, the fathers wounded, walk into Moncada from Barcelona with news. The radio goes at half-hour intervals, booming out: war news, government bulletins, tangos, Bing Crosby songs, "You're Driving Me Crazy."[8] As long as the government holds the radio, all is in order in Catalonia. There has been a tremendous battle in Barcelona, many dead, many wounded, but the generals are beginning to be beaten, the army is partly loyal, General Goded is speaking over the radio, confessing that his troops are beaten; the radio goes on, loud into the soft romantic night.[9]

On the train, a committee is set up to convey a letter of sympathy and thanks for courtesy to the town. Two members go down the length of the train, taking up collection for the use of Moncada.[10] Many have been wounded. The only stores open during the general strike are the chemists' shops. Almost everybody gives to the collection: a couple of centavos here, a duro there. The only exceptions are a few tear-stained frightened families, and the well-dressed Frenchmen who have been reading *Gringoire* all afternoon.[11] The Americans talk: this is what they

---

6. Thomas Cook & Son, a British travel agency.

7. The Rodney Hudson Girls were British dancing troupes featured in films and traveling variety shows in the 1920s and 1930s.

8. "You're Driving Me Crazy" (1930), a standard written by Walter Donaldson, was popularized by many covers and two 1931 animated short films' soundtracks. American crooner Bing Crosby did not release his own version until 1957.

9. Manuel Goded Llopis was one of the coup's leaders. Lluís Companys, the Catalonian president, forced him to announce his surrender over the radio. Goded was executed on August 12, 1936.

10. In her posthumously published novel *Savage Coast*, Rukeyser's protagonist Helen is one of two characters taking this collection.

11. *Gringoire*, a French right-wing weekly.

have been talking about, in little rooms in New York, in meetings in Union Square.[12] Everything is confused; John Reed could not tell what was happening during 1917, on top of a flight of stairs when something went on at the bottom, the revolution all around, almost silent, the rapid rumors.[13] Remember the waiter who was asked where he was during the Revolution? "It was during the special dinner, sir." One woman reads a French pamphlet on "The Problems of the Spanish Revolutionary Movement."

The committee takes the money and document in two languages to the mayor, who sends it on. It is too important for him to accept; he sends the committee down the green-and-white, modernist building—the Secretary of the Committee will accept it. He sits under the portrait of Lluís Companys, President of Catalonia. The Committee, tired men, watch while he types out formal thanks. "Tell him that some of us are sympathizers," somebody whispers. "No. No foreign nationals can intrude in revolutionary situations—in Paris on the 14th, word went out, too."[14] The passengers' committee shakes hands with the Committee, and goes back to sleep on the benches of the train.

> *Abajo el fascismo. Camaradas: Hay que actuar a fondo. El pueblo en masa debe levantarse como un solo hombre para barrer al fascismo. Frente a la avilantez de las fuerzas reaccionarias: Muera el fascismo.*
>
> Solidaridad Obrera, Barcelona, July 19th[15]

The roosters crowed all night, but at quarter of five they were stopped, as the train and their cages and the town shook with the bombing of the church. The peasant woman in third-class goes on with the fire she has been making to heat soup. The passengers begin to get up. News spreads. There have been five fascist officers killed in the early morning, and their captain has said as he was captured, "You can do as you please with me. I've killed two or three hundred of your men already." Their bodies are on view in a cellar.

---

12. Union Square, a public park on the edge of Greenwich Village, in Manhattan, that historically has been a site for political gatherings and protests.
13. American leftist John Reed's *Ten Days That Shook the World* (1919) provided a firsthand account of the Russian Revolution.
14. July 14 is Bastille Day, celebrating France's democratic revolution.
15. Translation from Spanish: "Down with fascism. Comrades: We must act soundly. United, the people must rise as one man to get rid of fascism. Oppose the reactionary forces' vileness: Death to fascism." *Solidaridad Obrera* (Workers' Solidarity) is an anarcho-syndicalist periodical still in circulation.

Cars begin to appear in the town, with U. G. T. and C. N. T., the initials of the united trade union groups which form a strong part of the Frente Popular, in great white letters on them.[16] They are all guarded—the heavy guns point at the passengers who are walking in the street. A truck with a machine-gun in it goes down the street, behind another car marked LLET—the official milk-wagon.[17] The town is warned that the fascists are retreating through the roads. Already the snap of bullets comes every few minutes, and the long echo of cannon passes from Barcelona through these hills. The train is given an hour-and-a-half to buy provisions, and then is to shut itself in.

In the stores, the fruit is running short, the town is buying bread and cheese and soda water, the foreigners stand helplessly around the fringes. Two little German children begin to fight with each other, and the scene becomes pathetic and intense: the town scrabbling for provisions, the foreigners, nerves going short, the little fair children in their playsuits knocking each other down. The mother stops them, cuffing the elder's head, and he screams and weeps. The shops begin to close again, after their short opening, which had been ordered by the mayor. The train shuts itself in.

All during the hot noon, the train waits for the attack. The tourists set up bridge games. Somebody reads D. H. Lawrence, somebody an old issue of *Variety*.[18] Shooting continues in the groves. During the afternoon, the train is given the use of the schoolhouse, a new building with water in which one may wash. The train is given its choice of place to sleep—the schoolhouse or the train. Some of the passengers make excursions, visiting peasants, and hide indoors when the houses are shot at. A few tourists, accustomed to luxury, are delighted by two things. The first is the removal of the train one hundred feet down the track. The town has permitted that for sanitary reasons. There has been little wind for two days. The other is the supply of gunny sacks in the town. An Englishman comes back, "So cheap—really such a bargain," with one over his shoulder, "It's really clean."

---

16. The CNT (National Confederation of Labor) and the FAI (Anarchist Federation of Iberia) came together as the CNT-FAI, and, along with the UGT (General Union of Workers) and other workers' parties, formed the Popular Front. The CNT and UGT are still active.

17. *Llet*, Catalan for "milk," not a political party's acronym.

18. In *Savage Coast*, Rukeyser's protagonist Helen reads D. H. Lawrence's novel *Aaron's Rod* (1922).

CHAPTER 10

The town is beginning to grow still and jumpy. In the street, boys are knocking a large doll about. The parochial school has strong doors, but they begin to give way. Priests have been firing on the people, fascists have been hiding in churches, and there are rumors: not a church left standing in Spain. The radio goes on. Trucks are promised for two teams, so that they may go to Barcelona. Nobody knows whether the games are taking place. The radio warns of enemy planes, enemy escapes. The train is empty, all the passengers stand before the schoolhouse, waiting for the truck, to see the teams off. It is perhaps more dangerous to try the road to Barcelona than to remain in the train, which, after all, preserves the appearance of neutrality. A few shots hurrah among the hills. Far off, clear along a line of olives, a little man is running, darting down into the grove. Suddenly, over the long range, a plane is heard—anybody's plane, the high sweet motor-sound infinitely strange and frightening. It is far off, and the hundred people are perfectly quiet. But in a second, even that fear is absorbed, an American and Englishman are quarreling about whether the fascists are brave, people are discussing the possibility of sending cables with the teams, if they arrive safely in Barcelona. The plane passes overhead, almost unnoticed. The speed and externality of every incident is unbelievable—the terror and habit of guns and warnings and fear descend on every system and are absorbed. All but the hatred of fascists, which increases.

That night the machine-guns fought in the town. The soldiers reappeared, as loyal troops, Guardia Civil, marching through the train all night, the yellow leather straps shining in the half-light.[19]

> *El pueblo . . . y ha escrito con su sangre una página inmortal en nuestra historia.*
>
> *El Diluvio,* July 22[20]

Order began to be evident in Moncada. The next day the houses of absentee landlords were opened with dispatch; no signs of bombing or pageantry. The boys would try to force the doors, and after that failed, one might climb a garden wall and go through a window. This would

---

19. When the war broke out, the Spanish Civil Guard, a national gendarmerie law enforcement force, was evenly split between Loyalists who supported the Second Republic and its Popular Front and Nationalists who supported Franco's fascist rebellion.

20. Translation from Spanish: "The people . . . have already written with their blood an immortal page in our history." *El Diluvio* (The Flood) was a Barcelona newspaper.

be done systematically. The passengers watch the street facing the station. Door after door is opened, the holy oleos removed, little plaster saints thrown on the street, a gun is found, a fine piece in an expensive case, and is taken. The townspeople, who have been crossing themselves when they hear shots, come round and finger the religious objects and finally smash them to the ground with as fine a superstition.

Suddenly, the sign of pass is the clenched fist, cars appear with "Partit Comunista" painted on their sides, the machine-guns go down the road, continuing to Barcelona. The Swiss team prepares to leave in a truck, and yodels in the street to an amazed populace. Another retreat is expected. Nobody knows where there are fascists. The clenched fist is everywhere.

A truck is ready for some of the others, who run to the train, collect baggage, run back to the truck. The valises are set up around the sides of the truck for fortification. The truck is warned to watch for sniping fascists and to duck at the sound of gunfire. The communist leader, a man with a pale intellectual face and a bruise-like mark on his temple, asks for strict proletarian order and discipline. A guard is with the driver, another boy with a gun stands in the front of the truck, ready. The American says, in this hysterical moment, in the voice of Groucho Marx, "Of course they know this means war!" The truck starts at full speed, following another and two cars.

The road is lined with fortifications—bales of hay top the walls, as ramparts, later barricades of paving stones fly the red flag, there are little machine-gun nests. The Ford sign at the roadside is a grotesque.[21] The clenched fist is everywhere. As Barcelona is reached, the white flags are apparent at all windows. Shots are heard, and as the man falls, the trucks swing wide, taking another road to the Hotel Olympic—immense building requisitioned for the athletes. In the streets, all the cars are armed and painted—the great squares show signs of battles, overturned cars stand where they stopped, there are a few dead horses, churches are burning all over the city. In the dusk, we come to Hotel Olympic.

---

21. Ford had factories in Spain. Despite the US Neutrality Act of 1935, which mandated the American government's nonintervention in foreign conflicts and prohibited the private sale of munitions to belligerent nations, Ford and other American corporations, including General Motors, DuPont, the Texas Oil Company, and Standard Oil, made unauthorized sales of vehicles and fuel to Franco's fascist forces. See Antony Beevor, *The Battle for Spain: The Spanish Civil War, 1936–1939* (New York: Penguin, 2006), esp. 138–139.

CHAPTER 10

> Barcelona, the wealthy capital of the four Catalan provinces, enjoys a splendid situation opposite the Mediterranean, between the rivers, the Besòs and the Llobregat, and the two natural watchtowers of the Tibidabo and Montjuïc mountains.
>
> Patronato Nacional del Turismo

Here the feeling is international and sympathetic; here the teams are arriving steadily, all with stories of a successful Popular Front in Catalonia. From the top of the building, Barcelona is laid out before you, dark and brilliant, the smoke rising from the churches, the squares illuminated, the Monumental y Arena across the way looking cavernous and a perfect place for snipers.[22] The heights above the city are very beautiful, the gilded ball where Columbus rises over the port is a black circle in the distance. The Olympic is on the Plaza de l'España, one of the two principal centers of the fighting. Cars are overturned in the square, guards stream into the building, girls of seventeen armed with rifles go out to take their places in the cars. It is very dark as we set out for the stadium. Two thousand foreigners, thrown on the city on the day of civil war, are to be taken care of, lodged here and fed there.

We went to the dinner with the French governmental delegate in a car brightly lit to identify us. There was not a window that was not spangled with bullet-holes, and two bullet-holes were in the rear window above a long stain of blood on the upholstery. The car carried the government letters, and we passed others—F. A. I., the anarchists, who are in the United Front, P. C., the trade unions, C. N. T. and U. G. T. The stadium was filled with athletes and stranded nationals eating beans. News went round—the word was "On to Saragossa," the fascist country. A workers' army was being organized to fight as one of the columns sent from all over northern and central Spain against Saragossa. There is no other news, no other way to get news: but Barcelona is solidly Popular Front. The only fascists are those who cruise the streets in cars marked like the others, giving the sign, and then firing from alongside, or those few unorganized rebels who fire from behind blind walls or high windows.

Barcelona is a workers' city today, occupied with putting down a fascist insurrection, conducting a general strike along the recognized lines.

---

22. Plaza del Toros Monumental, or La Monumental, a then-operational bullfighting arena.

> *Conference in the Palacio de Proyecciones: Objectives of Popular Sport and methods of developing it.*
>
> Program, People's Olympiad

A French athlete had been shot after a demonstration which the Olympic teams had made the day before, and was dying. The teams were meeting in their hotels, discussing procedure, voting to stay, voting to have the games. The French consul had insisted that the French—1,500 of them—leave on two French boats that were entering the harbor.

The athletes were forming great majorities intent on staying, on demonstrating the international People's Front by having their games. The next twenty-four hours was packed with the stress of a city sending armies out—the young, tired boys marched down the Ramblas at night as crowds stood and cheered and saluted them with their fists and shouts of "A Zaragoza!"[23] We knew Madrid was firm, and was sending more. In the morning, longer lines of soldiers went—and the Olympiad people and the sympathetic foreigners joined in a tremendous demonstration through the Ramblas and the Plaza de Cataluña, marked by fighting.

And during the speeches,

during the words of the Italian, passing his hand slowly over his hair, and flinging it far out as he claimed sympathy between his people and the Catalonians,

the *Vivas* flew open, from the army, from the armored cars, from the government officials, the soldiers in red-and-blue and silver standing among rooftops white with flapping laundry,

as the Norwegian spoke, the Belgian who had walked from Antwerp for the games,

as Martín spoke, telling of the athletes who had joined the Workers' Army and were gone to Saragossa,[24]

during all the speeches and the marching and the rides in gun-cars down the fashionable streets,

the city held itself firmly in order.

The French had gone, on boats alive with voices singing The Internationale, fists thrown up, slogans shouted of the Popular Front—on

---

23. La Rambla, colloquially called Las Ramblas, downtown Barcelona's major pedestrian thoroughfare. Translation from Spanish: "To Saragossa!"

24. Andrés Martín, an organizer of the People's Olympiad.

the long waves, retreating into the port, the slogan carried, "*Les Soviets Partout.*"[25]

The torn armies left the city, blankets over their shoulders, a few helmets here and there, several women, many men with red scarfs about their heads.

We made a demonstration, wearing black for the fighting dead.

The governments sent their boats.

It was easy to foresee the long voyages into the Mediterranean. But now Martín, his square face with the heavy yellow eyebrows large over the crowd, was shouting to a mass meeting:

"The athletes came to attend the People's Olympiad, but have been privileged to stay to see the beautiful and great victory of the people in Catalonia and Spain!

"These have come for games, but have remained for the greater Front, in battle and in triumph!

"Now they must leave, they must go back to their own countries, but they will carry to them . . .

> (the tense sunlit square, Martín about to start for Saragossa, the people shouting "Viva!" in the streets, the friends among workers, the soldiers who stopped to talk to foreigners, the salutes, international and strong)

they will carry to their own countries, some of them still oppressed and under fascism and military terror, to the working people of the world, the story of what they see now in Spain."

(*Life and Letters To-day*, 1936)

---

25. Translation from French: "Soviets everywhere." See Muriel Rukeyser, "Barcelona on the Barricades," in this volume, note 11.

CHAPTER 11

Words and Images (1943)

            The issues of the war have to be stated continually.[1] They are dynamic in themselves, and they require dynamic treatment. As our allies grew in their understanding of this war, their early plans for the cutting down of education—as in England—were changed. Total war it is; those who can express its issues must be used. And as we inquire into its definitions constantly, testing the meanings against conquest in North Africa, for example, or thinking of the issues of India and Detroit, we must also test—among other techniques—the images of the war.[2]

 One of the clearest means of communication is one for which we have not yet invented a name. It is the single image, as used in a

---

 1. In November 1942, Muriel Rukeyser began working at the Office of War Information (OWI)'s Graphics Workshop, a wartime propaganda agency. She designed its posters and the touring library exhibit *Words at War*, about language's democratic and anti-fascist power. In May 1943, she resigned, disagreeing with the agency's consumerist, undemocratic turn under its new director, an advertising executive. Rukeyser also addresses her OWI experience in her poem "Letter to the Front," in *CP*, 239-247.

 2. In summer 1943, race riots broke out in Detroit, a war production center, following white factory hands' work stoppages in protest of the hiring and promotion of Black workers. By the same summer, over three million Indians had died and millions more migrated internally, searching for food, work, and health care amid the high inflation and food rationing caused by Great Britain's wartime economic policies.

photograph or a painting—or the frame of film—to which words have been added to enlarge the context. The method is not the same as that by which most paintings are named. It is closer in its performance to what the dialogue does to a movie, to what the caption does to a good poster. The point is not in the *naming* of a picture, but in a reinforcement which is mutual, so that the words and the picture attack the same theme from slightly different approaches. Goya does it, when he calls a scene, through the side of whose frame pierce the rifles of the firing squad, "This is not to be looked at."[3] The best of our films do this; and certain portfolios of photographs, and certain picture books, in which the sharp text adds life to the pictures as the pictures add life to the words themselves, and a new and expressive form is before us.

This form is the basic form of the war poster. And when we see the fierce and vivid and constructive image—a face of the war—before us, we have, too, a point of conflict, if we are not yet agreed on the issues of the war. Because what we have is not the raw and brutal impact of the atrocity photograph, nor the cliché of the storytelling picture. We have an emotional image, *reinforced* from another direction by words, so that both make their strong appeal to the critical mind and to the wish, already moved by the facts of war.

Hardly anything has yet been written about these methods. One of the few recent statements, in an article in *El Tiempo*, points out the early errors in Mexico's treatment of fascist leaders as comic and amusing gangsters who imposed laws by bloodshed.[4] A basis for a graphics program includes these points, the article continues:

> We do not generally vibrate to a war-march, but we are moved by a child.
>
> Traditions that are stepped on make us desperate . . . A violated home pushes us to revenge . . . Contempt revolts us . . .
>
> A poster must be graphically eloquent, even without its slogan . . .

---

3. Francisco de Goya protested Napoleon Bonaparte's invasion of Spain with *The Disasters of War*, etchings depicting various wartime atrocities with brief text captions. Rukeyser alludes to Goya's etching *No se puede mirar* (1810).

4. *El Tiempo*, a daily newspaper in Chihuahua, Mexico. This article has not been located.

A poster can be attractive through its technique, execution, printing, or presentation; but if it is not moving, it does not meet its aim, and is a bad poster.

Every spectator must feel that the message is directly intimate to him; thus, he will accept its human and vital meaning.

Feeling, emotion, beauty, and severeness all have their negatives, which are: sentimentality, tepidity, and vagueness.

All anti-Nazi propaganda must provoke an energetic impulse.

The challenge is here given in terms of one fairly simple kind of expression. But we cannot forget that it has already been made to us in all the other forms, which reach us daily in the news: the ruin of cities, the death of man, great losses which must be replaced continually with meanings.

As far as posters are concerned, the key word is *continually*. If we are to provide war posters for America—and the civilian industry which corresponds to this war job, the advertising industry, has already vigorously shown that it realizes the importance of war advertising and war posters—we must look at the images. We must see them not merely image by image and poster by poster. These are images which need to be built up over a period of time, as an image is built up in a poem, as the action is built up in a play, as a product is built up in a year's campaign. The problem is not the same as it is in advertising, much as the advertising people wish to think so. The problem of war posters is not a selling problem, although selling ideas may be to some people one detail of the war. As a matter of fact, the division between two groups now active at home is the division between people who believe the war is something to be sold and people who believe the war is something to be fought. And a very good emblem of this conflict, and the issues about which it has formed, is to be found in the war posters we now see around us.

With the many ways in which food could be treated—posters about farmers, about inflation, about the relation of city buyers and grocers to farmers—we have, this month, the poster already described in *The New Republic*, whose caption reads: "We'll Have Lots to Eat This Winter, Won't We, Mother?"[5] The Southwest has already complained that its

---

5. The poster's subtitle actually reads: "Grow your own, can your own." It pictures a smiling white, blond mother canning vegetables with her identically dressed daughter.

needs are not being met; the posters which have reached predominantly Spanish and Indian communities, showing views of Independence Hall and the Minute Man, do not quite make their point, certain sections feel. This month, when discrimination is only one of the enemies we face in the manpower situation, we have a poster whose rather soda-fountain-looking girl proclaims: "I've Found the Job Where I Fit Best."[6] We have no posters on the United Nations, except panels of flags. We have had almost no government posters dealing with the enemy.

These lacks must be supplied. They go very deep. They exist because of confusion about the issues of the war, sometimes; but, more often, they exist because those people who have the editorial power of turning down clear and honest posters dealing with the basic issues of the war—our friends, our enemies, and what we fight for—are not willing to make clear statements. Posters have been made on these subjects, and they are the property of the Office of War Information. They are ready to be used. We need posters that will continually set before us the clarity and belief which strengthen us, and the tradition and future we fight for. We need poster people who believe in the issues of the war, and in the American people. We receive only harm ("sentimentality, tepidity, and vagueness") from people who feel that when they were in business they got "given" space for signs, since they had a good product which they could exchange for advertising space; and that, now they are in the United States Government, they are getting "begging" space.[7]

These attitudes of fear cripple our images, weaken our handling of ideas, and make us weaker in the war. We have here a very clear form. We can make bold images, forward-looking images. We can build up, over a period of months, campaigns of images that will explain our allies, not only as a set of flags, but in terms of their armies, their leaders, their people, and what they fight for. We can build up an explanation of domestic problems—first, in terms of what America is; then, as with the food problem, for example, by showing the farmers their great constructive power, by showing our consumers where "their" food is. We can tie in the problems of food, of coal, of warm underwear, with the war, every time. If we do that, we shall surpass ordinary advertising, and provide it with a program in which it can take its place as a detail of the war. We shall be relating these war issues to the war itself, and in doing

---

6. The poster features a smiling, young white woman wearing a headscarf and her hand on a machine. The subcaption reads: "FIND YOUR WAR JOB In Industry—Agriculture—Business."

7. Source for parenthetical citation unknown.

that, we shall be surpassing ourselves. We need to surpass ourselves in order to bring the war through to a sound peace. We can only do this by facing our own time, and by using our weapons.

As urgent as these questions were before the disbanding of the Graphics Division of the OWI, they are more urgent now, when the funds for domestic posters have been cut off. We have stopped necessary machinery before, only to find that we must set it up again. Even the profoundest critics of these posters knew that a government poster program was necessary. The advertising business recognized that need; although its reliance on worn-out technique was making its own kind of Maginot Line—its own reliance on technique instead of imagination.[8] *Collier's* says, in its July 24 editorial: "The high American standard of living and, in truth, the mighty industrial machine of America, is today the hope of all free people as a direct result of advertising."[9] Which is to say, "In the beginning was the Slogan." This is the empty-headed expression of what has so far been the leadership of the war-poster program. And now, in spite of what we have been able to do—public statements, letters to Senators, all the things which failed to keep the OWI Graphics Division going—we must have another poster set-up. The issues have been clearly shown, the symbols are simple and usable. And we need these expressions from our government; as a whole country, we need the images and words which will strengthen our lives, for war and for peace.

(*New Republic*, 1943)

---

8. On the Maginot Line, see Muriel Rukeyser, "The Fear of Poetry," in this volume, note 29.

9. Editorial ("I Will Advertise Thee What This People Shall Do . . ."), *Collier's*, July 24, 1943, n.p. Between July and November 1943, local papers nationwide reprinted or excerpted the editorial. *Collier's*, a popular weekly, mixed consumer ads with investigative photojournalism.

Chapter 12

War and Poetry (1945)

The subject of poetry cannot be restricted. There is no way to speak of war as a *subject* for poetry. War enters all our lives, but even that horror is only a beginning. The war is in our poetry only so far as it is in our imaginations, as a meaning, as a relationship, or simply as a fact. It has not been in much of our poetry because the meanings of this war have been lost; and through this the fashion in writing is aversion, wit, or easy mysticism and easy despair. We have been told by our governments—we have allowed our governments to tell us—to win the war first, and work out the meanings afterwards. This policy breeds more war, and nothing else.

For myself, war has been in my writing since I began. The first public day that I remember was the False Armistice of 1918.[1] And now the terms "soft peace," "hard peace," that are being passed as currency seem to me only other words for war, and war seems to me the after-image of many failures to react to truth at the time that truth first happens. We confess by this war that we did not react to fascism as it arrived. But now the fact that it might be a war against fascist ideas has slipped

---

1. On November 7, 1918, when Rukeyser was almost five years old, premature reports spread about a peace agreement between the Allies and Germany. The Great War officially ended four days later, when an armistice was signed.

away. So that the war for those concerned with life, the truth which is open to all, is still ahead. It is a struggle in which poetry also lives and fights.

A poet said to me, "You bring the world in too much. Poems should not be written about the war. Are you not afraid of guessing wrong?" I deny all of this. Again, I do not believe in any rule about the *subject* of poetry. If you do not love the world, you become the slave of the world. As for guessing wrong, I am not afraid of that. The war I think of is the common fight that is going on, the old same war, the struggle that gives these wars a touch of life—a fight which expresses itself in many ways among the people, always to make more freedom accessible to all. Peace, it seems to me, is not the lack of fighting. I want an end to false armistice. Peace, I think, is the force that works for creation and freedom, that fights war. I want that. I want peace which is a way in which peoples can work together for a wide creative life. I believe that poetry is a part of that, of the means which is peace, and of the living changing goal.

(*The War Poets*, 1945)

Chapter 13

A Pane of Glass (1953)

The six boys—men, really—came stamping down the snowy street. The air was hard and clear, the glassy places on the sidewalk rang. One of the boys laughed, and without breaking their fast walk, without looking, you would say, they threw their several snowballs across and into the doorway of the house I live in.

I was pulling the sled to the steps.

"Couldn't we go back to the Park?" my little boy asked. "For a couple of rides?"

"Well—" I began in doubt. It was getting colder, the whole lower part of the sky was turning orange; the six boys—really men, certainly eighteen or nineteen—were striding away on the other side; and in front of the house, an elderly German couple walked with pointed shoulders into the cold. Black icy places in the street; and the Park had been windy, my coat and skirt lashing while the little children poured down their hill on sleds.[1]

"Let's go in for a while, and then I'll take you to the party. And keep the sled under your bed again, for the morning."

---

1. Central Park.

The German couple had stopped short, and were facing each other, talking.

My little boy carried his sled up. Against the shiny glass of the door, the breaks stared out, soft and black.

"For no reason!" said the man, with his startled, burring speech.

"They were not angry, even!" said the German woman.

The snowballs had gone through the door in places, and one pane of the fanlight was shattered. On the floor inside, snow melting ran among the glitter of splintered glass.

The six boys had hardly glanced at the brick house. By now, the hall was cooling. The only sound was the baby upstairs trotting up and down and laughing. There was a silence of profound hangovers late on New Year's Day. My little son looked at me, and stood the sled against the wall, his stubby red boots grinding at glass.

"Let's just find them," I said. The German couple were still talking, with their high pointed shoulders declaring cold and outrage. They approved of my coming out again. They nodded, and went on with their walk.

"What will you say to them?" my little boy asked finally, as we turned the corner.

"I don't know," I told him. There they were—six of them, spread over the wide avenue and the traffic island, shouting. I felt cold and helpless. I walked over to the tallest one. He was wearing a leather jacket. His green clear eyes looked at me. I saw their distinct faces full of pride and question. I had no anger left.

"About the door down the street," I said. "Everyone feels like throwing snowballs today. But not through—that house is getting cold already, and it's full of little kids."

"What makes you think we did it?" asked the one in blue denim. He blew on his hands. "Anybody know about some snowball?"

"You can't prove which one of us threw it," said the short black-haired boy.

Which one. A few panes of glass, small-time stuff, kids' stuff, the grins are saying; we are six young men, far past all of this.

"That's a coward's trick," I started to say. But what do you ask them to do? Fix the glass? They mock and laugh. Pay—for what? Find—what? Something to do and be on New Year's Day?

"I'll know you next time," I said.

CHAPTER 13

"That's right, lady. Five six and a half," said Blue Denim, leaning his length against the pillar of the drygoods store.

My little boy stood waiting, brown and bearlike in the cold.

"Those big boys should be shamed," he was saying.

Shame! That is the cry of the parks, I thought. You hear the mothers and nurses all calling *Shame! Shame!* Where did you get it? I thought, looking at him. We won't do it like that.

We went home, talking. The sky was darkened now. All down our street the Christmas windows of the ground floors were lit—the Santa Claus riding over the white plastic hill; here, with a pointed red bulb turned on, all the approaches brought together: the crèche in one corner, the tree over here, the cathedral window in stained plastic centered, and an ivory Crucifixion high up and guarded by red and blue saints. Against the brick warehouse lay the first charred Christmas tree. Three little girls smiled as the short burning needles twisted rising, their keen pine scent burning through the cold.

In the chilly hallway, burnt smell of tree, glass ground down underfoot.

The super's wife answered the phone. "He'll be around in a half hour," she said. "He can patch up the door, anyway, and sweep the hall."

My little boy took off his stiff clothes. He put on his best suit, with very little help, and brushed down his hair. "Will there be many kids?" he asked.

I was wearing my long black skirt with the blue-green lining. I like to walk in that skirt. It must have been while we were dressing that it happened, but I did not see a sign of it on our street.

When we went down, it was as cold indoors as out. We walked the other way now, past the little grocery and the Home, across the avenue at the drugstore. These are mostly remodeled houses, with photographers and actors, TV people and cover artists, professionals.

The bars were shut, and the soda fountain. A few pigeons circled and landed at the next corner. Two couples hurried to the taxi stand.

My little boy went off, roaring with the son of the house through the crowd at the party. After a while, I looked out of the window, high over the street and the river. Smoke, lit white, blowing past the hospital sign; the mayor's house standing alone and snowy in the trees, its TV antennae low on the low Georgian roof; the other antennae, on the apartments and tenements near East End Avenue making alphabets and crucifixions.

A new man was saying to me, "... Like the mother in the shelter who said, 'Pay attention to the air raid.'"[2]

I laughed and answered. The rooms seemed to be full of painters. Standing on the edge, I could see them—the little square man with the white hair, telling people how soon his show would open; the man near the door, whose face was held together only by his exerted will, who kept frowning and explaining the film about himself; the lady all wire bracelets, and suddenly many women in green dresses; and there, listening, the lenient Puritan who had forgotten all of it, renounced it, and found himself in this room just the same.

The sound was mounting, a centered sound of a party going well. It was a sound moving over even the little boys who raced and went weaving through, hip-high, and could not be heard until they were very close; even over the lamp breaking; over the half-said things.

Now the man said to someone whose back had been pressed against his arm, "Yes, you're the one"; and to me, "He must listen to me! He's the man to invent it—the thing we need most of all just now: a glareless headlight."

Standing in that room, I thought of the six boys. They walked; they ran; they scattered through the streets.

When I got home, it was the freezing night. My heel went slipping and scratching on that floor.

I called the super. "He did mean to come," said his wife; "but there's been quite a commotion here; somebody seems to have given birth on the roof, and thrown it down the airshaft. The place has been full of cops.—He found it, Angelo found it."

I nailed the *Times* magazine section across one panel, and some corrugated paper from a Christmas present across another; and a pie-slice of brown paper over the fanlight section.

In the middle of the night, I woke out of dreamless sleep. The lights of a taxi slid on the ceiling. Where is that girl? I thought. What year did she have?

Angelo looked down from the ladder the next evening. "I'll have to show you how to do this," he said. His eyes glinted. He laughed at me.

---

2. In the 1950s, New York City mandated air raid drills simulating nuclear attacks. By 1954, they were run annually by the Federal Civil Defense Administration. In 1958, Rukeyser participated in a protest against the drills. See the last section of her poem "Waterlily Fire," in *CP*, 410.

CHAPTER 13

"No. You fixed it fine," he said, coming down. "Those were good pictures, in the *Times*."

Yes, he had found her sitting there. The tailor had gone downstairs to his shop. Just as he started to lock up again, he saw her face against the door. She asked to go back. Yes, that was where she had it, in the bathroom, and threw it out the window. Of course not; it was dead when they got to it. She was just sitting there, on the stairs of his house—"just like you now, here"—said Angelo. When he recognized her, she tried to get up and go. Lived up the street; a girl he saw around. Well, the detectives had been there all day, measuring and measuring. She wouldn't say a word, not whose it was, nothing. She'd have to, though. For the grand jury.

I heard the little boy playing cars upstairs. What with one miraculous deliverance and another, here I sat and he played cars.

Jim came out of the first-floor door. "Finished my script," he said, and put down the wastebasket. "Oh," he said, "Angelo. That glass was out yesterday. I wish we could get some action around here. Start the year right."

Angelo made the whole thing little with a turn of his wrist, and left. I told Jim.

"Threw it away!" Jim said. He laughed, and then cut it off, startled at himself. He laughed again. "Threw it away!" He laughed again, before he disappeared into the sound of children behind him. He put his head out of the door, his white face in order again. "What a mess!"

But Angelo in the pale sunshine downtown, among the gleaming marble of the Courts, was not the man on the ladder. Never had I seen this Angelo: his hair cut short and outlined; his shaved cheeks, with their straight lines drawn down plain, his sharp checked shirt. He clapped the policeman's shoulder. "You know what they say in Washington"—he was quoting a column in the afternoon paper—"they say it would be a pity if Taft died, because—"

He saw me coming, and looked again. I think it was the hat. "Oh," said Angelo, "the D.A. won't be here for forty minutes." He smiled, a public smile. He was being a civic character, at home in the world of detectives, files in the case of, and jokes with guards.

I thanked him and went to phone. I suppose I had some idea of finding somebody to help that girl. Could a psychiatrist . . . ? Could somebody be found to speak to her? And if she were told she was wanted, that her child had been wanted?

As I stood in front of the line of booths, not knowing whom to reach, I looked up, into Steve's face. After years, he looked at me with the same care. Here, in the soft-shining marble, we might still have been on the deck of that far ship, just evacuated from the city at peace, the great city so soon to fall. We had looked across the shore-waves to the city, and then at each other. He turned just such a look on me, and then the printer from Paris had said, "And where, in all this, is the place for poetry?"[3]

Only his face was not easygoing and a little fat now. He had emerged, a lawyer walking calmly through the halls.

"I know the case," he said. "I know one of the guys on it. There's something else," he said. "On the next block—you know, the church block—she threw her first baby, year before last, two years ago—threw it under the wheels of a car. There's a twist to this one: the car missed, the baby rolled clear, wasn't touched. They got her for abandoning the child. She's in Bellevue now, they're bringing her over for the hearing.[4] Do? They all say lock her up, keep her safe from herself, keep society safe. What do you want to do?"

"Oh," I said.

"Oh?" said Steve. "Change your mind? That's a different story, is it?"

Yes, I did; for a moment I did change my mind. But how do I dare? This will open, and open, and all be the same story.

"Come and have a drink," said Steve. "I want to hear about you."

"Next time," I said. "I know I can't get into the hearing—"

"Damn right," said Steve cheerfully. "Crime."

"Well. I've got a five-year-old coming home from school."

"Only one?" said Steve. "We've got two. Boy or girl?"

"Boy," I told him.

"Like that, don't you?"

"Yes," I said.

I got out of the El.[5] From the top of the iron steps, I looked across the neighborhood: the chained tall walk-ups, the strong curve of the asphalt plant, one vivid green building past the brewery, and all the reds, the greys, the blackened blond colors down toward the river and around to the sweep of the Triboro.[6] What will become of me? I had

---

3. Rukeyser recalls her leaving Barcelona in July 1936. She often repeated this story. For instance, see Muriel Rukeyser, "The Fear of Poetry," as well as "Barcelona on the Barricades" and "Barcelona, 1936," all in this volume. "Steve" is a pseudonym for Ernest Tischter, who also appears as Peter in Rukeyser's posthumously published novel *Savage Coast*.

4. Manhattan's Bellevue Hospital, the oldest American public health institution, popularly associated with its psychiatric facility.

5. The Third Avenue Elevated line, or "the El," serving Manhattan's and the Bronx's East Side, was phased out in the 1950s.

6. The Triborough (or Triboro) Bridge, renamed the Robert F. Kennedy Bridge, connects Manhattan, the Bronx, and Queens.

been thinking, but now, with a lifting of breath, What happens now? What is coming?

A close-running bunch of four boys and a girl in jeans, running like a team in purpose down the hill, put out their arms to knock over the ashcans. A spill of papers, a confession of food unused, and eggshells still beautiful, all were cast out across the sidewalk stone.

The river-light struck grey on water grey.

I thought of that girl. "Well, so long," Steve had said. "I'm sure you'll think of a way we can do something. Or *you* can. For her, or for all of us."

It was not until the next morning; and now, later, I look out of my window. The clean woman across the street is washing her venetian blinds again. The house is warm; the panes have been replaced downstairs, all but the one in the fanlight, a hard shape. My brown paper still is there. Up past where I stand drift the burning worms of fire—the needles of another tree transfigured. I feel as if I were on the edge of some way to speak to that girl, or speak for her, help somehow; help her, or my own knowledge of that day. But I have not really thought of anything definite.

That next morning, though, my little boy was putting on his socks. Our timing was good, and he was going to be able to play before school. He suddenly began asking.

"Mother," he said, "what are babies before they're babies?"

"Well," I said, "they grow to be babies. All the time before, they are growing to be babies out of something like a seed. Then they're ready to be born and be babies. Embryos, they call them."

"Something like a seed?"

"Yes," I said.

"Inside their mothers?"

"Yes."

Let him know this well, I thought. Let them all know it well.

"How do they get inside their mothers?" the little boy asked.

"Well," I said. "The father gives life to the seed, life is planted, it's something like planting. The man gives it to the woman."

"But how does the man get inside the woman?"

"All right," I said. "What does a man have to get inside a woman with?"

"Love," he said.

(*Discovery*, 1953)

Chapter 14

She Came to Us (1958)

She stood on the steps of New Lincoln School in New York City, waving happily at the crowd.[1] It was one day last February. All of us knew where she came from, and we knew that there, at this moment, her disgrace was being used against the rest. Right now, they were handing out cards that spoke for their fury—that said ONE DOWN, EIGHT TO GO. This girl was the "one down." Her name was Minnijean Brown, a sixteen-year-old student, expelled from Central High School in Little Rock, Arkansas.

She was one of the nine Negro students who had been going to Central High since September. Their first day there was a storm of feeling at riot pitch, with the National Guard trying to make a wall behind which these students could go to school. There was one photograph which

---

1. Rukeyser's archives contain several partial drafts and one full draft of this article. All versions anticipate New Journalism, or a subjective reportage of political and social events. This edition restores to her published article elements of her full draft, as noted below. For continuity, the editors have omitted the draft's prelude, a version of Rukeyser's unpublished story "The Week They Wore Their—," about a moral lesson called Hate Week conducted at the New Lincoln School five years before Minnijean Brown's arrival.

gave the scene: the dark girl going past the terrible open-mouth faces of women full of destruction. If you saw that picture, you remember it.[2]

Her coming here, five months later, was still not at all like the way a high school junior comes to school. She had been offered a scholarship for $525, tuition for that half-year, "providing that a proper home could be provided for her in New York City." Dr. John J. Brooks, director of New Lincoln, said that "as a pilot school for American education, we are concerned with principles of education as well as curriculum and teaching procedures." There was a principle of education involved as Minnijean Brown stood on the school steps that Monday morning, a strong, poised, handsome girl, dressed in a coat of a fresh blue with a corsage of orchids, beside her mother. She waved for the battery of photographers filling the sidewalk, crowding around the red Jaguar from the television network.

The school was excited, too. But through the city, there were several kinds of response. A boy in the school said: "A good thing. Our school invited that girl from Little Rock." A shopkeeper asked: "Will she be able to keep up with her studies?" And a woman listening: "Did they check on her grades when they gave her that scholarship?" A taxi-driver said: "Tell me this—why did they want the troublemaker?" And a soda-jerk: "That's a good school that does a good thing like that."

In Little Rock, when the nine Negro students were admitted, the school authorities pledged them never to "retaliate to verbal or physical harassment regardless of circumstance or degree." That meant, according to the local secretary of the National Association for the Advancement of Colored People, that Minnijean "could not raise a voice or a hand in defense of her very life without jeopardizing her future at Central. Yet those who contrived this agreement did nothing to deter her tormentors, who increased day by day."[3] She was "roughed up," kicked, threatened with violence, hit with a bowl of hot soup—twice—, hit in the back with a rock, and called endless names including "nigger bitch"—and expelled for spilling her lunch tray on two students who attacked her. No white student has been expelled from Central.[4] After

---

2. Rukeyser is describing *Arkansas Democrat* photojournalist Will Counts's Pulitzer Prize–nominated photograph of a white classmate verbally assaulting Elizabeth Eckford, one of the Little Rock Nine, as she was escorted by National Guardsmen into Little Rock Central High on September 4, 1957. The Associated Press ran the photo, now popularly known as "the Scream Image."

3. Draft specifies the NAACP official as Clarence Laws.

4. Restored sentence from draft.

Minnijean's expulsion, the signs came out in Little Rock. They were battle signals: ONE DOWN, EIGHT TO GO.

Minnijean had a chance to talk to her teacher that first morning at New Lincoln. They met privately, before the reporters arrived, and went on with the talk over coffee, before the last pictures were to be taken. Mrs. Carpenter liked the girl at once. Pauline Carpenter is a graceful, slender woman, with an accurate way of talking and moving that is very attractive. Her eyes are a changeable brown, flickering as she speaks, and her brown hair is folded smoothly up and over her head. "The thing that startled Minnijean most," she told me, "was my saying that she was expected to argue with her teachers. I told her she could ask questions about anything." What Minnijean said was: "I hope I can be just another student." The school promised her that she really could—after that first morning, no reporters, no photographers. They hoped they were not being naïve. For the acceptance of this girl after she had been thrown out of the entire Arkansas school system was stirring up many things, not likely to die down soon.

Governor Faubus had said publicly that the School Board in Little Rock "may have made a bad mistake."[5] He meant that Minnijean should have gone back to Horace Mann, the all-Negro school. "He doesn't mean that he thinks she shouldn't have been *expelled*—but just a little bit expelled," says Minnijean's mother, and her smile has a corner strong enough to carry her meaning.[6]

In Little Rock, the first day the girl could not go back to school, Mrs. Brown took her shopping for shoes. At forty, she has the same poise as her daughter, a lively assurance. "I hoped all the staring was over," she says, "but everything in that shoe store just stopped." They had had all the degrees of daytime unpleasantness whenever they went out. It was now evident in some of Mr. Brown's business life, too—he is a building contractor in Little Rock. But the horrors came at night. "They'd call us up, and say, 'We'll lynch her'—'We'll bomb the house.' Mostly at night. After a while, we told Minnijean not to answer the phone when it rang at night."

But it was the younger children she was worried about, too. They are three years old, nine, and ten. At first, the Browns thought they would not expose them to this, not tell them at all. But soon, says Mrs. Brown,

---

5. Orval Faubus, a Dixie Democrat and opponent of Black civil rights, was governor of Arkansas from 1955 to 1967.

6. This paragraph appears only in the published article.

they knew they couldn't keep it from them; so they told them, as gently as they could.

All during the school year, there was a lot of sadness for the nine Negro students. And growth, too. Minnijean's mother said that the girl found more strength than she had thought possible. Strength was necessary, every day, every morning. The nine families had not really known each other before this; but the solidarity among the children was there. When the scholarship was offered to Minnijean, she said, "I'll go to New York if the others want me to." The whole group decided together that she should go.

During the days before the flight east, there were two more telephone calls. One was to Mrs. Daisy Bates, president of the Arkansas NAACP, from a woman who asked what sizes Minnijean wore. The caller drove up to the Brown house on the last evening with a lot of new clothes—coats, hats, dresses, bags. She was a white woman, the owner of "the most exclusive shop in Pulaski Heights." Another call was made, and this Minnijean and Mrs. Brown did not know until after their flight. It was anonymous, a call made to the manager of the airport to say that there was a bomb on their plane. There was no bomb.

Mrs. Brown made only a quick visit to New Lincoln before she went home to Little Rock. She and her husband have respect for education, she says, and she knows that it is not a tour through the building that will let her know what is happening. "There are new school buildings in Little Rock," she says. "A new building isn't a school. We've heard a lot of that kind of talk. People think that a school's a building but it's not."[7]

Minnijean Brown hung up her coat with the orchids. In a violet dress she sat among her classmates with the books she would be using—Eugene O'Neill's plays, a life of Benjamin Franklin, *Immortal Poems*, a book on El Camino Real.[8] She wondered what would happen when they studied the Civil War. She knew she had heard about it from a Southern point of view; here it would all be Northern, she guessed, but Mrs. Carpenter had said they would use several books—Beard, Faulkner—and all discuss and ask questions.[9] She had never once asked questions about

---

7. A canceled footnote from earlier in the draft provides context: "The downtown building [Minnijean attended] was then [i.e., five years earlier, the time discussed in the draft essay's original prelude] the Boardman School, which shortly after merged with New Lincoln."

8. Draft also includes "the Beards' *American Civilization*," referring to Charles Austin Beard and Mary Ritter Beard's *The Rise of American Civilization*, 4 vols. (1927–1948).

9. Early twentieth-century progressive American historian Charles Beard and modernist novelist William Faulkner.

the Civil War. She would have more science than she had ever had; and maths, they said; and French this year, and biology.[10]

The class was talking about O'Neill.[11] There were objections from these sixteen-year-olds. Wasn't this too tragic? Minnijean volunteered. "Well," she said, "in life things don't always have a happy ending, do they? That's the way it is." And she volunteered to read. She loves to read, and can be seen as she really is when she reads poetry.[12] She likes to sing, too, and is glad the school will be doing Gilbert and Sullivan's *Princess Ida* this year.[13] But now she is reading the old song that begins:

> Love not me for comely grace,
> For my pleasing eye or face,
> Nor for any outward part . . .[14]

"She's an awfully nice girl," said Mrs. Carpenter to me.

And the school—what had it done to prepare for this? In the few days before Minnijean's arrival, Dr. Brooks had spoken to all the classes from the seventh grade up, telling them the facts and why the school was glad to welcome this girl.

For it was not a sudden or an empty gesture. The school's tenth anniversary comes later this spring, but this was not even seen as a sign of celebration. It goes deep into the reasons for the being of this kind of education, back into statements that Abraham Flexner, head of the Institute for Advanced Studies, made in 1920. It goes back to something that Dr. William H. Kilpatrick, the founder of New Lincoln, wrote for the *Teachers College Record* in March 1921:

> What is then demanded of the school? That it build in its pupils *breadth of view* in social and economic matters, the *unselfish outlook*, a *sense of responsibility* for improving affairs, and such an *ability to think* as will keep our pupils, grown to maturity, from being the

---

10. Last two sentences appear only in the published article.
11. Eugene O'Neill's *Long Day's Journey into Night* (1955), written between 1939 and 1941, had been recently published posthumously. In this context, Rukeyser's mention of O'Neill also calls to mind his early play *The Emperor Jones* (1921), which challenged white supremacy and the US occupation of Haiti.
12. Final coordinating clause only in the published article.
13. W. S. Gilbert and Arthur Sullivan's *Princess Ida; or Castle Adamant* (1884), a comic opera based on Lord Alfred Tennyson's long poem *The Princess* (1847).
14. Anonymous, Poem (Love me not for comely grace), in *The Golden Treasury of the Best Songs and Lyrical Poems in the English Language*, ed. Francis Turner Palgrave (London: Macmillan, 1875), 79.

prey of demagogues. [. . .] Practice in these is necessary to build them firmly. [. . .]

The school we have inherited has come down to us from a remote past when education was mainly designed on the one hand to inculcate docility and on the other to impart bare knowledge or skill. These things no longer satisfy. The duty of the school is now as large as is the life of the child who is to live in the democratic society of the future.[15]

It has meant something to the other students in this school to have Minnijean come, and to know that they are part of what is happening. To the younger children, it comes through in the simplest terms. A boy in the fifth grade overheard Dr. Brooks speaking about it to the high school, and told it this way: "He said there wasn't to be any yakking in the cafeteria." In the *Live Wire*, the paper of the lower school—mimeographed—a short statement on page three, under the heading "A New Student," is, again, Dr. Brooks speaking:

This is a dramatic incident in the life of the New Lincoln School. Our brief history has been full of adventuring of one kind or another. Our school always responds with enthusiasm to promising plans and fortunate circumstances. In this case we need more than enthusiasm; we need to be helpful, to be reasonable, restrained, and to act in good taste. I'm asking each member of our school's community to help make Minnijean's entrance to our school and her life here as normal, as unexcited, and as satisfying to her as possible.

To the other students it means many things. It means partly that they know that they are in a school that can act generously and with speed; they have seen a chance given to someone who was going to be cut off from all further education, for acting in a way many of them feel they would have acted. Most of all, it means to them this: they know they have a part in making the world. This is something that for a long time was a principle basic to our people, the principle on which the strength and responsibility of the individual in the life of this country

---

15. William H. Kilpatrick, "Teachers and the New World," *Educational Times* (London), April 1921, 175-178. Rpt. *Virginia Teacher*, March 1923, 57-62. Kilpatrick's article has not been located in the source Rukeyser specifies. Both Kilpatrick's quote and the paragraph by Rukeyser that introduces it are restored from draft.

was built. However, in our lifetime, this principle has come to be almost totally obscured. Here, in one stroke, among children and young people, it is made clear and active.

This girl is not a troublemaker. She has answered the troublemakers. She was set in disgrace for that. It is not her shame. The disgrace branches out past Little Rock to every one of us who is white and lets it exist, there and in our community; to everyone who thinks "Why did they take the troublemaker?" The disgrace belongs to all of us, for we all have that element in us. Attack can be met with passive resistance—and it looks as if the Negro people had made themselves the next "chosen people" in taking on themselves the great work of passive resistance in this country. But there will be times when somebody young and fiery will be the kind of champion who answers back, some young girl shouting back at those who say "Goddam," as it was said long ago in France, or "nigger bitch," as it is now said in Little Rock.[16]

Minnijean Brown fought back in Little Rock; there will be things for her to fight in New York, maybe as difficult, whatever they are. A letter about her came today—when the news arrived that a white girl had been expelled from Central High for making the cards saying ONE DOWN, EIGHT TO GO. The letter, from the son of two Vermont preachers, says, "Tell her I am proud of her, that all of us who stand for self, knowing thus we must stand for every other self, see in her our champion . . . Tell her how Jesus said: 'And every tree that beareth not good fruit shall be cut down and cast into the fire.' She is the good fruit when she fights back to make a better world for your son, for my daughter, for these warped and twisted of the earth, men who have made shame of man, the tool-user, man, the dreamer, man, the maker and mover."[17]

In her first week here, Minnijean asked the sixteen-year-old questions. What is the social life around here? Do they really want me to come to the party? Do they wear socks? She was told about socks—the three lengths, and what they are called locally. Yes, they want her at the

---

16. "Young girl" in France alludes to Joan of Arc, whom English occupiers executed for heresy in 1431. She was later canonized and is a French hero. Rukeyser's draft followed this sentence with a short paragraph: "But you cannot answer an element in yourself with passive resistance. That must be fought through, with all the resources each of us can summon up. We are outcast from ourself until we do."

17. Preceding paragraph, after first sentence, restored from draft. Rukeyser's correspondent is unknown.

party on Friday evening. But some of the students have invited her to go see *Long Day's Journey into Night*, and that is what she is going to do.[18]

She has noticed right away that the handshakes are different. In Little Rock, when people shook hands, they took her hand like this, with just their fingertips; their whole hands never touched hers. But perhaps that's the way they shake hands there. "I hope that they will see me as a *person*," she says. "I hope that I will have friends here. Last year, I had friends; but all during this time, with everything that's happened, I don't really make any friends."

Now she in her classroom is deep in talk about Shakespeare's sonnets. A class of about twenty students, eighteen of them white. Several of them volunteer to read. They say, one after another, the marvelous lines of the change of state—the poem which takes you, after the long despising, up in a great sweep at break of day.[19] Her classmates talk about this form, this sonnet—What does the tight structure do? Does it confine the poet? How can it mean freedom to him? They talk about the tightness of rhyme, the music within the lines, and the movement of the meaning.

Minnijean volunteers: she speaks about the poem as a whole, she comes through with an offering quality that is in her thought and in her experience. This is a girl who had been doing pretty badly in English at Little Rock—bad marks. She talks about the music and the rhyme. You cannot separate out any of these elements, she says, and hope to keep the beauty. The beauty is the entire thing, she says; and she volunteers to read the sonnet, too, sharing these meanings that the others have read, offering it to us for our meaning, the full and piercing lines:

> When in disgrace with Fortune and men's eyes,
> I all alone beweep my outcast state . . .[20]
>
> *(New Statesman*, 1958)

---

18. See note 11 above.
19. In draft, instead of "despising" Rukeyser first wrote "deepest sadness." She replaced that phrasing with two holo. emendations: "deepest and despised sadness" and then "despair."
20. William Shakespeare, Sonnet 29 (1609). Poem's second line restored from Rukeyser's draft.

Chapter 15

The Killing of the Children (1973)

Again and again during my brief time in jail in Washington, moments and people in Hanoi rushed up before me in full clarity.[1] They do as I say these words—the children at the turn in the road from Gia Lam Airport to Hanoi, the boy accepting the long stalk of flowers, the people swarming over the bombed bridge across the River Rouge to mend it, the children at my window in the hotel street. Eyes, filled with life, and a strong sanity. Did it come from that rushing to repair the bridge as soon as it was bombed, from the tones in which they said, "We have resisted for a thousand years. We can do this for a thousand more," and from the look with which they answered my question after I saw the shattered young boys at Bạch Mai Hospital— "How do you speak to these mothers?"—the look with which my host answered, "We have a saying, 'A good doctor is also a good mother'"—?

In jail they were before my thoughts. When I heard the crying of the prisoners in that big room which is sickbay of the Detention

---

1. In October 1972, Rukeyser went on an unofficial peace mission to Hanoi, North Vietnam, with poet-activist Denise Levertov and Jane Hart, a US senator's wife. After returning home, Rukeyser served a brief sentence at the Women's Detention Center in Washington, DC, for participating in the previous summer's protests discussed in this essay. Elements of this essay appeared in an earlier op-ed. See Muriel Rukeyser, "Free—What Do It Mean?," *Washington Evening Star* and *Washington Daily News*, November 30, 1972.

Center—crying as they spoke of missing their children. When I saw the young cat "hidden" very openly. He was a cream-colored and cinnamon cat named Contraband, and he made a flash of another life in that place. He did not know he was locked in.

My situation was different from that of the others. I was in as a matter of choice, and could have paid a fine instead. The trial and conviction following the peace action of Redress on June 27, 1972, in the Senate building was a matter of choice for all of us, too.[2] We had presented a citizens' petition calling for a redress of grievances, asking the Senate to suspend all its other business and devote itself to the most urgent question of stopping the war in Indochina—we called it "Vietnam" then, long ago last summer.

We presented our petition, being greeted by Senator Gravel and meeting with Senators Javits and Kennedy.[3] Then came our first choice: whether we would wait outside the Senate chamber, in the corridor, for an answer or not; and then, whether we would wait standing, or leave if we were asked to, or in a gesture of grief and protest, lie down on that cool mosaic floor.

In the back-and-forth of Hanoi and Washington, the coolness of that floor and the friends around me came back to me in the moist warmth of Hanoi, and on that evening when we were told that in two hours we would go to visit the prisoners of war in their camp.

Scene superimposed over scene. The sense of deep peace in the parks of Hanoi, those still lakes and the pagodas, the boy learning to fish while his father threaded his line, the lovers walking in the evening. And overhead the dread, as it had come from the moment we stepped from the plane, of the skies in which flew invisible the American planes. Our planes, and the fliers I had loved long ago, when I went to flying school and wrote my first book of poems—it is called *Theory of Flight*.[4]

---

2. Redress, a grassroots anti-war organization. After the events described here, Rukeyser promoted the affiliate group Project Nuremberg Obligation, whose platform was that individual citizens had a moral obligation to protest the US government's war crimes in Southeast Asia. See especially [Muriel Rukeyser et al.], Project Nuremberg Obligation fundraising letter, unpublished ts draft with Rukeyser's holo. notes, n.d. [c. August/September 1972], 4 pp., LC I:58.

3. Three Democratic US senators: Mike Gravel of Alaska, Jacob Javits of New York, and Ted Kennedy of Massachusetts.

4. Muriel Rukeyser, *Theory of Flight* (New Haven, CT: Yale University Press, 1935). In the 1930s, Rukeyser had attended flight school to get her aviation license. After the December 1941 bombing of Pearl Harbor, she tried to enlist in the US Air Force Auxiliary's Civil Air Patrol but was rejected.

"THE KILLING OF THE CHILDREN"

And now another evening, the park, and our interpreter saying to us as the sound of a plane came high over our heads, "It's all right. It's one of ours." The smiting realization that they are all "ours"—and that at home that must be sorted out every day. As it had to be sorted out new that evening, when we faced the prisoners across the table—men looking at us, taking our hands, speaking of their life from the moment their planes were shot down. The bombers, the pilots of those invisible high planes. For, five miles up, these men say, they do not feel the realities of ground below them, people down there, the explosion they give to earth. They do not see the bomb hit. They only do their job, they say, and turn and go. But here they are, made visible again, shot down, captured. And to their surprise, given first aid, given cigarettes, now their hands unbound, treated "decently," they say.

I face them, very conscious that in two weeks I will be going to jail. It is a brief sentence, thirty days, but there hangs over me the possibility that if I am not in court on the next day, it may turn out to have a penalty of five years. I look into the eyes of the prisoners.

But on that day, they ask me to speak in Hanoi on American writing and literature, and a large audience of writers comes to hear. For I have come with an errand, and a letter of authorization from PEN, the writers' organization.[5] The letter asks our hosts to set up with us, the American writers, a translation exchange program by which we will translate their writings and they will translate ours. And that is set up, happily and at once, with great warmth and cooperation from the writers in Hanoi.

And during my talk, a cable is brought that says I may have two weeks delay in beginning my sentence.

And when I come to surrender myself in Washington, the term is cut to four days.[6] Now in the Detention Center, the lights are turned off for the first night. In the night, you begin to know the other prisoners and the life of the jail.

---

5. PEN, an international organization with a human rights mission for literary authors and translators. Rukeyser served on the PEN American Center's Committee on Translation, and at its 1970 conference she presented "The Music of Translation," included in this volume. In 1975, she was elected the PEN American Center's first female president. She resigned after one term. Board members had criticized her use of her position to advocate for Kim Chi Ha, an incarcerated South Korean poet. See Muriel Rukeyser, "The Year—Signs without Scale," *PEN Newsletter*, 1976; Rukeyser, "The Gates," in *CP*, 561-570.

6. Rukeyser's sentence reduction, supported by her physician's petition, was due to her poor health. She was jailed in sick bay, rather than a cell.

CHAPTER 15

There are eleven cots in this room. My paper bag of a few objects is on the floor beside the cot. The books, the table, the TV. Now a girl comes over to talk to me. She is nineteen, she is black, she is here on the charge of killing her child, and has been waiting five months for trial. She crosses to my cot.

"What do 'free' mean?" she asks.

I look at her.

"You don't understand English!" she says.

"Yeah, I understand English."

"All right, what do 'free' mean?"

All our talk goes on from there.

And is still going on. I was able to work with her lawyers when I got out; and when she was moved to St. Elizabeth's Hospital and put in the section for the criminally insane, I was able to see her; and next week, I will testify at her trial.[7]

The young of Hanoi! Bombed, killed, mutilated, suffering, shattered in the hospital, evacuated to the villages. "We sent our younger children out," the father said to me. "At random, to the villages, to people we had never seen."

On Sunday evening, the bicycles. People on bicycles streaming into Hanoi, slowly, not biking aggressively; they are returning from the country, where they have been visiting their children on their one day off.

The woman doctor at Bạch Mai, who every Sunday visited her child fifty kilometers outside of the city.

And here, Lorraine, waiting for her hearing. She was pregnant at thirteen, and treated as retarded by her family, and she grieves for the child and the past. A young child she had, beaten to death.

But she too is the beaten child. And she needs the work and understanding that any of us can give.

And those other children? When I spoke to the writers about America, I expected to speak to them as my brothers and sisters. But I found myself saying, "You are my children, to whom my father has become a monster."

And my thought ran to those other young men and women, the Americans who were the only ones to support the Geneva Agreement—until

---

7. St. Elizabeth's Hospital for the Criminally Insane, in Washington, DC, was where poet Ezra Pound also was institutionalized from 1946 until 1958. On Rukeyser's relationship to Pound, see the editors' introduction to this volume.

now, after the ceasefire, when the rest of America is beginning.[8] Those war-resisters and war-refusers of all kinds—open refusers, evaders, "deserters," those who stood by the principles we were brought up on. How do they come back? Now that the prisoners of the war are beginning to return, how do the ones who would not kill come home?[9]

There must be a better word than "amnesty." Amnesty is a forgetting, and we do not forget. These men and the women who resisted with them are to be remembered. And established deep in American life, as a center and new beginning, as a chance to make our people again, to rebuild the spirit. I wish the war resisters could be put up for a Nobel Peace Prize.

I know that there is a defensive cry from the war-people saying that soldiers were killed in the place of the war-resisters who did not go to Vietnam.

And I think of a family that went south to Egypt at a time of fatality. It is like calling Joseph and Mary—and Jesus—to account for the slaughter of the Innocents.[10]

(Unpublished, 1973)

---

8. Rukeyser and other activists affiliated with Project Nuremberg Obligation believed the United States had violated the 1954 Geneva Agreement, which resolved France's colonization of Vietnam and instituted a demilitarized zone between the South and the North. A ceasefire between the United States and North Vietnam was signed in January 1973. A condition of the ceasefire was North Vietnam's return of American prisoners of war.

9. Rukeyser's activism entailed petitioning for amnesty for American men of draft age and their families who had left the country in protest of the war, as her son and his wife had.

10. In the New Testament, an angel appeared to Joseph after Jesus's birth and warned that Jerusalem's King Herod "will seek the young Child to destroy Him" (Matthew 2:13, New King James Version). Joseph fled to Egypt with Mary and the infant. Herod "put to death all the male children who were in Bethlehem and in its districts, from two years old and under" (Matthew 2:16, New King James Version). An angel recalled the Holy Family to Israel after Herod's death.

CHAPTER 16

The Uses of Fear (1978)

When they died, twenty-five years ago today, we all felt a tearing and a shudder, of great explosions threatened, of darkness, mystery, and confusion.[1] When the Rosenbergs were executed, many of us at once saw, and had seen all through the trial, the history of the Truman Doctrine ramifying without scale through all our lives.[2] This was long before we knew the letters of this couple to their sons—these are published now—or of the testimony, so long in following.[3] That can be seen now.

What was the climate in which they were killed?

---

1. Ethel and Julius Rosenberg were arrested for espionage in 1950, for sharing information about the Manhattan Project with the Soviets. Ethel's knowledge of and involvement with her husband's crimes remain doubtful. Both were executed on June 19, 1953. This edition is based on Rukeyser's corrected fc. Sentences cut from the published op-ed, titled "The Fear" (*New York Times*, June 19, 1978), have been quietly restored. Rukeyser's intended title, restored here, recalls themes of fear and use common to her work since her 1940 lecture series *The Usable Truth*, included in this volume.

2. The 1947 Truman Doctrine initiated US cold war containment policy by establishing a global sphere of influence to stop the spread of Soviet communism.

3. The Rosenberg sons' memoir prints their parents' letters, which maintain their innocence but contain no exculpatory evidence or countertestimony. See Robert Meeropol and Michael Meeropol, *We Are Your Sons: The Legacy of Ethel and Julius Rosenberg* (Boston: Houghton Mifflin, 1975). Rukeyser's published op-ed excludes mention of this volume.

The people I talked to then were these: men and women haunted by the mushroom cloud, not understanding either the science or politics of the atomic age, and feeling that doom hung over them; enormous numbers of those wanting to work for a world of deepening chances of life, but afraid of all the hints and more than hints of personal and public treachery that were in the air; the young who still would not accept other people's ideas of guilt or innocence, but would stick to their own definitions.

The nervousness and hysteria of any of these people could be worked on, in terms of anti-communism; and we can see the history of this vast dread, in huge movements, in the Truman Doctrine, in the soldiers we knew, in the private lives of all of us.[4]

I knew officers whose training in Russian at that time and for years before was, they believe, given them to fit them for war with the Soviet Union, our ally.[5] One issue of *Collier's* (not yet suspended) was edited by Robert Sherwood; its text and huge maps told and showed key points in Russia, strikes at which could most simply defeat the Soviet Union; there were, earlier, refusals to let persons I knew were passionately committed to the people of the United States, who were also radical, to go up on rooftops and spot German planes.[6] In very small, a book of mine about Willard Gibbs and science and imagination in America was in one instance attacked for speaking of Russian science, its thermodynamics and nitrate industry.[7] All my material in these pages had come from the New York Public Library; but, said the reviewer, it was patently a fact that no slave society could produce science.[8] The person who was

---

4. The published version changed "could be worked on" to "would be worked on."
5. Unidentified persons.
6. Robert Sherwood, playwright, screenwriter, and later a speechwriter for President Franklin Delano Roosevelt. Before *Collier's* ceased publication in 1957, anti-communists attacked the magazine for its editorials critical of the House Un-American Activities Committee (HUAC). Rukeyser references Robert E. Sherwood et al., "Preview of the War We Do Not Want," a special issue of *Collier's*, October 27, 1951. Intended to dissuade the Soviet Union from instigating a conflict, the article features journalist Edward R. Murrow, writer Arthur Koestler, and other prominent intellectuals "reporting" on an imagined World War III. Rukeyser corresponded with Sherwood about the issue and the anti-communist backlash it provoked. See Robert E. Sherwood, letter to Muriel Rukeyser, January 25, 1952, 1 ts. p., LC II:3. In the published article, Rukeyser refers to herself rather than anonymous "persons I knew" as looking out for German aircraft. She also openly acknowledges her radicalism but in the past tense: ". . . refusals to let me—true, I was a radical—go up on rooftops in New York to spot Nazi planes."
7. Muriel Rukeyser, *Willard Gibbs* (Garden City, NY: Doubleday, Doran, 1942).
8. Unidentified review.

sent to me said, Everybody calls you a communist; why shouldn't you be one? I said it was the worst reason I had ever heard for joining anything; and soon after my recruiter was writing a long series of articles against her past for a news syndicate.

Whittaker Chambers assumed that I was a spy in Spain, but didn't he assume that of everyone?[9]

Did the Rosenbergs really spy? some people asked. Do they still ask that? What is happening now is that the information, long denied, is becoming available. You can see the hundreds of thousands of pages of evidence at the Fund for Public Information. It was refused for a long time, but now the material is coming in from the F.B.I. and the C.I.A. This may be the largest difference between that time and this.

Then, they said we were paranoid if we said there was secret material or secret charges, as there were in the Rosenberg case. Now, it appears that all the charges made against them were made before there was evidence; that, in the atmosphere of changes, fearful family split, and increased pressure—particularly on Ethel Rosenberg—no evidence could be open, no appeal for clemency heard. Even the Jewish issue was raised; the attempt was made to get her to appeal to all Jews on these issues.

You know the facts as they were given, and how difficult it is to retain the sequence and characters of the trial. This is one of the most dramatic and murky parts of this terrible story. Most people that you speak to now cannot quite remember specific points or sequence.

The sons of the Rosenbergs, who have gone through their own transformation, learned much about people in the student movement and later, as they were sent on field trips by their professors. One son, sent to Catalonia, learned in that marvelous and generous country the conditions of close living between people and people, people and the soil of ordinary life. These sons of tragic learning are working, not only to find the whole truth of their parents' evidence, but for other such knowledge, with the Fund for Open Information.

With the opening of documents, we have a real difference with the closed tone of mystery and violence of twenty-five years ago. But we

---

9. Whittaker Chambers, fiction writer and playwright. In the 1930s, he edited the communist magazine *New Masses*, for which Rukeyser wrote reviews. In 1948, Chambers testified before HUAC about his involvement with American communist spies the previous decade. He implicated his ex-lover Alger Hiss as both a spy and a homosexual, thus sparking the US State Department's purge of lesbian and homosexual employees, now known as the Lavender Scare.

have ramifications all over the world of the causes and buried story of the Rosenbergs.[10]

There will be meetings, TV broadcasts, TV movies all next week. Look at your programs. Books are William Reuben's, the Schneirs', and the Meeropols', and the letters of Julius and Ethel Rosenberg, with her poem. And the story of her last act; her kiss given to the deathhouse matron. The most savagely anti-Rosenberg book is probably Louis Nizer's.[11]

The fear which surrounded and webbed the events of twenty-five years ago has to be answered factually; but really, it is belief that answers fear. Poets must bring to consciousness those things we cannot bear to face or talk about. One son said it was healing to be in Catalonia, where so many people had lived through their parents' execution under Franco; they could not talk about it also.

In our period, it is clear that if the Rosenbergs were innocent, they were being pushed to their death to make them lie. Then their refusal to lie and their sacrifice has given a gift to many Americans and many others, as William Reuben said, who had faith in the outcome, would speak out for them and join a developing struggle for freedom for us all.

Michael Meeropol, one of their sons, working now in Springfield, Massachusetts (the Greenglass relatives, who gave information—look at it yourselves, and see now whether you think it was false—are living "on the Island"), this son of the woman who said that her sons would know brotherhood and love said to me the thing that confirmed my belief in this time, and the difference between now and twenty-five years ago.[12] He said of the bushel of records at last coming in: "We are not afraid of anything that may turn up."

(*New York Times*, 1978)

---

10. Published article specifies "political causes."
11. Books mentioned: William A. Reuben, *The Atom Spy Hoax* (New York: Action Books, 1955); Walter Schneir and Miriam Schneir, *Invitation to an Inquest: A New Look at the Rosenberg-Sobell Case* (New York: Dell, 1968); Meeropol and Meeropol, *We Are Your Sons*; Ethel Rosenberg and Julius Rosenberg, *The Rosenberg Letters*, ed. Lewis John Collins (London: Dennis Dobson, 1953), with Ethel Rosenberg's poem "If We Die," 6; Louis Nizer, *The Implosion Conspiracy* (New York: Fawcett, 1974).
12. Greenglass was Ethel Rosenberg's maiden name. David and Ruth Greenglass, her brother and sister-in-law, implicated her during police interviews, purportedly to exonerate themselves. "The Island" refers to Long Island, New York.

Part III

Media and Democratic Education

A Photo-Text and Radio Scripts

CHAPTER 17

So Easy to See (1946)

*Photography-and-Text Collaboration with
Berenice Abbott*

                                                    In our time, there has been much talk about the difference between truth and reality.[1] We are familiar with contradictions, our society is based on them. And this division, with truth on the one hand and reality on the other, is known to us; it is as clear and obvious as moonrise and morning, or bombing in peacetime. The contradictions around us are not simply contradictions of meaning, but of the whole visible world. In the process of setting barriers between truth and reality, we have gone ahead with barrier-building. And now, all around us, we see the walls: between people and people, between art and science, between idea and idea. Those of us who mean in our lives the unity of people, the unity of nature and knowledge, mean also the

---

    1. In the early 1940s, Rukeyser began to work with photographer Berenice Abbott on a photo-text collaboration based around Abbott's Supersight photographs. This essay is one version of Rukeyser's introduction to their still-unpublished project, developed over a decade. Invented, built, and patented by Abbott, Supersight technology became the basis for later scientific photography. "The image of any three-dimensional object, when illuminated inside a closed dark box, in a darkened room, is transmitted or projected via an enlarging lens mounted on the side of that box. When received by a photosensitive surface outside the box that transmission creates an enlarged image of the thing itself, with no intervening 'noisy' medium to filter or dilute the image, as does, for example, grain in a negative." Julia Van Haaften, *Berenice Abbott: A Life in Photography* (New York: W. W. Norton, 2018), 249.

unity of imagination. In all the million individual flowerings of imagination and motive, of the human wish, there is the underlying unity. The common spring, the world-born source of power. Acknowledging that, we are drawn to look for those forms and meanings which will bring our reality and our truth together.

We are drawn to look. And the act of seeing opens new contradictions. For these eyes are mostly memory and partly moral, they bring their sentimentality and their traditions for furniture and set every scene for us a little, and then they are easy marks for seductions of color and tricks of light, nonsense of distance, fatigue, illness, age, the compromises of being alive. The eyes accept all of these, often they offer further compromises: weaknesses physical and political, blearing of sharp forms and detail, overlooking of meaning, rejection and censoring and canceling out. This is not a *visual* fact, this is the life of the eye as most people live it. And the arts called graphic, using paint, print, photography, are not merely visual—they reach us through total experience, experience of which novelty is a part. Whatever gives us the wholeness of experience enters our lives, through act, or sense, or art.

Through sight, powerfully, our lives are entered, all our waking time and even in dream—without our fallible eyes, with the dream-eyes that are so clear a criticism of the way we see. The idea of sight, here, is different from the idea of vision—its science is scarcely begun. It is as listening is to hearing. We hear all the sounds of the daytime, and in a city even deep at night I am full of voices and orchestras and wheels beyond the room; but when we reach a music constructed for some instrument which requires a further act and intensity of us, when the harpsichord gives us an intimate clear music and we make a meeting in ourselves with that sound, we know what listening is. As for vision—the visible world rains in its objects on our eyes, and we allow that fall, looking at our scene in an easy, clouded way, with our seeing full of our remembrance and our mood, and sometimes hardly seeing at all. We look at many things as we listen to jukebox music; but there is another kind of seeing. There is the fresh perception, and powerful and childlike eyes.

Anyone who has ever been threatened by death or blindness knows this flash of purer sight; the anticipation of darkness gives all life its truer, brighter forms, its clear colors. The blind know this, in their dreams; talking to sighted people, they describe sharpness and the hot red, the glad wild yellow. Anyone who, in love, sees with piercing clarity the turn of temple and eyeline, the cadence of cheek, the line of lip and lower lip on any face which has come to signify hope and excitement and all human meaning, sees this. Anyone who has been shaken and delighted by theatre or ballet or painting—by art—so that leaving the hall he sees in the street sharp, moving faces, brilliant and painful men and women and the evocative children, sees this.

These photographs, it seems to me, invite the sight in the way that crucial experience does.[2] They offer us the objects, simple and miraculous, and they do more than that: they offer us our own deep sight. Here are pictures of ordinary things, nothing is strange to us: a leaf, grass, a watch, a walnut, this apple . . . the list goes on and makes the book. But the apple, the walnut, the watch are here seen as the human eye *almost* can see them. Not quite: as Francis Bacon pointed out, spectacles can restore sight, microscopes and telescopes can enlarge a part of what we see, but we need an invention which will give us whole objects clarified beyond what the human eye can do, or can want to do.[3]

Berenice Abbott has made that invention, and here are the photographs. The apple is here, in its wetness and life, with its many textures, its flesh, its moment of ripeness—and its infinite suggestive correspondence with other textures and other flesh. "It *is* flesh!" one person said. "It's the moon!" said a child. I lived for a while in a room of an unfinished house where the carpenters and painters were still at work, and two or three of these pictures were on the walls. The painter came in and stopped short. "What's that?" he asked. And then he saw what it was. The carpenter had to see that, he said, and he called the carpenter in. "Nothing like that," said the carpenter of the apple, "has ever been seen in the world." He went out and got the contractor, brought him to face the apple, and said, "What do you make of that? Tell me what you think it is, don't tell me what it reminds you of."

Some have seen wood or a cock in the walnut, leather in the oak leaf, the lines of the eyebrow in the iron filings, fish-eye on butterfly-wing. But it is not only correspondences that are seen here; it is the close familiar thing seen new. One woman protested. "No, I don't want it,"

---

2. Rukeyser refers to Abbott's Supersight photographs of objects, including Rukeyser's eye and hand. She uses some of the following text in her untitled foreword to *Berenice Abbott: Photographs* (New York: Horizon Press, 1970), 9-11; and in her poem "An Unborn Poet," in *CP*, 591-592.

3. Francis Bacon, sixteenth-century English philosopher who argued for the scientific method. In her biography of his contemporary Thomas Hariot, Rukeyser argues the title figure countered Bacon's rigid, memory-based scientific approach to knowledge by instead foregrounding imagination and experience. See Muriel Rukeyser, *The Traces of Thomas Hariot* (New York: Random House, 1971), 61-65.

and she made a gesture, "I'm just now used to modern painting and the atom bomb, and I can't take *another* kind of seeing. It's too disturbing!"

But the housepainter's disturbance was of a different order. He asked, "Why didn't I know what they were, when I first saw the apple and the walnut? They're right in front of me, nothing is arty or faked; these are wonderful pictures. What's the matter with me, that I didn't see the *things*?" And after a while, "I'm a layman—How are you going to be sure the layman can see them? You'll have to prepare the people somehow."

Prepare people to look at what they know? Prepare them to see things that are deep in our lives, deep in childhood—a face, a wing, a hand?

Prepare people to see?

It is not simply that these photographs are done in extreme honesty; one need not say that with a first-rate work of art, in which one does not stop short, requiring honesty, or imagination, or the chance that meaning makes. We want all of these. Into creation go all the senses, the old hooded primitive, the intellectual imagination, and morality which is a flowing choice, as a line is a flowing point. And also that novelty which is needed—since we live in time—to let us recognize; to give us the sense of sameness as well as the sense of freshness.

Berenice Abbott has brought these gifts to her pictures. A portrait-photographer of inclusive delicacy and brilliance, artist of New York where she has set down steepness and the day of docks and streets and shops, she has beyond these two lives in photography searched for a meeting-place for art and science. This attempt to break down barriers that are indeed walls between truth and reality, artificial and political in their origins and meaning—this attempt has led her past laboratories and classrooms to photography of scientific process, and recently to the inventions presented in these photographs for the first time here. They are landmarks in the search, I believe; they are the first results of a process whose promise is scientific and commercial, and which will have further possibilities as new steps are taken. Berenice Abbott's attitude toward this new work, among the limitations of time and equipment, is that of the pure artist and inventor, full of recognition of the forces in our society that work against discovery and realism. "A machine art!" she will protest, in conversation about photography—"if there *were* a machine! They've perfected the bombsight; and we still gauge exposure, and focus, and open the shutter, in three *different* motions!" And, speaking of her need for stronger lights, that will be concentrated in a narrow ray, "We need a light as good as sunlight. Better than sunlight."

But these are workshop remarks, made casually, having to do with specific problems. More basic is this photographer's attitude toward realism. We have little enough reality in our physical life, she believes, and can have none in our spiritual life while this is still true for the people. Her work is part of a wide attempt to bring to spiritual life, and physical and intellectual life, this realism. Braque has said recently, "The true materialist, descending deeper into matter, lifts spirituality further up."[4]

At this point the search takes on other meanings. For the obstacles before your "true materialist" are social and political. I know this best in poetry. No matter how far our lives are involved in poetry, it is the fear of poetry that is immediate to all of us, that is part of life today in America. The resistance to these meanings and forms and symbols is a fierce and familiar thing, part of every day. And in poetry, it is to some degree a resistance to the use of symbols. In work like these pictures, nature is used as a symbol of itself; but the realism goes farther than we have yet gone. And there is always the danger of the real, which assumes a mythological character, an aspect of menace in a society that hides and evades and hurries toward compromise, hurries toward self-censorship. These pictures offer another attitude toward reality and toward truth. This attitude has implications that are generous in human and scientific meanings.

There is a morality here, as in all art; it is evident in us as selection. And what has been discarded here will be clear at a glance; what has been selected is the real. The objects have, as Emerson said, their "roots in central nature, and may of course be so exhibited to us as to represent the world . . . Now men do not see nature to be beautiful . . . They reject life as prosaic."[5] This is a new beginning, another acceptance of life. The acceptance does here what it always does; makes gifts, opens other doors, and offers other acceptances. There are these sources of power.

Our time demands this "true materialism." In many ways, the real is the most foreign to us. These pictures are tokens of foreignness. And at the same time they are brilliant tokens of reality and of the flower of the real, of possibility.

(Unpublished, 1946)

---

4. Georges Braque, "Pensées sur l'art," *Confluences* 4 (May 1945): 339. Braque was a French cubist painter, collagist, printmaker, and sculptor.
5. Ralph Waldo Emerson, "Art" (1851).

CHAPTER 18

From *Sunday at Nine* (1949)
Scripts for Two Radio Broadcasts

Good evening. This is Muriel Rukeyser. Tonight I am offering to you the first in a series of hours called *Sunday at Nine*. The program represents a new venture on the part of this station and myself, although the reading of poetry and the playing of music combine to make one of the oldest pleasures of the world.[1]

Radio has in the last years brought fine music into your home—first-rate contemporary music and indeed, a wide range of the music of many countries and many times. As we have grown used to asking for more and better and more brilliantly heard music, stations—like this one—have built programs around fine music. And, during these years of a growing feeling for music heard again and again, we have been aware of the place of radio in the story. We have been aware, too, of the place of the musician in our lives. It has changed. From the choice we used to have—of the music-maker seen as a decorative, romantic, and slightly foreign person, or as a useless, clowning long-hair, and still foreign to

---

1. *Sunday at Nine* was broadcast by KDFC San Francisco on four consecutive Sundays in August 1949. The first and final episodes' scripts, on Emily Dickinson and the blues, respectively, are reconstructed here. Master recordings have not been located, but Rukeyser's son, Bill, has recently discovered the as-yet-unpublished previously lost recordings of her spoken parts from episodes two and three, on Robert Frost and war poetry, respectively.

most of us—we have come, largely through radio, to know the musicians as givers and sharers in our life as a people.

But none of this warmth has come as yet into our feeling for poetry. What is poetry to us—even to those whose lives are deep in poems? It is still foreign, and we do not let it enter our daily life. Do you remember the poems of your early childhood—the far rhymes and games of the beginning, the little songs to which you woke and went to sleep? We all remember them. But, since childhood, to many of us poetry has become a matter of distaste. To recite is one thing: one of the qualifications for an announcer, listed by an enormous network among "good voice" and "correct pronunciation" is "the ability to read and interpret poetry." The other side of the picture is told perfectly in a letter written ninety years ago by the wife of the author of *Moby Dick*. Mrs. Melville said to her mother—and you can hear the misery of her words—"Herman has taken to writing poetry. You need not tell anyone, for you know how such things get around."[2] What is this distaste for poetry? If you ask your friends about it, you will find, as I have, that they will give you the same answers. Your friends may say that they have not the *time* for poetry. Now this is a curious position to take; for poetry, of all the arts that live in time—music, theatre, movies, writing—poetry is the briefest and most compact of these. Or your friends may say that they are bored by poetry. If you hear this, try one or two further questions. You will find that "bored" means different things. One person will confess that he has been frightened off forever by taking apart lines of poetry in school, and that now he thinks of a poem simply as a set of constructions that should have been much more. One will have come from a theatre of war to be confronted with verse like "Bobolink, bobolink / Spink, spank, spink."[3] One will tell you that, try as he will, he *cannot* understand poetry, and particularly, modern poetry . . . it is intellectual, confused, obscure. Almost any friend, if you ask a man, will finally tell you that there is something effeminate about the whole thing.[4] In all of these answers, you will meet a shying-away that amounts to a fear of poetry.

---

2. Howard P. Vincent, introduction to Herman Melville, *Collected Poems of Herman Melville*, ed. Vincent (Chicago: Packard, 1947), viii.

3. William Cullen Bryant, "Robert of Lincoln" (1855). Rukeyser's citation of this popular poem implicitly sets up her first episode since Emily Dickinson also wrote several poems referencing the bobolink, a variety of bird.

4. On ts draft, at the end of this sentence Rukeyser first typed "sissy" but replaced it, in holo., with "effeminate." In her contemporaneously written book *The Life of Poetry*, Rukeyser

Now a poem does invite, it does require, if it is any good. What does it invite? A poem invites you to feel. More than that: it invites you to respond. And better than that: a poem invites a total response from you. But it is not a mainly mental response; it is total, but it is reached through the emotions. A first-rate poem, a fine poem, will reach you intellectually . . . or may I say that when you reach it, you will reach it intellectually too . . . but the way is through emotion . . . through what we call feeling.[5]

What I would like to do in these evenings is to read to you, for a few minutes, from among the most immediate poems I know, and then, for the rest of the hour, to play recorded music—music which I have chosen to go with the poetry.[6] Much of what we will read is contemporary, and much is American. But, later, we will be turning many times to other places and other centuries; and, after three Sundays of reading poems which you may find in books, the fourth Sunday will always be another kind of evening. Three Sundays from tonight, for example, *Sunday at Nine* will offer an evening of the blues, their words and their music. And on other fourth Sundays, we will have movie poetry and movie music, children's poetry, street cries, theatre poetry . . . and so on. These programs are a new venture for me, and I am excited by the possibilities. I hope you will be, too; and that this new venture will give you a many-sided enjoyment. The opinions and the voice on *Sunday at Nine* will be, chiefly, mine. And now let us have the poems.

Episode One: Emily Dickinson

The legend of Emily Dickinson can now be seen receding like a trick movie sequence into the empty unreal distance.[7] With the publication of *Bolts of Melody*, and the disclosure of more of her story in *Ancestors' Brocades*, a full life begins to make coherence out of all the flashes and fragments of greatness we had until now.[8] The rareness of the woman,

---

addresses adults' fear of poetic emotion and the common belief that poetry is feminized and "sexually suspect." See Muriel Rukeyser, *The Life of Poetry* (Ashfield, MA: Paris Press, 1996), 11.

5. Rukeyser discusses "total response" in a nearly verbatim way in *The Life of Poetry*, written around the time she was preparing the *Sunday at Nine* broadcasts. See Rukeyser, *Life of Poetry*, 11.

6. Below, the [*Music*] cue indicates where recordings were played.

7. Episode broadcast by KDFC San Francisco on August 7, 1949.

8. Emily Dickinson, *Bolts of Melody: New Poems of Emily Dickinson*, ed. Mabel Loomis Todd and Millicent Todd Bingham (New York: Harper & Brothers, 1945); Millicent Todd Bingham, *Ancestors' Brocades: The Literary Life of Emily Dickinson* (New York: Harper & Brothers, 1945).

the rareness of her gift, and her view of life as rareness—of moment and communication—all come through. Emily Dickinson wrote this poem:

> Your thoughts don't have words every day,
> They come a single time
> Like signal esoteric sips
> Of sacramental wine,
>
> Which while you taste so native seems,
> So bounteous, so free,
> You cannot comprehend its worth
> Nor its infrequency.[9]

The gifts of Emily Dickinson seemed to be withdrawn. They were not: for we have them. The problem is simply one of display.

> The blood is more showy than the breath
> But cannot dance as well.[10]

Emily Dickinson was a recluse, yes. She lived in her house and her garden, locked away after an extremely social youth; and her queer concern, even for New England in her time, was truth. She knew how dangerous the light of truth.

> Tell all the truth but tell it slant,
> Success in circuit lies,
> Too bright for our infirm delight
> The truth's superb surprise;
>
> As lightning to the children eased
> With explanation kind,
> The truth must dazzle gradually
> Or every man be blind.[11]

If truth is a light, what is a poet, then? She writes:

> The poets light but lamps,
> Themselves go out;

Because Rukeyser read from *Bolts of Melody* on her program, that unauthoritative edition's versions, now in the public domain, are used here, even though the poems lack Dickinson's original punctuation, capitalization, lineation, and even variants in diction.

   9. Dickinson, Poem 435, in *Bolts*, 228.
  10. Dickinson, Poem 633 (fragment), in *Bolts*, 319.
  11. Dickinson, Poem 449, in *Bolts*, 233.

CHAPTER 18

> The wicks they stimulate,
> If vital light
>
> Inhere as do the suns,
> Each age a lens
> Disseminating their
> Circumference.[12]

Our age disseminates Emily Dickinson. We see the directness in which she lived. She was a recluse not because the outer world was too much for her; she lived at the center of her intensities, and told us of them, of almost all of them. She gave us her animals of emotion; and she gives us her cat, in all its cathood and ferocity, in its moment of hope—

> She sights a bird, she chuckles,
> She flattens, then she crawls,
> She runs without the look of feet,
> Her eyes increase to balls,
>
> Her jaws stir, twitching, hungry,
> Her teeth can hardly stand,
> She leaps—but robin leaped the first!
> Ah, pussy of the sand,
>
> The hopes so juicy ripening
> You almost bathed your tongue
> When bliss disclosed a hundred wings
> And fled with every one![13]

Look at her poems of animals. The wit that sparkled in her house, in her town of Amherst, will let her say, with a half-grave scientific air: "After all birds have been investigated and laid aside . . ."[14] And she will make the connection, over and over, between heaven and the season:

> Spring is the period
> Express from God.
> Among the other seasons,
> Himself abide,

---

12. Dickinson, Poem 432, in *Bolts*, 227.
13. Dickinson, Poem 117, in *Bolts*, 65–66. Rukeyser's selection introduced Dickinson's unsaid "intensities," especially lesbian desires, through this poem's sexual innuendo.
14. Dickinson, Poem 108, in *Bolts*, 61.

> But during March and April
> None stir abroad
> Without a cordial interview
> With God.[15]

But in this book, we have—and this is more true, to me, here, than ever before in her poems—we have that structure and continuity of meaning packing the bud which makes the penetrating poet:

> Bloom is result. To meet a flower
> And casually glance
> Would cause one scarcely to suspect
> The minor circumstance
>
> Assisting in the bright affair
> So intricately done,
> Then offered as a butterfly
> To the meridian.
>
> To pack the bud, oppose the worm,
> Obtain its right of dew,
> Adjust the heat, elude the wind,
> Escape the prowling bee,
>
> Great nature not to disappoint
> Awaiting her that day—
> To be a flower is profound
> Responsibility![16]

The poems we have heard—light, the cat, the flower, the spring—are an introduction to another set of meanings. Here is a poem which opens the door to a sense of greatness—that greatness which allows us all a sense of our own capacity:

> I thought that nature was enough
> Till human nature came,
> But that the other did absorb
> As firmament a flame.

---

15. Dickinson, Poem 52, in *Bolts*, 34.
16. Dickinson, Poem 78, in *Bolts*, 46.

CHAPTER 18

> Of human nature just aware
> There added the divine
> Brief struggle for capacity.
> The power to contain
>
> Is always as the contents,
> But give a giant room
> And you will lodge a giant
> And not a lesser man.[17]

Emily Dickinson's poems have a silence around them, like the silence of a still house. Her music is of several kinds. She is the soliloquy, the voice speaking alone among the darker sounds, as in the *Soliloquy* by Bernard Rogers. [*Music*][18]

The base of poets like Emerson and Emily Dickinson is, too, in the familiar hymns of their youth and their churchgoing families. [*Music*][19] And her town, Puritan and keen, is around her, and her fiery, volcanic family. Emily Dickinson gives us one clue to her withdrawn life when she speaks of "Vesuvius at home"; and some of the witty and intricate music of Scarlatti, even in an Italy so far from nineteenth-century Amherst, tells us a little of that background.[20] [*Music*][21] Music she heard, listening from the hall, was the piano music of Beethoven and Scarlatti and Bach. Now Gieseking plays a Bach partita. [*Music*][22]

---

17. Dickinson, Poem 149, in *Bolts*, 80.
18. Bernard Rogers, "Soliloquy for Flute and String Orchestra," Eastman-Rochester Symphony Orchestra, cond. Howard Hanson, recorded 1941, side 1 of *American Works for Solo Winds*, Victor Records VM-802, 78 rpm. 4:32 played. For this episode, the editors have reconstructed recording information, including tracks or sides played, from the program engineer's notes. Some notations are partial since most of the records were 78 rpm, a format not fully archived in musical recording databases. Readers can listen to most of the 78 rpm recordings fully documented here at Internet Archive's Great 78 Project: www.great78.archive.org.
19. Isaac Watts, "O Love That Wilt Not Let Me Go," London Tower Singers, LA-60, 78 rpm. 30 seconds played. Full recording information not available.
20. Poem 1705 ("Volcanoes be in Sicily"), which contains the phrase "Vesuvius at home," was included in an earlier collection, not *Bolts of Melody*. Dickinson's sister-in-law, Susan Dickinson, to whom the poet is believed to have had a lesbian attachment, transcribed the poem from a now-lost manuscript. See Emily Dickinson, Poem CXVII ("Volcanoes be in Sicily"), in *The Single Hound: Poems of a Lifetime*, ed. Martha Dickinson Bianchi (Boston: Little, Brown, 1914), 125.
21. Dominico Scarlatti, "Part 1" of *The Good-Humored Ladies Ballet*, London Philharmonic Orchestra, cond. Sir Eugene Goossens, n.d. [released 1938], side 1, Victor Red Seal VM-512, 78 rpm. 4:15 played.
22. Johann Sebastian Bach, *Partita No. 6 in E Minor, BWV 830*, Walter Gieseking, piano, n.d. [released 1934], sides 1 through 4, Columbia Records CMX-135, 78 rpm. 16:04 played.

Emily Dickinson, in a world of values, could have no idea of her success or failure in the future. That she wanted fame with a lifelong hunger, we know. But that was a gambler's chance, and on one of the thousand of little pieces of paper that hold her poems, is written this:

> We lose because we win.
> Gamblers,
> Recollecting which,
> Toss their dice again![23]

Her whole life was consciously lived between the pit, into which many dare not look, and the heavens many have not the hope to see. In one of her poems that knocks against our hearts, asking the great questions, Emily Dickinson says:

> A pit—but heaven over it,
> And heaven beside,
> And heaven abroad,
> And yet—a pit,
> With heaven over it.
>
> To stir would be to slip,
> To look would be to drop,
> To dream, to sap the prop
> That holds my chances up.
> Ah, pit! With heaven over it!
>
> The depth is all my thought,
> I dare not ask my feet;
> 'Twould start us where we sit
> So straight you'd scarce suspect
> It was a pit, with fathoms under it,
>
> It's circuit just the same:
> Seed, summer, tomb.
> Who's doom—
> To whom?[24]

---

23. Dickinson, Poem 533, in *Bolts*, 271.
24. Dickinson, Poem 532, in *Bolts*, 270-271.

You may want the chance to look at these poems. Some of them live more fully on the page—for all they are crowded with sound—and we feel that they were written *for* silence, *in* silence. This poem speaks of rareness and loneliness and all the hope of unrepeatable music.[25] But here are not the unheard melodies of Keats: this woman heard this strain:

> Better than music, for I who heard it,
> I was used to the birds before;
> This was different, 'twas translation
> Of all the tunes I knew, and more;
>
> 'Twasn't contained like other stanza,
> No one could play it the second time
> But the composer, perfect Mozart,
> Perish with him that keyless rhyme!
>
> So children, assured that brooks in Eden
> Bubbled a better melody,
> Quaintly infer Eve's great surrender,
> Urging the feet that would not fly.
>
> Children matured are wiser, mostly,
> Eden a legend dimly told,
> Eve and the anguish grandame's story—
> But I was telling a tune I heard.
>
> Not such a strain the church baptizes
> When the last saint goes up the aisles,
> Not such a stanza shakes the silence
> When the redemption strikes her bells.
>
> Let me not lose its smallest cadence,
> Humming for promise when alone,
> Humming until my faint rehearsal
> Drop into tune around the throne![26]

Here is one of the poems that is devout as any love poem, any religious poem, any seed-poem could reach to be:

---

25. Rukeyser had first written "unspeakable" rather than "unrepeatable." The original, suppressed version suggests Dickinson's and her own queerness.
26. Dickinson, Poem 454, in *Bolts*, 235.

He was my host, he was my guest,
I never to this day
If I invited him could tell
Or he invited me.

So infinite our interview,
So intimate indeed,
Analysis like capsule seemed
To keeper of the seed.[27]

The pain of her life, with its conscious loss, its immediate untold agonies—that pain is given us:

One crucifixion is recorded only;
How many be
Is not affirmed of mathematics
Or history.

One Cavalry exhibited to stranger;
As many be
As persons or peninsulas.
Gethsemane

Is but a province in the being's center;
India,
For journey or crusade's achieving,
Too near.

Our Lord indeed bore compound witness,
And yet,
There's newer, nearer crucifixion
Than that.[28]

"A pang is more conspicuous in spring," Emily Dickinson writes.[29] She is too strong in herself and her poetry to allow pain to remain without telling what carries it, to whom the terrible struggles come, and what withstands.

There is a strength in knowing that it can be borne
Although it tear.

---

27. Dickinson, Poem 281, in *Bolts*, 153.
28. Dickinson, Poem 513, in *Bolts*, 260.
29. Dickinson, Poem 475, in *Bolts*, 245.

> What are the sinews of such cordage for
> Except to bear?
> The ship might be of satin had it not to fight.
> To walk on tides requires cedar feet.³⁰

These poems are a chart of the strengths of the spirit. Have you seen the table of colors that express the degrees of heated steel? That table reminds me of these poems. Here is one of the great poems of our language, I believe, that speaks for the profundities of love and loss, and the places of the spirit's own right, and of the enlargement which is joy, even joy gone:

> The things that never can come back are several—
> Childhood, some forms of hope, the dead;
> But joys, like men, may sometimes make a journey
>   And still abide.
>
> We do not mourn for traveler or sailor,
> Their routes are fair,
> But think, enlarged, of all that they will tell us
>   Returning here.
>
> "Here!" There are typic heres, foretold locations,
> The spirit does not stand,
> Himself at whatsoever fathom
>   His native land.³¹

The Mozart *Duo in B-Flat* speaks in a voice like that one of hers. [*Music*]³² And for her country with its river running through the hills, and the accent of New England, here is Charles Ives's *Housatonic*. [*Music*]³³ A ground-voice to her many gifts, it is hard to choose. I wish we could hear the little music of the lock which opens the chest where all her poems were kept. But here is Bach, with the pure voice that reaches

---

30. Dickinson, Poem 468, in *Bolts*, 242.
31. Dickinson, Poem 529, in *Bolts*, 269.
32. Wolfgang Amadeus Mozart, *Duo No. 2 in B Flat Major for Violin and Viola, K 424*, Jascha Heifetz, violin, and William Primrose, viola, n.d. [released 1941], sides 1–5, RCA Victor DM 831, 78 rpm. 17:05 played.
33. Charles Ives, "The Housatonic at Stockbridge," track 7 on side 3 of *Four American Landscapes*, Janssen Symphony of Los Angeles, cond. Werner Janssen, n.d. [released 1949], Artist Records ART-100 / ART-JS-13, vinyl LP. 4:28 played.

directly, speaking with the openness of secrets we all know, in his *First Sonata*. [*Outro music*][34]

Episode Four: The Blues

Good evening. This is Muriel Rukeyser with the fourth hour of *Sunday at Nine*.[35] Tonight's poetry does not rise out of the pages of books. If you want to look at these words, you will have to take them down yourselves, in nightclubs, in the South, in the places, still apart, where Negroes live—or at home, from records. Every fourth Sunday of this program we will listen to poems that have, as yet, no written connection with literature—not in the textbooks and histories, at any rate. But these poems, these songs, in the darkness of their music, in what they say, have power. They reach us, our bodies and our lives. This evening will be given to the blues. In the last few years, the attitudes toward jazz and toward the blues have split sharply, and we no longer have a small, isolated audience to listen to these penetrating and native songs. Instead, we have two groups: one group still stays away from everything connected with jazz and thinks of literature, and music, only in relation to what are known as art forms. The other group is devoted to jazz. With the frenzy of any religious group early in the history of its movement, this group listens devoutly, has built up commentaries of the riff and the break, and has set up a critical hierarchy around the trumpet solo.[36] I am interested in the second group—the religious one—because I care very much about jazz and the blues. But I am curious about the gaps in their rapture. They are devoted to the blues. Every figure of this music, which preceded jazz, is familiar to them. The words alone—the words of the blues are forgotten, or at best glossed over.

Now it is impossible with these songs that shake you and reach you in fire and tears and in every kind of laughter—it is impossible to rip the words away from the music. In the first place, the form of the blues—a

---

34. Johann Sebastian Bach, "3e Mouvement: Andante," side 3 of *Sonate No. 1 en sol mineur pour clavecin et viole de gambe*, Isabelle Nef, harpsichord, and Antonio Tusa, viola da gamba, n.d. [c. 1948], Éditions de l'Oiseau-Lyre (France) OL 94/OL 95, 78 rpm. No time specified.

35. Episode broadcast by KDFC San Francisco on August 28, 1949.

36. Rukeyser's holo. script substitutes "will set up a critical hierarchy" for a canceled phrase: "will write stories and even novels." The original version anticipates jazz-related Beat Generation and African American literatures of the 1950s and 1960s, though the former usually heroized bebop legend Charlie Parker, a saxophonist, not a trumpeter.

basic verse form—is built on repetition. The first line is repeated. It is as if the line itself were used as a rhyme. The song goes:

> There's a change in the ocean, a change in the deep blue sea,
> There's a change in the ocean, a change in the deep blue sea,

and then the third line resolves the verse:

> You can bet yo' life there ain't no change in me.[37]

The songs we are having this evening are not *about* any subject; there is no driving theme, and although sadness has come to be identified with blues, there is a hot, untamable sadness which ranges from the homesickness of "Michigan water tastes like sherry wine" through the defiant shouting song of Lead Belly to the broken love of many of them, including the Mississippi of this music.[38] [*Music*][39]

Here is Bessie Smith in her power and unburied implacable song, full of triumph and full of despair, with "Young Woman's Blues":

> See that long lonesome road
> Lawd you know . . . it's gonna end.
>
> I'm a young woman
> And ain't done runnin' roun'.[40]

---

37. "The Crazy Blues" (1920), written by Perry Bradford and recorded by Mamie Smith and Her Jazz Hounds, was the first hit blues record. The editors preserve Rukeyser's misquotation of the original lyrics. The first line is not repeated, and Smith sings the third line as "I tell you folks, there ain't no change in me."

38. "Michigan Water Blues" (1923), written by Clarence Williams and performed by Sara Martin; popularized by Alan Lomax's recording of Jelly Roll Morton for Smithsonian Folkways (1938).

39. Script indicates "St. Louis Blues." Originally an instrumental blues by W. C. Handy (1916), Rukeyser probably selected a later lyric version like those by Paul Robeson (1933), Louis Armstrong (c. 1933), Billie Holiday (1941), or Bessie Smith (1925). Neither engineering cues nor a list of specific recordings are extant for this episode. Rukeyser's in-text annotations of track titles and recording artists are supplied in this edition's notes when provided. The editors have added composers and release dates, which Rukeyser did not annotate on her script.

40. Script does not indicate to play music, though the following mention of multiple songs having been heard suggest it was. Rukeyser's script cites excerpts from "Young Woman's Blues," written by Bessie Smith and performed by Bessie Smith and Her Blues Boys (1927). She transcribed these couplets as consecutive, but the second is the song's bridge and the first is the outro. If Rukeyser did play the record, then she let its queerness speak for itself rather than draw attention to the rest of the song's encrypted queer content ("Some people call me a hobo," "I ain't gonna marry / I ain't gonna settle down").

It seems to me that in many ways the songs we are hearing this evening are, to us, what the troubadours' songs were to Provence.[41] It has been said that only a few of the troubadours wrote poetry of any great literary merit. But they were the founders of modern lyric poetry. Only a small number of tunes have survived among the poems. The blues have taken a whole language, and made song. But the values are completely different. Even the love sung by the blues is vastly different from the love celebrated by the old French songs, with their emphasis on patience, discretion, and secrecy, even the secrecy of the name of the beloved. The songs of the troubadours were made for the court, we are told; the music traveled with the traveling entertainers who juggled and sang. The "courts" for which the blues were made were the tours and the band contests, the "palaces" of Basin Street, the River excursion boats, and the nightclubs.[42] Later, Tin Pan Alley learned to contrive blues: we'll hear Hollywood versions, Tin Pan Alley blues, and music that uses blues in extended composition.[43]

Will you remember to listen to the words? One man says that the music is pure and clean, the lyrics impure and dirty, and another believes that the blues are more valuable as a source of folk poetry than of folk music. You may hear some things easy to let pass. I think you will also hear much poetry, in its first emergence, raw, intense, reaching your life.

Have to count these blues, so I can say them all. We go on with Bessie Smith, singing "Midnight":

[*Music*]
Daddy, daddy, please come back to me
Your mama's lonesome as she can be.

---

41. In his early 1910 study *The Spirit of Romance* (New York: New Directions, 2005), Ezra Pound theorized that the pre-Renaissance Provençal troubadour tradition was modernist lyric's precursor. The year before Rukeyser wrote and broadcast *Sunday at Nine*, he had been awarded the Bollingen Prize for *The Pisan Cantos* (1948), for which her book *The Green Wave* (1948) also was nominated. The award caused much controversy because of Pound's fascism and trial for treason. See the editors' introduction to this volume.
42. *Palaces* is code for *brothels*. Basin Street was in New Orleans's red-light district. This site of interracial mixing and sex work was immortalized by Louis Armstrong and His Orchestra's "Basin Street Blues" (1929).
43. Tin Pan Alley, a Manhattan recording studio that commercialized the blues by separating the form from its original street and nightlife contexts. For "blues in extended composition," Rukeyser probably is thinking of *Four American Blues* (1926-1948, published 1949), composed by her friend Aaron Copland.

You left me at midnight, clocks were striking twelve,
You left me at midnight, clocks were striking twelve,
To face this cruel world all by myself.[44]

And now Bessie Smith sings "Cold in Hand":

[*Music*]
I got a hardworkin' man
The way he treats me, I don't understand ...
[. . .]
Now I don't want that man
Because he's gone cold in hand.[45]

Billie Holiday has been compared often to Bessie Smith. Her song is "Strange Fruit"; here she sings, first, "Long Gone Blues":

[*Music*]
I've been your slave
Ever since I've been your babe

But before I see you go
I see you in your grave.[46]

And now Billie Holiday sings her own "Billie's Blues":

[*Music*]
I love my man
I'm a liar if I say I don't
But I'll quit my man
I'm a liar if I say I won't[47]

Josh White has not been able to get permission from many nightclub owners to sing "T. B. Blues." The naked life comes through his inflection and his guitar:

---

44. "Midnight Blues," lyrics by Babe Thompson and performed by Bessie Smith and Fletcher Henderson (1923). Excerpt from lyrics added; they are not in Rukeyser's script.
45. "Cold in Hand Blues," lyrics by Jack Gee and performed by Bessie Smith with Louis Armstrong and Fred Longshaw (1925).
46. "Strange Fruit," classic anti-racist blues anthem elegizing lynching victims, with lyrics and music by Abel Meeropol and recorded by Billie Holiday (1939). Rukeyser does not play from that track but instead plays "Long Gone Blues," written and performed by Billie Holiday (1939).
47. "Billie's Blues," written by Billie Holiday and recorded by Holiday with Arty Shaw (1936).

[*Music*]
Mmmmmm the T.B.'s killin' me
Ah, Lord, the T.B.'s killin' me
Got the tuberculosis, consumption killin' me.[48]

And another Josh White song, "Fare Thee Well Blues":

[*Music*]
I had a gal, she was long and tall,
She moved her body like a cannonball.
Fare thee well, oh honey, fare thee well.[49]

One of the old blues, which I am drawn to again and again for its poem: "O come all you women and listen to my tale of woe / I got consumption of the heart, I feel myself sinkin' slow."
Sara Martin, singing "Death Sting Me." [*Music*][50]
The father of the blues, W.C. Handy, gave us the most far-reaching blues of all. Listening to his own version and that of Louis Armstrong is a very different matter from hearing Billie Holiday's or the Hollywood treatment. Bing Crosby does another thing with the song, filling it with his charm and his ease:

[*Music*]
I hate to see that evening sun go down
'Cause my baby, he's gone left this town.[51]

Jelly Roll Morton seems to me a unique singer. New Orleans music is here, and the man sitting at his loose and blue piano. [*Music*][52]

---

48. "T.B. Blues," written and recorded by Victoria Spivey (1927) and popularized by Lead Belly (1940); rerecorded by Josh White (1944). Rukeyser and White were close friends. In 1945, he provided music for the sole production of her unpublished anti-fascist play *The Middle of the Air*.
49. White's track was titled "Fare Thee Well" (1942), a traditional song first recorded with contralto vocals by Libby Hollman and White on guitar. He later rerecorded the track, providing his own vocals (1944). "Fare Thee Well Blues" is a different song, written by Mississippi Joe Callicott and Vol Stevens and recorded by Callicott (1930).
50. "Death Sting Me Blues," Sara Martin with Clarence Williams and His Orchestra (1928); rerecorded by Sara Martin with King Oliver's Orchestra (1928). Rukeyser misquotes the opening lines, which should read: "I want all you women to listen to my tale of woe, / I've got consumption of the heart, I feel myself sinking low."
51. "St. Louis Blues," written by W. C. Handy and recorded by Prince's Orchestra (1916); rerecorded by Handy (1923). Vocals were added to Handy's signature instrumental song in covers by Louis Armstrong (1926, with Bessie Smith on vocals; with Armstrong on vocals, 1929), Bing Crosby (1932, with Duke Ellington and His Orchestra), and Billie Holiday (1933).
52. Script does not indicate which track was played.

CHAPTER 18

On music paper, another style, in some ways only a decoration, comes in, and the earlier, unwritten music changes, reaches a wider audience, and then is lost or, if you like, absorbed into the bloodstream of the people. "Blues in the Night" is a *written*, contrived blues; it comes closest of the professional songs to the color and flow of the great ones, and it stakes out again the wide night-country, "from Natchez to Mobile, from Memphis to St. Joe, / Wherever the four winds blow"; and Gershwin orchestrated the material into the "Rhapsody's" big city music.[53] [*Music*][54]

But once more to the pillar, the source-music, the poetry behind much of our talk, much of our song—"St. Louis Blues." [*Outro music*][55]

(Unpublished, 1949)

---

53. Rukeyser quotes from "Blues in the Night," written by Harold Arlen (music) and Johnny Mercer (lyrics) and performed by Artie Shaw and His Orchestra (1941). The song was written for the Warner Brothers studio film of the same name.

54. "Rhapsody in Blue," composed by George Gershwin and performed by Paul Whiteman and His Orchestra (1924).

55. "St. Louis Blues," written by Handy. Script does not specify the version Rukeyser played. Most likely, she chose Handy's instrumental version, recorded first by Prince's Orchestra (1916) and then by Handy himself (1923).

Part IV

Modernist Interventions
On Gender, Poetry, and Poetics

CHAPTER 19

Modern Trends: American Poetry (1932)

Contemporary American poetry has divided itself into three trends: acceptance, despair, and hope towards something new and effective or towards death.[1] These motions have their latest origins in three poets—Archibald MacLeish, T. S. Eliot, and Robinson Jeffers—and in reaction to the temperature of the century's first fifteen years. The postwar time was a sound drowned in its own echoes. Imagism, with H. D.'s crispness and Amy Lowell's vibrations, was soon suffocated, and Vachel Lindsay's noisier brasses smothered, by time.[2] Their names remain, and much of their workmanship; but they stay at the same radius from the focal point of strictly contemporary poetry as Edgar Lee Masters and Stephen Crane did from them: a present influence, so ingrained in poetic essay that they do not lose because of lapses as memorable individuals.[3]

---

1. An editorial note indicates this article was to be the first in a series "on trends in modern art, culture and thought." The series did not continue; Rukeyser withdrew from Vassar College before the next semester's start.
2. Vachel Lindsay was not associated with Imagism, a poetic avant-garde launched by Ezra Pound in 1913 and the first to include American poets.
3. Popular turn-of-the-century poets Edgar Lee Masters and Stephen Crane are not usually counted as precursors of modernism.

CHAPTER 19

Their definitions of subject matter and treatment were more inclusive than anything since Chaucer and Shakespeare, and this comprehension has continued to be a source of strength. Carl Sandburg, who has been classified as an important unintelligent poet, gave readers the sight of the subtle planes of brickyards, of the power of thick chimneys blackened by use, the suggestion that an arc light might be confounded with a farther traditional moon, and not too much be forfeited.[4] Edwin Arlington Robinson dangled the hope that there might be an application of classicism in poetry to modern life before his audience, and cajoled them with the ease and sonority of *Lancelot* and *Tristram*.[5] Robert Frost lifted many of the prejudices against commonplace subjects.[6] It is all wrong to speak one sentence each of these people: their thoughts and rhythms twine to make the whole history of our poetry.

That history has passed down, out of a comfortable perspective, into our own years. It is impossible for us to judge with any sense of time—granted—but the leaders of three main floods stand.

Archibald MacLeish has become the accepted high-relief figure of one wing. Poems: *The Hamlet*, the lyrics of *Streets in the Moon* and *New Found Land*, and *Einstein* represent the final accomplishment built on an acceptance and realization of time and environment and the implications of these that contemporary poetry has reached.[7] He has asked, "And by what way shall I go back?"; and he has said in "The Too-Late Born":

We too, we too, descending once again
The hills of our own land, we too have heard
Far off—Ah, que ce cor a longue haleine—
The horn of Roland in the passages of Spain,
[. . .] and found
At Roncevaux upon the darkening plain

---

4. Carl Sandburg's populist modernism, though not erudite or obtuse, was not "unintelligent."

5. A popular early twentieth-century poet, Edgar Arlington Robinson integrated English Arthurian mythology into his long poems *Lancelot* (1920), *Tristram* (1927), and *Merlin* (1917).

6. For her later extended review of New England regionalist Robert Frost, see Muriel Rukeyser, "In a Speaking Voice," in this volume.

7. Collections by Archibald MacLeish: *Streets in the Moon* (1926), *The Hamlet of Archibald MacLeish* (1928), *Einstein* (1929), and *New Found Land: Fourteen Poems* (1930). Later, MacLeish and Rukeyser developed a professional relationship. See Muriel Rukeyser, "The Speed of the Image," in this volume, note 13.

The dead against the dead and on the silent ground
The silent slain—[8]

There is no eccentricity of viewpoint, no bravado of image. His poetry is not wild with sound nor involute in fragmentary meanings. But we feel the bravery of his comprehension, the daring that allows MacLeish to face the implications of his race, and breed, and culture, implications that fall heavily and find no answer in anything but their expression in symbols of grace and personal moment—the feel of America, the large walking of night across the sky, the knowledge that a thing is contained in itself always, without comparison, without contact from surface to surface—knowledge that is likely to stagger an unbuttressed mind.

T. S. Eliot in his early work, recognized some of these things. "Prufrock," parts of *The Waste Land*, and "Gerontion," with some of the shorter pieces, are summaries in exquisite and exact poetry of the pale inability of a frustrated season to feel adequacy in anything.[9] There is a gentleness about his work that gives us the most pity for his sense of brokenness: places like "Lips that would kiss / From prayers to broken stone" demonstrate this and the sadness of the end of "Prufrock," the shadowless rock, the tiger spring that means death, the endless sounds of brittle import, phonograph records, laughter in the next room, snatches of talk, mouthed and meaningless, and then the splendor of Leicester's barge, smoke writhing against a wall, sunlight weaving through a girl's hair.[10] Lately T. S. Eliot has decided in favor of Royalism, classicism, and the Church of England, and has returned to the influence of Laforgue and that bright boy of English letters, Ezra Pound: but, given release from the loyalties which sterilize him, there may be more poetry of the breed of his broader and greater work.[11] He has had a reaching power over the younger poets, in attitude as well as in form; and his "school of thought" will probably leave an incisive print on our poetry.[12]

---

8. Archibald MacLeish, "L'an trentiesme de mon eage" and "The Too-Late Born," *Streets in the Moon* (Boston: Houghton Mifflin, 1926), 14, 19. The second, much anthologized poem was later retitled "The Silent Slain."

9. Major early poems by T. S. Eliot: "The Love Song of J. Alfred Prufrock" (1915), "Gerontion" (1920), and *The Waste Land* (1922).

10. Quotation from T. S. Eliot, "The Hollow Men," in *Collected Poems, 1909–1962* (New York: Harcourt Brace, 1963), 81.

11. Jules Laforgue, nineteenth-century French Symbolist poet.

12. The Southern Agrarians and Fugitive poets singled out Eliot as an influence on their aesthetic and their conservatively "Romantic" attitudes opposing industrial modernity. See Donald Davidson, "A Mirror for Artists" (1930), in Twelve Southerners (Donald Davidson

Robinson Jeffers looks for material to stories of Greek proportions, and for locale to California, a place he uses to set scenes analogous to the country in their size, the furiousness of growth, the violence of struggle, the twin conflicting meanings of generation and death. Most of his long poems (*Tamar, The Women at Point Sur, Cawdor*) have as motives terrifying vehemence, passion bursting through law, marching events, with death and might remaining, swinging silences, looked-to, to be hoped for, to be loved.[13] "The Tower Beyond Tragedy" is one of the most deeply carved and huge poems of the language; and will bear any sort of comparison with *Mourning Becomes Electra*, whose theme Jeffers has used, and will invite contrast with the Greek tragedies.[14] Whether one agrees or not with the reaching to death which is one of the strongest characteristics of Jeffers's work, one is driven from the comfort of a life where forces so blind and so direct are seldom met, drawn by the compulsion of his poetry, shaken into complete subjection to the powers of the poem.

Of lesser influences in the country, people in the long range from Conrad Aiken, John Gould Fletcher, Wallace Stevens, William Carlos Williams, Elinor Wylie, Edna St. Vincent Millay, Allen Tate, Hart Crane, E. E. Cummings, there is a great deal to be said individually, and not too much as a group. The influence of the right wing of these is suffering a steady decline, while the radical members seem to be flourishing under the more or less shaky aegis of magazines like *transition*, *Pagany*, *Left*, and the better-settled *Hound and Horn*.[15] Some separate poems in this group have been far superior to second-rate, but the classification here depends on the general weakness of thought and workmanship. America has been unique in producing an inordinate number of one-poem,

---

et al.), *I'll Take My Stand: The South and the Agrarian Tradition*, 75th anniversary ed. (Baton Rouge: Louisiana State University Press, 2006), 28–60.

13. Robinson Jeffers's early long narrative poems *Tamar* (1924), *The Women at Point Sur* (1927), and *Cawdor* (1928) reimagine ancient myths as set in a seaside environment resembling his adopted home of Big Sur, California.

14. Jeffers's "The Tower Beyond Tragedy," in *The Roan Stallion, Tamar, and Other Poems* (New York: Horace Liveright, 1925), is based on Aeschylus's *Oresteia* trilogy. Rukeyser compares his version to Eugene O'Neill's popular Broadway adaptation *Mourning Becomes Electra* (1931).

15. Rukeyser names many modernist poets and three aesthetically oriented vanguardist little magazines edited by American-born or immigrant writers: Eugene Jolas's *transition* (1927–1938); Richard Johns's *Pagany: A Native Quarterly* (1930–1933); and Lincoln Kirstein and Varian Fry's *Hound and Horn* (1927–1934). *The Left* (1931), edited by George Redfield and Jay Du Von, was a short-lived, Iowa-based socialist magazine featuring radical politics and literature.

anthology, and garden-variety versifiers: one never has to wait very long to find a neatly done piece of work in one's pet magazine.—But this is a digression and has nothing to do with poetry.

Light verse has become a great bouncing baby in a pale-lipped and tragic-eyed family ever since Dorothy Parker got her first profits. The tradition goes back to the Elizabethans (as far as she and Samuel Hoffstein are concerned; the versification—that said with reservations—of Ogden Nash is a different matter).[16] The effectiveness of those earlier and acid Englishmen is one potentiality which modern America does not even claim to have exhausted—and the future of light verse might be something worth speaking about.

Labor poetry turns towards a different solution and represents a different class from any preceding group. At the present time, most current expression is rough artistically (this as distinguished from appropriateness of subject matter) and the clumsiness of expression seems not to be the most intelligent end possible. But this is a relatively new voice, and is almost without spokesmen. Norman MacLeod is its most genuine and promising exponent.[17] We should be able to know, in our time, some of the results of this poetry's evolution. It has already convinced many people that the scope of poetic material should be stretched as far as possible.

The foreign influences on our poetry have been mostly French and English and, with these, we have achieved an American expression which is no more nationally than it is artistically integrated. The trends point in cognate directions, and the divergences sometimes seem more disconnected than they are; but through single and united achievement of the foremost living American poets, there will be made, I think, a contribution of value to world literature.

(*Vassar Miscellany News*, 1932)

---

16. Dorothy Parker, Ogden Nash, and Samuel Hoffstein wrote popular poetry featuring humor, satire, and childhood-invoking rhymes and meters.

17. Poet Norman MacLeod, critically neglected today, was a major figure in New York who connected avant-gardists like William Carlos Williams and leftists like Horace Gregory. In 1939, he helped establish the Poetry Center at Manhattan's 92nd Street YMHA/YWHA, an important institution to Rukeyser's career.

Chapter 20

Long Step Ahead Taken by Gregory in New Epic Poem (1935)

Review of Horace Gregory's Chorus for Survival

The acclaim has all been for Auden, Spender, Day-Lewis, as the finest of the English revolutionary poets.[1] Now we put aside the telescope and look through our eyes: here, in America, Horace Gregory stands in the same relation to us as those three do to the English. With this new book, *Chorus for Survival*, he reaches a more ambitious place in poetry than any American has done since Hart Crane's *The Bridge*.[2] And, where the earlier poem was diffuse, consciously obscure, and shortsighted in its view of society and history, this long joined poem sustains itself in precise, energetic terms, seeing the country, from Emerson's limits, with his "curious scientific dreaming eye":

> Fixed on the landscape ash-tree, elm,
> And rippling grass like water at low tide:
> Trees' branches spars of Salem's ships that rode
> Jewel-edged at sunset into Asia's side

---

1. At the time, British poets W. H. Auden, Stephen Spender, and Cecil Day-Lewis were avowed socialists.
2. Horace Gregory, *Chorus for Survival* (New York: Covici, Friede, 1935), reviewed here, was structurally like Hart Crane's *The Bridge* (1930). Both epics consist of multiple poems, voiced by different lyric subjects at various points in American history.

—to our time's command to:

> Hear Y, the Communist at Union Square,
> Lenin's great hand against the sky, the lips declaiming:
> "Down, metaphysics down; up heart, up fire
> to burn out doubt and fear . . ."

—to a country whose museum is Park Avenue, whose subways and sweepstakes, Wisconsin fields and asphalt city squares are reality.[3]

From its promise of wealth and success in boom times ("*The neon sign 'Success' across our foreheads*") the writer travels, making in his own life the voyage from Wisconsin to New York, across to England, and Ireland, seeing the impossibility of denying country, as T. S. Eliot denies, of denying the past, of making himself anything but a confirming reflection of his country and his time.[4] And, finally, we have the return to this country, to the future after the panic of mock peace and bank crashes:

> *Turn here, my son*
> *(No longer turn to what we were)*
> *Build in the sunlight with strong men*
> *Beyond our barricade:*
> *For even I remember the old war*
> *And death in peace.*[5]

Chorus for Survival opens up a new form for the epic idea. There has been a demand for heroic structure that would be adapted to our life and to revolutionary thought; this book suggests and contains one solution, for its progress, as narrative and as formal scheme, builds up to a resemblance to the old epic that is no longer usable. It answers more than that in its implicit refutation, for example, of Robinson Jeffers's idea of

---

3. First quote and first block quote from Gregory, *Chorus*, part 14, 85. Told from the perspective of transcendentalist philosopher and poet-activist Ralph Waldo Emerson on his 1833 return to the United States from Europe. Second block quote from Gregory, *Chorus*, part 4, 35. Anticipating a labor strike, the narrator tries to reconcile a scientist's cool objectivity with an activist's "fiery" rhetoric.

4. Parenthetical quote from Gregory, *Chorus*, part 19, 122. Gregory's italics. T. S. Eliot became a naturalized British citizen in 1927. His *Waste Land* (1922) is an intertext for Crane's "The Tunnel," from *The Bridge*.

5. Gregory, *Chorus*, part 19, 122. Gregory's italics. In this final section of the epic, the narrator addresses his son and envisions American solidarity in a communist future. Before the quote, Rukeyser mentions the "mock peace" of the False Armistice, the four-days-premature declaration of the Great War's end on November 7, 1919; and the US stock market crash on October 24, 1929, which started the Great Depression.

the dead western world, and the trip westward as a journey to death.[6] It answers, also, the promise of earlier poems, losing the immediacy that was noticed in *Chelsea Rooming House*, enlarging the personal restrictions in *No Retreat*.[7] The poetry will be difficult to classify, with its resources of American and classical history, its wiry, graceful fluency, its political stand so close to the Communist Party, but with a national rather than a sectarian emphasis.

It is crowded with places and people; with pursuits and lyric quiet; musically and ideologically so varied as to sum up in a dynamic, accumulated ending. If we get lost here in the essentially leftist controversy over what is proletarian and what is not, we shall be lost indeed; this poem is written from the point of view of a poet whose writing is his trade, and is in the same class as its author, whose concentration has been on his work, and who has been actively close to the Communist Party in affiliated organizations, clubs, and strike work.

Chorus for Survival is an effort toward permanence that deserves its goal, a work that could be seized upon by the left-wing as one of its real advances in American poetry, in technique, in clarity of thought, in a national adaptation of the principles of revolutionary writers, and in a proud affirmation of the masses of this country:

> *As the map changes, through the cold sky,*
> *Lean from the cockpit, read*
> *The flower of prairie grass in seed*
> *(Though here is war*
>   *my hand points where the body*
> *Leaps its dead, the million poor,*
> *Steel-staved and broken*
>   *and no grave shall hold them*
> *Either in stone or sea; nor urn nor sand,*
> *Skyline of city walls, their monument,*
> *And on this field, lockstep in millions joined,*
> *New world in fire opens where they stand).*[8]

(Daily Worker, 1935)

---

6. Robinson Jeffers's misanthropic and pessimistic narrative long poems influenced Rukeyser. See Muriel Rukeyser, "Modern Trends: American Poetry," in this volume.

7. Gregory's first two collections, *Chelsea Rooming House* (1930) and *No Retreat* (1933).

8. Gregory, *Chorus*, part 19, 126. Gregory's italics.

CHAPTER 21

In a Speaking Voice (1939)
Review of Robert Frost's Collected Poems

Soon after he started to publish, in 1912, it was evident that Frost was to have a curative effect on the speech of poetry. A special effect. From the beginning, he said nothing that did not placate and soothe and reconcile. All the disturbances were natural, nothing was said that could not be stated without raising the voice. Patience and resistance and the pains of responsibility temper his lines, in lyric, short dramatic piece, or narrative, with his neighborhood stamped on all his work. Frost stands now, in this latest collection of his poems, as a mean in the measure, with no effort to rake up to consciousness, or to impose a unity of meaning from above; he stands at the level of articulation into conversation.[1] Average, if you like, in tone; reliable in the solid garden way, plus its articulation, so that the constant and delightful play of a combining charm is on the surface. He makes a place his own; coming from California to New England, he took over as unmistakably as Jeffers, traveling opposite, took over the Coast; but without the great expanded images, the stridings, the toppled forests and families and the victimized love.[2] Here is photography

---

1. Review of Robert Frost, *Collected Poems* (New York: Henry Holt, 1939).
2. Born in Allegheny, Pennsylvania, Robinson Jeffers wrote about his adopted home in Big Sur, California. Frost was born in San Francisco.

of the effects of snow and heat, sorrow, exuberance *to a point*, sun in the pines, on the bushes, lives turning slowly as leaves under warmth, householders living day-to-day; a realism of the senses, Frost gives us, blueprints of that countryside. New England, which he came to young, and claimed; the wild, neat states of exaggerated seasons.

There is not much development in over four hundred pages. There is reworking and turning over, and one looks naturally to farm comparisons. The first book has the voice already, and much of the later craft, in "Storm Fear," "October," "A Tuft of Flowers," "Mowing."[3] But the language is stilted; one questions how it could ever have appeared honest: "and lo," "fay or elf," "abide," "aloof," "zephyr," "limns," "The languor of it and the dreaming fond."[4] What saves the book and marks it is its flatness, inflection of casual speech, scapes laid on stroke by stroke:

> The crows above the forest call;
> To-morrow they may form and go.

and

> When the wind works against us in the dark,
> And pelts with snow
> The lower chamber window on the east . . .[5]

The next book, the successful *North of Boston*, which had its English furore and set Frost's standard, contains sixteen of the most sufficient, local, and convincing poems he has done. The list begins: "Mending Wall," "The Death of the Hired Man," "The Mountain," "A Hundred Collars," "Home Burial" . . .[6] If you open the book and read straight through, it is during these poems that you get taken up, catch the rules of conversation and attitude, and see the limitations the man has set himself. He comes through now, as a mild man to orient himself by the most permanent facts he can find: season force, constants in life and work and death to see him through his responsibilities. All of these poems, with three exceptions, are narrative, and dramatic, and conversation-pieces; the three are "After Apple-Picking," one of the

---

3. Poems from Frost's first collection, *A Boy's Will* (1913).
4. Outmoded words and phrases from Frost's *A Boy's Will*: "and lo" ("Reluctance," in *Collected Poems*, 43); "fay or elf" ("Mowing," in *Collected Poems*, 25); "abide" and "aloof" ("A Dream Pang," in *Collected Poems*, 22); "zephyr" and "The languor of it and the dreaming fond" ("My Butterfly," in *Collected Poems*, 42); "limns" ("The Trial by Existence," in *Collected Poems*, 29).
5. Frost, "October" and "Storm Fear," in *Collected Poems*, 40, 13.
6. Titles of the opening sequence of Frost's second collection, *North of Boston* (1914).

most beautiful poems Frost has ever written, "The Wood-Pile," and the final lyric.[7] The stories are lifelike, typical, moving against static backgrounds: the two startled people confronted by a face at the dark house; the descendants of Starks, met at a rainy reunion; the house with a room-size cage for the insane uncle; the clenched father who had dug his child's grave and come into the kitchen for weather-gossip; the collector drinking in a shared hotel room—exposing their lives in the calm monologue that Frost makes the world speak.[8]

The third book, *Mountain Interval*, has the short uneven poems whose top level is struck in "The Hill Wife," "Birches," and "The Bonfire."[9] England was put behind, and Frost was living in New Hampshire, famous, after the foreign success. Twenty years of obscurity and inability to get published were over. It seems now, from the outside and much later, that here was a place for choice. There was no turn; *Mountain Interval* was a variation on the one established theme; and *New Hampshire*, published seven years later, summed up all the previous work, taking the three books along together, repeating the early words with more affection, greater intimacy, a finer precision of the senses.[10] From the title-poem, through "Fire and Ice," and "Good-Bye and Keep Cold," and "Gathering Leaves," the level comes up in sureness of handling. *West-Running Brook*, published in 1928, and *A Further Range*, which appeared in 1936, take Frost back into the compact lyric, becoming more and more didactic, sorrowful, affectionate, and cross.[11]

Frost has his theme. He was recognizable from the beginning, and he never chose again. He stokes and banks, and gauges the fires; there is little work of enduring intensity. Fancy and imagination are very close in all his work; when the description is clean, striking the senses immediately, a lasting impression is made; but there is a double exposure, and behind the picture is a quiet and in many ways a desperate man, keeping his grip on his poems, but forcing them to be distal to his own much more intense problems and choices. The poems are end-products, and Frost has contempt for "poets / Who fall all over each other to

---

7. The volume's last poem is "Good Hours."
8. In the order mentioned, Rukeyser references Frost, "The Fear," "The Generations of Men," "A Servant to Servants," "Home Burial," and "A Hundred Collars," in *Collected Poems*, 112–116, 94–102, 82–87, 69–73, and 61–68.
9. Frost's third collection, *Mountain Interval* (1916).
10. Frost's fourth collection, *New Hampshire: A Poem with Notes and Grace Notes* (1923).
11. Frost's fifth and sixth major collections. He also published chapbooks during this period.

bring soil / And even subsoil and hardpan to market."[12] Markets are what he hates, but he has his product, and is at his counter; and when he chooses to be a plain New Hampshire farmer, in answer to the literary choice, "Choose you which you will be—a prude, or puke, / Mewling and puking in the public arms," he still does not choose to farm.[13] His obligation as poet has kept him at his self-controls, until one wonders whether he has not turned himself out a self-controlled prude, a self-controlled puke, by not choosing either of them, but choosing self-control. He falls into fears he says he has escaped. He writes, "I never dared be radical when young / For fear it would make me conservative when old."[14] And is conservative. Look, here is the mild man, quick to see, quick to love glints and delicacies, and sturdiness and thrift. He has no dependence on a shabby personal legend, none of the city shabbiness. He walks around an object, delimiting it, catching the surface well, doing this at the normal speed of walking and talking; not at the speed of the imagination, not seizing hold nor letting go fast.[15] This is not poetry that strikes immediately at invention and the spirit; it is delimiting, and at the end one knows the object in area and in impact on the senses; but whatever insight there is comes as recognition.

Frost took a country that he came to very young, and received it fresh on himself. It was lucky that he was not born in New England; he chose his home. He chose his work; caring enough for college to leave Dartmouth and return to Harvard, caring enough for academic standards and the classic, as Untermeyer points out in *Modern American Poetry*'s useful introduction to Frost, to get his best marks in Greek, and leaving it all behind in his work—except, perhaps, for the true bucolic flavor, which becomes New England flavor of apple and blueberry, snow and granite face—traveling, having his family, teaching, he cuts all of this out of his life in poetry, gripping hard for faith to New England simples.[16] With this passage of time, we see that he has the colors and sharp tastes of his countryside, and remember startled how he used to be accused of being colorless. But the strain and violence and sharp

---

12. Frost, "Build Soil: A Political Pastoral," in *Collected Poems*, 426. A previously uncollected dramatic poem from 1932, whose two speakers, Tityrus and Meliboeus, debate the relationship between socialism, agriculture, and poetry.
13. Frost, "New Hampshire," in *Collected Poems*, 210.
14. Frost, "Precaution" from "Ten Mills," in *Collected Poems*, 407.
15. See Muriel Rukeyser, "The Speed of the Image," in this volume.
16. See Louis Untermeyer, headnote for Robert Frost, in *Modern American Poetry*, 2nd ed., ed. Untermeyer (New York: Harcourt Brace, 1921), 174–177.

contrasts have been controlled out of his poems. They are in his country, and one sees them in his rejections; he has stayed away from them. He has his responsibility, he is firm in his craft, with a steady checking influence on the language of American poetry, in the line of recorded speech that includes Frost, Robinson, Masters.[17] Of the three, Frost evades most. He comes to the edge: read "The Bonfire," and "A Servant to Servants," and "Two Witches"—he almost goes over the edge. One need not require a line of development from Frost, any more than from Fearing—these are people working and always working with one implement.[18] But Frost has developed through certain apprehensions, with a certain nervousness. One thinks of Yeats, his generous full developing mind.[19] Frost stays close, and guards. He is a village-spirit, deep in village-life. I started to reread many of these poems (and they should be dated, and they should have an index) believing that I admired them and that they were not enough what I needed to hear to let me like them.[20] But as I read, I knew they were near, I did like them too; I was occupied by their warmth and mocking and turning, by the neat perception of physical detail, strict enough to let one smell these trees and animals, I saw that glare on snow. I wanted more, by then. Frost has articulated much that was not spoken for. Early in life, he drew his circle around himself, and plainly said, *I will deal with this*. The attitude does not come through as self-control, but as a rigid preconception of life. He wants his poem to have "the wonder of unexpected supply"; he says, "it begins in delight and ends in wisdom" in his note to this book, "The Figure a Poem Makes."[21] He cultivates his own garden, grouping with art so that everything there may be discussed in the same tone of voice. Meet him on these his own terms, and there is fine work, rewarding place-love, folk-love, solemn or gay recognitions. They are the recognitions of a man desperately determined that this is really all there is, and that this will be enough. It is not all, and it is not enough.

(*Poetry: A Magazine of Verse*, 1939)

---

17. Turn-of-the-century poets Edwin Arlington Robinson, known for many poems set in the fictive Maine community Tilbury Town (1896-1932), and Edgar Lee Masters, a midwesterner known for his *Spoon River Anthology* (1915).

18. Kenneth Fearing, leftist anti-fascist poet and friend of Rukeyser whose political poetry uses dark humor.

19. William Butler Yeats, nationalist Irish modernist who supported Home Rule and wrote of Irish traditions and myth.

20. Frost's *Collected Poems* does not date or index the poems.

21. Frost, "The Figure a Poem Makes," preface to *Collected Poems*, n.p.

CHAPTER 22

The Classic Ground (1941)
Review of Marya Zaturenska's The Listening Landscape

With this third book of poems, Marya Zaturenska has established a direction which was traceable in the difference between *Cold Morning Sky* and *Threshold and Hearth*.[1] In those earlier volumes, the lyric form she has made her home was developing: lucid and musical, and obliquely lit by the application of formal symbols to complex emotion. Those books were isolated in a strange way, although they won prizes. Markedly traditional on the surface, they issued at a distance from the one traditional parcel of writers in the country, who were occupied in fighting every other approach tooth and claw. Their dark and intricate under-content shut them off from the other lyrics that were being written to lie on the surface, in which form and content outdid themselves to be at rest and unity. These other lyrics accepted conventional treatments, and immediately surrendered themselves to conventional thought and emotion, in the pre-surrender which is coming to be an emblem of these times. Before the battle, nations give themselves up; before the censorship, writers impose their own restrictions on their spirits; and in poetry, this has its reflections and some-

---

1. *Threshold and Hearth* (1934) and *Cold Morning Sky* (1937) were the first two collections by Marya Zaturenska, a Russian immigrant and Horace Gregory's wife.

times its predictions, in a contemporary return to formalism before there is any need for its disguises.

To Marya Zaturenska, the form of her work has not arrived as a compromise or a late choice: *The Listening Landscape* carries on the style of ten years ago in what may now be seen as an even growth. This poetry is extremely deceptive, and, I believe, has not been clearly read. Here we have lyrics sealed in their transparency, through which may be seen the amazing and troubled images of the world. Readers have been confused through their misunderstanding of the lyric itself, and I suppose the quarrel about form and content has thrown off many readers. Because here there is a double process going on. Form has been unified with content, and at the same time another strain has been imposed; under the restrictions of the unity, the image struggles to be freed again. The same thing happens here with the symbols themselves. We read in these poems rose, bough, and moon, petal, and sea; but under them the contemporary stress:

> Slowly the god arises from sleep, the unsaving spear in his hand,
> Awaits the assault of the beast, the wail of the *Magna Mater*,
> Reechoing through the cedars.[2]

And this, the ending of "St. Dorothy Presents the Fruit and Flowers of Paradise":

> ... On that vast orchard hurled,
> The sunbursts and the longings of the world!
> You who have witnessed her death, denied her immortality,
> Draw nearer, see revealed that downrushing, living sea,
> Toward which our blood tides move; furtive, sullen slow,
> Till revelation quickens our sight, and the bronze trumpets blow.[3]

Another reason for the misplacement of these poems has been the range of reference in them. *The Listening Landscape* draws on Hans Christian Andersen, Poussin, Ryder (in the fine lines of "Forest of Arden"), Linnaeus, and Kafka, classical mythology and the two generations of

---

2. Marya Zaturenska, "Watchers in the Sacred Wood," in *The Listening Landscape* (New York: Macmillan, 1941), 21.
3. Zaturenska, "St. Dorothy Presents the Fruit and Flowers of Paradise," in *Listening*, 68. Much of the collection is inspired by Romantic writer Dorothy Wordsworth's letters and diaries.

the war through which we are going.[4] But, again, the sources feed the form; the meanings are renewed. "Head of Medusa" is a profoundly disturbing version of the myth; Perseus arrives ("foe or deliverer?") under a sexual mask, as a murderer whose act is the only possible deliverance.[5] In "Child in the Crystal" the image of the infant Time, which so seldom reaches us now except in the debased form of a cheap magazine cover for the New Year issue, is again able to carry lines like these:

> Thy Sire is manifest through fire, but thou in the fire's light,
> Thy great descent is made clear in the dews and stars of the night,
> Thy beauty brief and dear,
> Quicksilver in water, ecstasy pointing to dark, in rust and smoke.[6]

This range and its compression are another indication of the way in which the poet's personality has been resolved, as the creative strain in the form is an indication. Here is a woman who has imposed upon a wide critical attitude and a background of learning the composure and strict flexibility of the lyric form, submitting constantly to its restrictions, but injecting more and more, as her work goes further, the color and meaning that we have falsely learned to associate with experimental work.

In this book, she has included several poems that are so much broader in scope that I imagine critics who wish to pigeonhole her in one classification will overlook them altogether. But such poems as "Century of Athletes" and "The Unsepulchred" and the extremely beautiful and suggestive sequence "Leaves from the Book of Dorothy Wordsworth" make it plain that Marya Zaturenska is choosing her limitations.[7] They are not being forced upon her, as they are upon some of the poets who are, on the surface, experimental. The Dorothy Wordsworth poems invoke Coleridge:

> Not as when I saw him at the last,
> The grotesque, dropsical body worn with sick desires,

---

4. Zaturenska alludes or dedicates poems to children's writer Hans Christian Andersen ("Quiet Countries; The World Hans Christian Andersen," in *Listening*, 11–12); painters Nicolas Poussin ("Landscape After Poussin," in *Listening*, 15) and Albert Pinkham Ryder ("Forest of Arden," in *Listening*, 18); botanist Carl Linnaeus ("Summer to Lapland," in *Listening*, 84–85); and modernist Franz Kafka ("Silence and the Wayfarer" and "Century of Athletes," in *Listening*, 44–45, 79–81).

5. Zaturenska, "Head of Medusa," in *Listening*, 33.

6. Zaturenska, "Child in the Crystal," in *Listening*, 14.

7. Zaturenska, "Century of Athletes," "The Unsepulchred 1914–1918," and "Leaves from the Book of Dorothy Wordsworth," in *Listening*, 79–81, 82–83, 52–58.

> The broken will, the eyes
> Burning with fitful fires,
> But as in youth we met . . .

—and the loved brother:

> Wandering through summer fields watching the gypsies roam
> Through moorland wind;
> Each day a renewal of wonder, each day the growing
> Of a checked passion . . .

—and the moorlands, the islands, the poems, the approaching destruction in madness, in a unique and illuminating treatment of that neglected life.[8]

Distinct and terrible, the images of this time find a classic reflection, giving them distance and the clarity of grace and wisdom, that clarity which life has not yet given them. I hope this book will be read for what it is. I hope for the book that it may be seen in its full darkness and sunlight; seen against an age which Marya Zaturenska names:

> Century of athletes where the young men run
> To action in a noisy wrestling ring,
> All intellectual passion cast away
> In that barbaric ecstasy of hate . . .

—and for which she makes a wish which summarizes her work:

> When fountains of despair run dry, when chance,
> War, ruin, misery, their cycles round
> Men turn again to music, sun, and dance,
> The burning roses on the classic ground.[9]

(Decision, 1941)

---

8. Zaturenska, "Coleridge" and "First Memories" from "Leaves from the Book of Dorothy Wordsworth," in *Listening*, 55, 53.

9. Zaturenska, "Century of Athletes" and "The Golden Rose," in *Listening*, 79, 86.

Chapter 23

Nearer to the Well-Spring (1943)

Review of Rainer Maria Rilke's Sonnets to Orpheus, *translated by M. D. Herter Norton*

> [...] They [*Sonnets to Orpheus*] are, as could not be otherwise, of the same "birth" as the *Elegies*, and their sudden coming up, without my willing it, in association with a girl who had died young, moves them still nearer to the well-spring of their origin; this association is one more connection towards the center of *that* realm the depth and influence of which we, everywhere unboundaried, share with the dead and with those to come...
>
> —Letter from Rilke to Witold von Hulewicz, November 13, 1925

On February 5, 1922, the first of the two sequences of *Sonnets to Orpheus* was finished, and Rilke sent them to the mother of the dead girl, Vera Knoop. He had entered into the death of this young dancer. Learning of the details of her death at the time of his daughter's marriage; reading Valéry's *L'Ame et la danse*, with its quotation from Socrates speaking of the dance as pure metamorphosis, he remembered this dancer as a nameless flower, pausing as if she were being cast in bronze, at last entering the hopelessly open portal—the unconscious Eurydice, dead and shadow, news of whose death was the news which made these poems fall in a stream.[1] Scatterings of the *Duino Elegies*, they were written in two marvelous bursts of sonnets during the same days

---

Rukeyser's epigraph, here abbreviated, is from Rainer Maria Rilke, letter to Witold von Hulewicz, November 13, 1925, trans. J. B. Leishman, qtd. in M. D. Herter Norton's "Notes," in Rainer Maria Rilke, *Sonnets to Orpheus*, trans. Norton (New York: W. W. Norton, 1942), 132. Rilke's emphases. All Muriel Rukeyser's quotations are from this edition. For the full letter, see Rainer Maria Rilke, *Letters of Rainer Maria Rilke, 1910–1926*, trans. Jane Bannard Greene and M. D. Herter Norton (New York: W. W. Norton, 1948), 372–376.

1. Paul Valéry's *L'Ame et la danse* (Dance and the Soul, 1921) is a prose conversation between Greek philosopher Socrates and his disciples Eryximachus and Phaedrus.

as the arrival of the *Elegies*.² The first sequence, of twenty-six, was written after Rilke's letters had complained continually of his inability to concentrate, because of the effect of the war. The last of these complaints occur in two letters written on January 28, 1922. From February 2 to February 5, the twenty-five sonnets were written—hardly written, almost spoken, among the long and powerful music of the *Elegies*, which were now also being finished. And, in another burst, from February 12 to February 20, the second sequence, of twenty-nine sonnets, was done.

In a great crisis, at Muzot, this book was written down. In the grip of this crisis, Rilke again broke through his isolation. Speaking in the *Elegies* for angels in their full height and menace, he speaks here for the root, the shadow, the transience, for the song which visits death, visits the gleaming earth, can pass only as song, only as Orpheus. For Eurydice, pure and unconscious, is human to the end, even in afterlife. But the poet, the wound, Rilke-Orpheus, rent and scattered, cannot be destroyed; in the end, he can only be heard, heard everywhere.

There is little use in tracing the poems and myths that echo through these sonnets; both Mrs. Norton's and Leishman's notes, as well as Rilke's letters, do that for us.³ Valéry's dead are here—the shadowy people at the roots of trees, their lost words, their unique selves—the dead of *Le Cimetière marin* are close to Rilke's dead, as the dead of the Greek ancestors, dormant and fluid, in a fruit, a dance, a mirror, a trace of earth.⁴

> But to us existence is still enchanted; at a hundred
> points it is origin still.⁵

In love, in change, in Orpheus singing. Rilke saying it, in the third sonnet:

> Song, as you teach it, is not desire,
> not suing for something yet in the end attained;
> song is existence. Easy for the god.
> But when do we *exist*? [. . .]⁶

---

2. Rilke's *Duino Elegies* (1923) provided Rukeyser the model for her *Elegies* (1939-1949, in *CP*, 297-330). Each project consists of ten poems written over a decade. Just as Rilke had written *Sonnets to Orpheus* (1922) when completing *Duino Elegies*, Rukeyser composed her long poem "Orpheus" (1949), in *CP*, 285-296, while finishing her *Elegies*.

3. In 1936, J. B. Leishman published the first English-language translation of Rilke's *Sonnets to Orpheus* with Leonard and Virginia Woolf's Hogarth Press.

4. Paul Valéry, *Le Cimetière marin* (The Graveyard by the Sea, 1920).

5. Rilke, "Sonnet 10," from "Second Part," in *Sonnets to Orpheus*, 89.

6. Rilke, "Sonnet 3," from "First Part," in *Sonnets to Orpheus*, 21. Rilke's emphasis. Quotation abbreviated; Rukeyser cites the entire poem.

All the pieces of his fear, all the withdrawals, are here; but in this book, since the object is acknowledged dead, there is no threat; and since he as poet is all-powerful, death may be visited and seen as origin. The early magic is here, with its strong symbols, its cries, and the bread and milk of its mysteries. "Nothing can harm for him the valid symbol," says a line near the end of the sixth sonnet, and the seventh begins in the familiar tone, "Praising, that's it!"[7] That Rilkean praise which must arrive with all lament; lament, which moves in the world of praising, and which, together with praising, can sing the image.

The richness of these sonnets is very great, even in translation.

> No matter if the farmer works and worries,
> where the seed is turning into summer
> he never reaches. The earth *bestows*.[8]

This gesture of gift and blessing is balanced by the warning of: "not till a pure whither / outweighs boyish pride / of growing machines" will "one who had neared the distances / *be* his lone flight's attaining."[9] But from the line "Killing is a form of wandering sorrow" to "the head and the lyre" of Orpheus killed, to the "O come and go" of the dancer, is a succession of movement and image.[10] This sequence must be found all at once and taken completely, in its imagery. Here is the long unfolding of a single image-cluster, transformed and killed and taken up again, sustained by Rilke through wartime. Analogies of isolation are here, and the convalescent breathing of a poet who has come through war to release and poetry again. Much of that breath is lost in translation; Mrs. Norton says disarmingly in her Foreword that she still believes that "the closest adherence to the poetry itself is best achieved through the most literal possible rendering of word, phrase, image, far as the result may prove to remain from the final perfection . . ." and I have printed two sonnets here, in full, attempting in a short space to illustrate this definition.[11] Mrs. Norton does not speak of music.[12]

---

    7. Rilke, "Sonnet 6" and "Sonnet 7," from "First Part," in *Sonnets to Orpheus*, 27, 29.
    8. Rilke, "Sonnet 12," from "First Part," in *Sonnets to Orpheus*, 39. Rilke's emphasis. Quotation abbreviated.
    9. Rilke, "Sonnet 23," from "First Part," in *Sonnets to Orpheus*, 61. Rilke's emphasis. Quotation abbreviated.
    10. Rilke, "Sonnet 11," "Sonnet 26," and "Sonnet 28" from "Second Part," in *Sonnets to Orpheus*, 91, 121, 125.
    11. Norton, foreword to Rilke, *Sonnets to Orpheus*, 10. Rukeyser's transcription of full sonnets not reproduced in this edition.
    12. See Muriel Rukeyser, "The Music of Translation," in this volume.

Rilke's definition of religion, as "a direction of the heart," surely applies to poetry; and a "literal rendering" can as surely ignore the direction of a poem as a statement about the "facts" of war can ignore the issues of the war, when "facts" and "literalness" depend on relationship.[13] One wishes, then, for a third poem, after the original and the literal translation—an equivalent poem, an English poem.

But Mrs. Norton is making an architectural gift to us of Rilke, book by book. Gift by gift, he increases, even when his faults and softness increase.

(*Kenyon Review*, 1943)

---

13. Religion "is not knowledge, not content of feeling [. . .], it is not duty and not renunciation, it is not restriction: but in the infinite extent of the universe it is a direction of the heart." Rilke, letter to Ilse Blumenthal-Weiss, December 28, 1921, in Rilke, *Letters*, 277. In her second independent clause, Rukeyser reprises but misquotes Norton's foreword.

CHAPTER 24

A Simple Theme (1949)

Review of Charlotte Marletto's Jewel of Our Longing

                      The difficulty of dealing, in art, with the most common experiences shows itself in the thinness of our literature of childhood. Here is your universality, here is your common denominator, and the complexity of meanings, and the symbols of growth, promise, consciousness. Where are the children? In Mark Twain, in Booth Tarkington, in Thomas Wolfe, in William Carlos Williams, in Henry Roth, in Carson McCullers, in Dickens; take up the list.[1] And in poetry? In de la Mare?[2] In Blake they are; and I saw the children standing before them at the Blake show, standing heads thrown back, hands clasped behind them, staring up at the children and the angels and at Job.[3] But to speak of our own time. The poetry of childhood scarcely exists.

---

    1. Novels about infancy, childhood, and adolescence: Mark Twain's *The Adventures of Tom Sawyer* (1876) and *The Adventures of Huckleberry Finn* (1884); Thomas Wolfe's *Look Homeward, Angel* (1929); Booth Tarkington's *Penrod* (1914); William Carlos Williams's *White Mule* (1937); Henry Roth's *Call It Sleep* (1934); Carson McCullers's *The Member of the Wedding* (1946); and Charles Dickens's *Oliver Twist* (1837–1839), *David Copperfield* (1849–1850), *Great Expectations* (1860–1861), and others.

    2. British author Walter de la Mare wrote stories and poetry for children, including *Songs of Childhood* (1902).

    3. In *Songs of Innocence* (1789) and elsewhere, Romantic poet William Blake drew on images of childhood. Rukeyser references an exhibit of Blake's illuminated poetry volumes

There is no poetry of birth in the literature that reaches us. In our own time, we can count the poems on our fingers; there is a great blank behind us, in our classic and religious literature. There we might expect to find the clues to human process and common experience. In our religious literature, birth is not faced until the moment after: we are given the scene with the kings and the animals and Joseph, Mary holding the newborn; the Pharaoh's daughter discovers the newborn.[4] I cannot think of a scene of birth (and we edit out the little children nowadays) in Greek drama, or all the way up to Gargantua; of any representation in graphic art other than the tribal statues, African, Mexican, Polynesian.[5] I cannot think of anything in films, or in the literature that tries to give us the stream of consciousness; or in music. I cannot think of anything in Western poetry, other than formal Nativity odes, until this century. I may be mistaken here, and I shall be glad to know of the existence of any poems of birth or pregnancy. But it seems to me that there is a great lack, one that has scarcely been noticed. Havelock Ellis speaks of the necessity for documents concerning the psychic state during pregnancy; he refers to one novel which he says is autobiographical, although he does not tell us its name.[6] I think offhand of another, Enid Bagnold's *Door of Life*; and I think of the poems of Anne Ridler, and of Genevieve Taggard and Marie Welch; and the lines in Spender and Edith Sitwell and Gabriela Mistral.[7]

This is an entire area of experience which has not reached poetry. And it should hardly be necessary to say that this is a universal, and at the same time a scene one hardly ever sees in this civilization. How many of you have ever seen a birth, or have been conscious while you gave birth? I look at my line about birth's being a universal; one is on

---

at Manhattan's Morgan Library & Museum, whose extensive Blake holdings include his *Book of Job* (1826).

4. Rukeyser refers to Christ's Nativity and infant Moses's discovery by Thermouthis.

5. Gargantua, title character from French Renaissance writer François Rabelais's *Gargantua and Pantagruel* (c. 1532–1564), a fantasy pentalogy about giants.

6. Havelock Ellis, British pioneer of sexology and progressive social reforms related to gender and sexuality. Contrary to Rukeyser's claim, in a footnote Ellis does name the volume as Ellis Meredith's *Heart of My Heart* (1904), "a seemingly autobiographical account of a pregnant woman's emotions and ideas." Havelock Ellis, *Studies in the Psychology of Sex*, vol. 5: *Erotic Symbolism, The Mechanism of Detumenescence, The Psychic State in Pregnancy* (Philadelphia: F. A. Davis, 1906), 229, note 4.

7. Enid Bagnold, *The Door of Life* (1938). Undetermined poems by most of the other figures mentioned, including Stephen Spender. On Anne Ridler's poem, see note 11 below.

the edge of the absurd the minute one tries to relate the experience of birth to the silence about it in poetry. But why is an absurdity felt here?

And why is there a silence?

In the books about the artist, and I have Otto Rank's *Art and Artist* before me, there is absolutely no allowance made for the possibility of the woman artist.[8] And in the crop of recent books about women (with the exception of *Woman and Music*) the possibility of dealing with the experience of parturition (even the vocabulary is not fully made, along with the sexual terms of women) is simply not there.[9] In the index to Rank, you will find as neighboring listings: "Woman as Muse," "Womb-Symbolism." Apart from its comic value, the listing of these concepts badly needs addition and adjustment for women. But *that is all there is.* And we go on to the birth-trauma.[10]

Now birth as trauma has an important repressive role in our art—our literature, in particular. Few of the women writing poetry have made more than a beginning in writing about birth. There is exceptional difficulty in giving form to so crucial a group of meanings and experiences. And the young men in poetry seem, for the great part, to suffer so from the fear of birth that we have a tabu deep enough in our culture to keep us even from speaking about it as a tabu.

I do not like to speak about poetry according to subject. I feel that our entire current criticism is on the wrong track, here, that the criticism of poetry has dealt either with subject or with a set of static terms. It could more fruitfully, I believe, speak of relationship and then go on in terms of dynamics. The poetry of birth will have to be one of relationship. Perhaps this is one of the next steps, for us.

Anne Ridler says, in "For A Child Expected," "The world flowed in." It is the poetry of the world flowing in, and of "what we began / Is now its own," which will make a beginning.[11] I heard a literary young man say, "In pregnancy a woman is all self-love; she is in a bath of narcissism." You can see what is at work there. You can see it in a hundred references, in a hundred books dealing with death. There is a terrible fear

---

8. Psychoanalyst Otto Rank's *Art and Artist: Creative Urge and Personality Development* (1932). On Rank, also see Muriel Rukeyser, "Many Keys," in this volume.

9. No volume titled *Woman and Music* published in the 1940s has been located.

10. Rank theorized that humans, from birth, create meaning out of their longing to recapture a lost unity. See Otto Rank, *The Trauma of Birth* (1924; reis., New York: Routledge, 2014).

11. Anne Ridler, "For a Child Expected," in *A Dream Observed and Other Poems* (London: Poetry Society, 1941), 16.

of birth abroad. It is close to the fear of poetry; and I do not know how closely it is connected with the agonies of our wars and with the daily crushing of the fiery life. I know that there are strong bonds here; and the matter before me, the poetry of birth, seems to me to be one clue.

This book, *Jewel of Our Longing*, is another attempt to deal with birth.[12] Charlotte Marletto uses the water-images to which one turns, during pregnancy, and often she comes close to the characteristic motion of that state, the rocking between selflessness and self that is the answer to my literary young man. She says,

> [...] a convergence of flesh
> or that I walking outside of body
> have no name...

and, in the poem called "Conception," "I am shed down the wind / circling upon Self."[13] She tries, again and again, for the images of fusion and the terms that will describe the body of pregnancy, which seems almost unspecialized, as one thinks one's body in infancy might have been, seeing with the whole body, tasting with the whole body. This truth, we come to know scientifically, is a truth of the person. The mind is the acting man, it has been said, and we may go on with that.

These poems, however, are frustrated almost always by the inadequate attempt to make a form to communicate pregnancy and its emotions. The word-combining is not careful; and the music is thrown away. It is so easy, and fatal, in coming to a subject which frightens so many people, to fall into autobiographical sentimentality and "expression," without having given the emotion to the reader. There is also an anatomical fallacy in these poems, which are written in an overdecorated "modern" idiom with all its errors. Lips are rivers fingering; there is "lip-sculptured foam / bright-braceleted once more by sun."[14] The traps are all illustrated here: we have the "cervix-hall," "cerebral halls," "orgastic waves," "cephalic shores," and the wild line, "shocking his

---

12. Charlotte Marletto, *Jewel of Our Longing* (West Los Angeles: Wagon & Star Press, 1948). In a contributor's note to an issue of *Voices: A Quarterly of Poetry* (Spring 1944, 62), Marletto is described as a "graduate nurse" living in California. This was her only collection, published one year after the birth of Rukeyser's son.

13. Marletto, "This Wheeling Seed" and "I Who Am Amen," in *Jewel*, 28, 63. Marletto's final ellipsis in "This Wheeling Seed." The second quoted poem is not titled "Conception" but instead contains three sections glossed as "Conception," "Gestation," and "Parturition."

14. Allusion to Marletto, "Millefiori," in *Jewel*, 9: "lips all running rivers / fingering secret coves beneath the stone." Quote from Marletto, "Goddess Forever Green," in *Jewel*, 17.

schizospheres together."[15] But there are moments in broken phrases, when Charlotte Marletto forgets the details of anatomy and sentiment, and says, "Flesh my intercessor," and speaks of the "totem of sense" and the "apocryphal animals."[16] Page after page is marred, made fancy, ruined and in bad taste; but all of this work is here to do, here is the unborn as Muse, all these poems are to be made,

> this the season of mockingbird
> singing poignant variations
> on a simple theme . . .[17]

(Poetry: A Magazine of Verse, 1949)

---

15. All quotes from Marletto: "cervix-hall" from "Being Mortal," in *Jewel,* 20; "cerebral halls" from "This Asterisk on Flesh," in *Jewel,* 22; "orgastic waves" and "cephalic shores" from "Invasion of Symbols," in *Jewel,* 29; "shocking his schizopheres together" from "The Circle of Aleph and Zaleth," in *Jewel,* 25.

16. First quote from Marletto, "As Thorned Hunger," in *Jewel,* 46. Last two quoted phrases from Marletto, "Invasion of Symbols," in *Jewel,* 29.

17. Marletto, "Lotus Song," in *Jewel,* 7. Marletto's ellipsis.

Chapter 25

A Lorca Evening (1951)

Lorca's theatre is surrounded, as the house of Bernarda Alba is surrounded, with heat and starvation, the sexual cries of summer, and the wildness of animals, meaning the heart of man.[1] Even when you stand among the whitewashed walls of a scene, the songs are outside. When the reapers go past, the hoarseness and the repetition should drive the audience mad, as they drive mad five young girls locked in a house of mourning, an airless house, a house without a man. The slashing of grain in the fields, the hot sounds of the cicadas rubbing their legs together—or whatever they do—are in these plays, as clearly as the rose of which María says, in *Yerma*,

---

   1. Rukeyser prepared this originally untitled talk for the Lorca Memorial, a private event held at Manhattan's 92nd Street YMHA/YWHA on February 1, 1951, to celebrate Spanish modernist poet and playwright Federico García Lorca, who was murdered by fascist paramilitary in 1936. The event featured presentations by Rukeyser and three other speakers, plus Katina Paxinou's planned performance of a scene from Lorca's final play, *The House of Bernarda Alba*. See Poetry Center (New York), Lorca Memorial Program (privately printed, 1951), LC II:19. Holo. note on draft indicates Rukeyser wrote this talk to give in Paxinou's absence. She probably had been invited to give a different talk, about the Spaniard's 1930 visit to Rukeyser's alma mater. An outline is archived with this manuscript and a translation of Lorca's Vassar lecture on *duende*. See Muriel Rukeyser, Notes on Lorca at Vassar, unpublished ts outline, with unpublished ts translation of Federico García Lorca's Vassar lecture on *duende*, 5 ts (carbon) pp., n.d. [1951], LC I:43.

CHAPTER 25

> Lord, make blossom the rose,
> leave not my rose in shadow.[2]

The theatre is close to all Mediterranean theatre. Lorca's theatre, like the Greek theatre—upon which, again and again, he builds—celebrates the holy powers which cannot be denied. The holy powers of life, whose denial means every time doom coming down like lightning on a dark-green sky. Many of his people—the dried-up man who will not give Yerma her child, the woman Bernarda Alba whose torrent of domination rains down on the family—do deny these powers. They act against life, the outside life and the life of the house. And then the blood begins, or the madness, the emptiness which leaves Bernarda in her house, calling among the silence, "Silence! Silence!"[3]

Lorca's theatre is close to the classic theatre of Greece in form as well as in theme. The daughters, the maid of Bernarda Alba, do more than serve the purpose of the Greek chorus. They are the chorus and leader.[4] The passion and clarity of that theatre is in Lorca's scenes, a combination of purity and violence which emerges, not as brutality—recent handling of Greek themes has translated everything into brutality and cruelty—but as form. A control and sense of law in which denial and repression are the worst violence, and can lead only to doom.

This law, which is natural and is to be found in Greek theatre and in Lorca's theatre, is not acknowledged in most of the plays which we may see if we look through the theatres—or the movies. The violence we admit leads to other violence, yes. Guns lead to guns. But this is a theatre of emotions, in which life leads to life, and the denial of life leads to death. Blood means life, and tyranny over the blood will lead to the spilling of it.

But imagine *Bernarda Alba*, for example, translated to New England! In Lorca's play, although the daughters are in jail, although every repression and jealousy and hostile passion is alive on that stage—those women do not once question their own nature. They do not question their sexuality because they are locked away from themselves, with the

---

2. Federico García Lorca, *Yerma*, in *Three Tragedies of Federico García Lorca*, trans. James Graham-Luján and Richard L. O'Connell (New York: New Directions, 1947), 145. María's lines become a refrain for a chorus of women.
3. Lorca, *The House of Bernarda Alba*, in *Three Tragedies*, 190. Rukeyser misquotes: Bernarda Alba exclaims "Silence!" several times but not in succession.
4. Ts improvisation cue: "go on about formal likeness."

same key that locks them from the world beyond the door—the world of the reapers, of summer, and of love.

And if the life is blood, the summer that raises it is hope—a fierce hope, the hope of Doña Rosita at the end of the play, when she says: "I lost all hope of marrying the one I loved with all my blood, the one I loved and still do. [. . .] I want to flee. I don't want to see. I want to be left serene, empty. Doesn't a poor woman have the right to breathe freely? And yet, hope pursues me, encircles me, bites me; like a dying wolf tightening his grip for the last time."[5]

But Lorca is not the poet of denial; the rose, the fullness, breathes through his plays like music—the red capes, the balconies, the saffron and cloves, Belisa saying, "His skin must be dark, and his kisses must perfume and burn at the same time—like saffron and cloves," saying, "Sometimes he passes underneath my balconies and moves his hand slowly in a greeting that makes my breasts tremble," saying,

Love, love,
Enclosed within my thighs,
The sun swims like a fish.
Warm water in the rushes,
love.[6]

(Unpublished, 1951)

---

5. Federico García Lorca, *Doña Rosita, the Spinster; or the Language of the Flowers*, in *From Lorca's Theatre: Five Plays by Federico García Lorca*, trans. Richard L. O'Connell and James Graham-Luján (New York: Charles Scribner's Sons, 1941), 245–246. Rukeyser reproduces Rosita's full monologue, much abbreviated here.

6. Lorca, *The Love of Don Perlimpín and Belisa in the Garden*, in *From Lorca's Theatre*, 62, 50. On verso, Rukeyser's holo. note: "Only live things, burning in their blood, with all their outlines intact."

Chapter 26

Many Keys (1957)

On Women's Poetry

Certain music, a band playing on a village green, with the instruments coming in, each from its own distance, and some of the trumpets really far away on rooftops, was heard by Charles Ives.[1] And Emily Dickinson took hymns, making so personal a thread of faith out of the sounds she heard that for a hundred years there would be people to complain that her ear was off. These ways of music, perfectly evident in the poems, in Ives's music, come flowing in, were taken and used fully, are offered new to us.[2]

That music joins the influences at work on our lives today.[3] Sometimes there plainly, often transformed; we can take it and implicate it

---

1. This edition's subtitle not on fc but instead supplied by editors. On *The Nation*'s commission and suppression of "Many Keys," and for additional variants from the ts draft that are not noted below, see Eric Keenaghan, "There Is No Glass Woman: Muriel Rukeyser's Lost Feminist Essay 'Many Keys,'" *Feminist Modernist Studies* 1, nos. 1-2 (2018): 186-204, doi.10.10 80/24692921.2017.1368883.

2. Also on ts draft: "They may be called influences, and tracked back. The game is played in criticism: you know what kind of critical training must not be broken, you know how up-to-date and sterile the equipment must be kept[.]"

3. Also on ts draft: "What Emily Dickinson saw and heard can be traced in the poems of her imitators as plainly as in the books and plays and dances based on her life; but when it comes to us purely through her, in her work which transformed her 'influences,' and when we take it and transform it through ourselves, it is harder to find and more valuable."

232

whole; or resist it and leave it out, working against it; or transform it through ourselves into its next art.

Looking at any art we see at once a range of ancestors, ancestors of this liveliness. We can see, too, the influence that becomes history, the experience assimilated and reoffered as part of form.

The forming powers of response can be seen in any art, any part of life. They may be seen with an additional clarity, I think, in poetry by women in America at this time. I do not want to separate out a group for the sake of likenesses, or by date, or—least of all—for a statistical sampling. But if you will look at the books, or the poems in anthologies, by women who may be thought of as artists, you will find an ease in tracing the forming powers of certain forces through their work and their lives. For one thing, the group of actual artists is small, even smaller than the comparable group of men. For another, there are fewer literary influences than you might expect, and some of the same writers emerge almost everywhere. The range is to be found in two kinds of influence; and these have hardly begun to be explored. One is the variety of nonliterary material: observations, images absorbed from dreams or landscapes and with a brilliant integrating gesture given as meaning, and the details of daily life made personal; the other, fascinating and difficult to trace, consists of those influences rejected in the writer's work. We hardly have the biographical methods, or the critical beginnings, to let us perceive the struggle against influences, and how these reactions may be used, turning rebellion, hostility, the desires begun in hatred and fear into the movements that, reaching art, may surpass these origins.

Another reason to set apart a flight of poets is the concentration of method that will let us ask our questions. What links these wishes? To what forms do they tend? What objects are sacred here? Where are we led by these beliefs?

It is easy enough to find the long tradition. We all, women and men, know it in ourselves. It is that of the woman as listener. Trained to perfect herself in receiving, educated as appreciator, she classically was exalted, set on a mountain as Muse; one of those for whom Pegasus struck open with his hoof the moon-shaped Well of Poetry; one of those who taught the Sphinx the riddle which finally lay in wait for answering Oedipus. That the answer to the riddle was known to such women, and simply confirmed by Oedipus, is not taught either to girls or boys. That the poets who drank from that spring were men, we know very well. In this same tradition, curiously, when one great poet was a woman, she was called the Tenth Muse.[4] But the woman-poet draws on her sources, making no more mention of the Muses than do the Japanese. She is glad to be Muse, on occasion, although it is not an easy life; she is glad to be recipient, certainly this can be delightful, although to be exclusively a recipient will guarantee atrophy at least, and all the viciousnesses with it.

But Sappho was here. And before her, the lyrics of the Old Testament: Miriam's song, and Deborah who sang with Barak of "great searchings of heart."[5] It is David, though, and the writers of the Psalms and the Song of Songs who bring us to this place. As Misch says in his rich sourcebook on autobiography, at the outset of personal poetry the individual experience is there, but given in terms of its results.[6] Then Sappho's songs opened an art of the "secret melody in the soul, creatively echoing its life, so that every stirring of the emotions became a miniature cosmos and formed itself into supreme poetry." Among the papyri with the fragments of Sappho found in our century is one in which "the audience is, as it were, the writer herself." This is one of the starting points of self-portrayal.[7]

To do this, to write as if oneself were the audience and to make communication, means that one has dived deep enough to reach the place where obscurity, that terrible middle depth, is passed, deep enough to be where all is shared again.

Here men and women are open to each other, of course. But the ideas inherent in this go along with the central training of women: oneself as audience, any one life as an expression which may be understood at such a depth that it can be seen as having form. In considering

---

4. Also on ts draft: "In that gesture, her relation both to the sources of her poetry and to the living women she knew is indicated. The poetry of women was another relation to a muse."

5. "Miriam's Song" (Exodus 15:20–21, New King James Version), a fragment praising God after Moses parts the Red Sea. "The Song of Deborah and Barak" (Judges 5:2–31, New King James Version) celebrates the Jews' victory over the Canaanites.

6. Georg Misch, *A History of Autobiography in Antiquity*, 2 vols., trans. E. W. Dickes (New York: Routledge, 2002). In an early chapter, "The Discovery of Individuality," Misch mentions Sappho. Contrary to Rukeyser's assertion, Misch concludes that two male poets, Archilochus and Solon, originated autobiographical lyric, not Sappho. See Misch, *History*, 1:76.

7. Additional paragraph follows here in ts draft: "The ideas here: of the writer as audience, of one life as an expression which may be understood at such a depth that it can be seen as having form—these are ideas that are particularly close to the lives of women. They do not go past the socially accepted forms of a woman's life even in the most conventional society, except that women who do not have to work are often brought up to limit their interest in art to products of 'good taste,' and women who do have to work are often brought up to limit theirs to the means of 'self-improvement.'"

a group of poets who are women, and in going to the influences of their lives, we have a chance to see what the possibilities here are. Do these women have any special relation to any art? Involved in art, may they be able to declare for women who are expressed primarily in their personal lives?

In a group brought up primarily to be audience, there are shared attitudes toward experience and toward art. The role of the listener is felt strongly, and is conceived as having qualities which can evoke further action, further communication. This is the listener who is necessary, as necessary as the listener who heard out the Ancient Mariner, under his compulsion to tell what manner of man he was.[8] This is a listener who answers, traditionally, as Muse, evoker; who answers, sometimes, as artist, and breaks that barrier.

For there has been a dialogue of poems, a drama of poems. It expresses dialogues on this earth, at times open and at other times part of the buried life. In Japanese poetry, which does not turn to a muse any more than does the poetry of women in the West, poems are go-betweens in love affairs; women answer. At one time, the men wrote in Chinese, the women doing the work that in Europe we link with Dante, "to express the genius of the time in the native language," says Donald Keene.[9] In Lady Murasaki's time, the "English" past has only *Wulf and Eadwacer* to speak for women—unless you count Grendel's mother.[10]

Our contemporary American poets who are women speak in their own voices, and there would be screams, from writers and publishers too, if you printed an unsigned book of their chosen poems. You could not sort out literary influences. And what would happen to the controversy about Anne Lindbergh?[11] But some things could be sorted out.

---

8. In Samuel Taylor Coleridge's ballad "The Rime of the Ancient Mariner" (1798), the title figure's song is forced on an unnamed Wedding-Guest. Held in suspense, he "cannot choose but hear" and so "listens like a three years' child: / The Mariner hath his will."

9. Donald Keene, *Japanese Literature: An Introduction for Western Readers* (New York: Grove, 1955), 73. Rukeyser ties Keene's quote about eleventh-century Lady Murasaki Shikibu, author of *The Tale of Genji* (c. 1008-1021), to Dante Alighieri's *De vulgari eloquentia* (c. 1302-1305), a tract on vernacular Italian poetry.

10. *Wulf and Eadwacer*, an anonymous Old English lyric compiled in the tenth-century Exeter Book, is believed to be a woman's elegy, riddle, or early ballad. Rukeyser also alludes to the monster Grendel's unnamed mother from the Old English epic *Beowulf* (c. 700-1000 CE).

11. Anne Morrow Lindbergh, wife of aviator Charles Lindbergh, wrote the popular book *Gift from the Sea* (1955) and was the namesake of the protagonist of Rukeyser's anti-fascist play *The Middle of the Air* (drafted 1944-1948, produced 1945). The "controversy" regards how Anne Lindbergh's book *The Wave of the Future* (1940) urged American nonintervention during the

You would have such poets as Josephine Miles, Elizabeth Bishop; Marie Welch, Claire McAllister, Isabella Garner; May Swenson, May Sarton, Naomi Replansky; Babette Deutsch, Margaret Walker, Helen Wolfert; Léonie Adams, Louise Bogan; Marya Zaturenska, Marianne Moore. Other names will occur to you at once.[12] But in a vocabulary of influences, what could you not say about Blake and Vaughan and Herbert?[13] About the openly acknowledged sources of natural history and the records of travel? About the ballads and the persevering French forms, the sonnet and the hieroglyph of wings or the edge of the sea? The syllabic metric of the Mediterranean, the Bible parallels, and the spark leaping between the poles of the shortest Japanese form?

Away from the books in one sense—if you know the lives of these artists, you will find the left-out influences, cadences suppressed, directions in art rejected, groups and fashions renounced in favor of the unfriended integrities that, at one time or another, have to be chosen by every poet.[14] And, because they are poets, because they are women, you will find the almost illegible but unmistakable records of the times that they chose commitment to life instead of to art, and were able to move on later to another level of poetry. But I will come to this again.

Away from the books, too, one must make distinctions regarding the traditional work of women, in its relation to these forms. This, also, is influence. Although some of these poets have taught or worked in libraries, it is the other work that enters here: the concern with housework, the quality of life that is in daily cooking and cleaning. The recurrences here, the necessity to start continually from the beginning, the thanklessness that exists in these drudgeries while one is rebelling against them—I think these come into the attitudes of women toward form in writing.

They come into attitudes toward experience of women and of all those who grow up as the artist grows, in almost constant conflict between modes of life and modes of creativity. We all know the hesitation before experience which is one of the most deeply felt truths of the adolescent girl. She goes through a discipline so implacable toward her

---

Second World War and ambivalently treated fascism as a flawed but feasible future alternative to democracy and communism.

12. Rukeyser's holo. notes for the essay also list and strike H. D. (a.k.a. Hilda Doolittle).

13. Nineteenth-century Romantic William Blake and seventeenth-century metaphysical poets Henry Vaughan and George Herbert.

14. Ts draft also notes "sources of natural histories and records of travel, all the prose, the library" as influences on female poets.

growing powers, in our civilization, that only the disciplines of art are fair mirrors of it, or the spiritual discipline that brings one consciously to the next level of one's life. But on the writing of the young who express the images of this hesitation you will often find the teacher's single word, IMMATURE.

American writing is full of hesitation before the terms of experience of our life. Very often, and conspicuously in novels, you see it camouflaged as a grasping for cruelty and corruption of consciousness. The disguise slips easily, in poems; the movement of the meanings—what is called the music—lets the falseness show at once. It is like the falseness of crude imitation in its effect. But, in the work of women, imitation is seen more often. You can think of many women in whose work can be found the "immaturity" which tries to express conscious denial for the sake of something more alive, significant of more. The expression of this process in terms of form is now taking place in the poetry of women. Partly from a sense of waste—seeing the depression as waste, seeing the wars as waste unless they are fought

> . . . till I have conquered in myself what
> causes war, but I would not believe it[15]

—partly from a search for the forms that will express all the subtleties of the central movements of the being, this work is proceeding.

It is not new, and of course it does not belong to women. It can be seen clearly in the use and misuse of the sonnet form, the sonnet seen philosophically, as dialectic resolution of two simultaneous meanings; meanings which could be as opposite, as parallel, as the juxtapositions of the Old Testament. It can be seen in a recent correspondence about Kathleen Raine's poems, with W. S. Merwin finally saying, against "organic form," "That is why there are two words for Nature and Art."[16] The wit-writing of men's poetry—often alien to women when it denies the irrational, and deeply fascinating to women when it includes the marvelous and wise "irrational" element, as Donne does—stands at

---

15. Marianne Moore, "In Distrust of Merits," in *New Collected Poems*, ed. Heather Cass (New York: Farrar, Straus & Giroux, 2017), 172-173. Rukeyser's ellipsis. In 1943, this anti-war poem first appeared in *The Nation*, the same venue that commissioned "Many Keys."

16. Poet W. S. Merwin, source not located. In a recent review, Merwin had panned British poet and William Blake scholar Kathleen Raine's *Collected Poems* (1956) for its "shapeless" poems, steeped in "vagueness" and "bleak mysticism." See W. S. Merwin, "Romantic Distrust," *New York Times Book Review*, January 27, 1957.

one end of this range.[17] At the other stand the forms which allow for another order of experience. They do not work against rhyme, as has often been assumed; they are likely to call for the return of sound *more than once*, more than the minimum of rhyme, and not only or mainly at the ends of lines. They allow for recurrences of sound, and for movement through recurrences which are not repetitions because they exist in time, in changed circumstances. They justify Frank Lloyd Wright and Gertrude Stein and everyone behind these who has known that there is no repetition in nature, or in art.[18]

There *is* waste in nature, waste in art, and plenty of waste in the lives of women. Waste is an influence, and the making of poetry works against waste. In poetry, as everywhere else, there are swamplands of the fourth-rate, the third-rate, and endless suburbs of the second-rate. What one hopes for is the first-rate, and the lives that will produce it. To the work on the making of forms must be added the work of the individual on himself.[19]

There are individuals who construct themselves to be artists, and from that time on live according to this commitment. He, she, will act out what he can; and will make experiences and forms which then will act on him, so that he travels a road determined by the exchange between work and a character which, in the beginning, was created by himself. In American poetry, the characters formed by Walt Whitman and Emily Dickinson have the highest visibility. It is on these legends that they literally risked their lives, in self-rebirth as a new type. It is this risk which their detractors cannot forgive them. The basic creation,

---

17. John Donne, English metaphysical poet.

18. Frank Lloyd Wright pioneered organic architecture. Modernist Gertrude Stein used repetition to break linguistic and mental habits.

19. On ts draft, additional paragraphs follow that elaborate on gender:

> In a person brought up to be a listener—or Muse—whose response takes existence as art, there will be more than the ordinary creative guilt-feeling (in Rank's words for the penalty). The *cost* of creativity will be emphasized more, as it is to almost all women. [Rukeyser's emphasis]
>
> (Everything that I am saying applies to the artist, man or woman; it is simply that, in our civilization at this time and even more in the past, it applies slightly more acutely to women. None of it excuses bad art, or corrupt consciousness, anywhere. What I hope is that the truths I am attempting to indicate here are the promise of future creative levels and future forms.)

On artists' guilt for pursuing their individual desires rather than promoting collective ideology, see Otto Rank, *Art and Artist: Creative Urge and Personality Development* (1932; reis., New York: W. W. Norton, 1989), esp. 389-392.

made in this way, is that of a character who could write the poems that they would wish to write. The movement was toward a future requirement.

This movement, which organizes the embryo, is certainly not male or female. But it is part of the instinctual life which, in this society, may not be lost in the growth of women as often, perhaps, as in the growth of men; although certainly the great poets of it have been men. If it comes to be expressed in the art of women—and some of the signs exist in the poets I have named—new resources of the forms must surely appear, and new forms for these resources follow as the buried life of our time is brought to consciousness.

At the point at which the barriers are broken, an energy and daring must be summoned up in order to meet experience. All the influences that reinforce her energy will have to be available now to the woman who enters and continues in an art.[20] One crisis is likely to come as her formal education ends, and the support or friction of a ready audience (for her who has often seen herself as audience) is suddenly removed. How many brilliant girls, the astonishers of their schools, end and subside! Another time—apart from the psychic and economic crises of all our lives—comes in the long rearrangement of life that predictably will come to women who write, after the birth of their children. This change of level may take about ten years, and, like the others, can stop the function of the artist or be taken as "influence."[21]

These are two crucial times. What ancestors affirm one's life in these? What is chosen and built-in, what thrown away?

And what kind of poetry emerges from such commitments?

There is another crisis—the most significant one of the artist's mature development, says Rank, and it comes into being through the conflict between life and art. In a fertile chapter, Rank writes of the victory over the idea of deprivation.[22] With the end of doubt in this conflict comes the freeing of the artist from the needs which enter most often into his first turning toward art. This crisis is familiar to all artists. It is met in the life of most women who do any kind of creative

---

20. Also on ts draft: "The images of strength that persevere, in dream and in waking; the concentration that the ability to love and search have left her as a gift; the power to select and bring together, beginning always from a new beginning, so that in her art she may offer communication without depending on the sharing of a specific event—all these must be evoked in herself through every means she has."

21. When Rukeyser wrote "Many Keys" in 1957, her son, William Laurie, was ten years old.

22. Rank, "Deprivation and Renunciation," in *Art and Artist*, 415-431.

work—in fact, of most women who work—not once, but many times. Often, it is one of her recurrences, and the ways in which she meets it determines, each time, her entire future.

Emily Dickinson's legend is based on her qualities in this encounter. To anyone who imitates her stance or her poetry of these struggles and transcendence, Emily Dickinson is a "bad influence." But these are the evil translations of recurrence. It is such translation that has made Whitman, or any first-rate poet, or any man or woman who has risked his life, "a bad influence."

But, if you hear the music in your own way, use it, and offer it new, the image is made, it takes on its new life. Part of this is birth-image—from Anne Bradstreet's "The Author to Her Book,"

> And for thy Mother, she alas is poor,
> Which caused her thus to send thee out of door,

but there is the weaning-image, the going out:

> I took my Power in my Hand
> And went against the World . . .

and the image of being native to oneself:

> I will play a part no longer . . .

and the image of consciousness, seen as evil in its corruption, as in Marie Welch's

> The black of magic
> Is in not knowing
> Oneself
> The magician.[23]

For a man, for a woman, the image goes out into the world. As this happens, the poet has his return to life, and then a gathering-together for the next work, with whatever nourishes his powers. These nourishments, too, are called influences; "the earth," says Emily Dickinson,

---

23. Quotations, in order of citation: Anne Bradstreet, "The Author to Her Book" (1650); Emily Dickinson, Poem 540 (1862); Walt Whitman's "Native Moments" (1860) from the "Children of Adam" cluster in *Leaves of Grass*; and a then-unpublished poem by Rukeyser's close friend Marie de L. Welch, "The Black of Magic," *New York Quarterly*, Winter 1973, 70. All Rukeyser's ellipses.

"has many keys."[24] The gathering is seen as withdrawal, and—for most women—the withdrawal from daily life is extremely difficult. It can mean extra financial pressure for a man or for a woman; in addition, the receptive and recurrent nature of a woman's life exists, to prevent her from living "like a beast or a hermit" and to make more inaccessible the conditions under which her art may be followed.[25] Then the tortures may come; they do not belong specifically to women or men, you can find them catalogued for the poets of our time in Kenneth Rexroth's "Thou Shalt Not Kill."[26]

To use the possibilities so that life is allowed and nourished; the life also of the forms. To make the forms so that experience is seen to include the world, so that all things of daily life are seen in their essential and full vitality (so that the mysticism of the material will not survive as a deadening force among us); to understand the withdrawals before experience, when they are made in generalization, in the impersonal and anti-sexual, and when they are made for the sake of more life. To move as listeners, until criticism becomes a response to the world with *that particular work of art* in it. To explore the recurrent, to explore the receptive in its full relationship to all creative aspects of life. To move with the receptive until it finds its forms, so that the buried life finds its poetry, in all its voices, approaching alive and now.

(Unpublished, 1957)

---

24. Dickinson, Poem 1775 (1865). See Emily Dickinson, Poem 139, in *Bolts of Melody: New Poems of Emily Dickinson,* ed. Mabel Loomis Todd and Millicent Todd Bingham (New York: Harper & Brothers, 1945), 75.

25. Rukeyser probably references Lebanese author Khalil Gibran's "The Hermit and the Beasts," in *The Wanderer: His Parables and Sayings* (New York: Knopf, 1932). Wild beasts reproach a hermit for preaching about love even though he, lacking a mate, knows nothing of it.

26. On Kenneth Rexroth's poem "Thou Shalt Not Kill," see Muriel Rukeyser, "Lyric 'Rage,'" in this volume.

CHAPTER 27

Lyrical "Rage" (1957)

Review of Kenneth Rexroth's In Defense of the Earth

The fineness of Kenneth Rexroth's *In Defense of the Earth* depends on several virtues. They are virtues which are rare in this year but which are apparent in almost every one of the Rexroth poems: a lyric-mindedness that has been prepared by many disciplines to summon up its music; a learning that eats the gifts of the world, knowing (like the laboratory baby before the food) how many cultures must be drawn on to make human fare; and that quality which has been talked about so much in speaking of Kenneth Rexroth and of those he has known in San Francisco: rage.[1]

The poems included in the collection are the whole background of lyrics written by Kenneth Rexroth since 1949.[2] Here is the exquisite "Great Canzon":

> . . . She, when she goes
> Wreathed in herbs, drives every other

---

1. After hosting the October 1955 Six Gallery reading in San Francisco, Kenneth Rexroth was regarded as the Beat Generation's godfather. The 1957 obscenity trial for Allen Ginsberg's *Howl and Other Poems* (1956), whose title poem was premiered at that reading, grabbed national attention the same year as Rukeyser's review of Rexroth.
2. Since 1949, Rexroth had published three volumes: *The Art of Worldly Wisdom* (1949), *The Signature of All Things* (1949), and *The Dragon and the Unicorn* (1952).

> Woman from my mind—shimmering
> Gold with green—so lovely that love
> Comes to rest in her shadow, she
> Who has caught me fast between
> Two hills, faster far than fused stone.[3]

And here are "the web" and "hidden crippled bird," landmarks of the time when Morris Graves and Rexroth first knew each other and wanted the journey to Japan; here are the moving poems for his wife, Marthe, and for the little daughter, particularly "The Great Nebula of Andromeda," "A Maze of Sparks of Gold," and "A Sword in a Cloud of Light," with its Christmas crowds on Fillmore Street, its Orion "spread out / On the sky like a true god," and ending:

> Believe in all those fugitive
> Compounds of nature, all doomed
> To waste away and go out.[4]

There are here also the whiplash "Bestiary"; a group of epigrams and translations; and the four-part memorial for Dylan Thomas with its shattering *ubi sunt* for the poets of these years, dead of all the deaths or

> stopped writing at thirty . . .
> How many went to work for *Time*?
> How many died of prefrontal
> Lobotomies in the Communist Party?
> How many are lost in the back wards
> Of provincial madhouses?
> How many on the advice of
> Their psychoanalysts, decided
> A business career was best after all?
> How many are hopeless alcoholics?[5]

---

3. Kenneth Rexroth, "The Great Canzon for Marthe," in *In Defense of the Earth* (New York: New Directions, 1956), 17. Translation of Alighieri Dante's "Canzone 1." Rukeyser's ellipsis.

4. Morris Graves, abstract expressionist painter influenced by his travels in Asia in the 1920s and 1930s. Rexroth translated Japanese and Chinese poetry but did not visit Asia until the 1970s. First quoted phrases ("the web," "hidden crippled bird") from Rexroth, "Marthe Away," in *Defense*, 12. Final quotations from Rexroth, "A Sword in a Cloud of Light" from "The Lights in the Sky are Stars," in *Defense*, 22.

5. Rukeyser mentions two sections: Rexroth, "A Bestiary" and "Epigrams and Translations," in *Defense*, 60–67, 75–80. She quotes from Rexroth, "Thou Shalt Not Kill," part 3, in *Defense*, 56–57. Rukeyser's ellipsis. The long poem memorializes Welsh poet Dylan Thomas

244   CHAPTER 27

The last part of the poem is for Dylan Thomas himself, and it carries its heaped-up accusation for murder against the specific anti-poetry, anti-religion—but you had better read this for yourself, since any description will sound like the frothing and rage with which the poem has been charged.

This would be rage, in the speaking man; and a shout and rant of frustration. But here, in the sparse, controlled poems it is something else and more: it is the sharp willingness to speak of the committed man. There is little enough control around anywhere this year, and less commitment.[6] The sound of commitment comes through as the sound of anger. In these brief and disciplined poems of Rexroth's we have the background and tradition of "Howl" and *On the Road*.[7] The influence and the lyric commitment are shown naked here. They reach us, in love, jeering, bringing in other poetry from China and Japan. Read:

> Lions terrify most men
> Who buy meat at the butcher's—[8]

and

> What happened to Robinson,
> Who used to stagger down Eighth Street,
> Dizzy with solitary gin?
> Where is Masters, who crouched in
> His law office for ruinous decades?
> [. . .]
>   Timor mortis conturbat me.[9]

It does not matter that Alethea made that same last crack in *The Way of All Flesh*; it is surely a crack as old as the Bible.[10] But, in context this

---

and uses tropes from Ginsberg's "Howl," including *Time* magazine, lobotomization, and madhouses. See note 1 above. *Ubi sunt* is Latin for Rexroth's refrain, "where are they."

  6. Leftist "commitment" seemed impossible. In September, Congress passed the Civil Rights Act of 1957, furiously protested by Dixie Democrats. The anti-communist Red Scare also continued, and the nuclear arms race accelerated.

  7. Together, Ginsberg's poem "Howl" (1956) and Jack Kerouac's novel *On the Road* (1957) established the Beats as the American literary counterculture's vanguard. See notes 1 and 5 above.

  8. Rexroth, "Jackal" from "A Bestiary," in *Defense*, 63. Rukeyser's em dash.

  9. Rexroth, "Thou Shalt Not Kill," part 2, in *Defense*, 54. Quotation abbreviated. Rexroth names twentieth-century poets Edward Arlington Robinson and Edgar Lee Masters. In this part of the long poem, the Latin refrain *Timor mortis conturbat me* ("Fear of death disturbs me") ends every stanza.

  10. Samuel Butler's *The Way of All Flesh* (1903), a British novel satirizing Victorian attitudes about life and morality. Overton, the narrator, not Alethea, notes early on that, as

year, the lines knock against our lives. And now the poets come on, in their deaths and lives: Jim Oppenheim, Orrick Johns, Elinor Wylie, Sara Teasdale, Jack Wheelwright, Bodenheim, Edna Millay, Genevieve, Harry, Hart, and the rest of Rexroth's line of poets.[11]

The title is right; this book is written "in defense," and the parts are love, anger, willingness to act to protect. In these poems the qualities come through with marvelous strength, clarity, and music. This review has been held for long enough to let readers see how many critics talk of these poems in terms of rage, and talk of "Howl" and *On the Road* in terms of vitality. Again, this is not rage, but the commitment of a poet, coming through in the classic terms of our thought, in terms of our poetry of nature, and in terms of some attitudes identified here with Oriental religion—quite simply, attitudes largely neglected in our lives. Or, even more simply, in the words of a poet older than Rexroth, Robert Frost:

> Someone had better be prepared for rage.
> There would be more than ocean-water broken
> Before God's last *Put out the Light* was spoken.[12]

Kenneth Rexroth is dealing with the plans of women and men in these magnificent poems, which are harsh, full of grace and certainty and grief: poems of the mountain nights, of the vast crystal of knowledge encompassing the limitless crystal of air and rock and water; of the people to be loved, the mountain animals, the nights of stars, and, on Fillmore Street, the night, the moon, the crowded earth.[13]

(Saturday Review, 1957)

---

children, they liked the idea of someone else's death. Others' funerals meant that they had not died and, as mourners, they even would receive a consolatory treat.

11. Modernist poets named in "Thou Shalt Not Kill," part 2, including Maxwell Bodenheim, Genevieve Taggard, Harry Crosby, and Hart Crane.

12. Robert Frost, "Once by the Pacific," in *Collected Poems* (New York: Henry Holt, 1939), 314.

13. Fillmore Street, a San Francisco thoroughfare. In 1956, the Fillmore District was singled out for race- and class-motivated gentrification.

Chapter 28

A Crystal for the Metaphysical (1966)
Review of Marianne Moore's Tell Me, Tell Me: Granite, Steel, and Other Topics

Marianne Moore's *Tell Me, Tell Me: Granite, Steel, and Other Topics* performs a rare act: these poems and brief essays supply another part in the definition of a structure, accurate and personal.[1] [. . .] In this new work, her fourteenth book (to be published November 4), the objects appear to face each other; forms that had seemed crystals, twin crystals, take on a further growth. The polarity is clearer and greater than one had guessed. She sets up an opposition. [. . .]

Many of her poems are "metaphysical newmown hay"; and Marianne Moore has offered the charge against herself with gallantry, answering it with the crystal structure, the delicate, courageous wit of poems.[2] [. . .]

In clarity the poems claim their form.
[. . .]

---

1. This edition is an abridged version of Muriel Rukeyser's review of Marianne Moore, *Tell Me, Tell Me: Granite, Steel, and Other Topics* (New York: Viking, 1966). Moore's volume features brief essays that gloss the poems with autobiographical narratives, thus creating the "twin crystal" structure Rukeyser describes. The full review heavily cites the poems and essays from *Tell Me, Tell Me*, as well as earlier essays by Moore. This edition's omissions are marked by bracketed ellipses, and, for readability, this edition supplies only limited annotations about that cut material.
2. Moore, "Tell me, tell me," in *Tell Me*, 43.

This poem ["The mind, intractable thing"], in its praise and harsh confessing grace, sets extreme qualities alongside those that Miss Moore has long given us: probity, scrupulousness, limits set and honored by the self, a sense of exotic dailiness, a pattern to which the poet has been committed in personal bravery, a vital diffidence. For here the mind and the poet, and witchcraft, wordcraft, rouse us by so powerful a suggestion that every cry is answered. We know this in familiarity on the stage, when Tennessee Williams and Albee, in cannibal attack, offer us the vision of love between people, of marriage, by showing us the hour massacred.[3] Or Houdini, as strong magician of escape, who said he had to master two things: fear and every muscle of his body.[4] These poems have mastery of things comparable, ultimate danger. What is mastered here, and what the poems of Marianne Moore suggested might be mastered, are "disparagers, death, dejection," and chaos, against which she has struggled for compactness.[5]

[. . .]

The line-by-line handling of Miss Moore's poems is now our history: her medieval device of rhyme-breaking; the syllabic standard, the form in which she gathers her freedom. But with these poems and meaning that face each other we can see something more: a style of the spirit for which there are precedents, and none closer than the one celebrated in the first poem of this book, the poem called "Granite and Steel," and again in "In Lieu of the Lyre."[6] [. . .]

In early autumn 1966 a visit to Marianne Moore was rather like an answer to the poem by Elizabeth Bishop "Invitation to Miss Marianne Moore": "From Brooklyn, over the Brooklyn Bridge, on this fine morning, / please come flying."[7] She lives now near the Henry James part of Greenwich Village; not that there is any James stretch now, but the overtopping and smothering of the city that he foresaw have its several gaps, housefronts, a long broad sky.

---

3. Contemporary literary and Broadway playwrights Tennessee Williams and Edward Albee.
4. In the 1940s, Rukeyser had begun to develop a play about Hungarian American escape artist Harry Houdini (né Erik Weisz). *Houdini: A Musical* (Ashbury, MA: Paris Press, 2002) premiered in 1973.
5. Moore, "The mind, intractable thing," in *Tell Me*, 10.
6. Moore, "Granite and Steel" and "In Lieu of the Lyre," in *Tell Me*, 3–4, 7–8.
7. Elizabeth Bishop, "Invitation to Miss Marianne Moore," in *The Complete Poems, 1927–1979* (New York: Farrar, Straus & Giroux, 1983), 82.

CHAPTER 28

"Miss Moore's not likely to answer the bell," said the man downstairs. But she did. Here, newly returned to Manhattan after living in Brooklyn almost forty years, she was frail and strong in a pale blue dress. We sat under the square clockface, facing the yellow velvet, tufted sofa. Kind, ironic, of acute and direct speech, she gave me gracefulness. We spoke of the new book, whose galleys I had been reading. What might she do next? Maybe write her memoirs, Miss Moore said.[8] Her files were all in the next rooms, boxes to the ceiling in one, she said; the sorting-out of moving was still going on. However, she really lived here now, although her church was still in Brooklyn, and people there were talking to her about coming back and asking her why she hadn't told them that she was thinking of leaving.

We spoke of several poets for whose writing she has affection. For whom she cares. Robert Francis.[9] Elizabeth Bishop, now in the Northwest.[10] Many good poets now, don't you think so?

Of politics, of the war in Vietnam, and of the reception given for her recently by Ambassador Goldberg, at which I heard her say, after the terms of praise with which she had been introduced, "Overestimated! Always overestimated!"[11] She said she did not really like her marvelous poem "In Distrust of Merits" because it is "didactic": "I care about speaking up. I never wanted to evade anything."[12]

We spoke of TV and the interviews, close and personal, that come into one's room; the interview with Jean Renoir, of which she has written in this new book. [...][13]

We spoke of the interview with Roy Campanella, in which Mike Wallace asked him in his suffering, "Do you believe that God was

---

8. Around the time of Rukeyser's review, Moore had begun a memoir, incomplete and still unpublished. See Charles Molesworth, *Marianne Moore: A Literary Life* (New York: Atheneum, 1990), 449–450.

9. Robert Francis, author of "The Pitcher" (1953), a popular poem about baseball. Moore was an enthusiast and addresses the sport in the poem "Baseball and Writing," in *Tell Me*, 28–29.

10. In 1966, Bishop, Moore's mentee, briefly left her adopted home of Brazil to teach in Seattle.

11. In 1962, Arthur Goldberg, US ambassador to the United Nations, hosted a large party celebrating Moore's seventy-fifth birthday. See Molesworth, *Marianne Moore*, 434.

12. Quotes are from Rukeyser's interview with Moore. Moore's poem "In Distrust of Merits" (1944), in *New Collected Poems*, ed. Heather Cass (New York: Farrar, Straus & Giroux, 2017), 171–173, expresses doubts about whether the Second World War was just.

13. French director, screenwriter, and actor Jean Renoir is cited by Moore in her essay "Profit Is a Dead Weight," in *Tell Me*, 24.

punishing you?" And Campanella answering, "No, I believe that actions follow as a direct result of laws of physics." With dignity.[14]

Of baseball: I was not curious about her interest, but the scoreboard knowledge for which she is celebrated. I praised it as the only *orbital* game.

Of art, imagination, and long achievement. Of the phrase to which she comes back again and again, the most difficult central phrase. It is in the hymn that says, "Rejoice evermore."[15] (Echoes of "Nevertheless" start up, of the crow who will not learn to say "Nevermore.") "Evermore!" she said.[16] "Think of it! And if it is a mother with a son blown to unrecognizable bits in Vietnam . . ."

Around us the signs of the place, rare and many, filling one's senses. Haunting, curious moment; beginning when one was a child, reading Louis Untermeyer's *Modern American Poetry* and finding Marianne Moore with "a scarab of the sea"—the seagull greeting "men long dead."[17] This moving, frail, strong woman and the cluster about her, all speaking so clear: the small bone figure of the Arctic musk-ox, the Mexican toad, the yellow rose painted by E. E. Cummings, the sea, the ballpark, in her room the dark beaver in snowy winter giving off a dark light, the photograph of T. S. Eliot as a young boy, the green wax candle.[18] The book she gives me, the thin fine English print, its feel in my hand after she writes in it. Now she lights the great wax candle; the flame springs up, warm flower-yellow, deepens; down the tower-shaped candle the shadow drops.

[. . .]

---

14. Roy Campanella, a Black catcher for the Brooklyn Dodgers, was paralyzed in a 1958 car accident. The following year, he was profiled on *The Mike Wallace Interview*, a television series.

15. Albert Benjamin Simpson, "O Let Us Rejoice in the Lord Evermore" (date unknown): "It is better to sing than be sighing, / It is better to live than be dying; / So let us rejoice evermore." The hymn obliquely cycles back to Moore's questioning of the moral effectiveness of the Second World War in her poem "In Distrust of Merits." See note 12 above.

16. In the full review, Rukeyser discusses Moore's story "My Crow, Pluto—A Fantasy" and its corresponding poem "To Victor Hugo of My Crow Plato," in *Tell Me*, 32-34, 35-37. Both of Moore's texts allude to Edgar Allan Poe's poem "The Raven" (1845) and its classic refrain "Nevermore."

17. Marianne Moore, "A Talisman," in *Modern American Poetry: A Critical Anthology*, 3rd ed., ed. Louis Untermeyer (New York: Harcourt, Brace, 1925), 445. Untermeyer first included this 1912 poem and three other early pieces by Moore in his anthology's third edition after having omitted her work from its previous editions. Rukeyser was twelve years old when this edition was published.

18. Most famous for his poetry, E. E. Cummings was also a painter.

The poet who believes in the materials of the world—written material—in such a way that his desire to include drives him to use them selectively, but in their own voice, is at once faced with questions.[19] How to claim, to make the material one's own, and still leave it to walk among its origins?

The traditional assertion—that all materials belong to the artist—is true in a sense. This is actually an assertion that the artist does not want to own the world but to use the world. It includes the entire range of life in horror and love.

And of the delights and irritations of Marianne Moore's poems? In what relation to the world does this woman stand? Is it as wry, odd zookeeper? Is it as poet interested chiefly in the edges of things, bringing them together to offer them to us juxtaposed as joints of crystal are, the edge-lit world of meeting planes, severely maintained axes of alignment?

One thinks of Eliot and the ways in which he acknowledges the world of sources; Marianne Moore, Louis Untermeyer notes, "unlike Eliot... scrupulously puts her quotations between inverted commas."[20] Paradoxically, no poet owes more to more sources than Miss Moore, and yet no author is more original.

This use of the world, incorporating the achieved angles of existence into the work, opens all the questions of taking and making. In writing about these poems, in which one hopes to be able to remove the scaffolding, one deals with the fusion of materials. With luck, in writing about Willard Gibbs, Charles Ives, the Ajanta paintings, one can—after a very short time, in a generation—take away the scaffold of information.[21] But one's own sources—it is these that Miss Moore scrupulously and honorably retains; and this family of sources must be examined, for she goes prospecting for flavors among the description of things visible, for the pleasures of the assorting eye among the

---

19. Here, Rukeyser refers to the sourcing of found language and the use of citation in Moore's poetry. The published review quotes in full Marianne Moore, "A Note on the Notes," in *What Are Years* (New York: Macmillan, 1941), 46.

20. Louis Untermeyer, headnote for Marianne Moore, in *Modern American Poetry: Mid-century Edition*, 7th ed., ed. Untermeyer (New York: Harcourt, Brace, 1950), 368. Rukeyser's ellipsis. Rukeyser quotes material added by Untermeyer to the original 1925 headnote for this later edition. See note 17 above.

21. Rukeyser refers to her own poems "Gibbs," "Ives," and "Ajanta," in *CP*, 182–185, 195–198, 207–211.

spirit's counting of syllables in a strange and telling awareness of time, not by beat but by actual procession of sounds going by. Henry James and Beatrix Potter, the actual owners of an actual cat—the range of her sources is very wide.[22]

In his essay on Marianne Moore in the new *William Carlos Williams Reader*, edited by M. L. Rosenthal, Williams speaks of the "definite place where the matters of the day may meet if they choose or not, but if they assemble it must be there."[23] It is for him a place of "white penetration" where the thrust goes through all colors.[24] There, where the sources become something new, the poem exists.

Writing of novelty, which must be inspired, Wallace Stevens observed, "There is one most welcome and authentic note; it is the insistence on a reality that forces itself upon our consciousness and refuses to be managed and mastered. It is here that the affinity of art and religion is most evident today. Both have to mediate for us a reality not ourselves. This is what the poet does. The supreme virtue here is humility, for the humble are they who move about the world with the love of the real in their hearts."[25]

That art of the supreme virtue is declared in the ways in which the world is given in the poet's voice. It can be seen in Marianne Moore.

(Saturday Review, 1966)

---

22. Rukeyser is noting Moore's references to Beatrix Potter's *The Tailor of Gloucester* (1902) and Henry James in "Tell me, tell me," in *Tell Me*, 44.

23. William Carlos Williams, "Marianne Moore," in *The William Carlos Williams Reader*, ed. M. L. Rosenthal (New York: New Directions, 1966), 387.

24. Williams, "Marianne Moore," 385.

25. Wallace Stevens, "About One of Marianne Moore's Poems," in *The Necessary Angel: Essays on Reality and the Imagination* (New York: Vintage Books, 1951), 99. Rukeyser misquotes and interpolates much new material into this passage from Stevens, thus altering his meaning.

CHAPTER 29

Poetry and the Unverifiable Fact (1968)

I'm glad to be here on an evening of poetry weather; somehow whenever there is a poetry reading it seems to rain.[1] And the bounty and the discomfort and the people who come out in it and the reasons for their coming out, I think, have to do with what we are here for, in talking about poetry in relation to fact, verifiable and unverifiable.

It is a happiness to me to be here. The things I have heard and seen before coming here come together in a way I care very much about, the comings-together. I knew about the library, some of the stories of the publications, of the Stuart book, sent to me by Henriette Lehman, of Mark Curtis's work on the history of Oxford which has that vibration in the present that to me is history.[2] I belong to a society of historians,

---

1. Lecture delivered on February 13, 1968, at Scripps College in Claremont, California.
2. Scripps College's Denison Library has a special collection on the history of women's colleges, as well as archives for modernist T. S. Eliot, Victorian poets Robert and Elizabeth Barrett Browning, and fin de siècle illustrator Aubrey Beardsley. Henriette de Saussure Blanding Lehman directed the San Francisco Conservatory of Music and was a trustee of Mills College. She had sent Rukeyser a copy of Scripps College president Mark Curtis's *Oxford and Cambridge in Transition, 1558–1642* (1965) while Rukeyser was researching *The Traces of Thomas Hariot* (1971). Rukeyser discusses Hariot in "Opening Convocation," her second Scripps lecture, delivered on February 15, 1968, not included in this volume. See Muriel Rukeyser, "Opening Convocation," *The Clark Lecture, 1968: An Address by Muriel Rukeyser, Scripps College Bulletin* 42, no. 4, extra ed. no. 3 (1968): 23–36.

but I have had nothing to do with them since they defined history, a historic event, as an event which is finished, since it seems to me that these events, like the events in poetry, live in the present.[3] And that is one of our few reasons for real interest, for coming out on a rainy night.

The third connection I make with this place is through Marjorie Downing, whom I liked in the very beginning in relation to poetry, particularly her feeling for Hopkins and the way she speaks about Hopkins, and again through liking her and her family, but in a new phase of friendship because of something she said to me once.[4] I asked her, as I ask people, about her early wish, what she wanted to be. And she said, "A religious."[5] She looked at me and considered. Then with a marked special look, she said: "Well, really also a sea captain." She said, "I like ships. I knew it wasn't possible—but I wanted that."

And I said, "These are difficult things to bring together."

And she said, "Oh, no. It's easy—dean of a women's college!"

It is these comings-together that have to do with the extraordinary resonances, the parable that poetry actually is in our lives, the recurrences. People have asked me whether I use rhyme. Rhyme itself, as it has come down to us through European tradition, is one returning of sound. One return has never been enough for me. I wanted sound established and recurring many times, as the recurrences in our lives come many times; and that sequence of return seemed to me romantic, if you want to talk in those terms; fact, if you want to talk in those terms; poetry and the wish for form, the need for form.

I wonder very much about the needs for poetry—what brings us out to such an evening as this which is not compulsory. And I think "they" lie to us very much about these necessities and the nature of the thing itself. "They" tell us in every way possible, not only in classes and through books but in songs and in jokes, in the way people look, that poetry is a rare and curious and very peculiar thing in which to have interest, in which to engage, to which to be committed. They say it is peculiar. They say it is sexually questionable for a man to do it. They say it is sexually questionable for a woman to do it.

---

3. Rukeyser was a member of the Society of American Historians.
4. Marjorie Downing, dean of Scripps College. See Marjorie Downing, "The Nature Poetry of Gerard Manley Hopkins, S.J." (master's thesis, Catholic University of America, 1939); Downing, "Inscape and Instress: Further Analogies with Scotus," in *Gerard Manley Hopkins*, ed. James F. Scott and Carolyn D. Scott (St. Louis: Herder, 1968), 32–43.
5. Nun.

What is the nature of this lie? A company has made a fortune on the premise that everybody takes snapshots. And I wonder about this other thing. I wonder—all critical standards, all criteria aside—I would like to ask you something. How many of you here have ever—without any thought for critical standards—how many of you have ever in your lifetime written a poem? Would you put up your hands, please? Thank you.

I am always nervous when I ask this question. I ask now in rooms whether small or big, and generally there is a moment of panic before the hands begin to move, more slowly often than on this evening. Almost all the hands go up. There are three or four generally who do not put their hands up. If I wait afterwards, and with favorable winds, the three or four will come up and speak to me and say something like this: "I was fifteen. It was a love poem. It stank."

But this is quite different in nature from what we are told. "They" say that this is something that people do not do; I think from the evidence this evening that it is actually something else, that it is actually a human activity. People do this, almost everybody writes a poem at some time in his lifetime. It is quite a different sort of thing from what we are told.

I speak of the writing of poetry as part of a deep indication of what the nature of our lives actually is—what the reverberations and recurrences are, what the facts, verifiable and unverifiable, are, and how we share these with each other. And it seems to me that this experience is the entrance into the present moment, which is the real—this moment, this moment which we share, this rainy hour that we share, that has never existed before. It is our actual living present with everything that we bring to it, and that as history enters this moment through us, if we are the means.

So what we call poetry, which also cannot be defined. I would be glad to try. I think of all the people who have defined it in all the ways we know—from the attempts to name the recurrences of the spirit, to the line about the hairs standing up, to Louis Untermeyer on the platform, who said when he was asked from the audience whether he could define poetry: "Certainly, I can. Poetry is—Poetry is—" and then said, "Can you define *chocolate?*"[6]

---

6. Rukeyser references the first version of Marianne Moore's "Poetry" (1919), which defines the art as "useful" because it produces physical reactions: "Hands that can grasp, eyes / that can dilate, hair that can rise / if it must." Marianne Moore, "Poetry," in *New Collected*

And that is simple compared to what we have to consider this evening. But this, about what enters the moment with us and on what terms we come to the moment in our own experience, unknown to each other, partly known. When I say *unverifiable fact*, it is that "partly known" that we each hold for every other person—the signs of the recognition in recurrence, in what is immediately recognizable to someone else, in what is recognizable across the world, across race and life story, and the nature of beliefs, and all that which is brought to the moment.

Poetry is a very good parable of the coming to experience. It holds to the rhythms of experience. It is the shortest of all the arts that live in time. You will find people who are really stopped before the quality of the bringing-together of thought and imagination, and the recurrence of the attempt to find, that come into poetry. The two stock answers of such stopped people will be: "I haven't had anything to do with that since I was at least thirteen (or fourteen or fifteen)," or "I have no time for poetry."

Now the first answer is a very interesting one that you should go behind if you can, because the ways in which people are stopped, stop themselves, have to do very often with early adolescence—very often with the moment, if there is a moment, of puberty, in which they worry and grieve about what they should be feeling: and I am speaking of the depths of the center, its poetry, and poetry can be of any lightness that you want, you know. It can be of any suspense. As a matter of fact, the thriller, which is a perfectly good image of poetry—in itself a suspense of images—offers us a term in which we can speak to people who will not talk directly about the poem.

But these two answers about stoppages in adolescence, or about not having the time for this art which is so quick and brief generally in time, should be gone behind. I think if you do go behind them, you will often find that the quarrel is between the person and his own belief, in his own experience; and that there is a relation with one's own experience here that is a base for this attitude toward art and this attitude toward the world; because the necessity has to do with believing your own experience, with trust in your own experience and with the rhythms of

---

Poems, ed. Heather Cass (New York: Farrar, Straus & Giroux, 2017), 27. Louis Untermeyer was an early champion of Rukeyser's work and added her to the sixth edition of his anthology *Modern American Poetry* (New York: Harcourt, Brace, 1942). Also see Louis Untermeyer, "The Language of Muriel Rukeyser," *Saturday Review of Literature*, August 10, 1940, 11–12.

experience. Certainly the things that are difficult have the relations of the rhythms of our own feeling, the bodily rhythms, in which breathing, for example, and the rhythms of the heart, will provide many kinds of base for music.

Now they will speak of music, the music of poetry, what the sound is. If you look at that, if you look at the very complicated preparation musically in a poem, you will find that the best, the tightest poems will prepare in every way for their own climaxes, prepare in thought, prepare in the way the feeling moves, and prepare in the way the meaning moves in sound. And that is the music, the movement of meaning itself. Very often the title itself is part of that preparation. But underneath that is a wish that is native to us, shared by all of us, a wish for the discovery of our own forms, of the form of our experience. And it seems to me that poetry has this to offer, as many of the other arts have, as music certainly has, without the verbal meaning; as movies have. The density of the texture of experience can be given in a poem as in a parable. The movement, the curve of emotion in a poem, is close to something deeply human; it is the finding; it probably has to be lived with without ever completely being defined.[7]

And that brings me to the second part of what I would like to talk about—which is really a relation with the unknown, with the partly known, with the uncertain, with the unverifiable. Now I care, and I know you care, very much—we live in a period of caring about the document, about the documented fact, the kind of fact that can be assimilated in memory, that can sometimes, if you like, be programmed into machines, that can be verified. And you can think of many of these today, things that happened today in your lives—things that can be verified.

But there are also other things, of which one is dreams, things that cannot be verified by anyone else, but which you can give, which you can share with other people, by this skill, by this way of discovering form, by this way of making an experience which is not simply memory, but which is making something new to which you and another person, the reader, can come wanting—in a way—the same state of being. This is the thing that Collingwood calls "the principle" in *The Principles of Art*,

---

7. On poems' "curve of emotion," see Muriel Rukeyser, "The Fear of Poetry" and "The Music of Translation," both in this volume.

where he says, "We get from art a way of understanding what it feels like to be a person who thinks these things."[8]

I think that statement brings the understanding, the feeling, and the thinking into the relationship that I would hope for. For these things are clusters. You have that here physically in the cluster colleges, which I think is the physical type of what is coming.[9] And the fact that the cluster is made to center around the materials, the library, is life; it is that kind of life that does not exist in many colleges, and which is coming, it seems rather quickly in other places, but which, in a poem, cannot be diagrammed a-b-c-d, a movement going from one point to another to another, but rather as a constellation moves, as many lives in their movement, and related always with another constant, a constant which tends to be forgotten and neglected, often despised— which is the unknown, which is a constant in science, as it is in art and the uncertain.

I know President Curtis has spoken about the things I have been living in, the life of somebody in the past, part of a buried life. I thought of all the reasons why I came to this. He was kind enough not to tell you one of the reasons that I gave him—which was that I needed to read this book, and I went to person after person, saying, "You could do this. This needs to be written." And as I talked, I came further into it, and finally the only way I could read it was to write it.[10]

And so one does these bringings-together of kinds of meanings that have been separated in many of the ways of thinking about education where separate fields are defined, lines are made between them. Now I do not think those lines exist in nature, as we say. I do not think that what they call the imagination of science and the imagination of poetry are distinct.[11] And I think that the unifying work, the work that moves us towards the deepest imagination, is the work of which George Sarton

---

8. Paraphrased from R. G. Collingwood, *The Principles of Art* (New York: Oxford University Press, 1938). For more on Collingwood, see Muriel Rukeyser, *The Life of Poetry* (Ashfield, MA: Paris Press), 29, 48–49, 92.

9. Scripps College is part of the Claremont Colleges, a consortium of schools in the greater Los Angeles area.

10. Rukeyser is narrating the origin of her then-in-progress book, *The Traces of Thomas Hariot* (1971). See note 2 above.

11. See C. P. Snow, *The Two Cultures* (New York: Cambridge University Press, 1959). Rukeyser is referencing Snow's well-known thesis.

spoke, saying that if there is progress, it is progress toward the unity of the imagination, the unity of people, the unity of the world.[12]

This has been called very naïve, oversimplified; and it can be seen as that: a chalking-in of very complicated relationships. The minute you have a piece of work, a work of art, a human being before you, then the terms make themselves useful as material, material to take hold of, experience; and one wants not only to take hold of it but to learn to trust it. And that trust of experience is, I think, needed in life as in art.

One of its beginnings is in breath itself, and this is what it is made out of; that is what is shared, also. In a child's book the other day I saw the statement that "all of us are breathing air that Leonardo breathed."[13]

In this timespan the breathing of Leonardo has been mixed with the air that hangs to the world. That is shared, curious breath, a relation to the past, a relation to something we all share. Very often students will deny the linkage. I think of a group of students with whom I have been working this past winter. These students in New York were reading Hart Crane, were reading *The Bridge*, and they started with great excitement; and this began to fall away. He was dead, in the first place. He was an older poet, of another time. They wanted their contemporaries. They wanted to read each other's work. They very much wanted to read their own work to people. They came to a phrase like "fiery parcels."[14] They looked out at New York, where you can see those "fiery parcels" any evening as you can in any city today. They began to fall away completely from this work which they thought of as in the past.

At that point I had what I can recommend to anybody working with students: I had flu; and it's very easy to have at this point, and if you don't have it, it might be a good idea to say you have it, to stay away for a week, at the point at which people who are reading together come to this place in their lives. For what they did was to disregard the assignment given, disregard everything that had happened, start reading their own work to each other, and say to me when I came back the following week: "We learned. We established a rapport. We read our own poems,

---

12. Sarton described "the idea of unity" and "the humanity of science" as two of his guiding principles. George Sarton, *Introduction to the History of Science*, vol. 1 (Washington, DC: Carnegie Institution of Washington, 1927), 9.

13. Italian Renaissance artist and inventor Leonardo da Vinci. Rukeyser's source unidentified.

14. Hart Crane, "To Brooklyn Bridge," in *The Bridge: A Poem* (1930; repub., New York: Liveright, 1992), 2.

which is what we wanted to do"; and they went on believing in this rapport.

Now I'm going back on what I said; this is the other side of it. Because what had happened was that the four or five most articulate people in that room *had* established rapport with each other, but the people who were silent were not yet known, were not known in any way to each other. And these disclosures went on and on as they went on reading. And as they went further they came to an end of wanting their own work read and they brought in William Carlos Williams, they brought in Ezra Pound, they brought in the Russian poets, they brought in each what he had been reading, and the past came in with that vibration which is memory in a curious way, and which enters the presence with its resonance.[15]

A matter that comes to us in relation to poetry, certainly in relation to everything that hangs over and in the imagination of the people we know at this time, a time of war, is a matter of powerlessness—the powerlessness of the poet, the powerlessness of speaking about what seems to us the actual nature of the war and what it is doing to our people. The powerlessness is probably a constant. It has a power within it, and that, I think, is related to the kind of poetry we are talking about. I speak of a raining hour, a raining night, but there is *that* rain, too, and we know what that is, and we know what is happening to the people we speak to.[16] And we see it in the people who, whatever their attitude about the war now, declare for their own imagination what is happening in their own lives. And it seems to me if that were taken fully into our selves, taken into action, it might be the end of all mechanism and mechanistic thinking.[17] I think of all the people I speak to who say: "Why, yes, it was a mistake from the beginning, but what can be done now?"

---

15. Pound and Williams were contemporaries of Crane. Rukeyser breaks here to read from two poems: "Song" ("A voice flew out of the river . . ."), in *CP*, 405; and parts 1 and 2 of "Are You Born?", in *CP*, 379–380, 399.

16. "*That* rain" signifies US carpet bombing in Vietnam. In the wake of the defeats suffered during the Tet Offensive (January to March 1968), mainstream America's support for the war began to decline sharply the year of this talk.

17. In the 1960s, the New Left and the American counterculture viewed the military-industrial complex and mainstream sociocultural attitudes as technocratic. Such critiques are rooted in earlier Popular Front and Second World War-era criticisms of the state as mechanistic.

One thinks of what powerlessness is and the powerlessness of poetry. It seems to me there *is* a power at the center of all of this—whatever people's opinions may be here—and that this power is different in nature from the powers we are taught in many places, the powers that are spoken about, for example, in broadcasting and in the press—the enormous heavy, rather dead powers over us at this time. And that within that there is a power as small, perhaps, as powerless, perhaps, as the power of the infant; and that newborn, the infant, has been spoken of classically as powerlessness. "Infant" is given us as a weak word. I don't think it is a weak word. I think it contains enormous strength—not only a strength of desire which is evident in the newborn, but this power, which is like the power of poetry, the power to evoke. What does the newborn evoke? What does that crying which is so irritating to so many people? What is that irritation? What power is in it?

I think of a passage from Jonathan Hanaghan, in a book called *Society, Evolution, and Revelation*, who quotes Fenichel as saying: "The human infant is born more helpless than other mammals. He cannot live if he is not cared for."[18] Hanaghan goes on to say:

> [. . .]
> The helpless cry of a human baby is not weak and ineffective and archaic. It is the most profound and powerful force in nature. [. . .] It is an utter cry for help and protection, a call first answered by the nipple's tingle to give mother's milk and by overflowing mother- and father-love passing into the infant spirit.
> [. . .] And his self-preservation cry has created the beloved human community on earth, a prefiguring of the divine City of God on earth for it is to be especially noted that the infant has achieved self-preservation by self-abandonment to the answering beloved parents. Further, the infant's self-preservation instinct has served his sexual instinct. His libido has been drawn forth from its narcissistic commitment.[19]

---

18. Otto Fenichel, *The Psychoanalytic Theory of Neuroses* (1945; reis., New York: Routledge, 2006), 31. Fenichel, a German Marxist psychoanalyst, was an associate of Erich Fromm and Wilhelm Reich, both of whom were influences on Rukeyser.

19. Jonathan Hanaghan, *Society, Evolution, and Revelation: Original Insight into Man's Place in Creation* (Dublin: Runa Press, 1957), 19. Quotation abbreviated. Rukeyser and Hanaghan, a Freudian who founded the Irish Psychoanalytic Society, briefly corresponded after she learned of his privately printed book in 1958 while visiting Puck Fair in County Kerry, Ireland. She cites his book in her fictionalized 1965 memoir *The Orgy*. See Muriel Rukeyser, *The*

And I offer to you this as dealing with powerlessness, the powerlessness that has the power to evoke; and that is, I think, the weakness and strength of the art of poetry which is taken as so small a thing with so small an audience. We know the audience is small but we know the people come to it out of some necessity, and that this necessity draws the meaning deep into their lives. I do not compare it actually with the infant cry, about which I believe has the strength that Hanaghan is talking, but I think in all of these kinds of powerlessness that we know in life around us now, and that is deep in the imagination of this time so heavily assaulted with the description of the machine as human, with the power, and the seductive heavy power of these things, each in ourselves.

I wake very slowly in the morning, and this is why I think I do it: I think I am a very violent woman, and I think that every morning I try to be non-violent one day more.[20] It's rather like Alcoholics Anonymous saying, "Just one day more."

And I think this thing of trying to be as human as one can be, making oneself aware daily, all the time, of the real commitment to each other, to the resonance in the world, to the world we breathe.

I think of what Bruno said—and Giordano Bruno comes very much into this work I am doing now—and particularly a late poem of his just before he was caught by going back to Venice and the Inquisition, a wonderful poem, read very little. It's very hard to come by. It is called *De immenso*, and it has marvelous things all through it.[21] I think of one line—and your people here will know seventeenth-century Latin much better than I will ever do. (It is one of the things I fall flat on my face about every three minutes!) But the line says: "*Est animal sanctum, sacrum et venerabile, mundus.*" And I think it means that the world is a living creature, an animal in the deep sense (seventeenth-century Latin)—sacred, holy, to be loved. And I think that these unifying things, and the security—the actual security that comes from dealing with them

---

Orgy (Ashfield, MA: Paris Press, 2007), esp. 79–80, 101–107. Also see Jack Morgan, *New World Irish: New Directions in Irish and Irish American Literature* (New York: Palgrave Macmillan, 2011), 203–219.

20. Rukeyser later retells this anecdote in her 1973 poem "Waking This Morning," in *CP*, 471.

21. Giordano Bruno, sixteenth-century Italian Dominican friar convicted of heresy and burnt at the stake. His book-length poem *De immenso et de innumerabilibus* (On the immense and infinite, 1591), written while exiled in England, doubles as a work of religious philosophy and cosmology. On Bruno, see Muriel Rukeyser, *The Traces of Thomas Hariot* (New York: Random House, 1971), 108–110.

and dealing with them in change—as one goes through a poem and it changes, that this has something to do with human security, swimming in the world. And I think in everything I do of that poem of the newborn.[22]

You have heard a definition of the Humanities before. I thought of Jews and the Jewish people as not perhaps a thing you can say anything about, in a way, and I have been startled by something that has happened, not to me but to a poem of mine, this month. There's been a revision, a new edition of the Jewish Prayer Book which was just published in London and which has just reached me. And they have used a sonnet of mine in this Prayer Book, and it is so strange to see this, you know, unsigned, assimilated, absorbed into the body of poetry, in a way. And it is what one hopes for in general for the best of anything one can do—that it simply be taken into the body of poetry.[23]

A great deal of the form, of the nature of form that I have spoken about, is not a static form, not form as we have sometimes heard about it, but form that casts forward, too, formed in terms of our lifetimes, that is, the kind of form that forms us for the next phase of our lives. We know it perfectly well in the formation of our own bodies, in the embryo forming not for childlife but for mature grown life.[24]

In this kind of form we take to ourselves every means possible. In the attempt of the young now to be finished with the hypocrisies of the grown, you can see everywhere the attempt to find different means of getting at the truth, true experience, whether it is classic means, drunkenness, drugs, art forms that break the forms—all the ways of doing it.[25] And I think again and again these days of what to me is a central poem in our history of taking the means and letting go the means. It is a poem that I have never heard spoken of in this way or taught in this way. It is

---

22. Here, Rukeyser reads her 1939 poem "M-Day's Child," in *CP*, 177–178, which she prefaces in her lecture as "a child poem of another kind altogether."
23. Here, Rukeyser reads her "Poem" ("To be a Jew in the twentieth century"), the seventh part of her sequence "Letter to the Front," in *CP*, 243. After its initial publication in her 1944 collection *Beast in View*, this poem was added without authorial attribution to *Service of the Heart: Weekday Sabbath and Festival Services and Prayers for Home and Synagogue*, ed. Rabbi Chaim Stern and Rabbi John D. Rayner (London: Union of Liberal and Progressive Synagogues, 1967). Later, it was included in American Reform and Reconstructionist prayer books.
24. On fc, an aside gestures to Rukeyser's second talk, not in this volume: "(I want to come to this two days from now.)"
25. Rukeyser alludes to late 1960s American hippie counterculture. The previous summer had been the Summer of Love in San Francisco's Haight-Ashbury neighborhood.

a poem that we all read for the first time in high school, that we all read again in college. It is by Keats. It is the "Ode to a Nightingale."[26] And I suggest this poem as something that is so deep in the present that it can be gone to again in a different way.

Again the title places the entire thing. *Nightingale* is a very hard word to use. "Nightingale" here is a bird that is named once and never again.[27] He is called "bird" after this in the poem—and this the poem of the means, by a young man who knows all the means (he is a medical student), it begins with the drugging sensation, "as though of hemlock I had drunk." And what is it, what does he give us as that? Is it happiness, is it the ecstasy itself? No, it is the very beginning, and he gives it to us as identification, of "being too happy in thine happiness."

This is very curious. What is that to be "too happy"? People do not talk in that way now. But he gives it to us right in the beginning. (I'm referring to this poem assuming we all know it well.) This is really in the tradition. It can be spoken about almost, but not quite, as the main thing, as the main thing that we refer to each other. There is a play in New York called *Rosencrantz and Guildenstern Are Dead*.[28] And it's perfectly easy in that to assume all the action of the play of *Hamlet* going on in the back of the play, with the young, with the students Rosencrantz and Guildenstern wishing that life would be coherent, wishing that life would not be just these little episodes, and we being able to feel all of *Hamlet* going on behind the scenes.

I give you the Keats poem in the same way. But go back and look at it, because after "dull opiate" is wine; after drugs it is wine, not strong wine here but wine, and wine mixed with water, with Hippocrene, with water from the spring of the muses.[29] And from that, and each time taking it fully and letting go, that is what makes the stanza in the poem, taking the drugs, and the misery of "Here, where men sit and hear each other groan."

And if you ask people: "Where is that? Where do men sit and hear each other groan?", you will get several answers from your friends. But

---

26. Romantic poet John Keats, "Ode to a Nightingale" (1819).
27. The word *nightingale* only appears in Keats's title.
28. *Rosencrantz and Guildenstern Are Dead* (1966), English playwright Tom Stoppard's spinoff of Shakespeare's *Hamlet*, had opened on Broadway the previous fall, in October 1967.
29. Keats, "Ode to a Nightingale": "O for a beaker full of the warm South / Full of the true, the blushful Hippocrene." In Greek mythology, the Hippocrene fountain sprung when the hooves of Pegasus, the winged horse, struck Mount Helicon. Its waters were thought to inspire poets.

always among these answers will come *hospital*. That is where men sit and hear each other groan. And that is what Keats knew very well, and he knew the death of his brother besides, and he knew the death of his mother. The young poet, and after that it is poetry itself that he takes hold of for the most experience, for the ecstasy, and lets go of it. I read it once in California, and I came to the line: "Not charioted by Bacchus and his pards," and I said, "You know what *pards* are?" And they looked at me, very California, very affectionate, very kind, and said, "Oh, yes, it's a western term. It means partners!"[30]

"But on the viewless wings of Poesy"—and this is the young poet, the most intense poet—we have no more intense, we have no more wonderful—and letting go of poetry and the coming to the senses, to the selves, to the verifiable facts of sense and crossing them out this way, saying, "I cannot see what flowers are at my feet"; and then giving us the flowers, not through sight but through smell, holding to the senses, holding to the keen verifiable senses. You can go and verify these things. This is not the unverifiable fact.

But he is the young realist. He is not the romantic poet they will give you, "half in love with easeful Death, as the romantic cry, as meaning in love with easeful Death."[31] But it is not that. This is the young poet of saying actually: "But here there is no light," giving us the truth and giving it to us in monosyllables, which the fashion of his time said were not possible in poetry.[32] "But here there is no light," and he broke it again in one of the famous lines you had in school: "But where the dead leaf fell there did it rest."[33] "But here there is no light," and giving us everything in the dark—everything that we feel and smell and hear; and everything that is then echoed through time, in a marvelous stanza which gives us three kinds of time, three kinds of history: king and clown, which is actual historic time; and Ruth amid "the alien corn," which is Bible time, the time of parable, the inner time of dream

---

30. Although the archaic word *pards*, or drinking companions, sounds like the American Western slang term *partner*, they are not directly related.
31. Keats, "Ode to a Nightingale": "I have been half in love with easeful Death, / Call'd him soft names in many a mused rhyme[.]"
32. Keats, "Ode to a Nightingale": "But here there is no light, / Save what from heaven is with the breezes blown[.]"
33. Keats, "Hyperion" (1820):

> [. . .] No stir of air was there,
> Not so much life as on a summer's day
> Robs not one light seed from the feather'd grass,
> But where the dead leaf fell, there it did rest.

and parable; and then the enchanted time and the word "forlorn."[34] And this is the young romantic poet, and a word the people don't dare use at this point. Where have you heard "forlorn"? But he says "forlorn" and "forlorn" is the bell, and "forlorn" is the Zen stroke on the head. And what does it do? It calls him back to what? He says: "to my sole self."[35]

And it is at this point that he lets go of the bird. Look at the poem. He lets go of all the means. The bird is "easeful summer." The bird is "deep song."[36] The bird is his identification as a poet; and he lets go last of this; coming to the great question—and I ask it of you, and ask it of each other: "Do I wake or sleep?" That is the question that is asked when you get to the unverifiable fact.

> Was it a vision, or a waking dream?
> Fled is that music:—Do I wake or sleep?[37]

I would like to ask you one by one. The answerers come up almost always with one answer: "Wake." And it seems to me *that* is the answer one gets to, that one reaches when the verifiable fact and the unverifiable fact come together. That is the second question. Number One was, "How many of you have ever written a poem?", and number Two is, "Do I wake or sleep?"

This brings us to the present as the "Ode to a Nightingale" brings us to the present moment, in which possibility is established again and the making of a relation with the unknown—a relation in which one can live, knowing the unknown to be a constant, not having to have the certainty again that we have been taught in many ways. I think of a

---

34. Keats, "Ode to a Nightingale":

> Perhaps the self-same song that found a path
>   Through the sad dark heart of Ruth, when, sick for home,
>   She stood in tears among the alien corn;
>   The same that oft-times hath
>   Charm'd magic casements, opening on the foam
>   Of perilous seas, in faery lands forlorn.

35. Keats, "Ode to a Nightingale": "Forlorn! the very word is like a bell / To toll me back from thee to my sole self!"

36. The phrases "easeful summer" and "deep song" do not appear in Keats's poem, despite Rukeyser's quotation marks. Death, not summer, is described as "easeful" in the poem. "Deep song" evokes Spanish modernist Federico García Lorca's poetics of *cante jondo*, a region's spirit that possesses poets and thus makes their songs true.

37. Keats, "Ode to a Nightingale," concluding lines.

story of William James, speaking in Boston and asking for questions at the end. A lady asked, "What does the world rest on?"

And he said, "I don't know. What *does* the world rest on?"

She said, "A rock."

He got interested and said, "What does that rock rest on?"

And she said, very straight-necked: "Another rock."

And he said, "And that rock, what does it rest on?"

And the lady said, "Young man, let me make myself clear. It's rocks, all the way!"[38]

That is the secure and the insecure. But at the depth, when one goes to the depths of the rhythms of experience, these recurrences, the discovery of form, that is true each for ourselves, and a relation with the unknown which can change and still be a constant. Then we come to a very curious depth in life, and we find at this depth that—I'll do it in terms of poetry—that the poems that have been obscure, the poems that have been shallow, the poems that have not been possible to share with, however much opening we give them, however much we bring to them—these poems, whether we write them or read them, yield to poems at a further depth at which, curiously, all things can be shared. And there the things one hesitates to show, one thinks of as private (I think of many things I have written that I have not wanted to show at the beginning, poems other people have seemed most to want)—and I think of them in the art that I come to.[39]

(*The Clark Lecture*, 1968)

---

38. Rukeyser narrates this anecdote from memory. See William James, "The Sentiment of Rationality," in *The Will to Believe and Other Essays in Popular Philosophy and Human Immortality* (1897; reis., New York: Dover Publications, 1956), 104.

39. Rukeyser ended her talk by reading four poems from her new book *The Speed of Darkness* (1968): "The Poem as Mask," in *CP*, 413; "The Conjugation of the Paramecium," in *CP*, 414–415; "In Our Time," in *CP*, 417; and "Poem" ("I lived in the first century of world wars"), in *CP*, 430.

Chapter 30

The Music of Translation (1971)

Mr. Flood, Mr. Payne, translators, writers, poets: yes, it cannot be done, and yes we will go on doing it.[1]

The matter of music and the matter of meaning—I think they are not opposed. I don't think the dualities are really opposed and I think the music here has a great deal to do with the meaning as it moves.

The movement of the meaning of what we are doing.

As children, it seems to me we have all come to translations in the same way that we came to the writings in English. Knowing indeed that the French works were against the French background. Feeling our way into something that had happened in France, knowing that the Asian

---

1. Talk delivered on May 13, 1970, at the PEN American Center's Conference on Literary Translation in New York City. Rukeyser begins by addressing Charles Bracelen Flood, the organization's president, and Robert Payne, chairperson of the PEN Translation Committee and the conference's organizer. By this time, Rukeyser had translated the poetry of Octavio Paz (Mexico), Arthur Rimbaud (France), Nelly Sachs (Germany, Sweden), and Gunnar Ekelöf (Sweden). See Muriel Rukeyser, trans., *Sun Stone*, by Octavio Paz (New York: New Directions, 1957); *Selected Poems*, by Octavio Paz, trans. with others (Bloomington: Indiana University Press, 1966); *Selected Poems*, by Gunnar Ekelöf, trans. with Leif Sjöberg (New York: Twayne, 1967); *Configurations*, by Octavio Paz, trans. with others (New York: New Directions, 1971); and *"the difficulties involved": Muriel Rukeyser's Selections from A Season in Hell*, by Arthur Rimbaud, ed. Chris Clarke (New York: Lost & Found, 2019). Rukeyser's early Rimbaud translations have been posthumously recovered. On her unrecovered Sachs translations, see note 6 below.

267

languages were far outside and the collision of the strokes of meaning made as if pictures. All of these are "as if" because the physicality of what we are coming to is perhaps not a physicality as if we are coming to the work entire, to ourselves entire, and to something that is named. We have the "translator-traitor" name-throwing always behind us. And I think we might very well come to it openly.

Perhaps it is not so bad to be called traitors. Many of us have become used to this. We have to translate news; as the government says, to kill is to save, to go in to pull out, and so on.[2] We have been translating all the time. And we are called traitors: many of us are called traitors for being against wars and so forth, because what treason is it to translate? It is some kind of mandarin thing to which we are traitors, but underneath that and I think—to get to the music here—one must dive far underneath into a place where we share experience.

I know in writing poems, the poems that I very often thought of not showing to anybody become the poems that are taken hold of later on. They are not, in another dirty word, they are not the obscure ones that don't go deep enough. For when you dive deep enough into experience you come to a place where we share our lives. And so in language there is something underneath our languages which is shared and this is curious, this is subtle, this is a secret, and also this is known to all of us.

There is something under that. We make mistakes with it all the time. We work for perfection and we fall flat every three minutes. There is no perfection here and we want it.

We want to bring that over. Treason and resurrection and bringing over, these are translations. It is a mythological effort to bring a music over into another life. And it involves one's own lost languages. As if we knew all languages. For example, I do not know Hebrew and when I hear the cantillation of the beginning of the Song of Songs and it says *Shim ha-shirim* I know that means Song of Songs, there's something in me as if it were a lost language of my own. Well, is it? German was the private language of my parents and I flunked German in college because the taboo of not knowing what my parents were saying, that they wanted me not to know, was very strong. And it was not theirs.

---

2. In 1968, the Associated Press quoted an anonymous US Army officer as saying of American aggressions in Vietnam's Mekong Delta, "It became necessary to destroy the village in order to save it."

It was third generation. And you know what happens in this country. We're all translators.

We are the translated people.

And if we are third generation as I am, we know the second generation tried terribly hard to be everything they were not and bleached out all language, all poetry, all jokes *back there*, all cooking of *back there*, not to talk with your hands, Muriel, only Mediterranean people do that. And the mistakes go back the other way. You can get awfully pretentious—sound awfully pretentious. I can sound awfully pretentious in France if Alain Bousquet does as he did translate a title of mine which was called *U.S. 1* which is a little too much of a national—it's a road, you know, it means a coastline to me. It means our conflict, it means my conflict, it means what happens on the Atlantic Coast; but when this comes out in France as *U.S. moi, U.S. 1* which came out as *U.S. I* and so on, that makes something one is not exactly.[3] These things can all happen. All these mistakes, terrible mistakes.

A man cannot be translated, but it is possible through how you say a translator to have a child and certain things can be brought through. Again, every mistake, every ignorance, every falling flat on one's face comes through. It comes through in language. And here we are trying to bring over a significant music, signifying to someone unknown, to you my reader, unknown to me, that perhaps I'm born now, but what makes it significant. In the work entire, one modulated "curve of emotion," as Lawrence said; curve of music in which the last word of the poem can sometimes show you where the tonic is, what lattice as in crystal structure this lives on.[4]

What the poem climbs up to. Oh, take Milton's sonnet on his blindness which has all the waiting and losing and burying and hiding and finally comes to the one word, "wait": not what they tell us in school, it isn't that at all.[5] You come to the word "wait," and on the word

---

3. *U.S. 1* (1938) was Rukeyser's second poetry collection. French poet and critic Alain Bosquet included Rukeyser in his *Anthologie de la poésie américaine* (1956, Anthology of American Poetry) and *Trent-cinq jeunes poètes américaines* (1960, Thirty-five Young American Poets).

4. "The translator is best when he has the plain curve of emotion—preferably dramatic—to convey." D. H. Lawrence, "A Review of *Contemporary German Poetry*, Selected and Edited by Jethro Bithell," in *D. H. Lawrence's Poetry: Demon Liberated, A Collection of Primary and Secondary Material*, ed. A. Banerjee (New York: Macmillan, 1990), 39. Rukeyser uses the phrase "curve of emotion" to describe poetry's relational nature. See Muriel Rukeyser, "The Fear of Poetry" and "Poetry and the Unverifiable Fact," both in this volume.

5. John Milton, Sonnet 19 ("When I consider how my light is spent") (c. 1652-1655). The narrator reflects that "man's work or his gifts" "serve [those] who only stand and wait," not

"wait" the marvelous structure of the sonnet is there, the fact that he is writing poems again is there, the whole thing comes through, absolutely before you. Well, it is that movement, that music, that has to be brought over. And it's a marvelous and terrible game. It can be done at times at which one is unable to write one's own poems and has something one cares for very much. Something marvelous there can be set out before one and worked with. Not spun out of one . . . but in front of one.

And Nelly Sachs, tormented, pursued for the chimneys and the people like sand and the sand itself sharp and abrasive and beautiful and many-colored in her poems. And she believed, in Sweden, that the German police were after her. She asked to translate her poems and a publisher here said I must translate the whole book or none.[6]

All these questions of the quests, one's absolute wish, they say it's going to be presented and then as I was saying before, the people to whom this is going to be significant. The one person, one's listener, to whom this is going to be significant. It doesn't happen often in bringing works entire through. It doesn't happen in bringing a word through. The example that Jespersen uses is "uncle," the Latin word *avunculus*—the root he says generally comes through.[7] People remember the saying and bring this part of the word through. Not here, they remember the "dear little" as if it were a Russian "dear little uncle." We don't get *avus* except in the adjective. We get "uncle," part of "dear little." Our dear littles are the dead writers in this. My pleasure, my joy, and my torture has been working with living poets so one has the frightfulness and blowups and marvelous letters and roses coming from other countries and a frightful letter from Paz came yesterday saying, "what do you mean you're going to print a page of my afterthoughts in the paper edition of my selected poems?" (It's a book we did ten years ago that was to come out in a paper edition.) "I have no afterthoughts and by the way,

---

just those who discharge others "without rest" to do their bidding.

6. Nelly Sachs, German holocaust survivor and 1966 Nobel Laureate. She died the day before Rukeyser's talk. In 1967, two English-language volumes of Sachs's poetry, each involving multiple translators, were published by Farrar, Straus and Giroux. That year, Rukeyser claimed she had been "stopped" from printing her Sachs translations, whose "literal versions" had been completed with unnamed collaborators. Those texts have not been located. See Muriel Rukeyser, letter to Alan Brilliant (Unicorn Press), October 24, 1967, 2 ts carbon pp., LC II:5.

7. Danish linguist Otto Jespersen argues that the word *uncle* has a common root across many languages. See Otto Jespersen, *Language: Its Nature, Development, and Origin* (New York: Henry Holt, 1922), 156–157.

could you rewrite the book completely and could we change the name of the book from *Selected Poems* to something else?"[8]

But this thing of a living voice brought over where one possibly can make a music, and one does not want a faulty music, one wants the clear music, not of clarity, it was said yesterday when the thing is not clear, it must not be translated as clear.[9] But something of the work entire, the word, each word, in itself whatever that is, and with it suggestion, with it silence, with it potential, because it is the thing at its potential.

What it gives us.

What we have in our early reading, this warming of an unknown life present and entire as it all is. As these works in unknown languages are. I think of what must be a frightful translation of the Vietnamese epic *Kim Vân Kiều* and I puzzle that with a script I can't read on one side of the page and a kind of awful prose which cannot possibly be what it is, and now Cambodian poetry.[10] I don't know that I know a single Cambodian poem, and they will be telling us all kinds of things about the Cambodians, and we will not know a thing—could we have a project to translate Cambodian poetry? Could that be made now?

And other translations. I found a box, while in my nerves before speaking I was pacing up and down and drinking water. At the water cooler outside there is this, as an example of the kind of translation that we have. Here's a box with a sign on it—Coffee Stir Sticks. It sounds like a bad translation from the Chinese. Well, what is it? Coffee Stir Sticks. I know what it is. It says, "300 count." You know, maybe it was

---

8. Rukeyser was involved with three translated volumes of Octavio Paz's poetry. See note 1 above. She was the sole translator of the first volume, *Sun Stone* (trans. 1957), consisting of a long poem. For the other two, *Selected Poems* (trans. 1966) and *Configurations* (trans. 1971), she wrote the introductory essays and was one of several contributing translators. The paperback edition of *Selected Poems* was retitled *Early Poems, 1935–1955* (New York: New Directions, 1973). Paz did not provide an afterword.

9. At the same conference, on the previous day, Latin Boom translator Gregory Rabassa argued against incorporating both untranslatable foreign words and domesticating equivalences. Like Rukeyser, he argues instead for listening closely to the original text and making a similar "impression" in the target language: "The translator with a tin ear is as deadly as a tone-deaf musician." Gregory Rabassa, "The Ear in Translation," in *The World of Translation: Papers Delivered at the Conference on Literary Translation*, 81–85 (New York: PEN American Center, 1971), 84, 82.

10. Eighteenth-century epic by Nguyên Du, also called *The Tale of Kieu*. Rukeyser refers to the following prose version, the only full English translation available at that time: Nguyên Du, *Kim Van Kieu*, trans. Lê Xuân Thuy (Saigon: Khai-Tri, 1963). Rukeyser's anti-war activism included her involvement with Vietnamese poetry translation projects.

made in Hong Kong, I don't know. But here is the kind of translation that we have and all our headlines say this all the time. But when you go to each word—I think of the story about Hans Christian Andersen who took an awful lot of beating about everything he wrote and he liked to go to houses and he liked to read the stories and he wanted grownups there and children there and there was a critic there once—there often is a critic, and this one did his job on the story and a little girl looking at the work while the critic was going at it said, "Here's one little word you didn't scold." The word was *and*. You can do that. But there is the work entire. In the translations of Hans Christian Andersen, Rumer Godden speaking about them said they don't come over clear.[11] They have to be transparent, they have to be wonderful translations, and she said something, I don't know how you would translate this. She said they come over as *pawky*. Now I suppose there's a word in every language that we have for *pawky*, but I don't know how to translate that. And yesterday when Isaac Bashevis Singer was doing that and we laughed and we clapped and he was doing all the words for *poor* in Yiddish and I thought of what we do.[12] "I'm going where the climate fits my clothes," and "My pockets think I'm dead." We all have our ways of saying *poor*. But what he was saying was that the killed, the six million, his audience, had been killed.[13] His language has been killed. He didn't say that. He made jokes. That's the way he works. We laugh our heads off and yet an hour later . . . But this is a curious refreshment. This is visiting another culture. Boas used to say the only way to have a holiday really is to go to another culture.[14] This is a holiday that brings something to us as translators, not us as readers because again, one is the twelve-year-old finding the things of the world and realizing in a curious way, a floating way, that these come from other people and other languages. Rilke said, "I believe that no poem in the *Sonnets to Orpheus* means anything that is not fully written out there, often, it is true, with its most secret

---

11. See Rumer Godden, *Hans Christian Andersen: A Great Life in Brief* (New York: Knopf, 1955), 17. Godden cites translator R. P. Keigwin's remark that the atmospheric descriptors in Andersen's poems do not have exact English equivalents.

12. "How many expressions are there in English for *poor*? You can say: 'a poor man, a pauper, a mendicant, a panhandler,' and this exhausts all that can be said about it. But in Yiddish you can say: 'a poor *shlemiel*, a begging *shlimazel*, a pauper with dimples, a *schnorrer* multiplied by eight, a *schlepper* by the grace of God [. . .].'" Isaac Bashevis Singer, "On Translating My Books," in *World of Translation*, 109-113, quotation on 109-110.

13. "The six million" refers to the Jewish genocide of the Holocaust.

14. During the 1950s, Rukeyser worked on several uncompleted projects about cultural anthropologist Franz Boas, including a biography, a selection of his letters, and a reader.

name. All 'allusion' I am convinced would be contradictory to the indescribable 'being-there' of the poem."[15] That "being-there" is what we are trying to bring over.

It can only be done by the *things*. It is working through the flesh. With all its mistakes, it's like bringing up a child. You know, one knows one's own howlers in doing the work and sees the howlers all around one very easily, more easily than one sees one's own often. But, it must be done, it can be done. There is only one poem in the world that I know that can really be translated. And it's the only abstract poem; when I was teaching, students would ask, would speak very often about abstract poetry, concrete poetry (what I think of as poured poems); but there is one abstract poem. It's Christian Morgenstern's "Fish's Night Song":

```
      U U
      - - -
    U U U U
      - - -
    U U U U
      - - -
    U U U U
      - - -
    U U U U
       - -
      U U
        —16
```

That can be translated, yes, you can do it by opening and shutting your mouth or anything else you have. But that is it. And there are these things that move from sound to the meaningless words. We have them, we know what they are. We got them in the old days, a few years ago a woman was not supposed to say it, but well, in the early centuries and the nineteenth, you had O for a meaningless space-holder or something to give it sound and exaltation, and then you had *ah*—"Ah, what

---

15. Rainer Maria Rilke, letter to the Countess Sizzo, June 1, 1923, qtd. in M. D. Herter Norton, foreword to Rainer Maria Rilke, *Sonnets to Orpheus*, trans. Norton (New York: W. W. Norton, 1962), 11. On translations of Rilke, see Muriel Rukeyser, "Nearer to the Well-Spring," in this volume.

16. German writer Christian Morgenstern's "Fish's Night Song" (1905), an early visual poem, was supposedly derived from fish's language. Rukeyser's version corrected here.

avails the sceptred race."[17] That kind of thing. We have something else now. Here is one example which Frances Keene was good enough to show me in the translation that Eshleman did of Vallejo.[18] The line in the poem is "Pero me busca y busca. ¡Es una historia!" and Eshleman has had the generosity to translate it. "But she looks and looks for me. What a fucking story!"[19] Well, that doesn't exist in the original, and it's a dishonor to the word which is dishonored anyway as a kind of monkey insult or superiority sign, but it is used as a placeholder, and we get an awful lot of that. This in translation seems to me an abomination. And when you're translating poems you long for something to solve your torment, every few breaths. Because with almost any other language, you need something for this place, and if it exists, it exists only by turning it and putting in something which generally is not a good idea.

The things that one finds as solvings are generally not good ideas. And you have to think how to bring over something that depends on breathing, throwing against one's heartbeat, thrown against all the muscles in one's body and this is only a way of speaking. What we are talking about is something entire. One's self entire. Jespersen speaking of languages says, you have to remember that it's the mouth and the air passages and the lungs and the abdomen and the body cavity.[20] It's more than that. That's just a beginning. Collingwood says it about painting.[21] We say painting is seen through the eye and done with the hand—nonsense. A painting is made by a man walking up and down in space before another space and working on it and turning his back on it and walking away and sleeping and doing all these other things, and it's seen in the same way. These are entire. The movement in the

---

17. The opening line of Walter Savage Landor's "Rose Aylmer" (1806).
18. Frances Keene, the vice chair of the PEN American Center's Translation Committee.
19. César Vallejo, "Poem to Be Read and Sung," in *Poemas humanos: Human Poems*, trans. Clayton Eshleman (New York: Grove, 1968). Later, for Vallejo's *Complete Posthumous Poetry* (1978), Eshleman retranslated the poem and removed the explicative.
20. See Jespersen, *Language*, 414–415, on the physical vocalization of interjections, including the apostrophe O or *Oh*.
21. Philosopher R. G. Collingwood argues that Paul Cézanne, who "began to paint like a blind man" and "uses color not to reproduce what he sees in looking at them but to express almost in a kind of algebraic notation what in this groping he has felt," disproves the idea that painting is just a visual art. R. G. Collingwood, *The Principles of Art* (New York: Oxford University Press, 1938), 144. Also see Muriel Rukeyser, *The Life of Poetry* (Ashfield, MA: Paris Press, 1996), 29, 48–49, 92.

Translation Bill of Rights from unit to unity is the true movement here.[22] And it is the movement in the translation of poetry, and this is not to exclude prose. This is the total thing, and it depends on every breath we take, and that is a figure of speech. So, there is the thing of an equivalent music, and what is that? Do we try to pull through the tradition in the translations of Emily Dickinson in Italian? The attempt is made to offer a hymn music because Emily Dickinson's poems are based on a hymn music familiar to New Englanders of a certain religion and a certain time. What is that in Italy? What does that bring through? Is the Italian reader like the general average man who forgot the stem of *avunculus* and everybody knows the stem will be the part that's kept? But we have received the word. The stem is the part that has been lost, thrown away. We have to be willing to lose in this. We have to be willing to see a great deal die. We have to trust our forgetting as we all trust our forgetting. We know that these things are in us, somewhere. I can't say that the tradition of China is in us somewhere, it has to be shown to us. But there are correspondences and the work to bring the music through counts on these correspondences and counts on—I've heard people say instinct and intuition but I really don't think there's any such thing. I think it's noticing, noticing very much the thingy quality of poetry, these are physical things. We are physical beings dealing with each other. Suzuki in answering the question about the Buddha offering the lotus was asked, "Isn't that fragile?" And he said, "I speak to you, you speak to me, is that fragile?"[23]

And these things have the tensile strength of a single life.

Now, Isaac Singer speaking yesterday was talking about his lost language. His lost people. And when he said in a charming, hostly manner, "I will translate you, you will translate me," this is a deep, deep

---

22. The event's program lists Robert Payne as presenting "On a Bill of Rights for Translators." PEN American Center Translation Committee, Program for the PEN Translation Conference, May 11-15, 1970, PEN America, 2020, https://pen.org/wp-content/uploads/2020/07/1970-PEN-translation-conference-program.pdf. That document is printed in the proceedings as an unattributed poem. Rukeyser here invokes the lines: "The unit in translation is the entire work: / and the imagination of the translator is concerned / above all with this unity." "Bill of Rights," in *World of Translation*, 8.

23. D. T. Suzuki, Japanese monk who popularized Zen Buddhism in the United States. Rukeyser's anecdote comes from a 1958 televised appearance where Suzuki responded to a question about the Buddha's Flower Sermon. Also see Rukeyser's poem "Fragile" from "Waterlily Fire," in *CP*, 409.

urgent cry.[24] I want to end with a poem called "The Writer."[25] I wrote it, actually, for him, whom I don't know at all, really. But I read that *New Yorker* review tearing him apart—his lost language and his lost people—and I thought of all of us and what music we are trying to carry through and out of what and how we have been willing to risk our terrible mistakes and our terrible failures all the time, and go on making it and make it, knowing it is about perfection, knowing that we cannot hope for it, it is impossible, but we will go on doing it.[26]

(*The World of Translation*, 1971)

---

24. Singer doesn't say this verbatim. His talk concludes with an account of the importance of authors valuing their translators, working collaboratively with them, and appreciating the inevitability of mistranslation.

25. The lecture and published essay conclude with Rukeyser's poem "The Writer," in *CP*, 502.

26. Review not located. Rukeyser may be misremembering a recent, mixed *New York Times* piece on Singer. See Thomas Lask, "The Novel as Process," review of *The Estate*, by Isaac Bashevis Singer, *New York Times*, November 1, 1969.

CHAPTER 31

Thoreau and Poetry (1972)

Thoreau, whom we come to honor, speaks to us today.[1] You have been hearing, seeing the traces of Thoreau in our own time. I imagine much of what I am going to say to you may be recapitulation. But I want to recapitulate for you, from this place where I stand, the effort of a person, in conscious life, to make something that can flash again and again with an integral moment in its flashing. Thoreau speaks to us of the great difficulty of our own lives to pull themselves into that integrity, speaks in that flash of reality, which is the present moment always, which is now, which is the only real, and of which Thoreau was deeply conscious.

I do not know how you have been hearing about him. You have heard from people whose lives are deep in his work and life. Professor Harding, whose work one must know to find this, is here, and Mr. Feinberg, whose work has helped to make this possible, and Carl Bode, who

---

1. This essay appeared in the proceedings of a May 1967 festival at Nassau Community College celebrating nineteenth-century transcendentalist Henry David Thoreau. The book's foreword notes how as public opinion about the Vietnam conflict was shifting, Thoreau's ideas about civil disobedience resonated with students. See Walter Harding, foreword to *Henry David Thoreau: Studies and Commentaries*, ed. Harding, George Brenner, and Paul A. Doyle (Rutherford, NJ: Fairleigh Dickinson University Press, 1972), 7-9.

made the poems available and remade the edition of the poems.[2] Many people, many people living and dead—I think of Matthiessen, whom I knew and who reached Thoreau from where *he* lived in a way that comes into this deeply.[3] The process goes back; it goes back to Thoreau's own recognition of the young Whitman. He came not only to the poems but to Brooklyn; he came here—he speaks of the beach at Rockaway—he lived at Staten Island; he came to Emerson: "The American Scholar" was the address that he heard while he was still at college.[4] And before that, we reach what he reached—the people he reached and their work. I name Goethe, Coleridge, Thomas Browne, because it is these currents that make the process. And it is not simple; it is not a man walking in the woods, as we say "a man walking in the woods." Because every word of Thoreau's would have to be gone to, and gone to according to your own life, according to the difficulties, the parts of one's self that one dislikes, the parts of one's self that won't fit in with all the rest, except with extraordinary and skilled, disciplined, wild effort. Because he was aware, he treated openly the difficulties that he had, the difficulties that are open to us all, in his illness—that is, T.B.[5] How to live with it? The difficulty in facing his own body, which he felt awkward with; the difficulty visible in even a drawing of Thoreau. You can see a lot of it.

There are discrepancies. These are his materials. There are discrepancies in what I have to deal with, with you today, in the way the poems are and in what he believed poetry must be. A lot of this does not "match"; and it is a fact of the not matching which is of value to us, and is deep in this curious man who was like us in that he didn't "match."

How to live with that; how to make a life in this world!

I want to come to "in Wildness is the preservation of the World."[6] You can't come to that without his saying the suburban, very suburban

---

2. Walter Harding, Thoreau Society Secretary; Charles E. Feinberg, a private collector of Walt Whitman's and Thoreau's letters; and Carl Bode, editor and scholar of Thoreau.

3. F. O. Matthiessen, Harvard University professor and Rukeyser's friend, committed suicide in 1950.

4. Ralph Waldo Emerson gave his address "The American Scholar" to Harvard University's Phi Beta Kappa society in 1837.

5. Thoreau struggled with chronic tuberculosis for nearly three decades. Rukeyser delivered her talk after her first stroke, in 1964, which temporarily impaired her speech and ability to write.

6. Henry David Thoreau, "Walking" (1862). Rukeyser's surviving notes, her published essay, and the original editors' notes for the published collection do not indicate the edition of any of Thoreau's writings that Rukeyser referenced. Her notes' page numbers for cited

remark that we all know: "I wish my neighbors were wilder," he said.[7] It's that he didn't have enough of it in himself—he wanted it. He didn't have it in his country—he wanted it. It is the wish, it is the desire, that doesn't match what one sees, this desire of which he is the great artist and saint. And if this leads to the life at Walden, if this leads to civil disobedience, if this leads to the poems, to poetry, if this leads to pieces of a book with titles like "Economy," "Solitude," "Walking," what is this, what does it say to us?[8]

It is not the hermit saint, unified, integrated, finding regularity of verse, making the best pencils that anybody could make at that time, living in friendship with Emerson, living in love so that they are twin stars, no longer planets.[9] It is the man frustrated in friendship, irritating beyond belief; frustrated in love, both his brother and himself turned down by the woman they loved.[10] In love with his own people who were, finally, in Civil War, the culmination of the struggle during his lifetime and long before.

He faces the moment with everything that does not match, that does not fit, and sees this meeting as the potential.

This potential has to be dealt with if one is dealing with reality.

Thoreau wanted to deal with reality. More than walking on the earth and mud and muck, although he would have that; he said he must have that. He said he would find the reality, the rocks, underneath so that you could say, "This is it," of the reality you found.

I want to come to him through poems, and even the people who speak most fully and with most understanding about his poems are likely to say something disparaging in the next moment. Even the people who believe they love his poems will say something that pulls most of it back right after and will take you to his prose. I say there is a huge

---

poems correspond to Henry David Thoreau, *Collected Poems of Henry David Thoreau*, ed. Carl Bode (Chicago: Packard, 1943). Rukeyser's quotations for this edition are sourced from public domain versions. Full bibliographic information for Thoreau's noncanonical journals is supplied.

7. Henry David Thoreau, journal entry, February 27, 1851, in *The Writings of Henry David Thoreau: Journal, Vol. II, 1850–September 15, 1851*, ed. Bradford Torrey (Boston / New York: Houghton Mifflin / Riverside Press, 1906), 171.

8. "Economy" and "Solitude" are chapters in Henry David Thoreau's *Walden; or, Life in the Woods* (1854). "Walking" is not part of *Walden*, though they often are published together.

9. Thoreau innovated the use of inferior graphite in lead pencils, a fact Rukeyser reprises later.

10. In 1839, Thoreau and his brother separately proposed to Ellen Sewall. She declined both.

distinction, even in the rhythms—the rhythms of the prose, say, are wilder than the rhythms of the poems, which are, if you will excuse me, suburban in relation to the forest of the prose. Emerson said that these poems were the best poems to come out of our American forest.[11] But they come out of many things. They come out of the pressure on Thoreau to be a pastoral poet. This was a pastoral strip made in the attempt to make a civilized strip of America. He was reaching for something beyond him as we reach for something beyond us. And it is *that* that did the work on him; it is *that* kind of poet that he is. He will say what he loves in prose, and it's a curious sort of person whom he loves, and he says this of his maxims, "They are not philosophy, but poetry."[12] This is not Goethe; this is not Coleridge; this is Raleigh, Sir Walter Raleigh, and this is one of the ways in which I come to Thoreau.[13]

Raleigh longed for the New World. Raleigh! How could Thoreau have anything in common with Raleigh, a marvelous silver and crimson man, the man whose arrogance is deep of his downfall; with the pearls in his ears; with the fortune spent on his clothing; with a fortune thrown away as a gesture that every child knows as a story—he threw his cloak down before Queen Elizabeth when she came to a plashy place. Raleigh was a seagoing boy, a west-country boy. His family were Grenvilles and Gilberts.[14] He wanted the New World. He wanted these unknown forests, the unknown shores. "Rockaway," says Thoreau. We know Rockaway.[15] It is something quite different by now. It is the coast of the New World, stretching beyond a possible Northwest Passage, stretching beyond the people—unknown people. Red men—what's that? Infinite riches—what's that? Wildness—what's that?

Raleigh never got there. Raleigh was not allowed to leave. Queen Elizabeth would not let him leave. She kept him as Captain of the Guard, all sparkling, outside the court chamber. But young Hariot is how I come

---

11. Emerson's assessment of Thoreau's poetry was mixed: "His poetry might be bad or good; he no doubt wanted a lyric facility and technical skill; but he had the source of poetry in his spiritual perception." Ralph Waldo Emerson, "Thoreau," *Atlantic Monthly*, August 1862, 246.

12. Henry David Thoreau, journal entry, March 15, 1842, in *The Writings of Henry David Thoreau: Journal, Vol. I, 1837–1846*, ed. Bradford Torrey (Boston / New York: Houghton Mifflin / Riverside Press, 1906), 333.

13. At the time of her talk, Rukeyser was researching *The Traces of Thomas Hariot* (1971), wherein seventeenth-century explorer and poet Sir Walter Raleigh figures prominently. Rukeyser later footnotes her recently published book when she mentions Hariot.

14. English noble families and courtiers since the fifteenth century.

15. Beach in Queens, New York.

to Raleigh, young Thomas Hariot, a scientist, the kind of scientist that we have not even imagined yet, because we say men are specialized; a man makes pencils—all right, he is a pencil-maker; a man lives by the side of water, whether it is a pond or the sea—all right, he is a fisherman. Now Hariot was one of the people who had not specialized. Hariot was the young scientist who was the explorer who *did* come here. It is as if we had trained one of our astronauts, one of our poets, one of our scientists, that is, to be an astronaut, to go to the moon, to go wherever, and to write the report—chart it—write whatever it is, tell us.[16] Not describe—we call it describe—*not* describe. Give us an experience so that we have an experience that lets us understand what it feels like to be a man thinking these things.[17]

Raleigh sent the expedition out—this was 1585, it is over three hundred years before Thoreau was doing all this—and Raleigh stayed in England. But Raleigh, in what he wrote, in what he caused people to do, speaks to Thoreau. Thoreau says of the Raleigh writing—I think I can say it without having it before me—says, "It is a branch of greenness laid across the page. It is as if a green bough were laid across the page."[18]

And Raleigh, this man so outwardly different, with so many complexities in his nature, with that pride, with that ability to incorporate his body into his thinking, spoke to Thoreau and formed many of the wild and fresh and difficult ideas of a new world so that Thoreau will say of the difficulties, of the things one reaches for (and this is when he is writing about Raleigh), "What is Truth? That which we know not. What is Beauty? That which we see not. What is Heroism? That which we are not."[19]

It is *that* kind of man who is able to deal with the unknown, with that which he is not, as part of himself. This is how one climbs. This is how Thoreau climbed. This is how we come to what he wanted poems to be. There are two distinct things here, and he allows for both: what he wants them to be and what he makes.

---

16. Rukeyser added this detail to the published essay. The moon landing occurred two years after her original talk, on July 20, 1969.

17. Rukeyser's footnote: Cf. R. G. Collingwood, *Principles of Art* (New York: Oxford, 1938).

18. Rukeyser misremembers a passage from Thoreau's posthumously published 1843 lecture on Raleigh: "It is as if a green bough were laid across the page, and we are refreshed as if by the sight of grass in midwinter or early spring." Henry David Thoreau, *Sir Walter Raleigh*, ed. Henry Aiken Metcalf (Boston: Bibliophile Society, 1905), 89.

19. Thoreau, *Sir Walter Raleigh*, 89.

This is what he says he wants poems to be (he is speaking of Raleigh's poems): "They are in some respects more trustworthy testimonials to his character than state papers or tradition; for poetry is a piece of very private history, which unostentatiously lets us into the secret of a man's life, and is to the reader what the eye is to the beholder, the characteristic feature which cannot be distorted or made to deceive."[20] We are told this about the camera, "which cannot be distorted or made to deceive," and we all know pictures, we all know snapshots, movies. We know what the camera cannot do. But this is the eye, and this is poetry. It is a way that poetry is *not* spoken of very often, "the characteristic feature which cannot be distorted or made to deceive. Poetry is always impartial and unbiased evidence. The whole life of a man may safely be referred to a few deep experiences."[21] It is in this way that Thoreau speaks to us.

Is that true? Is that true for you? That the whole of your life can "be referred to a few deep experiences"? Thoreau doesn't use the word "safely" very often. He is not interested in safety except in this line just quoted. But safely, surely! Think of your main "deep experiences." They are the expressive things. Even if you think of them as "happening to" you, they are the ways in which you have expressed yourself. That is what Thoreau gives us in his view of poetry and in his poems— a momentary flash in which, if a man prepares for it, a life can be expressed to other lives.

Now he does not say, although we know from his life and what he has written and his way of living, he does not speak very much of the discipline that goes into it. He speaks of it obliquely ... not obliquely at all, perfectly straight to it. He will tell us, detail by detail, of what he has observed—that is, what has acted on him. He will say what he cannot tolerate in the society around him, and what he is willing to do to place his body and his life at the situations he cannot tolerate.

His poems can be taken as evidence of this. I would like to quote a few of these poems to you.

---

20. Thoreau, "Sir Walter Raleigh," 69.
21. Thoreau, "Sir Walter Raleigh," 69. The passage's beginning, not quoted by Rukeyser, clarifies her point: "[F]or poetry is a piece of very private history, which unostentatiously lets us into the secret of a man's life, and is to the reader what the eye is to the beholder, the characteristic feature which cannot be distorted or made to deceive."

"I Am a Parcel of Vain Strivings Tied," we are given as the title of this.[22] It is the first line of the poem. These poems have all been taken from among the prose—most of them—jottings, and they should be read that way, because this is a life in writing in which the relationship between prose and poetry is acknowledged openly, always:

> I am a parcel of vain strivings tied
>   By a chance bond together,
> Dangling this way and that, their links
>   Were made so loose and wide,
>   Methinks,
>   For milder weather.[23]

The next poem is called "The Thaw":

> I saw the civil sun drying earth's tears,
> Her tears of joy, that only faster flowed.
>
> Fain would I stretch me by the highway-side,
> To thaw and trickle with the melting snow,
> That, mingled soul and body with the tide,
> I too may through the pores of nature flow.
>
> But I, alas, nor trickle can nor fume,
> One jot to forward the great work of Time,
> 'T is mine to hearken while these ply the loom,
> So shall my silence with their music chime.[24]

And with the sorrows and discrepancy that goes into those comes also a man's own idea of hell. This is Thoreau:

> No earnest work that will expand the frame,
> And give a soundness to the muscles too?
> How ye do waste your time![25]

---

22. Thoreau did not title all his journal poems. Rukeyser references titles supplied by scholar Carl Bode, a conference participant and editor of the volume where her essay first appeared. He also had edited Thoreau's *Collected Poetry* (1943; enlarged, 1965). This edition sources the poems from the journals where they first appeared. Manuscript poems recovered by Bode are noted.

23. Thoreau, untitled poem from "Friday," in *A Week on the Concord and Merrimack Rivers* (1849). Quotation abbreviated; Rukeyser cites the entire poem.

24. Thoreau, "The Thaw" from journal entry, January 11, 1839, in *Writings: Journal, Vol. I*, 71.

25. Thoreau, "No Earnest Work That Will Expand the Frame," in *Collected Poems*, 191. Recovered manuscript poem. Quotation abbreviated; Rukeyser cites the entire poem.

CHAPTER 31

Two more. This is called "Loves Invalides". . . This is the other side. These are the other sides, if you like, of Thoreau, the things—the material—out of which he made, finally, his simplicities:

> Loves invalides are not those of common wars
>   More than its scars—
> They are not disabled for a higher love
>   But taught to look above.[26]

And this is a very short one called "I Was Made Erect and Lone":

> I was made erect and lone,
> And within me is the bone.
> Still my vision will be clear,
> Still my life will not be drear.
> To the center all is near.
> Where I sit there is my throne;
> If age choose to sit apart,
> If age choose, give me the start;
> Take the sap and leave the heart.[27]

He said in his journal on March 25th, a Friday, 1842: "Great persons are not soon learned, not even their outlines, but they change like the mountains in the horizon as we ride along."[28] His greatness comes reflected to us from what he did and what he thought. We have this evidence: he spoke for one's body and one's thoughts, what one writes, one's thoughts or what one lives out in action. This action, as you know, became the great river of disobedience as a means to front *the other* in life, *the other* in society.

Disobedience is of course only a negative way of putting it. The positive way is the fronting: the fronting of life, with hostility reduced all the way down, since one knows what hostility makes in another person. One knows what kind of animal one is and how one responds to hostility. One knows what it whips up in oneself.

I know it is only the violent person who understands nonviolence—who has to wake up every morning and be nonviolent for one more

---

26. Thoreau, "Loves Invalides Are Not Those of Common Wars," in *Collected Poems*, 168. Recovered manuscript poem. Quotation abbreviated; Rukeyser cites the entire poem.

27. Originally concluded the longer poem "Solitude" from journal entry, April 11, 1843, in Henry David Thoreau, *The First and Last Journeys of Thoreau*, vol. 1, ed. Franklin Benjamin Sanborn (Boston: Bibliophile Society, 1905), 135.

28. Thoreau, journal entry, March 25, 1842, in *Writings: Journal, Volume I*, 347.

day.[29] It is only the person who knows what it is to be irritating, to be hostile, who knows what the long physical battle is to put down—not put down, but to deal with hostility in oneself, to use all the parts of it which are usable, because there *are* ways to use war in oneself.

One can make art of this. This is one of the ways of art, to use the warlike, to use the ways of active struggle. It can be shown; it can be given to other people; it can be given in art.

But in the hostilities, in such a war as Vietnam in which the imagination has not yet been released to solve it—it is a political action like the political actions of which Thoreau wrote.

We have the qualities in ourselves to deal with political struggle. The ways which are taken as being hysterical, which are the civilized ways of dealing with political struggle, such as demonstration, speaking, putting your life where your opinions are—these are taken as hysterical and childlike. It is perfectly apparent what is hysterical and childlike. Not childlike, because it is not what children do. It is what wild hostility in oneself does, undealt with, not met with the imagination as Thoreau insisted on meeting it. And simply not paying a tax, walking into jail, is one of the ways to deal with it, so that one prepares oneself for jail. As the California poet Marie Welch said, we would be better off if we did our work improving the conditions of jails, because many of us may go there.[30]

Thoreau saw the life of a poet as part of these ways of responding. And those of you who are students know it in yourselves. You are told always that your student time is a preparing for life—to be something else, to live in some other way. We know the ways of the phases of life, and how in each phase of a man's life he becomes something different. In nature, in a way, as ice, in nature, becomes water—becomes steam, and is all one's life. Thoreau will laugh at some of the preparations. And you know how many times in life you have been told to hold still; don't let your real feelings come into this—you are preparing for another part of life. Thoreau says, "This spending of the best part of one's life earning money in order to enjoy a questionable liberty during the least valuable part of it, reminds me of the Englishman who went to India to

---

29. Rukeyser repeats this sentiment in her 1973 poem "Waking This Morning," in *CP*, 471. Also see Muriel Rukeyser, "Poetry and the Unverifiable Fact," in this volume, note 20.

30. Marie de Laveaga Welch, a California poet, probably said this in a private conversation with Rukeyser, her close friend and ex-lover.

make a fortune first, in order that he might return to England and live the life of a poet. He should have gone up garret at once."[31]

Here is another poem—I read you poems; Thoreau wrote poems, and he said that the real poem is what the poet himself has become. Now, he would argue the other way, too, and say, when you have the poem you don't need the biography. He will give you both sides; he will give you all the discrepancies. But he has said, among the discrepancies, the real poem is what the poet himself has become.

This poem was written and then lengthened. I am going to present it to you in its shorter form, which I love. It is the poem called "Wachusett." This is as it is in the journals:

> But special I remember thee,
> Wachusett, who like me
> Standest alone without society.
> Thy far blue eye,
> A remnant of the sky,
> Seen through the clearing or the gorge,
> Or from the windows of the forge,
> Doth leaven all it passes by.
> Nothing is true
> But stands 'tween me and you,
> Thou western pioneer,
> Who know'st not shame nor fear,
> By venturous spirit driven
> Under the eaves of heaven;
> And canst expand thee there,
> And breathe enough of air?[32]

And this quatrain:

> I've searched my faculties around,
> To learn why life to me was lent:
> I will attend the faintest sound,
> And then declare to man what God hath meant.[33]

---

31. Thoreau, "Economy," in *Walden*.
32. Thoreau, untitled poem from "Monday," in *A Week*.
33. Henry David Thoreau, "Mission," in F. B. Sanborn, "Thoreau's Unpublished Poetry," *Critic*, March 26, 1881, 75. Printed with variations as an untitled poem in Thoreau, *Collected Poems*, 195.

And also this poem. I'd like to read the last lines first and then go back to the beginning, because the strength of what he meant deeply is in small, in seed, in these last lines:

Implacable is Love,—
Foes may be bought or teased
From their hostile intent,
But he goes unappeased
Who is on kindness bent.

It starts with its opposite, of course. It's called, from its first line, "Let Such Pure Hate Still Underprop," and the epigraph is "Friends, Romans, Countrymen, and Lovers":

Let such pure hate still underprop
Our love, that we may be
Each other's conscience,
And have our sympathy
Mainly from thence.

We'll one another treat like gods,
And all the faith we have
In virtue and in truth, bestow
On either, and suspicion leave
To gods below.

Two solitary stars,—
Unmeasured systems far
Between us roll,
But by our conscious light we are
Determined to one pole.

What need confound the sphere,—
Love can afford to wait,
For it no hour's too late
That witnesseth one duty's end,
Or to another doth beginning lend.

It will subserve no use,
More than the tints of flowers,
Only the independent guest
Frequents its bowers,

CHAPTER 31

> Inherits its bequest.
>
> No speech though kind has it,
> But kinder silence doles
> Unto its mates,
> By night consoles,
> By day congratulates.
>
> What saith the tongue to tongue?
> What heareth ear of ear?
> By the decrees of fate
> From year to year,
> Does it communicate.

and now I'm jumping to the end:

> There's nothing in the world I know
> That can escape from love,
> For every depth it goes below,
> And every height above.
> It waits, as waits the sky,
> Until the clouds go by,
> Yet shines serenely on
> With an eternal day,
> Alike when they are gone,
> And when they stay.
>
> Implacable is Love,—
> Foes may be bought or teased
> From their hostile intent,
> But he goes unappeased
> Who is on kindness bent.[34]

I want to stop with these poems, but I want to leave you also with the moment that follows, "in Wildness is the preservation of the World."[35] They don't quote that passage. They stick to the first sentence as if it were a maxim.[36] But it is part of something; and to prepare for that,

---

34. Thoreau, untitled poem from "Wednesday" (The Atlantides), in *A Week*. Rukeyser skips three stanzas at the point she indicates.
35. This quote is not from Thoreau's *A Week on the Concord and Merrimack Rivers* but instead is from "Walking." See note 6 above.
36. The first part of Thoreau's sentence reads: "The West of which I speak is but another name for the Wild [. . .]" See Thoreau, "Walking."

something else that he said in *Walden*: "We need to witness our own limits transgressed, and some life pasturing freely where we never wander."[37] And then to the great statement on wildness, which comes from the man he is to the wildness which we all imagine, "in Wildness is the preservation of the World. Every tree sends its fibres forth in search of the Wild."[38]

(*Henry David Thoreau: Studies and Commentaries*, 1972)

---

37. Thoreau, *Walden*.
38. Thoreau, "Walking."

Chapter 32

Glitter and Wounds, Several Wildnesses (1973)
Review of Anne Sexton's The Book of Folly

At a reading at the Guggenheim Museum, Anne Sexton—after three books of poems—finished one of her poems and said, "But it is not true." That hall feels cold and artificial. It was a beautiful woman standing there, in a beautiful dress. The expectation and the gossip around one was of confessional poetry. Now this is a curious genre, one taken to promise a new order of the secret, and one finds secrets that everyone knows; taken to promise emergent men, emergent women, who may bring to speech the lives of these generations; too, one is often given disposable poems, made without the structural reinforcements, those lattices on which the crystal grows.

However, when Anne Sexton said, "But it is not true," a waver went through the audience. No, I cannot say that, I can speak only for myself. I thought, "It may very well be true." She had cut through the entire nonsense about confessional writing, and returned me to the poem.

The issue in most of Anne Sexton's poems has been survival, piece by piece of the body, step by step of poetic experience, and even more the life entire, sprung from our matrix of parental madness. It is these people, who have come this way, who have most usefulness for us, they are among our veterans, and we need them to look at their lives and at us. It is the receivers of these "confessions" who are the welcomers and the further damagers of the poets among whom Anne Sexton stands, with her father, her mother, the trains of relatives, doctors, nurses, lovers who populate this landscape, and the children in whom we find the same traits, with a difference: they may be dealing with them differently, their poems may be otherwise.

The two books of poems before *The Book of Folly* (published in 1972 and now before us) gave us a gathering-together of forces.[1] I remember the signs. There had been books even earlier: *Live or Die* was shown to me in manuscript with the page on whose back Saul Bellow had written a letter.[2] It was on the front of that page—a draft of his novel—that Anne Sexton had found her title, and it was in the work that was before a group of us at that moment that the instigation for her next work, running along with the poems in *Love Poems*, came.[3]

For Herbert Kohl, speaking to us as we worked for the Writers-Teachers group, said as he said to the high school students he knew, "Why not write fables? Or make something based on fables and childhood stories?"[4] Anne Sexton's *Transformations* followed that reminder.[5] I do not know whether her play, *Mercy Street*, was written after that period, or whether the production I saw was based on earlier writing, but the density of the works—the play of the early flailing life in which our father's fantasies overcome our own, and the poems of the next phase of our other childhood fantasies, inherited from Grimm and the rest—this reality, has fed the last two books.[6]

Love Poems opens with a statement of theme in "The Touch."

For months my hand had been sealed off
in a tin box. Nothing was there but subway railings.

---

1. Anne Sexton, *The Book of Folly* (Boston: Houghton Mifflin, 1972), her sixth collection and the last published during her lifetime, reviewed here. Sexton's previous two books were *Love Poems* (1969) and *Transformations* (1971).

2. Sexton, a fan of Saul Bellow's fiction, corresponded with him and sent him an early manuscript of *Live or Die* (1966). She drew her collection's title from Bellow's novel *Herzog* (1964), as Rukeyser soon mentions. See Diane Wood Middlebrook, *Anne Sexton: A Biography* (New York: Vintage, 1992), 161–162.

3. Circa 1970, Rukeyser wrote an unpublished review of Sexton's *Love Poems* (1969). She repurposes some of its material here.

4. Herbert Kohl founded the Writers and Teachers Collaborative in 1967. Rukeyser, Sexton, June Jordan, and Grace Paley taught for the organization at P.S. 75 in the Bronx.

5. *Transformations* (1971) rewrites classic fairy tales as feminist poems.

6. *Mercy Street* premiered in 1969 at the American Place Theatre, located in midtown Manhattan's St. Clement's Episcopal Church. The title poem from Sexton's posthumous volume *45 Mercy Street* (1976) postdates the play. On Rukeyser's comment about "the last two books," see note 1 above.

CHAPTER 32

> Perhaps it is bruised, I thought,
> and that is why they have locked it up.

The hand lies there like an unconscious woman. It has "collapsed": "Nothing but vulnerable. // And all this is metaphor." And then we are given all the people and reasons for the trouble:

> Then all this became history.
> Your hand found mine.
> Life rushed to my fingers like a blood clot.
> Oh, my carpenter,
> the fingers are rebuilt.
> They dance with yours.
> They dance in the attic and in Vienna.
> My hand is alive all over America.
> Not even death will stop it,
> death shedding her blood.
> Nothing will stop it, for this is the kingdom
> and the kingdom come.[7]

In the next poem, "The Kiss,"

> Before today my body was useless.
> ... Where there was silence
> the drums, the strings are incurably playing. You did this.
> Pure genius at work. Darling, the composer has stepped
> into fire.[8]

These excerpted lines have some of the breath of her speech and her assumption of relation, but it is in the sequence of the book itself that the declaration here is made. It goes on with the architectural statement of Herbert's *The Temple*: "The Breast," "That Day," and one of the few poems in which a woman has come to the fact as symbol, the center after many years of silence and taboo: "In Celebration of My Uterus."[9] We have allowed the language of sex when it was accompanied—really superseded—by wit; or, in this year, accompanied by strobe lights and lack of words on the stage; or, in film, when it is ripped away from the rest of life, ripped away from the exchange of fantasies that is

---

7. Anne Sexton, "The Touch," in *Love Poems* (Boston: Houghton Mifflin, 1969), 1–2.
8. Sexton, "The Kiss," in *Love Poems*, 3. Rukeyser's ellipsis, omitting more than ten lines.
9. All titles from Sexton's *Love Poems*. Rukeyser compares them to the English metaphysical poet George Herbert's *The Temple: Sacred Poems and Private Ejaculations* (1633).

deep in relation; or, as in *Portnoy's Complaint*, when it is really prison literature, so that one's genitals become the image of the world, the only beautiful thing, the only loved thing.[10] In Anne Sexton's poems, the world is here—Capri, Vietnam, Boston, Africa, Washington, the house, the bedroom—and the other person is here, or absent so strongly that he is "a weird stone man / who sleepwalked in, whose features did not change."[11] Although Anne Sexton wrote poems in high school, she soon stopped. What happened to let her come through this Afterlife of the American Girl, to take the reality and dance it, physical it, allow it always its whiskey and its gold skin, its psalms and the Papa and Mama dance?

There are traps here. There is always the chance to fall over into total sanity, a kind of fashionable grotto, the death of Elinor Wylie, in which the world is "gorgeous" and "crystal."[12] But here is a woman who *was* a model, who *was* a librarian. Sometimes you think it is going to be the marriage of E. E. Cummings and Marion Morehouse that is doing the writing.[13] But these poems always ride steady again, furious and seductive; the woman is swimming, lying on the water,

> The walls of that grotto
> were everycolor blue and
> you said, "Look! Your eyes
> are seacolor. Look! Your eyes
> are skycolor." And my eyes
> shut down as if they were
> suddenly ashamed.[14]

It is that movement that brings the poems through the narcissism, the breakage, the wounds. Into what? Song and connection and delight, brought through by a poet who has transformed acrid experience into

---

10. Rukeyser's quick references: wit and eroticism were common in seventeenth-century metaphysical poetry like George Herbert's; the opening of New York City's Loft in 1970 launched the disco scene; New York City vice officers began a crackdown on proliferating porn theaters in 1972, following the release of Gerard Damiano's blockbuster *Deep Throat* (1972); Philip Roth's novel *Portnoy's Complaint* (1969) includes an infamous scene in which the narrator masturbates with a piece of liver.

11. Sexton, "December 2nd" from "Eighteen Days Without You," in *Love Poems*, 47.

12. Elinor Wylie, a popular American poet celebrated in the 1920s for her personal beauty and subjected to various scandals due to polygamy and remarriages. "Gorgeous" does not appear in Wylie's poems, but the word "crystal" recurs frequently.

13. Modernist poet E. E. Cummings was married, from 1934 until his death in 1962, to the first American supermodel, Marion Morehouse.

14. Sexton, "The Nude Swim," in *Love Poems*, 15.

her own words and her own touch reaching another person.[15] Reaching the reader superbly, as in this poem of one of the days of absence in the group "Eighteen Days Without You":

> Then I think of you in bed,
> your tongue half chocolate, half ocean,
> of the houses that you swing into,
> of the steel wool hair on your head,
> of your persistent hands and then
> how we gnaw at the barrier because we are two.
>
> How you come and take my blood cup
> and link me together and take my brine.
> We are bare. We are stripped to the bone
> and we swim in tandem and go up and up
> the river, the identical river called Mine
> and we enter together. No one's alone.[16]

The Book of Folly draws on all Anne Sexton's earlier work, and a fertile transformation can be seen.

> Once there was blood
> as in a murder
> but now there's nothing

gives us a theme.[17] The parts are here, one's mother's breasts, Mary's breasts for Jesus, "His penis sang like a dog," and the angels, the rather Spanish angels, "Angel of blizzards and blackouts, do you know raspberries . . . ?" and the larger statement, which when it comes, sounds too much like Sandburg,

> We are America.
> We are the coffin fillers.

---

15. Rukeyser's footnote: "Reaching past her earlier poems in mastery, echoing the earlier knowledge of 'The Truth the Dead Know,'

> My darling, the wind falls in like stones
> from the whitehearted water and when we touch
> we enter touch entirely. No one's alone.
> Men kill for this, or for as much . . . ."

Anne Sexton, "The Truth the Dead Know," in *All My Pretty Ones* (Boston: Houghton Mifflin, 1962), 3. Rukeyser's ellipsis.

16. Sexton, "December 11th" from "Eighteen Days Without You," in *Love Poems*, 58.

17. Sexton, "The One-Legged Man," in *Book of Folly*, 16.

> We are the grocers of death.
> We pack them in crates like cauliflowers.

But it goes on, a little further,

> And the woman?
> The woman is bathing her heart.
> It has been torn out of her
> and because it is burnt
> and as a last act
> she is rinsing it off in the river.
> This is the death market.[18]

The "confessional poem" is beginning to turn into something, and I think we have waited for this for a long time.

I heard a woman-poet say, "It's really the distinction between those woman poets who are attractive and those who really aren't like poor — — isn't it?" Well, of course it isn't, but that adheres to the name in its own time, and beyond. When the live woman is attractive, is part of her own and Sylvia Plath's fable, works with a music group, trails clouds of Robert Lowell, has a Pulitzer and various epaulets, you have also an actress-persona, and actress before you.[19]

But when the live poet is a woman writing sonnets of angels:

> Angel of fire and genitals, do you know slime,
> that green mama who first forced me to sing,
> who put me first in the latrine, that pantomime
> of brown where I was beggar and she was king?
> I said, "The devil is down that festering hole."
> Then he bit me in the buttocks and took over my soul.

and, in "Going Gone,"

> Although you are in a hurry
> you stop to open a small basket

---

18. Sexton, "Jesus Asleep," "Angel of Blizzards and Blackouts," and "The Firebombers," in *Book of Folly*, 95, 61 [Rukeyser's ellipsis], 15. Rukeyser compares the two quoted passages from "The Firebombers," which opposes US-inflicted atrocities during the Vietnam conflict, to Carl Sandburg's modernist poem "Chicago" (1914), an indictment of labor injustice during the industrial era.

19. Sylvia Plath and Robert Lowell often are called confessional poets. From 1968 to 1974, Sexton fronted Anne Sexton and Her Kind, a "touring chamber rock group," reading her poems to rock music. See Middlebrook, *Anne Sexton*, 143.

CHAPTER 32

> and under layers of petticoats
> you show her the tiger-striped eyes
> that you have lately plucked,
> you show her your specialty, the lips,
> those two small bundles,
> you show her the two hands
> that grip each other fiercely,
> one being mine, one being yours.
> Torn right off at the wrist bone
> when you started in your
> impossible going, gone.

—then one sees that the long walk out the other side of the struggle, madness, into the other struggle, to use madness, has made a poet who no longer looks at the audience to see how the confession is going.[20] For those confessions had to have their "other"—and the other, the audience, fattened on confessions, not even eating, they were not nourished by them, not using them in any way at all.

It has remained for the poet to use the early confessions and make a second poetry out of them. We see the gossip produced by that period all around us, and we also see the result of several battles, in their slightest, lightest terms, as well as the ones we all know. Still men talk about Emily Dickinson—last week, on a remote island in Canada, I heard a doctor and a student ask each other whether she really slept with him, she certainly wanted to, all her life. And I had a book-length manuscript from a woman poet—the stamps the package carried were twelve Emily Dickinsons and one Planned Parenthood.[21]

The contortions here, the deaths, the fathers, the silences, all turning into

> Father,
> we are two birds on fire

give us the versions of any one experience—even in the stories that begin to enter these books, here in "Dancing the Jig" and the others.[22] The

---

20. Sexton, "Angel of Fire and Genitals" and "Going Gone," in *Book of Folly*, 57, 20.
21. Rukeyser's mention of Planned Parenthood invokes *Roe v. Wade*, the US Supreme Court's January 1973 ruling protecting women's reproductive rights.
22. Sexton, "Begat" from "The Death of the Fathers," in *Book of Folly*, 53. *The Book of Folly* includes three stories: "Dancing the Jig," "The Ballet of the Buffoon," and "The Letting Down of the Hair."

variousness reminds me of the great example out of Coleridge, who wrote to his wife, "a stye, or something of that kind, has come upon & enormously swelled my eye-lids, so that it is painful and improper for me to read or write," and wrote to Wordsworth,

> O, what a life is the eye! what a strange and inscrutable essence!
> Him, that is utterly blind, nor glimpses the fire that warms him;...
> Even for him it exists! It moves and stirs in its prison!
> Lives with a separate life: and—"Is it a Spirit?" he murmurs:
> "Sure, it has thoughts of its own, and to see is only a language!"[23]

I think of his "confessionals" and the nonsense that critics have issued about him, speaking of his incompleteness when he is the one who knows of the search for completeness.

What, then, is the place reached now by the women who have gone through the steps, as Anne Sexton has? What processes are brought together? Can these poems bring the moment through? *Folly*, the word in its title, speaks for the book. Sanity and madness as daily life—the folly that offers

> ... air to have.
> There are gulls kissing the boat.
> There is the sun as big as a nose.
> And here are the three of us
> dividing our deaths,
> bailing the boat
> and closing out
> the cold wing that has clasped us
> this bright August day.[24]
>
> *(Parnassus*, 1973)

---

23. Samuel Taylor Coleridge, letter to Sara Coleridge, December 2, 1798, in *The Collected Letters of Samuel Taylor Coleridge*, vol. 1, *1785–1800*, ed. Earl Leslie Griggs (1956; reis., New York: Oxford University Press, 2000), 449; Coleridge, "Written during a Temporary Blindness in the Year 1799" (1828). Rukeyser's ellipsis.

24. Sexton, "The Boat" from "The Death of the Fathers," in *Book of Folly*, 45. Rukeyser's ellipsis.

CHAPTER 33

The Life to Which I Belong (1974)
Review of Franz Kafka's Letters to Felice

Put away all questions of *should*. I cannot deal with them. Should these letters have been published; or Kafka's books?[1] Should Max Brod have kept his promise? And Emily Dickinson's packets of poems? And Byron's papers in John Murray's fireplace? And Lady Burton?[2] Should this child have been born, whose mother said, "No, I will not have the child"?[3]

They do exist, and I cannot talk about *should*. I need these letters; I take Max Brod's responsibility on myself. What a piece of pretentiousness! Simply, I read and read these letters, and try to imagine the lost others, and the letters from Felice, the young woman who lived far away in Berlin, with war, work, many kinds of separation between them, and

---

1. Franz Kafka, *Letters to Felice*, ed. Erich Heller and Jürgen Born, trans. James Stern and Elisabeth Duckworth (New York: Schocken Books, 1973). The volume contains Kafka's correspondence to his fiancée, Felice Bauer, plus a few letters to Bauer from Max Brod, Kafka's literary executor. Brod ignored Kafka's order to destroy all his manuscripts, including what would become all his major literary works, after his death.

2. Emily Dickinson's poems, gathered as sewn fascicles, were collected posthumously. The sole copy of Lord Byron's memoirs was burned upon his death by his publisher, who feared connection with the poet's libertinism. The scandalous autobiography of Lady Isabel Burton, wife of explorer Sir Richard Francis Burton, was published a year after her death.

3. Muriel Rukeyser wrote this review one year after the US legalization of abortion through *Roe v. Wade* (1973).

all the time this heroic life being poured on her in an attempt not like any other I know.

This "review" has been put off for months, while all the others were being published. I have seen little squibs that say that these are sad letters, tragic letters of a marriage attempt that was doomed from the start. Something is happening here that is quite different in nature from all that.

These letters are the attempt to show the entire person to the beloved, in preparation for an enduring relationship. Preparation for marriage, as living together might be thought of as real in itself, and also a preparation. Sometimes these two people spoke of "going to Palestine," also.[4] Five years in Prague, with a permanent relation to writing and with a tidal, deep, foreboding relation to this woman, to his family, and to some partly-known, partly-unknown opponent within himself. This opponent turns out to be tuberculosis, death, suppression of the written work; and also the last wills and commands and even a suicide letter. The "opponents," along with his friend and ally, Max Brod, may have been Kafka's protectors. But we know that part of the story: the stories were published, and the unfinished novels. They were saved and turned loose into our world, and a future world. Max Brod did go to Palestine, to Tel Aviv, and lived to see this process moving fully, the full life of his surpassed promise.[5]

For whom were these letters and fictions written? For whom is a child conceived? This is rhetoric, having nothing to do with the young man Kafka.

When Franz Kafka met Felice Bauer in the summer of 1912 in Prague, he was working for the Workmen's Accident Insurance Company (as he continued to do). A recent entry in his diary had said: "The moment I were set free from the office, I would yield at once to my desire to write an autobiography."[6] The letters to Felice are, in a certain way, that autobiography. They must be taken with his other writings and his diaries. But Kafka wrote them to Felice. It was she who had to receive them. She had to come to the decision about marrying him. Twice they were engaged, and finally the engagement and the letters ended.

---

4. Quote not from Kafka's letters. His first letter recounts that, upon their meeting, Bauer made "a promise to accompany him next year to Palestine," and he repeatedly mentions their unrealized trip thereafter. Kafka to Felice Bauer, September 20, 1912, in *Letters*, 5.

5. In 1939, Max Brod and his wife fled Nazi-occupied Prague to Palestine.

6. Franz Kafka, diary entry, December 16, 1911, in *Diaries 1910–1913*, ed. Max Brod, trans. Joseph Kresh (New York: Schocken Books, 1965), 181.

CHAPTER 33

"A hail of nervousness pours down upon me continuously," he writes, after "Oh, the moods I get into, Fräulein Bauer!" and he adds, "What I want one minute I don't want the next. When I have reached the top of the stairs, I still don't know the state I shall be in when I enter the apartment. . . . But oh, what has happened to the trip to Palestine?"[7]

In October of their first season, the letters are becoming necessary. He understands his continual and "circular complaining."[8] It is the way he moves. New emergences are beginning to tear at him. A letter is not answered, it has been lost; he knows he must write to Felice, he must know what she is doing when the letter arrives, when she writes to him, when she doesn't write. He, in Prague, follows her in all imagining as she goes to the theatre in Berlin—all good except for one, at which he had yawned, a yawn wider than the stage—and at her office, and on her journeys—why had she gone first-class?—and in her packing, and what she is going to read.

It is long past his death, we know Kafka, we pretend to be wise after the fact, and we see the signals of terrible danger. Can a man tell his beloved *this much* about himself, all the fever of his dread, all the diseases of his hope and his body? What kind of beloved will accept this surf of precise anxiety, the detail of truth? Could an older woman with a family take this? Who? George Sand?[9] Some wise woman with a house, money, her own children? A man? Verlaine?[10] A dragon?

October 31, 1912—"Dear Fräulein Baeuer, Just look, how many impossibilities there are in our letters."[11]

November 1, 1912—". . . . Just as I am thin, and I am the thinnest person I know (and that's saying something, for I am not stranger to sanatoria), there is also nothing to me which, in relation to writing, one could call superfluous, superfluous in the sense of overflowing."[12]

Max Brod, in that same month, writes a letter to Felice that at first glance seems defensive and possibly harmful, too descriptive of Kafka's drawbacks, really an act of disservice. But this letter of Brod's continues: ". . . conflicts arise which one must try and help him to overcome with understanding and kindness, aware that such a unique and wonderful

---

7. Kafka to Felice Bauer, September 28, 1912, in *Letters*, 6-7. Rukeyser's ellipsis.
8. Kafka to Felice Bauer, October 23, 1912, in *Letters*, 10.
9. George Sand, nineteenth-century French novelist, née Amanthine Lucile Aurore Dupin.
10. Paul Verlaine, nineteenth-century French Symbolist poet and lover of Arthur Rimbaud.
11. Kafka to Felice Bauer, October 31, 1912, in *Letters*, 19.
12. Kafka to Felice Bauer, November 1, 1912, in *Letters*, 21. Rukeyser's ellipsis.

human being deserves to be treated in a different way from the millions of banal and commonplace people.... Franz suffers greatly from having to be at his office every day until 2 o'clock. In the afternoon he is exhausted, so all that is left for the 'profusion of his visions' is the night. This is tragic. And there he is, writing a novel that puts everything I know in the way of literature in the shade. What might he not achieve if he were free and in good hands!"[13]

The figure of Franz Kafka begins to take on darkness, lightness, ardor, a dramatic grace, as these scenes fill. One identifies, as in a fine play, with both people—in the finest plays, it is with everyone that one identifies. But not the parents, who go through Kafka's pockets and read his letters, who come down heavily, oppressively upon his life with the demands of their disappointments. It is not until much later in this book that the reader suddenly learns that Kafka, who is thirty, is living in a room that is between the living room and his parents' bedroom. Slowly, one understands that his mother has made inquiries in Berlin about Felice Bauer, and "one hears particularly that you are an able cook."[14] The question then comes up: will Felice want to cook the vegetarian meals that Franz eats?

The warnings come: his sense of unreality, his illnesses, his need to write every day. The apartment he finds for them, in wartime Prague, has no kitchen. The whole setting-forth of the way of life that Kafka needs, in order to do his work, in a tight regime that will allow him to earn a living, to rest and eat, and then to get to work until the deep hours of the night.

It is the war that is tearing at them. "Once the war has come to an end without causing too much destruction, presumably conditions will be quite favorable," Kafka writes in March 1915.[15] But he warns Felice that she must not hope for—is it beautiful children? is it any children?

All the time, the writing is growing, the flat, marvelous stories, the novels and parables. Alongside these torments, this drama which Kafka has set up to make it all impossible for them both. He must have a doctor's examination; but if the medical report is good, he will know not to believe it.

---

13. Max Brod to Felice Bauer, November 15, 1912, in Kafka, *Letters*, 43. Rukeyser's ellipses.
14. Kafka to Felice Bauer, July 1, 1913, in *Letters*, 282.
15. Kafka to Felice Bauer, March 3, 1915, in *Letters*, 447.

He writes to Felice's mother, "As I have often observed, heard, and said, I am not altogether easy to get on with, not even for myself..."[16]

And now the encroachment of silence. "Dearest, not a single word, for days and days."[17] Suddenly, glimpses of possibility, trips, plans, promises, letters speaking of Flaubert, Dickens, the chances of their happiness.

In this superb translation by James Stern and Elisabeth Duckworth, trust is made for the reader of the English version. But in the pits of expression, Kafka says to Felice about another apartment he has found in Prague, "you would have to do" for a short time "without a kitchen of your own, and even without a bathroom."[18] In the next letter, the stab comes. The opponent.

In September, 1917, the first "hemorrhage of the lung" arrives.[19] After the headaches and suffering, what Kafka calls "neurasthenia," the diagnosis is of tuberculosis in both lungs.[20] Kafka now sees himself clearly as two combatants, "as you know," he writes to Felice, and tells her that the better of the two belongs to her.[21] "A decisive stab" has been delivered by one of the combatants, and he rushes to accept the decision.[22]

The drama of the long struggle belongs with *The Trial*, *The Castle*, *Metamorphosis*, the *Parables*, and the other stories.[23] Franz Kafka and Felice are here as characters of ramifying reality, full of gifts and forebodings, of great riches to us, dangerous beyond belief and charged with dailiness that we know from his stories and our dreams and waking lives.

What I would really like to do is to keep a diary of events during the time of thinking about Kafka's letters. The endless thinking about Felice. What happened to her in America? Are her children in New York?[24]

---

16. Kafka, postcard to Felice Bauer's mother, November 14, 1916, in *Letters*, 533. Rukeyser's ellipsis.
17. Kafka, postcard to Felice Bauer, November 21, 1916, in *Letters*, 534.
18. Kafka to Felice Bauer, n.d. [December 1916/January 1917], in *Letters*, 542.
19. Kafka to Felice Bauer, September 9, 1917, in *Letters*, 543.
20. Kafka does not describe his illness this way in 1917. In March 1913, though, he used the term *neurasthenia* in relation to his insomnia. See Kafka to Felice Bauer, March 21, 1913, in *Letters*, 227. Later letters tie the hemorrhages to his chronic sleeplessness and headaches.
21. Kafka to Felice Bauer, n.d. [September 30 or October 1, 1917], in *Letters*, 544.
22. Kafka to Felice Bauer, n.d. [September 30 or October 1, 1917], in *Letters*, 545.
23. Fiction by Kafka: *The Trial* (1925, posthumous), *The Castle* (1926, posthumous), *The Metamorphosis* (1915), and *Parables and Paradoxes* (1961, posthumous).
24. Bauer fled to Switzerland with her husband and children in 1931 and then moved by herself to upstate New York five years later.

That man who passed me on 48th Street yesterday, could he have been Felice's son?—he had something of her look. Certain facts make their entrances among the dreamlike realities of the *Diaries* and *Letters*. Here is Kafka, sending his manuscript off—or, rather, Max Brod, sending the book off—to Kurt Wolff. And *here*, today, is Helen Wolff suddenly met on 48th Street—that extraordinary woman with whom I have a certain work to do, to my happiness.[25]

For months, I could not think at all about these letters, or write. This happened, too, when I first read *Metamorphosis*. His hand—somebody's hand—was about my throat for a long time. Don't make assumptions, Muriel, don't think that because your parents, too, were Bohemian-German Jewish that these smiters you read are not there for everyone who reads. But let nobody think that I will tell what happened in my parents' living room the night of my thirtieth birthday.[26]

Kafka saying, "And since that is the life to which I belong, it can never be exhausted by scrutiny."[27]

(*American Poetry Review*, 1974)

---

25. With her husband, Kurt, Kafka's German publisher and the founder of the American press Pantheon Books, Helen Wolff emigrated to New York City in 1941. She was a trustee at the PEN American Center, a literary and human rights organization with whose Translation Committee Rukeyser was involved. See Muriel Rukeyser, "The Music of Translation," in this volume. Rukeyser became the first female president of PEN one year after this review appeared.

26. We still do not know.

27. Kafka to Felice Bauer, December 15, 1912, in *Letters*, 105.

CHAPTER 34

Women of Words: A Prefatory Note (1974)

Why should there be a book of poems by women?[1] "If they are any good," a publisher (male) says, "they can stand up in an anthology with men." What will such a book be, a kind of wastebasket?

Why does a woman write a poem? This question has not come up during all the rising questions now being asked; and this moment, the time of publication of this book, may be the last moment for such questions. You will hear queries about equal rights, about dominance, about orgasm—Is there a vaginal orgasm? The answer to that is: Since there is orgasm every other inch of the body, why not there?

But deeper, as deep as these, are the questions concerning the poems of women, and they are answered here. Or partly answered. Because this race of women, the women poets, have opened a music in their lives that out of a mixture of strength and weakness, sex and protest, visibility

---

1. This essay is Muriel Rukeyser's preface to the second-wave feminist poetry anthology *The World Split Open: Four Centuries of Women Poets in England and America, 1552–1950*, ed. Louise Berkinow (New York: Random House, 1974). A line from her 1968 poem "Käthe Kollwitz," in *CP*, 463, lent the volume its title: "What would happen if one woman told the truth about her life? / The world would split open." The anthology closes with Rukeyser's 1939 poem "Ann Burlak," in *CP*, 191–195, about a labor organizer.

and invisibility, offers us a glimpse of possibility that we may be on the edge of claiming.

Have you ever known the curious happiness and sadness of the young woman poet, who is such a source of confusion to her family and the people around her, if they are culturally tied, hobbled, spancelled, as the Irish say? Have you ever lived in a jail for women, and felt the solidarity and frustration of that suffering, imposed so wildly and lopsidedly?[2] Have you known the double joy and despair of women as daughters and poets? Or the joy and until recently the despair of women homosexuals; or wives or mothers? These may be extremes of what we see here, but they may not be. These cries, these formalities, these bursts of song, this formal music, seen in a brief sampling of four hundred years, will let you make your own decision. We have had Men of Letters; here are the Women of Words.

We have seen many of these writers before. They have appeared in glorious anthologies—I think of Louis Untermeyer's, with his critical building and introducing of the poets I first met—or in books by women devoted to one woman poet, like Marya Zaturenska's work on Christina Rossetti.[3] But here they stand in a procession that says extraordinary things to us.

That procession begins, for me, with Miriam and Deborah and Sappho.[4] The last will be found in Louise Berkinow's sharp and fascinating introduction, but the other two—who dealt with triumph and justice—are not mentioned.[5] It is the haunting beauty of that long procession that stays with me, along with certain poems and songs which you will find here. That beauty has been selected out for you. You do not feel it when all the poems, by women and men, are grouped together.

How do poems by women reach students in the schools today? One undergraduate said to me, "There are no women poets until after

---

2. Rukeyser alludes to her brief incarceration in 1972, following her arrest at an anti-war protest. See Muriel Rukeyser, "The Killing of the Children," in this volume.

3. On Louis Untermeyer, see Muriel Rukeyser, "Poetry and the Unverifiable Fact," in this volume, note 6. Socialist poet Marya Zaturenska wrote the biography *Christina Rossetti: A Portrait with Background* (New York: Macmillan, 1949). For a review of Zaturenska's poetry, see Muriel Rukeyser, "The Classic Ground," in this volume.

4. On the influence of biblical figures Miriam (from the book of Exodus) and Deborah (from the book of Judges), as well as ancient Greek poet Sappho, see Muriel Rukeyser, "Many Keys," in this volume.

5. The anthology's introduction mentions Sappho only in relation to posthumous collections' omission of certain poems by Christina Rossetti. See Louise Berkinow, introduction to *The World Split Open*, 5.

Easter." In this book, Queen Elizabeth, Aphra Behn, and a few others, come "before Easter," and if the book were opened to poetry in translation, of course there would be many more.

And here we come to poems by black women, mill workers, blues singers, set with the "literary" forms. Many musics.

Often there are gaps, for the heroes can be the "ten anonymous women," of my "Ann Burlak" poem in the thirties.[6] And some of the questions are not here—"Will the male voice answer?" Marya Zaturenska asks in a poem.[7] And Sara Bard Field, Elizabeth Bishop, Léonie Adams, Marie Welch—they come in the same procession.[8] The poets I have just named were publishing widely before 1950, the cut-off date of this book. It is a good stopping-place, the end of one stage of what I called in "Ajanta" (1941) "the journey, and the struggles of the moon."[9] The journey reached a turning-point; the moon—in all the senses with which we reach her—took on new meaning.

But, even after those years, I remember reviews of books by women poets grouped in a "liberal" magazine under the title "Ladies' Day."[10]

There are traces in the poems here of the attempt to get through the burden of sorrow that the speech—speech alone—of women has brought on them; attempts to get through the hostility engendered by that frustration; attempts to find one's own voice, clear of those choking emotions. These are poems, not simply of protest, not simply of the cunt, but of the person entire, the woman.

Yesterday, in a city park, I saw fifty flying children, girls, boys, running along the stone in what looked like free patterns. One girl lifted up a small bright cape, and ran. Maybe these children will be spared the weight of the burden that even their parents—brought up since

---

6. The title figure "speaks to the ten greatest American women," all described as "anonymous." Rukeyser, "Ann Burlak," in *CP*, 193.

7. "Clear woman's voice, long fingers whitely straying, / Over the speaking keys, do you hear the answer? / Will the male voice answer?" Marya Zaturenska, "Woman at the Piano," in *Golden Mirror* (New York: Macmillan, 1944), 36.

8. Twentieth-century American women poets, who do not appear in Berkinow's anthology and who, except for Bishop, still lack critical attention.

9. Rukeyser, "Ajanta," in *CP*, 211.

10. See Oscar Williams, "Ladies' Day," *New Republic*, October 23, 1944, 534-536. This group review of Rukeyser, H. D., Marianne Moore, Marya Zaturenska, and others describes their new works as "little books." Also see M. L. Rosenthal, "Ladies' Day on Parnassus," *The Nation*, March 16, 1957, 239-240. This chauvinist group review of Katherine Hoskins, Kathleen Raine, and Moore appeared in *The Nation*, the same year that the magazine rejected Rukeyser's groundbreaking essay on women's poetry, "Many Keys," in this volume.

1950—have felt. Maybe their poems. Or does it take forty years in the desert, clear of that "Egypt" of women, those idols, those fleshpots, those pyramids of death and power, before we can make an art that is not branded?

But that is the next book. Here is this one, a good one.

(The World Split Open, 1974)

Appendix

Bibliographic and Archival Information for Selections by Muriel Rukeyser

Full bibliographic information about each of this volume's selections is supplied below, in order of appearance. All extant draft materials were consulted in the preparation of this edition, but only significantly different drafts of previously published items are noted below. For a key to the editorial abbreviations, see the List of Abbreviations at the start of this volume.

Front Cover

The Four Fears (1955), 8.5" x 11" gouache painting. Box II:20, Muriel Rukeyser Papers, Manuscript Division, Library of Congress, Washington, DC, hereafter cited as LC, followed by series and container number.

Author's Introduction

Untitled statement. In "Under Forty: A Symposium on American Literature and the Younger Generation of American Jews," 4–9. *Contemporary Jewish Record* 7, no. 1 (February 1944): 3–36.

Part I. The Usable Truth: Five Talks on Communication and Poetry

The Usable Truth: Five Talks on Communication and Poetry. Lectures, Vassar College, Poughkeepsie, NY, October 29–November 1, 1940. *Fc*: The Usable Truth. Unpublished ts draft with Rukeyser's holo. notes, October 29–November 1, 1940. LC I:43. The last four lectures are previously unpublished. "The Fear of Poetry" was published in *Twice a Year*, Fall/Winter 1941, 15–33, with Rukeyser's poems "Reading Time: 1 Minute 26 Seconds" and "Lyric from *Mediterranean*." An abbreviated excerpt of

"Communication and Poetry" was published as "The Usable Truth" in *Poetry: A Magazine of Verse*, July 1941, 206-209. https//www.jstor.org/stable/20582634. Rukeyser's fc for the Vassar talks supplies ct for the last four lectures in this edition. The published article "The Fear of Poetry" supplies the first lecture's ct.

Part II. Twentieth-Century Radicalism: On Politics, Society, and Culture

"The Flown Arrow: The Aftermath of the Sacco-Vanzetti Case." *Housatonic: A Magazine for and about New England*, August 1932, 9-10, 24-26.

"From Scottsboro to Decatur." *Student Review*, April 1933, 12-15.

"Women and Scottsboro." Previously unpublished, 1933. *Fc*: Women and Scottsboro. Unpublished ts draft with Rukeyser's holo. corrections, n.d. [1933]. Muriel Rukeyser Collection of Papers, Henry W. and Albert A. Berg Collection of English and American Literature, New York Public Library, Astor, Lenox, and Tilden Foundations, New York, New York.

"Barcelona on the Barricades." *New Masses*, September 1, 1936, 9-11. Part of "Liberty versus Death in Spain," a multi-author feature on the Spanish Civil War.

"Barcelona, 1936." *Life and Letters To-day*, Autumn 1936, 26-33. *First recovered version*: Muriel Rukeyser. *"Barcelona, 1936" and Selections from the Civil War Archive*. Edited by Rowena Kennedy-Epstein, 9-22. New York: Lost & Found, 2011.

"Words and Images." *New Republic*, August 2, 1943, 140-142.

"War and Poetry." In *The War Poets: An Anthology of the War Poetry of the Twentieth Century*. Edited by Oscar William, 25-26. New York: John Day, 1945.

"A Pane of Glass." *Discovery*, April 1953, 29-37.

"She Came to Us." *New Statesman* (UK), November 8, 1958, 625-626. *Draft*: She Came to Us. Unpublished ts draft with holo. notes, n.d. [c. 1957-1958]. LC I:16. Archived with two incomplete unpublished ts drafts of a story titled "The Week They Wore Their—." This edition's version restores material from the full unpublished draft that was omitted from the published article.

"The Killing of the Children." Previously unpublished, n.d. [1973]. *Fc*: The Killing of the Children. Ts draft, n.d. [1973]. LC I:16. Also see

Muriel Rukeyser. "Free—What Do It Mean?" *Washington Evening Star* and *Washington Daily News*, November 30, 1972.

"The Uses of Fear." Originally published as "The Fear." *New York Times*, June 19, 1978. *Fc*: The Uses of Fear. Ts draft with Rukeyser's holo. corrections, June 1978. LC I:16. This edition restores Rukeyser's original title and material omitted from the published version.

Part III. Media and Democratic Education: A Photo-Text and Radio Scripts

"So Easy to See." Previously unpublished, n.d. [1946]. *Fc*: Introduction [to So Easy to See, incomplete collaboration with Berenice Abbott]. Unpublished ts draft, n.d. [1946]. LC II:12. *Draft*: Seeing Things. Unpublished holo. draft, n.d. [c. 1946]. LC II:12.

From *Sunday at Nine*. Previously unpublished, 1949. *Fc (Series introduction and episode 1)*: KDFC Sunday at Nine (Emily Dickinson Program—Aug. 7). Unpublished ts production script with Rukeyser's holo. notes and unidentified holo. engineering cues, n.d. [August 1949]. LC I:42. *Draft (full series)*: Sunday at Nine: First Four Programs. Unpublished ts and holo. drafts of scripts, n.d. [1949]. LC II:14. Scripts for the series introduction and the first and last episodes have been selected for this edition. Rukeyser's unpublished holo. draft script supplies the ct for this edition of the final episode, for which there are neither extant production scripts nor engineering cues.

Part IV. Modernist Interventions: On Gender, Poetry, and Poetics

"Modern Trends: American Poetry." *Vassar Miscellany News*, May 21, 1932.

"Long Step Ahead Taken by Gregory in New Epic Poem." Review of *Chorus for Survival*, by Horace Gregory. *Daily Worker*, March 19, 1935.

"In a Speaking Voice." Review of *Collected Poems*, by Robert Frost. *Poetry: A Magazine of Verse*, July 1939, 218-224.

"The Classic Ground." Review of *The Listening Landscape*, by Marya Zaturenska. *Decision*, June 1941, 81-83.

"Nearer to the Well-Spring." Review of *Sonnets to Orpheus*, by Rainer Maria Rilke, translated by M. D. Herter Norton. *Kenyon Review*, Summer 1943, 451-454.

"A Simple Theme." Review of *Jewel of Our Longing*, by Charlotte Marletto. *Poetry: A Magazine of Verse*, July 1949, 236-239.

"A Lorca Evening." Previously unpublished, 1951. *Fc*: Unpublished untitled ts draft of talk on Federico García Lorca, February 1, 1951. LC I:43. Also see Muriel Rukeyser. Notes on Lorca at Vassar. Unpublished ts outline, with unpublished translation of Federico García Lorca's Vassar lecture on *duende*, n.d. [1951]. LC I:43.

"Many Keys." Posthumously published, 2017; written, 1957. *Fc*: Many Keys. Unpublished ts draft, n.d. [1957]. LC I:16. *Draft*: Many Keys. Unpublished ts draft [first full draft], n.d. [1957]. LC I:16 and I:44. *Notes*: The Glass Woman. Unpublished holo. notes, n.d. [c. 1956-1957]. LC I:34. *First recovered version*: Muriel Rukeyser. "Many Keys." Edited by Eric Keenaghan, in Keenaghan, "There Is No Glass Woman: Muriel Rukeyser's Lost Essay 'Many Keys,'" 193-198. *Feminist Modernist Studies* 1, nos. 1-2 (2018): 186-204. doi:10.1080/24692921.2017.1368883.

"Lyrical 'Rage.'" Review of *In Defense of the Earth*, by Kenneth Rexroth. *Saturday Review*, November 9, 1957, 15.

"A Crystal for the Metaphysical." Review of *Tell Me, Tell Me: Granite, Steel, and Other Topics*, by Marianne Moore. *Saturday Review*, October 1, 1966, 52-53, 81. This edition is an abridged version of the published review.

"Poetry and the Unverifiable Fact." In *The Clark Lecture, 1968: An Address by Muriel Rukeyser, Scripps College Bulletin* 42, no. 4, extra ed. no. 3 (1968): 1-21. The issue also includes Rukeyser's lecture "Opening Convocation," 23-36.

"The Music of Translation." In *The World of Translation: Papers Delivered at the Conference on Literary Translation*, 187-193. New York: PEN American Center, 1971.

"Thoreau and Poetry." In *Henry David Thoreau: Studies and Commentaries*. Edited by Walter Harding, George Brenner, and Paul A. Doyle, 103-116. Rutherford, NJ: Fairleigh Dickinson University Press, 1972. Based on a talk at the Thoreau Festival, Nassau Community College, Long Island, New York, May 1967. *Notes*: Muriel Rukeyser. Unpublished untitled ts and holo. notes on Henry David Thoreau, n.d. [c. 1967]. LC I:34.

"Glitter and Wounds, Several Wildnesses." Review of *The Book of Folly*, by Anne Sexton. *Parnassus: Poetry in Review*, Fall/Winter 1973, 215-221. *Draft*: "... and not be afraid of her bed." Unpublished ts and holo. draft review of *Love Poems*, by Anne Sexton, n.d. [c. 1970]. LC I:17.

"The Life to Which I Belong." Review of *Letters to Felice*, by Franz Kafka. *American Poetry Review*, May-June 1974, 8-9. Originally published with Rukeyser's poems "How We Did It," "Then," "Before Danger," "The Iris-Eaters," "Not to Be Printed, Not to Be Said, Not to Be Thought," "Recovering," "Trinity Churchyard," "Parallel Invention," and "Ives."

"Women of Words: A Prefatory Note." Preface to *The World Split Open: Four Centuries of Women Poets in England and America, 1552–1950*. Edited by Louise Berkinow, xiii–xv. New York: Random House, 1974.

Notes on Contributors

Muriel Rukeyser (1913-1980) was an American writer, activist, and public intellectual. Born in New York City, she lived most of her life in that metropolis, with short periods spent in upstate New York during her college years (1930-1932) and in the San Francisco Bay Area (1945-1949). Rukeyser's first book of poems, *Theory of Flight*, won the Yale Younger Poets Award and was published in 1935. She would go on to publish more than a dozen other poetry collections, the last being *The Gates: Poems* in 1976. In 1947, Rukeyser gave birth to her son, William Laurie Rukeyser, out of her desire to raise a child on her own. From the 1950s on, she had an open relationship with, but maintained a separate household from, her literary agent Monica McCall. Throughout her life, Rukeyser pursued a variety of careers—ranging from political reportage, magazine and film editorships, wartime service for a federal propaganda agency, radio broadcast and production, screenwriting for film and television, education, and nonprofit leadership. No matter her occupation, though, writing was the chief means of her livelihood. Although she is best known for her poetry and self-identified principally as a poet, in actuality she was prolific in a variety of forms—ranging from poetry, short and long fiction, children's books, drama and musicals; to journalism, biographies, and literary and political nonfiction; to screenplays, radio scripts, and teleplays. All her writings contributed to her evolving, career-long vision of the complex interrelationship between conventional and experimental literary formalism and social justice, which encompassed her fierce commitment to racial, class, and gender equity, sex positivity, and anti-war views. Much of what she wrote never appeared in print, often because of editors' and publishers' politically or ideologically motivated suppression. The bulk of Rukeyser's previously published nonpoetic writings has not yet been recovered. Having experienced several strokes and suffered for years from diabetes and heart disease, Rukeyser died in 1980, at the age of sixty-six.

NOTES ON CONTRIBUTORS

Eric Keenaghan is the author of *Queering Cold War Poetry* (Ohio State University Press). His writings about American modernism, cold war and New American poetry, and LGBTQ+ poetry, poetics, and politics have appeared in many collected volumes and in such journals as *PMLA*, *Modernism/modernity*, *Textual Studies*, *Journal of Modern Literature*, and *Translation Studies*. He is associate professor in the English Department at the University at Albany, State University of New York. Contact him at ekeenaghan@albany.edu.

Rowena Kennedy-Epstein is the author of *Unfinished Spirit: Muriel Rukeyser's Twentieth Century* (Cornell University Press), and she recovered and edited Muriel Rukeyser's unpublished Spanish Civil War novel, *Savage Coast* (Feminist Press). An NEH Public Scholars fellow, she is writing the first biography of Rukeyser (Bloomsbury). She lives in the UK, where she is associate professor of gender studies and twentieth- and twenty-first-century women's writing at the University of Bristol.

Selected Bibliography

"General Published Sources" includes works referenced by the editors in their introduction and annotations. Classic literary works in the public domain or available in multiple editions have been excluded from the editors' notes and this selected bibliography. "Select Works by Muriel Rukeyser" includes only published and unpublished works by Rukeyser that are referenced in the editors' introduction or annotations. "Select Sources Referenced and Reviewed by Rukeyser" includes entries for known sources cited by Rukeyser, including canonical authors' paraliterary published essays, journals, and letters. When known, entries for specific editions cited or reviewed by Rukeyser are provided. Bibliographic information about recordings played during *Sunday at Nine* appear only in the editors' annotations to those broadcasts, not in the bibliography.

General Published Sources

Abbott, Berenice. *Changing New York*. Edited by Bonnie Yochelson. New York: New Press, 2008.

Ahmed, Sara. *Living a Feminist Life*. Durham, NC: Duke University Press, 2017.

Barbian, Jan-Pieter. *The Politics of Literature in Nazi Germany: Books in the Media Dictatorship*. Translated by Kate Sturge. New York: Bloomsbury, 2013.

Barrett, William. "A Prize for Ezra Pound." *Partisan Review*, April 1949, 344–347.

Beevo, Antony. *The Battle for Spain: The Spanish Civil War, 1936–1939*. New York: Penguin Books, 2006.

Berkinow, Louise, ed. *The World Split Open: Four Centuries of Women Poets in England and America, 1552–1950*. New York: Vintage, 1974.

Brooks, Van Wyck. "On Creating a Usable Past." *Dial*, April 11, 1918, 337–341.

Carter, Dan T. *Scottsboro: A Tragedy of the American South*. Revised ed. Baton Rouge: Louisiana State University Press, 2007.

Cohen, Robert. *When the Old Left Was Young: Student Radicals and America's First Mass Student Movement, 1929–1941*. New York: Oxford University Press, 1993.

Corrigan. Robert A. "Ezra Pound and the Bollingen Prize Controversy." *Midcontinent American Studies Journal* 8, no. 2 (Fall 1967): 43-57. https://www.jstor.org/stable/40640705.

SELECTED BIBLIOGRAPHY

Daniell, F. Raymond. "Bailiffs Isolate Scottsboro Jury." *New York Times*, April 2, 1933.

——. "'Observers' Leave Scottsboro Trial." *New York Times*, April 3, 1933.

Däumer, Elisabeth, ed. "Muriel Rukeyser Centenary Issue." *Journal of Narrative Theory* 43, no. 3 (Fall 2013): 287–425. https://www.jstor.org/stable/i24482959.

Däumer, Elisabeth, and Bill Rukeyser. *Muriel Rukeyser: A Living Archive*. Eastern Michigan University, Department of English, 2022. http://murielrukeyser.emuenglish.org/.

Dickinson, Emily. *The Letters of Emily Dickinson*. Vol. 2. Edited by Thomas H. Johnson and Theodora Ward. Cambridge, MA: Belknap Press of Harvard University Press, 1958.

Doherty, Thomas. *Show Trial: Hollywood, HUAC, and the Birth of the Blacklist*. New York: Columbia University Press, 2019.

Downing, Marjorie. "Inscape and Instress: Further Analogies with Scotus." In *Gerard Manley Hopkins*, edited by James F. Scott and Carolyn D. Scott, 32–43. St. Louis, MO: Herder, 1968.

——. "The Nature Poetry of Gerard Manley Hopkins, S.J." Master's thesis, Catholic University of America, 1939.

Eberhart, Richard. "Pound's New Cantos." *Quarterly Review of Literature* 5 (1949): 174–191.

Eisenstein, Sergei. "Dickens, Griffith, and the Film Today." In *Film Form: Essays in Film Theory*, edited and translated by Jay Leyda, 195–255. New York: Harcourt Brace Jovanovich, 1949.

Eliot, T. S. *Selected Prose of T. S. Eliot*. Edited by Frank Kermode. New York: Harcourt Brace Jovanovich, 1975.

Emerson, Ralph Waldo. "Thoreau." *Atlantic Monthly*, August 1862, 239–249. https://www.theatlantic.com/magazine/archive/1862/08/thoreau/306418/.

Federal Bureau of Investigation. Muriel Rukeyser, file no. 77-27812. n.d. [1942–1978].

Gander, Catherine. *Muriel Rukeyser and Documentary: The Poetics of Connection*. Edinburgh: Edinburgh University Press, 2013.

——, ed. "Muriel Rukeyser's *The Life of Poetry*." *Textual Practice* 32, no. 7 (September 2018): 1075–1253.

Haas, Britt. "The Scottsboro Boys: Demands for Equality from the Deep South to New York City." In *Fighting Authoritarianism: American Youth Activism in the 1930s*, 61–81. New York: Fordham University Press, 2017.

Harding, Walter. Foreword to *Henry David Thoreau: Studies and Commentaries*. Edited by Harding, George Brenner, and Paul A. Doyle, 7–9. Rutherford, NJ: Fairleigh Dickinson University Press, 1972.

Hayford, Harrison. "Usable or Visible Truth." *Modern Language Notes* 74, no. 8 (1959): 702–705. http://www.jstor.org/stable/3040391.

Herzog, Anne F., and Janet E. Kaufman, editors. *"How Shall We Tell Each Other of the Poet?": The Life and Writing of Muriel Rukeyser*. New York: Palgrave Macmillan, 1999.

SELECTED BIBLIOGRAPHY

Holmes, John Haynes. Introduction to *America Arraigned!* Edited by Lucia Trent and Ralph Cheyney, 13-19. New York: Dean, 1928.
KDFC. "The Story of Classical KDFC." Classical California KDFC. Accessed September 30, 2022. kdfc.com/culture/story-classical-kdfc/.
Keenaghan, Eric. "The Life of Politics: The Compositional History of *The Life of Poetry* and Muriel Rukeyser's Changing Appraisal of Emotion and Belief." *Textual Practice* 32, no. 7 (2018): 1103-1126. doi:10.1080/09502 36X.2018.1477109.
———. "There Is No Glass Woman: Muriel Rukeyser's Lost Feminist Essay 'Many Keys.'" *Feminist Modernist Studies* 1, nos. 1-2 (2018): 186-204. doi:10.1080 /24692921.2017.1368883.
Kennedy-Epstein, Rowena. *Unfinished Spirit: Muriel Rukeyser's Twentieth Century*. Ithaca, NY: Cornell University Press, 2022.
Kenner, Hugh. *The Poetry of Ezra Pound*. Norfolk, CT: New Directions, 1951.
———. *The Pound Era*. Berkeley: University of California Press, 1971.
Kertesz, Louise. *The Poetic Vision of Muriel Rukeyser*. Baton Rouge, LA: Louisiana State University Press, 1980.
Kierkegaard, Søren. *Concluding Unscientific Postscript to the Philosophical Crumbs*. Edited and translated by Alastair Hannay. New York: Cambridge University Press, 2009. German original published 1846.
MacDonald, Dwight. "Homage to Twelve Judges: An Editorial." *politics*, Winter 1949, 1-2.
Marletto, Charlotte. Contributor's biography. *Voices: A Quarterly of Poetry*, Spring 1944, 62.
Matthiessen, F. O. *American Renaissance: Art and Expression in the Age of Emerson and Whitman*. New York: Oxford University Press, 1941.
Mead, Margaret. *And Keep Your Powder Dry: An Anthropologist Looks at America*. New York: Berghahn Books, 2000.
Merwin, W. S. "Romantic Distrust." Review of Kathleen Raine, *Collected Poems*. *New York Times Book Review*, January 27, 1957.
Middlebrook, Diane Wood. *Anne Sexton: A Biography*. New York: Vintage, 1992.
Molesworth, Charles. *Marianne Moore: A Literary Life*. New York: Atheneum, 1990.
Moore, Marianne. *New Collected Poems*. Edited by Heather Cass. New York: Farrar, Straus & Giroux, 2017.
———. *What Are Years*. New York: Macmillan, 1941.
Morgan, Jack. *New World Irish: New Directions in Irish and Irish American Literature*. New York: Palgrave Macmillan, 2011.
Mullen, Bill V., and Christopher Vials. "Introduction: Anti/Fascism and the United States." In *The US Antifascism Reader*, 1-21. New York: Verso, 2020.
Nguyên Du. *Kim Van Kieu*. Translated by Lê Xuân Thuy. Saigon: Khai-Tri, 1963.
Olson, Charles. "Projective Verse and Letter to Elaine Feinstein." In *Selected Writings*, edited by Robert Creeley, 15-30. New York: New Directions, 1967.

SELECTED BIBLIOGRAPHY

Patchen, Kenneth. *The Journal of Albion Moonlight*. New York: New Directions, 1961.
PEN American Center Translation Committee. Program for the PEN Translation Conference, May 11–15, 1970. PEN America, 2020, https://pen.org/wp-content/uploads/2020/07/1970-PEN-translation-conference-program.pdf.
Physick, Ray. "The *Olimpiada Popular*: Barcelona 1936, Sport, and Politics in an Age of War, Dictatorship, and Revolution." *Sport in History* 37, no. 1 (2017): 51–75. doi.10.1080/17460263.2016.1246380.
Poetry Center (New York). Lorca Memorial Program. Privately printed, 1951. Box II:9. Muriel Rukeyser Papers, Manuscript Division, Library of Congress, Washington, DC.
Pound, Ezra. *Pound's Cavalcanti: An Edition of the Translations, Notes, and Essays*. Edited by David Anderson. Princeton, NJ: Princeton University Press, 1983.
———. *The Spirit of Romance*. New York: New Directions, 2005.
Rosenthal, M. L. "Ladies' Day on Parnassus." Review of Katherine Hoskins, Kathleen Raine, and Marianne Moore. *The Nation*, March 16, 1957, 239–240.
Sacco-Vanzetti Defense Committee Bulletin 1, no. 18 (n.d. [September 1927]).
Snow, C. P. *The Two Cultures*. New York: Cambridge University Press, 1959.
Stern, Rabbi Chaim, and Rabbi John D. Rayner, eds. *Service of the Heart: Weekday Sabbath and Festival Services and Prayers for Home and Synagogue*. London: Union of Liberal and Progressive Synagogues, 1967.
Stout, James. *The Popular Front and the Barcelona 1936 Popular Olympics: Playing as If the World Was Watching*. New York: Palgrave Macmillan, 2020.
Untermeyer, Louis. "The Language of Muriel Rukeyser." *Saturday Review of Literature*, August 10, 1940, 11–12.
———, ed. *Modern American Poetry*, 6th ed. New York: Harcourt, Brace, 1942.
Van Haaften, Julia. *Berenice Abbott: A Life in Photography*. New York: W. W. Norton, 2018.
Williams, Oscar. "Ladies' Day." Review of Muriel Rukeyser, H. D., Marianne Moore, Marya Zaturenska, and others. *New Republic*, October 23, 1944, 534–536.
Winter, Ella. *And Not to Yield: An Autobiography*. New York: Harcourt, Brace, 1963.

Select Works by Muriel Rukeyser

Published Books and Chapbooks

Beast in View. New York: Doubleday, Doran, 1944.
The Book of the Dead. Morgantown, WV: West Virginia University Press, 2018.
The Collected Poems of Muriel Rukeyser. Edited by Janet E. Kaufman and Anne F. Herzog with Jan Heller Levi. Pittsburgh: University of Pittsburgh Press, 2005.

SELECTED BIBLIOGRAPHY

Configurations, by Octavio Paz. New York: New Directions, 1971. Introduction and contributing translator.

"the difficulties involved": *Muriel Rukeyser's Selections from A Season in Hell*, by Arthur Rimbaud. Edited by Chris Clarke. New York: Lost & Found, 2019. Translator.

Elegies. New York: New Directions, 2013. First published 1949 by New Directions (Norfolk, CT).

The Green Wave. Garden City, NY: Doubleday, 1948.

Houdini: A Musical. Ashfield, MA: Paris Press, 2002.

The Life of Poetry. Ashfield, MA: Paris Press, 1996. First published 1949 by Current Books/A. A. Wyn (New York).

One Life. New York: Simon & Schuster, 1957.

The Orgy: An Irish Journey of Passion and Transformation. Ashfield, MA: Paris Press, 1997. First published 1965 by Coward-McCann (New York).

Orpheus. San Francisco: Centaur Press, 1949.

Savage Coast. Edited by Rowena Kennedy-Epstein. New York: Feminist Press, 2013.

Selected Poems. Norfolk, CT: New Directions, 1951.

Selected Poems, by Gunnar Ekelöf. New York: Twayne, 1967. Co-translator with Leif Sjöberg.

Selected Poems, by Octavio Paz. Bloomington: Indiana University Press, 1966. Republished as *Early Poems, 1935–1955*. New Directions, 1973. Introduction and contributing translator.

Sun Stone, by Octavio Paz. New York: New Directions, 1957. Translator.

Theory of Flight. New Haven, CT: Yale University Press, 1935.

The Traces of Thomas Hariot. New York: Random House, 1971.

Willard Gibbs. Garden City, NY: Doubleday, Doran, 1942.

Published Essays, Articles, and Stories

"Adventures of Children." *Coronet*, September 1939.

"Barcelona, 1936" and Selections from the Spanish Civil War Archive. Edited by Rowena Kennedy-Epstein. New York: Lost & Found, 2011.

"Barcelona on the Barricades." *New Masses*, September 1, 1936, 9–11.

"A Call to Action." *Student Review*, March 1933, 6–7. Coauthor of unsigned article.

"The Club." *Ellery Queen's Mystery Magazine*, August 1960.

"The Color of Coal Is Black." *Vassar Miscellany News*, March 12, 1932.

Darwin and the Writers. Edited by Stefania Heim. New York: Lost & Found, 2003.

"The Education of a Poet." In *A Muriel Rukeyser Reader*, edited by Jan Heller Levi, 277–285. New York: W. W. Norton, 1994. First published in *The Writer and Her Work*, edited by Janet Sternburg, 217–230. New York: W. W. Norton, 1980.

"The Fear of Poetry." *Twice a Year*, Fall/Winter 1941, 15–33.

Foreword. In Berenice Abbott, *Berenice Abbott: Photographs*, 9–11. New York: Horizon Press, 1970.

"Free—What Do It Mean?" *Washington Evening Star* and *Washington Daily News*, November 30, 1972.
"Gauley Bridge: Four Episodes from a Scenario." *Films: A Quarterly Discussion and Analysis* 1, no. 3 (Summer 1940): 51-64.
"Little." *Ladies' Home Journal*, February 1965.
"Start of Strife in Spain Is Told by Eyewitness." *New York Herald Tribune*, July 29, 1936.
"Students Fight for Free Speech at City College." *Vassar Miscellany News*, November 5, 1932.
"The Telephone Company." *Life*, July 17, 1939. Unattributed author.
"Trudi on the Road." *New Theatre* 3, no. 2 (1936): 6.
"The Usable Truth." *Poetry: A Magazine of Verse*, July 1941, 206-209. https://www.jstor.org/stable/20582634.
"We Came for Games." In *Savage Coast*, edited by Rowena Kennedy-Epstein, 281-298. New York: Feminist Press, 2013. First published in *Esquire*, October 1974.
"Worlds Alongside." *Coronet*, October 1939.
"The Year: Signs without Scale." *PEN Newsletter*, 1976.

Produced Films

All the Way Home. Directed by Lee R. Bobker. Dynamic Films, 1957. Scriptwriter.
Stop Japan! Directed by Joris Ivens. New York: Garrison Films, 1936. Uncredited scriptwriter.

Unpublished Drafts

Arabian Nights: An American Comedy. Unpublished play, 1975. Box I:35, Muriel Rukeyser Papers, Manuscript Division, Library of Congress, Washington, DC.
A Dark Night, A Perfect Night. Unpublished short story, n.d. [c. 1955]. Box I:16, Muriel Rukeyser Papers, Manuscript Division, Library of Congress, Washington, DC.
I Could Have Kissed Him. Unpublished short story, n.d. [c. 1955]. Box I:16, Muriel Rukeyser Papers, Manuscript Division, Library of Congress, Washington, DC.
The Middle of the Air. 4 versions. Unpublished drafts, 1944-n.d. [1948]. Boxes I:40 and II:14, Muriel Rukeyser Papers, Manuscript Division, Library of Congress, Washington, DC.
Notes for a poetry and music series of FM programs for KDFC Saus[alito]. Unpublished holo. draft, December 2, 1948. Box II:14, Muriel Rukeyser Papers, Manuscript Division, Library of Congress, Washington, DC.
Notes on Lorca at Vassar. Unpublished ts outline, with unpublished ts translation of Federico García Lorca's Vassar lecture on *duende*, n.d. [1951]. LC I:43, Muriel Rukeyser Papers, Manuscript Division, Library of Congress, Washington, DC.

SELECTED BIBLIOGRAPHY

Parkhurst Notebook. Unpublished notebook, 1955. Box I:30, Muriel Rukeyser Papers, Manuscript Division, Library of Congress, Washington, DC.

Project Nuremberg Obligation fundraising letter. Unpublished ts draft with Rukeyser's holo. notes, n.d. [c. August/September 1972]. Box I:58, Muriel Rukeyser Papers, Manuscript Division, Library of Congress, Washington, DC. Unattributed coauthor.

Sunday at Nine: First Four Programs, n.d. [1949]. Unpublished ts and holo. drafts of scripts for radio broadcasts. Box II:14, Muriel Rukeyser Papers, Manuscript Division, Library of Congress, Washington, DC.

Table of contents for Selected Poems. Unpublished holo. draft, n.d. [c. 1950-1951]. Box I:35, Muriel Rukeyser Papers, Manuscript Division, Library of Congress, Washington, DC.

The Voice of the Child—Outline. Unpublished ts outline, n.d. [c. 1955]. Box II:13, Muriel Rukeyser Papers, Manuscript Division, Library of Congress, Washington, DC.

We Came for Games. Unpublished ts outline for short story cycle, n.d. [c. 1973-1974]. Box I:16, Muriel Rukeyser Papers, Manuscript Division, Library of Congress, Washington, DC.

Correspondence

Burton, Naomi (Curtis Brown, Ltd.). Letter to Muriel Rukeyser, November 28, 1945. Box II:5, Muriel Rukeyser Papers, Manuscript Division, Library of Congress, Washington, DC.

Deverill, E. G. K. (KDFC/Sundial Broadcasting Corporation). Sales form letter for *Sunday at Nine*, n.d. [1949]. Box II:14, Muriel Rukeyser Papers, Manuscript Division, Library of Congress, Washington, DC.

Howe, Quincy (Simon and Schuster, Inc.). Letter to Muriel Rukeyser, March 28, 1941. Box I:7, Muriel Rukeyser Papers, Manuscript Division, Library of Congress, Washington, DC.

MacCracken, Henry Noble. Letter to Muriel Rukeyser, August 16, 1940. Box I:5, Muriel Rukeyser Papers, Manuscript Division, Library of Congress, Washington, DC.

Porter, Katherine Anne. Letter to Muriel Rukeyser, August 30, 1940. Muriel Rukeyser Collection of Papers, Incoming Correspondence: Porter, Katherine Anne, The Henry W. and Albert A. Berg Collection of English and American Literature, New York Public Library, Astor, Lenox, and Tilden Foundations, New York, New York.

Rukeyser, Muriel. Letter to Alan Brilliant (Unicorn Press), October 24, 1967. Box II:5, Muriel Rukeyser Papers, Manuscript Division, Library of Congress, Washington, DC.

———. Letter to the Editor. *New York Times*, April 7, 1933. Coauthored with Edward Sagarin.

Sherwood, Robert E. Letter to Muriel Rukeyser, January 25, 1952. Box II:3, Muriel Rukeyser Papers, Manuscript Division, Library of Congress, Washington, DC.

Select Sources Referenced and Reviewed by Muriel Rukeyser

Anderson, Maxwell, and Harold Hickerson. *Gods of the Lightning*. New York: Longmans, Green, 1928.

Associated Press. "Expects Little War Poetry." *New York Times*, February 25, 1940.

Bingham, Millicent Todd. *Ancestors' Brocades: The Literary Life of Emily Dickinson*. New York: Harper & Brothers, 1945.

Bishop, Elizabeth. *The Complete Poems, 1927–1979*. New York: Farrar, Straus & Giroux, 1983.

Braque, Georges. "Pensées sur l'art." *Confluences*, May 1945, 339–341.

Coleridge, Samuel Taylor. *The Collected Letters of Samuel Taylor Coleridge*, vol. 1, *1785–1800*. Edited by Earl Leslie Griggs. New York: Oxford University Press, 2000. First published 1956 by Clarendon Press (New York).

Collingwood, R. G. *The Principles of Art*. New York: Oxford University Press, 1938.

Crane, Hart. *The Bridge: A Poem*. New York: Liveright, 1992. First published 1930 by Black Sun Press (Paris).

Dickinson, Emily. *Bolts of Melody: New Poems of Emily Dickinson*. Edited by Mabel Loomis Todd and Millicent Todd Bingham. New York: Harper & Brothers, 1945.

——. *The Single Hound: Poems of a Lifetime*. Edited by Martha Dickinson Bianchi. Boston: Little, Brown, 1914.

Dollard, John. *Caste and Class in a Southern Town*. Madison: University of Wisconsin Press, 1988.

Dos Passos, John. *Facing the Chair: Story of the Americanization of Two Foreign-Born Workmen*. Boston: Sacco-Vanzetti Defense Committee, 1927.

——. "They Are Dead Now." *New Masses*, October 1927, 7.

Editorial ("I Will Advertise Thee What This People Shall Do . . ."). *Collier's*, July 24, 1943.

Eliot, T. S. *Collected Poems, 1909–1962*. New York: Harcourt, Brace, 1963.

Ellis, Havelock. *Studies in the Psychology of Sex*, vol. 5: *Erotic Symbolism, The Mechanism of Detumescence, The Psychic State in Pregnancy*. Philadelphia: F. A. Davis, 1906.

Fadiman, Clifton. Review of *Proletarian Literature in the United States: An Anthology*, edited by Granville Hicks et al. *New Yorker*, October 12, 1935.

Fearing, Kenneth. "U.S. Writers in War." *Poetry: A Magazine of Verse*, September 1940, 318–323. https://www.jstor.org/stable/20582262.

Fenichel, Otto. *The Psychoanalytic Theory of Neuroses*. New York: Routledge, 2006. First published 1945 by W. W. Norton (New York).

Frost, Robert. *Collected Poems*. New York: Henry Holt, 1939.

Gibran, Khalil. *The Wanderer: His Parables and Sayings*. New York: Knopf, 1932.

Godden, Rumer. *Hans Christian Andersen: A Great Life in Brief*. New York: Knopf, 1955.

SELECTED BIBLIOGRAPHY

Gregory, Horace. *Chorus for Survival*. New York: Covici, Friede Publishers, 1935.

Hanaghan, Jonathan. *Society, Evolution, and Revelation: Original Insight into Man's Place in Creation*. Dublin: Runa Press, 1957.

H. D. [Hilda Doolittle]. "A Note on Poetry." In *Oxford Anthology of American Literature*, edited by William Rose Benét and Norman Holmes Pearson, 1287-1288. New York: Oxford University Press, 1938.

Herring, Robert. "Editorial." *Life and Letters To-day*, September 1940, 197-200.

———. "News Reel." *Life and Letters To-day*, September 1940, 201-214.

James, Williams. "The Sentiment of Rationality." In *The Will to Believe and Other Essays in Popular Philosophy and Human Immortality*, 63-111. New York: Dover, 1956. First published 1897 by Longman, Greens (New York).

Jeffers, Robinson. *Roan Stallion, Tamar, and Other Poems*. New York: Horace Liveright, 1925.

Jespersen, Otto. *Language: Its Nature, Development, and Origin*. New York: Henry Holt, 1922.

Kafka, Franz. *Diaries 1910–1913*. Edited by Max Brod. Translated by Joseph Kresh. New York: Schocken Books, 1965.

———. *Letters to Felice*. Edited by Erich Heller and Jürgen Born. Translated by James Stern and Elisabeth Duckworth. New York: Schocken Books, 1973.

Keene, Donald. *Japanese Literature: An Introduction for Western Readers*. New York: Grove, 1955.

Kierkegaard, Søren. *Fear and Trembling and The Sickness unto Death*. Translated by Walter Lowrie. Princeton, NJ: Princeton University Press, 2013. German original published 1843. English translation first published 1941 by Doubleday (New York).

Kilpatrick, William H. "Teachers and the New World." *Educational Times*, April 1921, 175-178. Reprinted in *Virginia Teacher*, March 1923, 57-62.

Lask, Thomas. "The Novel as Process." Review of *The Estate*, by Isaac Bashevis Singer. *New York Times*, November 1, 1969.

Lawrence, D. H. "Pornography and Obscenity." In *Late Essays and Articles*, edited by James T. Boulton, 236-253. New York: Cambridge University Press, 2004.

———. "A Review of *Contemporary German Poetry*, Selected and Edited by Jethro Bithell." In *D. H. Lawrence's Poetry: Demon Liberated, A Collection of Primary and Secondary Material*, edited by A. Banerjee, 37-39. New York: Macmillan, 1990.

Life magazine, October 14, 1940.

Lorca, Federico García. *From Lorca's Theatre: Five Plays by Federico García Lorca*. Translated by Richard L. O'Connell and James Graham-Luján. New York: Charles Scribner's Sons, 1941.

———. *Three Tragedies of Federico García Lorca*. Translated by James Graham-Luján and Richard L. O'Connell. New York: New Directions, 1947.

MacLeish, Archibald. *Streets in the Moon*. Boston: Houghton Mifflin, 1926.

Mahan, Captain A. T. *The Influence of Sea Power upon History, 1660–1783*. Boston: Little, Brown, 1890.

SELECTED BIBLIOGRAPHY

Marletto, Charlotte. *Jewel of Our Longing*. West Los Angeles: Wagon & Star Press, 1948.

Maxwell, James Clerk. "Science and Free Will." In *The Life of James Clerk Maxwell with a Selection from His Correspondence and Occasional Writings*, by Lewis Campbell and William Garnett, 434–444. London: Macmillan, 1882.

Meeropol, Robert, and Michael Meeropol. *We Are Your Sons: The Legacy of Ethel and Julius Rosenberg*. Boston: Houghton Mifflin, 1975.

Meiklejohn, Alexander. "In Memoriam." *New Republic*, September 5, 1928, 69–71.

Melville, Herman. *Collected Poems of Herman Melville*. Edited by Howard P. Vincent. Chicago: Packard, 1947.

———. *Correspondence*. Edited by Lynn Horth. Evanston, IL: Northwestern University Press, 1991.

Millay, Edna St. Vincent. "Fear." *Outlook*, November 9, 1927, 293–295, 310.

Misch, George. *A History of Autobiography in Antiquity*. 2 vols. Translated by E. W. Dickes. New York: Routledge, 2002.

Moore, Marianne. *Tell Me, Tell Me: Granite, Steel, and Other Topics*. New York: Viking, 1966.

Nizer, Louis. *The Implosion Conspiracy*. New York: Fawcett, 1974.

Palgrave, Francis Turner, ed. *The Golden Treasury of the Best Songs and Lyrical Poems in the English Language*. London: Macmillan, 1875.

Pavlov, Ivan Petrovich. *Conditioned Reflexes*. Translated by G. V. Anrep. New York: Oxford University Press, 1927.

Rank, Otto. *Art and Artist: Creative Urge and Personality Development*. New York: W. W. Norton, 1989. First published 1932 by Knopf (New York).

———. *The Trauma of Birth*. New York: Routledge, 2014. First German edition published 1924, English edition published 1929 by Kegan Paul, Trench, Kubner (London).

Reuben, William A. *The Atom Spy Hoax*. New York: Action Books, 1955.

Rexroth, Kenneth. *In Defense of the Earth*. New York: New Directions, 1956.

Ridler, Anne. *A Dream Observed and Other Poems*. London: Poetry Society, 1941.

Rilke, Rainer Maria. *Duino Elegies*. Translated by J. B. Leishman and Stephen Spender. 4th ed. London: Chatto & Windus, 1963. First published 1939 by Hogarth Press (London).

———. *Letters of Rainer Maria Rilke, 1910–1926*. Translated by Jane Bannard Greene and M. D. Herter Norton. New York: W. W. Norton, 1948.

———. *Sonnets to Orpheus*. Translated by M. D. Herter Norton. New York: W. W. Norton, 1942.

Rosenberg, Ethel, and Julius Rosenberg. *The Rosenberg Letters*. Edited by Lewis John Collins. London: Dennis Dobson, 1953.

Sacco, Nicola, and Bartolomeo Vanzetti. *The Letters of Sacco and Vanzetti*. Edited by Marian Denman Frankfurter and Gardner Jackson. New York: Penguin, 2007.

Sarton, George. *Introduction to the History of Science*, vol. 1. Washington, DC: Carnegie Institution of Washington, 1927.

Schneir, Walter, and Miriam Schneir. *Invitation to an Inquest: A New Look at the Rosenberg-Sobell Case*. New York: Dell, 1968.
Sexton, Anne. *All My Pretty Ones*. Boston: Houghton Mifflin, 1962.
———. *The Book of Folly*. Boston: Houghton Mifflin, 1972.
Sherwood, Robert E. et al. "A Preview of the War We Do Not Want." *Collier's*, October 27, 1951.
Sinclair, Upton. *Boston: A Novel*. 2 vols. New York: Alfred and Charles Boni, 1928.
Stevens, Wallace. "About One of Marianne Moore's Poems." In *The Necessary Angel: Essays on Reality and the Imagination*, 91–103. New York: Vintage Books, 1951.
Thoreau, Henry David. *Collected Poems of Henry Thoreau*. Edited by Carl Bode. Chicago: Packard, 1943.
———. *The First and Last Journeys of Thoreau*, vol. 1. Edited by Franklin Benjamin Sanborn. Boston: Bibliophile Society, 1905.
———. "Mission." In F. B. Sanborn, "Thoreau's Unpublished Poetry." *Critic*, March 26, 1881, 74–75.
———. *Sir Walter Raleigh*. Edited by Henry Aiken Metcalf. Boston: Bibliophile Society, 1905.
———. *The Writings of Henry David Thoreau: Journal, Volumes I (1837–1846) and II (1850–September 15, 1851)*. Edited by Bradford Torrey. Boston / New York: Houghton Mifflin / Riverside Press, 1906.
Trachtenberg, Alan. *Brooklyn Bridge: Fact and Symbol*. New York: Oxford University Press, 1965.
Trent, Lucia, and Ralph Cheyney, eds. *America Arraigned!* New York: Dean, 1928.
Twelve Southerners (Donald Davidson et al.). *I'll Take My Stand: The South and the Agrarian Tradition*, 75th anniversary ed. Baton Rouge: Louisiana State University Press, 2006.
Untermeyer, Louis, ed. *Modern American Poetry*. 2nd ed. New York: Harcourt, Brace, 1921.
———. *Modern American Poetry: A Critical Anthology*. 3rd ed. New York: Harcourt, Brace, 1925.
———. *Modern American Poetry: Mid-century Edition*. 7th ed. New York: Harcourt, Brace, 1950.
US Department of Commerce and Bureau of the Census. *Mortality Statistics: 1932*. Washington, DC, 1935.
Vallejo, César. *Poemas humanos: Human Poems*. Translated by Clayton Eshleman. New York: Grove, 1968.
Watson, David Lindsay. *Scientists Are Human*. London: Watts, 1938.
Weeks, Robert P., ed. *Commonwealth vs. Sacco and Vanzetti*. Englewood Cliffs, NJ: Prentice-Hall, 1958.
Welch, Marie de L. "The Black of Magic." *New York Quarterly*, Winter 1973, 70.
Williams, William Carlos. "Marianne Moore." In *The William Carlos Williams Reader*, edited by M. L. Rosenthal, 384–393. New York: New Directions, 1966.

The World of Translation: Papers Delivered at the Conference on Literary Translation. New York: PEN American Center, 1971.

Zaturenska, Marya. *Christina Rossetti: A Portrait with Background.* New York: Macmillan, 1949.

———. *Golden Mirror.* New York: Macmillan, 1944.

———. *The Listening Landscape.* New York: Macmillan, 1941.

Index

Abbott, Berenice, 21–22, 179–183
abortion, 20, 298
Abraham (biblical figure), 97
activism. *See* anti-fascism; anti-racism; feminism; labor; leftist politics; radicalism; student activism
Adams, Henry, 65n16, 90n1
Adams, Léonie, 236, 306
advertising, 47, 108, 147–149
Ahmed, Sara, 28
Aiken, Conrad, 206
Akiva ben Josef, Rabbi, 8, 31
Albee, Edward, 247
Albert Memorial, 65
anarchism, 103n1, 105, 128–129, 136
Andersen, Hans Christian, 272
Anderson, Maxwell, 95, 106
anti-Americanism, 3, 24
anti-communism, 1–4, 8, 20, 33n7, 35, 172–174, 244n6. *See also* HUAC
anti-fascism, 1–2, 4, 7–8, 10, 15–17, 25, 134n2
anti-imperialism, 4, 7, 11, 31n4, 111
anti-left hysteria, 2, 16, 106n7
anti-racism, 4, 10, 17, 24–25, 198n46. *See also* civil disobedience; racism and racial justice
antisemitism, 7–9, 24, 34–35
anti-war activism, 10–12, 16–17, 167–171, 271n10, 285, 305n2. *See also* peace
Arlen, Harold, 200n53
Armstrong, Louis, 196n39, 197n42, 199
atomic bombs, 22, 173
Auden, W. H., 65n16, 88n26, 95, 95n13, 208
audience: size of, 94–95; women as, 234–235

Bach, Johann Sebastian, 194–195
Bacon, Francis, 181, 181n3

Bagnold, Enid, 225
Bahá'í Temple, 65
Baraka, Amiri (LeRoi Jones), 25
Bates, Ruby, 113n1, 123, 125. *See also* Scottsboro Boys case
Bauer, Felice, 298–303
Beardsley, Aubrey, 252n2
Beat Generation, 242n1, 244n7
Beauvoir, Simone de, 15
Behn, Aphra, 306
belief: communication and, 74–75; poetry and, 67–76, 81–83, 89
Bellow, Saul, 291n2
Beowulf (epic poem), 235n10
Berkinow, Louise, 27–28, 304n1, 305
Bible, 65, 97, 244, 264, 305; Old Testament, 234, 237
Billings, Warren K., 111–112
Birth of a Nation, The (1915), 62
bisexual poet-activists, 27. *See also* queerness
Bishop, Elizabeth, 9, 236, 247–248, 306
Black aesthetic forms, 24–25, 195–200
blacklisting, 1, 4n11, 20
Blake, William, 64, 224, 236
Boas, Franz, 5, 17, 115n4, 272
Boch, Otto, 17, 132n12
Bode, Carl, 277–278, 283n22
Bodenheim, Maxwell, 245
Bogan, Louise, 236
Bollingen Prize, 1, 3–4, 6–7, 9, 24, 197n41
Bonus Army, 108n19, 119n10
Bousquet, Alain, 269
Bradford, Perry, 196n37
Bradstreet, Anne, 240
Braque, Georges, 183
Brod, Max, 298–300, 303
Brodsky, Joseph, 124. *See also* International Labor Defense; Scottsboro Boys case

329

INDEX

Brooks, Van Wyck, 50n20
Brown, John, 51, 73, 88, 90–91
Brown, Minnijean, 18–19, 159–166. *See also* Little Rock Nine
Brown, Sterling, 25
Browne, Thomas, 278
Browning, Elizabeth Barrett, 252n2
Browning, Robert, 252n2
Bruno, Giordano, 261
Bryant, William Cullen, 185n3
Buddhism, 275
Burton, Lady Isabel, 298
Butler, Samuel, 244n10
Byron, Lord, 298

California Labor School, 1, 13, 15
Cameron, Angus, 4n11
Campanella, Roy, 248–249
canon, 4, 10, 28
Carossa, Hans, 51–54, 73–74, 76, 90–91
censorship, 3–4, 84, 180, 183, 216
Cézanne, Paul, 274n21
Chambers, Whittaker, 174
Charles I, King, 46
Chase, Stuart, 65n16
Cheyney, Ralph, 109–110
children, 224–228, 239, 260–262, 301–303. *See also* motherhood; pregnancy and birth
civil disobedience, 11–12, 277n1, 279, 284–285
civil rights, 161n5, 244n6. *See also* racism and racial justice
Clark, Eleanor, 9
Clark, Eunice, 9
classicism, 204–205, 219–223, 230
Cohen, Robert, 9
Cold War, 16, 172n2. *See also* anti-communism; HUAC
Coleridge, Samuel Taylor, 64, 83, 218, 235n8, 278, 280, 297
Collingwood, R. G., 256–257, 274
Columbia University, 13–15, 17
Comfort, Alex, 24
communication: belief and, 74–75; breakdown in, 92–93; ethics of, 60; fear of, 39–43, 51, 55; indirect, 45n10; poetry and, 14, 39–43, 51, 55, 57–64, 68, 74–75, 82, 90–100, 234–235
communism, 209–210. *See also* anti-communism
conscription law, 14, 44n7, 54

Con Spirito (literary magazine), 9
Contemporary Jewish Record (periodical), 8, 30–35
Copland, Aaron, 197n43
Coronet (magazine), 10
counterculture: American, 259n17, 262n25; literary, 244n7
Crane, Hart, 27, 65n16, 206, 208, 245, 258
Crane, Stephen, 203
Crosby, Bing, 199
Crosby, Harry, 245
Cullen, Countee, 115n4
Cultural Front, 10, 12
Cummings, E. E., 92, 206, 249, 293
Curtis, Mark, 252
Czolgosz, Leon, 111

Daiches, David, 88n26
Daily Worker, The (newspaper), 26, 210
Day-Lewis, Cecil, 208
Deborah (biblical figure), 305
Decision (periodical), 219
de la Mare, Walter, 224
democracy, 3, 7–8, 21–25, 34, 59, 145n1
Deutsch, Babette, 236
Dewey, John, 70n6
Dickens, Charles, 224
Dickinson, Emily, 23–25, 42n4, 185n3, 186–195, 232, 238, 240–241, 275, 296, 298
Dies Committee, 8. *See also* HUAC; Red Scare
di Prima, Diane, 27
Discovery (literary magazine), 11
dispossession, 19–20
Dollard, John, 73n13
Donne, John, 237–238
Dos Passos, John, 106, 106n9
Douglass, Aaron, 115n4
Dovzhenko, Alexander, 63
Downing, Marjorie, 253
dream-singing, 76, 97. *See also* Ghost Dance movement
Dryden, John, 58n2, 89
Duckworth, Elisabeth, 302
Duncan, Robert, 28, 128n4
Du Von, Jay, 206n15

Eberhart, Richard, 4, 24
Eckford, Elizabeth, 160n2
education, 18–19, 159–166, 257

INDEX

Einstein, Albert, 106n9
Eisenstein, Sergei, 63
Ekelöf, Gunnar, 267n1
Eliot, T. S., 3, 26–27, 63, 72–73, 75, 83, 95, 95n13, 203, 205, 209, 249–250, 252n2
Elizabeth, Queen, 306
Elizabethan period, 280–281
Ellis, Havelock, 225
Emerson, Ralph Waldo, 48, 65, 73–74, 83n12, 183, 190, 208–209, 278–280
emotion, 44, 146–147, 216, 256; poetry and, 42n3, 63–65, 72–73, 80, 186, 188, 227, 234, 256, 269, 306
Engdhal, J. Louis, 123. *See also* International Labor Defense; Scottsboro Boys case
epic poetry, 26–27, 208–210, 235n10, 271
Eshleman, Clayton, 274
experience, 2, 10–11, 27–28, 58–59, 70–71, 180–181, 224–226, 233–241, 254–268, 281–282, 293

fascism, 3, 24, 33–34, 150. *See also* Spanish Civil War
fear, 39–40; of communication, 39–43, 51, 55; of death, 108; of poetry, 39–56, 64, 82, 183, 185; uses of, 172–175; war and, 43–47
Fearing, Kenneth, 65n16, 87n23, 88n26, 215
Feinberg, Charles E., 277
feminism, 1–2, 4, 7, 10–12, 23
Fenichel, Otto, 260
Field, Sara Bard, 306
films, 12, 15, 59–65, 92
Flanagan, Hallie, 95n13
Fletcher, John Gould, 206
Flood, Charles Bracelen, 267
Forché, Carolyn, 18
Foreign Correspondent (1940), 61–64, 62n10
France, 54; Nazi occupation of, 15, 83n13. *See also* Maginot Line
Francis, Robert, 248
Franco, Francisco, 135n4, 175. *See also* Spanish Civil War
free speech movement, 9
Fromm, Erich, 260n18
Frontier Films, 10, 60n5
Frost, Robert, 24–26, 81n10, 204, 211–215, 245

Fry, Varian, 206n15
Fugitive poets, 81n10, 205n12
Fuller, Hank, 113n1
Funaroff, Sol, 95n11

Garner, Isabella, 236
gender equity, 8–9, 11, 26–29. *See also* feminism; motherhood
Ghost Dance movement, 76n17
Gibbs, Willard, 5, 22, 173, 250
Gibran, Khalil, 241n25
Ginsberg, Allen, 242n1, 244n5, 244n7, 245
Glück, Robert, 19
Godden, Rumer, 272
Goethe, Johann Wolfgang von, 278, 280
Goodman, Paul, 128n4
Goya, Francisco de, 146
Graham, Martha, 95n13
Grahn, Judy, 27
Graves, Morris, 243
Great Depression, 115n5, 125n8, 209n5
Gregory, Horace, 26–27, 65n16, 81n10, 95n11, 207n17, 208–210, 216n1
Grendel, 235
Guiteau, Charles, 111

Hamlet (Shakespeare), 263
Hanaghan, Jonathan, 260–261
Handy, W. C., 199
Harding, Walter, 277
Hariot, Thomas, 5, 181n3, 252n2, 280–281
Harlem Renaissance, 25
Harpers Ferry raid, 90–91
Hart, Jane, 11, 167n1
Hawthorne, Nathaniel, 15, 50, 74–75
Hayes, Alfred, 88n26, 95n11
Hayes, Ellen, 105
Hays, Arthur Garfield, 105
H. D. (Hilda Doolittle), 80–81, 203, 236n12, 306n10
Hemingway, Ernest, 86
Herbert, George, 236, 292, 293n10
Herring, Robert, 85nn15–16, 134n1
Hickerson, Harold, 106
Hiss, Alger, 174n9
Hitchcock, Alfred, 15, 60–61
Hitler Youth, 52, 73, 91
Hoffstein, Samuel, 207
Holiday, Billie, 196n39, 198–199

INDEX

"Hollywood 10" hearings, 1, 4n11
Holmes, John Haynes, 107
Holocaust, 272n13
Homer, 48
homophobia, 7, 23, 174n9
homosexuality. *See* queerness
Hoover, Herbert, 108n19, 115n5
Hopkins, Gerard Manley, 253
Hoskins, Katherine, 306n10
Houdini, Harry, 247
Hound and Horn (literary magazine), 206
Housatonic (magazine), 9, 16
Houseman, John, 95n13
HUAC (House Un-American Activities Committee), 1, 4, 8, 173n6, 174n9
Hughes, Langston, 25
human rights activism, 11-12
Hurston, Zora Neale, 17

illness, 9, 180, 278, 299, 301-302
imagination, 12, 14-15, 35, 39, 42, 44-49, 55-57, 74, 78-82, 88-89, 99, 173, 180-182, 213-214, 257-259, 285
Imagism, 80, 81n9, 82n11, 203
immediacy, 51, 98, 210
imperialist war state, 11, 15, 111. *See also* war
indigenous peoples, 76
inequality, 20, 76. *See also* gender equity; racism and racial justice; social justice
influences, 6, 8, 27-28, 64n14, 70n6, 106, 206-207, 210n6, 232-241, 260n18. *See also* canon
International Labor Defense (ILD), 124, 126
Italy, 31, 135n4. *See also* fascism
Ives, Charles, 194, 232, 250

Jackson, Andrew, 111
James, Henry, 247, 251
James, William, 266
Jarrell, Randall, 3
Jeffers, Robinson, 26, 79-80, 95, 203, 206, 209-211
Jespersen, Otto, 270, 274
Jewishness, 8, 30-35, 174, 262, 272; Yiddish, 272
Jim Crow. *See* segregation
Johns, Orrick, 245
Johns, Richard, 206n15
Johnson, Oakley, 9

Jolas, Eugene, 206n15
Jones, LeRoi. *See* Baraka, Amiri
Jordan, June, 27, 291n4
joy, 194, 270, 305
Joyce, James, 83n14
juvenile courts, 12, 20, 156-157

Kafka, Franz, 27, 72, 97-98, 298-303
KDFC (radio station), 21, 23, 184n1
Keats, John, 192, 263-265
Keene, Donald, 235
Keene, Frances, 274
Keigwin, R. P., 272n11
Kelvin, Baron (William Thomson), 71
Kenner, Hugh, 4
Kenyon Review (journal), 223
Kerouac, Jack, 244n7, 245
Kierkegaard, Søren, 15, 45, 72, 73n12, 75, 97
Kilmer, Joyce, 64, 70n4
Kim Vân Kiều (epic poem), 271
King, Carol Weiss, 124. *See also* International Labor Defense; Scottsboro Boys case
Kirstein, Lincoln, 206n15
Kohl, Herbert, 291
Korzybski, Alfred, 65n16

labor, 9-10, 295n18; organizers, 110n25, 111n29; strikes, 112, 136, 209n3
Laforgue, Jules, 205n11
Landor, Walter Savage, 274n17
languages, 268-269. *See also* translations
Laughlin, James, 24
Lavender Scare, 174n9. *See also* homophobia; Red Scare
Lawrence, D. H., 46, 269
Laws, Clarence, 160n3. *See also* NAACP
Lawton, John Howard, 105
Lead Belly, 196
Left, The (literary magazine), 206
leftist poetics, 81n10, 106n7
leftist politics, 1-4, 10-12, 16, 106n10, 121n15, 210, 244n6. *See also* anti-fascism; anti-racism; anti-war activism; civil disobedience; communism; New Left; radicalism; Sacco-Vanzetti case
Lehman, Henriette de Saussure Blanding, 252
Leishman, J. B., 221
lesbian poet-activists, 27. *See also* queerness
Levertov, Denise, 11, 28, 167n1

INDEX

Life (magazine), 10, 86
Life and Letters To-day (periodical), 10, 17, 86–87, 127, 134n1
Life is Beautiful (1930), 61
Limón, Ada, 18
Lincoln, Abraham, 51, 88, 111
Lindbergh, Anne, 235
Lindsay, Vachel, 203
Little Rock Nine, 18–19, 159–166
Locke, Alain, 17, 115n4
Lomax, Alan, 196n38
Lorca, Federico García, 26, 229–231, 265n36
Lorde, Audre, 27
Lowell, A. Lawrence, 103
Lowell, Amy, 82, 203
Lowell, Robert, 295
Luce, Henry, 86n21
lynching, 117, 120–121, 198n46

MacCracken, Henry, 13
MacDonald, Dwight, 3
MacLeish, Archibald, 26, 64, 95–96, 203–205
MacLeod, Norman, 207
MacNeice, Louis, 86
madness, 83–84, 93–94, 219, 230, 296–297. *See also* schizophrenia
Maginot Line, 45, 54, 149
Mahan, Alfred Thayer, 78
Mailer, Norman, 19
Marletto, Charlotte, 27, 224–228
marriage, 247, 299–301
Martin, Sara, 196n38, 199
masculinity, 19, 81n10, 152–155
Masters, Edgar Lee, 203, 215, 244n9
Matthiessen, F. O., 83n12, 278
Maxwell, James Clerk, 49, 94
Mayer, Elizabeth, 53n27
McAllister, Claire, 236
McCarthy, Mary, 9
McCausland, Elizabeth, 22
McCullers, Carson, 224
Melville, Herman, 5, 15, 50, 65n16, 69–70, 74–76, 85, 99, 185
Mercer, Johnny, 200n53
Meredith, Ellis, 225n6
Merwin, W. S., 237
Miles, Josephine, 236
Millay, Edna St. Vincent, 81n10, 105–106, 106n9, 108, 206, 245
Milton, John, 48, 269–270
Miriam (biblical figure), 305

Misch, Georg, 234
Mistral, Gabriela, 225
Montgomery, Olen. *See* Scottsboro Nine
Mooney, Tom, 111–112, 125
Moore, Marianne, 27, 236, 246–251, 254n6, 306n10
morality, 159n1, 168n2, 180, 182–183, 244n10, 249n15
Morehouse, Marion, 293
Morgenstern, Christian, 273
Morton, Jelly Roll, 196n38, 199
motherhood, 1, 11, 20, 28, 31–32, 123–125, 128, 161–162, 167, 301–302. *See also* children; pregnancy and birth
Mozart, Wolfgang Amadeus, 194
Murasaki Shikibu (Lady Murasaki), 235
Murray, John, 298
Muses, 226, 228, 234–235, 238n19, 263
music, 184–185, 190, 192, 194, 232–233; blues, 24–25, 195–200; jazz, 195; of poetry, 256; translations and, 267–271
Myles, Eileen, 19

NAACP (organization), 160, 162
Nash, Ogden, 207
Nation, The (periodical), 28, 306n10
National Student League, 9, 118n8
Naumburg, Nancy, 21
Nazi Germany, 33–34, 52, 73, 135n4. *See also* World War II
Nelson, Maggie, 19
New Critics, 81n10
New Journalism, 19, 159n1
New Left, 12, 259n17
New Masses (magazine), 10
New Narrative, 19
New Republic (periodical), 306n10
New Statesman (periodical, U.K.), 11, 18
New Theatre (magazine), 10
New Theatre League (organization), 10, 95n11
Newton, Isaac, 59
New York City, 30, 152–158; juvenile courts, 12, 20; literary scenes, 12
New York Herald Tribune (newspaper), 10
New York Times (newspaper), 16, 104
Nguyên Du, 271n10
Niebuhr, Reinhold, 115n4
92nd Street YMHA/YWHA, 207n17, 229n1

INDEX

nonviolence, 11–12, 108n19, 284–285. *See also* civil disobedience
Norris, Clarence. *See* Scottsboro Nine
Norton, M. D. Herter, 220–223

Office of War Information (O. W. I.), 2, 12, 18, 64n13, 144–149, 145n1
Old Testament, 234, 237
Olson, Charles, 28
Olympics (1936), 134n2. *See also* People's (Workers') Olympiad
O'Neill, Eugene, 163
Oppenheim, James, 245
Oxford Book of English Verse, 47

Pagany (literary magazine), 206
Paley, Grace, 291n4
Parker, Charlie, 195n36
Parker, Dorothy, 106n9, 207
Parkhurst, Helen, 20
Patchen, Kenneth, 14
Patterson, Haywood, 113n1, 117, 124–125. *See also* Scottsboro Nine
Patterson, Janie, 123–124. *See also* Scottsboro Boys case
Pavlov, Ivan Petrovich, 70
Paxinou, Katina, 229n1
Payne, Robert, 267, 275n22
Paz, Octavio, 267n1, 270
peace, 47, 150–151; poetry and, 77–89. *See also* anti-war activism
PEN American Center (organization), 169, 267n1, 274n18, 275n22, 303n25
People's (Workers') Olympiad, 10, 17, 85n15, 127, 130–137, 141–144
perception, 18, 98–99; visual, 180–181
photography, 21–22, 179–183
Planned Parenthood (organization), 296. *See also* reproductive rights
Plath, Sylvia, 295
plays, 91–92, 94–95. *See also* theater
poetry: abstract, 273; aesthetics and poetics of, 26–27; American, 237–238; American, trends in modern, 203–207; anti-war activism and translation of, 271n10; belief and, 67–76, 81–83, 89; communication and, 14, 39–43, 51, 55, 57–64, 68, 74–75, 82, 90–100, 234–235; concrete, 273; confessional, 290–297; definitions of, 254; emotion and, 42n3, 63–65, 72–73, 80, 186, 188, 227, 234, 256, 269, 306; epic, 26–27, 208–210, 235n10, 271; fear of, 39–56, 64, 82, 183, 185; found language and, 250; immediacy in, 98; Japanese, 235; lyric, 197, 242–245; magazines, 206–207; modernist, 16; movements in, 81–83; music of, 256; New American Poetry, 28; pastoral, 280; peace and, 77–89; resistance and, 15; science and, 257; social, 79, 81n10, 87; social transformation and, 26–29; sonnets, 237; Thoreau and, 277–289; unverifiable facts and, 252–266; war and, 24, 77–89, 150–151; "where, in all this, is the place for poetry?," 17, 20, 41–42, 45, 54, 56, 157; women's, 232–241, 304–307; workshops on, 13–14
Poetry: A Magazine of Verse, 14, 215, 228
political repression, 1–2, 12. *See also* anti-communism
politics: aesthetics and, 1–29; contemporary sociopolitical climate, 12; postwar sociopolitical climate, 1–4. *See also* anti-fascism; anti-racism; anti-war activism; civil disobedience; communism; leftist politics; New Left; radicalism; Sacco-Vanzetti case
Popular Front, 27, 128n4, 131, 136, 139n16, 140n19, 142–144, 259n17
Porter, Katherine Anne, 56
Potter, Beatrix, 251
Pound, Ezra, 3–4, 6, 24, 65n16, 72, 80n8, 82n11, 170n7, 197n41, 203n2, 205, 259
Powell, Ozie. *See* Scottsboro Nine
Powell v. Alabama (1932), 124n5. *See also* Scottsboro Boys case
pregnancy and birth, 1–2, 19–20, 63, 112, 155–158, 224–228, 298. *See also* children; motherhood; reproductive rights
Price, Victoria, 113n1, 123, 125. *See also* Scottsboro Boys case
prison-industrial complex, 11–12
Project Nuremberg Obligation (organization), 171n8
propaganda, 18, 145–149
prostitution. *See* sex work

queerness, 1, 5, 7, 23, 25, 27–28, 187–188, 190n20, 192n25, 196n40, 305

Rabassa, Gregory, 271n9
Rabelais, François, 225n5
racism and racial justice, 7, 9-11, 16-19, 24, 111-126, 145n2, 159-166. *See also* anti-racism; lynching
radicalism, 1-2, 5, 7-10, 12, 16-21, 105, 108. *See also* leftist politics; Sacco-Vanzetti case
radio programs, 21, 23-25, 184-200
Raine, Kathleen, 237, 306n10
Raleigh, Sir Walter, 280-282
Rank, Otto, 226, 239
Rankine, Claudia, 18
Ransom, John Crowe, 81n10
rape, 9, 114n2, 124, 126
Read, Herbert, 128n4
realism, 97-98, 182-183, 212, 264
Redfield, George, 206n15
Redress (organization), 168
Red Scare, 244n6. *See also* anti-communism
refugees, 12, 14-15, 35, 41, 44, 46, 52, 54-55, 87-88
Reich, Wilhelm, 260n18
religion, 35, 74-75, 223, 225. *See also* Jewishness
repetition, 65-66, 196, 238
Replansky, Naomi, 236
reproductive rights, 20, 296n21, 298. *See also* pregnancy and birth
revolution, 63, 105, 129, 137-138. *See also* Spanish Civil War
revolutionary poetics, 25, 27, 208-210
Rexroth, Kenneth, 27, 128n4, 241-245
rhyme, 19, 48, 166, 185, 196, 238, 247, 253; repeating, 65-66
rhythms, 75, 204, 255-256, 266, 280
Rich, Adrienne, 27
Richards, I. A., 65n16
Ridge, Lola, 106n9
Ridler, Anne, 225-226
Rilke, Rainer Maria, 26, 71, 220-223, 272-273
Rimbaud, Arthur, 65n16, 267n1
Roberson, Willie. *See* Scottsboro Nine
Robeson, Paul, 196n39
Robinson, Edwin Arlington, 204, 215, 244n9
Roe v. Wade (1973). *See* reproductive rights
Roosevelt, Franklin Delano, 92n5
Rosenberg, Julius and Ethel, 16, 172, 174-175

Rosenthal, M. L., 251
Rossetti, Christina, 305
Roth, Henry, 224
Roth, Philip, 293n10
Rukeyser, Muriel: children's books, 5; criticism on, 6; Jewishness, 8, 30-35; journalism, 7, 16-21; motherhood, 1; photo-essays, 21-22; political activism, arrests for, 118-121, 167-170; as public intellectual, 26; queerness, 1, 5; radical politics, 1-2, 5, 7-10, 12, 16-21
—BIOGRAPHIES: *One Life*, 5
—PAINTINGS: *The Four Fears*, 28
—PLAYS: *Arabian Nights*, 64n14; *Houdini: A Musical*, 5; *The Middle of the Air*, 1, 95n13, 199n48, 235n11; *The Traces of Thomas Hariot*, 5, 257n10; *Willard Gibbs*, 5, 71n8, 90n1, 173
—POETRY, 2-7, 13; "Ajanta," 250n21, 306; "Akiba," 31n4; "Ann Burlak," 304n1, 306; "Are You Born?," 259n15; *The Book of the Dead*, 5, 9, 21, 27; "Easter Eve, 1945," 2; *Elegies*, 5, 5n13; "Elegy in Joy," 2; "Eyes of Night-Time," 2; "From 'To the Unborn Child,'" 53n27; "Gibbs," 250n21; *The Green Wave*, 1-3, 5, 197n41; "Ives," 250n21; "Käthe Kollwitz," 28, 304n1; "Leg in a Plastic Cast," 66n19; "Letter to the Front," 69n3, 145n1, 262n23; "M-Day's Child," 262n22; "The Minotaur", 66n19; "Nine Poems for the Unborn Child," 2; *Selected Poems*, 5n13, 10; "Song," 259n15; *Theory of Flight*, 13, 168; *A Turning Wind*, 13; *U.S. 1*, 13, 269; "Waterlily Fire," 155n2; "Water Night," 2; "The Writer," 276
—PROSE, 3-29; "Barcelona, 1936," 17, 134-144; "Barcelona on the Barricades," 17, 127-133; "The Classic Ground," 27, 216-219; "The Club" (story), 19n44; "A Crystal for the Metaphysical", 27, 246-251; "The Flown Arrow," 16, 103-112; "From Scottsboro to Decatur," 17, 113-122; "Glitter and Wounds, Several Wildnesses," 27, 290-297; "In a Speaking Voice," 26, 211-215; "The Killing of the Children," 16, 20, 167-171; *The Life of Poetry*, 5, 13-15, 23, 185n4; "The Life to Which I Belong", 27, 298-303; "Little" (story),

336   INDEX

—PROSE (continued)
19n44; "Long Step Ahead Taken by Gregory in New Epic Poem," 208–210; "A Lorca Evening", 26, 229–231; "Lyrical 'Rage,'" 27, 242–245; "Many Keys," 28, 232–241, 306n10; "Modern Trends: American Poetry," 26, 203–207; "The Music of Translation", 26, 267–276; "Nearer to the Well-Spring," 26, 220–223; "Opening Convocation" (lecture), 252n2; *The Orgy* (memoir), 5; "A Pane of Glass" (story), 19–20, 152–158; "Poetry and the People" (lectures), 13–14; "Poetry and the Unverifiable Fact" (lecture), 26, 252–266; *Savage Coast* (novel), 5, 10, 20n48, 157n3; "She Came to Us," 18–19, 159–166; "A Simple Theme", 27, 224–228; "So Easy to See," 21–22, 179–183; *Sunday at Nine* (radio broadcasts), 21, 23–25, 184–200; "Thoreau and Poetry," 26, 277–289; *The Usable Truth* (lectures), 1–3, 13–16, 26, 29, 39–100; "Belief and Poetry" (lecture), 67–76; "Communication and Poetry" (lecture), 14, 90–100; "The Fear of Poetry" (lecture), 14, 39–56, 96n15; "Poetry and Peace" (lecture), 77–89; "The Speed of the Image" (lecture), 57–66; "The Uses of Fear", 16, 172–175; "War and Poetry," 18, 150–151; "We Came for Games" (story), 6n15, 17n39, 19n44; "We Came for Games" (story cycle), 19n44; "Women and Scottsboro," 17, 123–126; "Women of Words: A Preface," 27, 304–307; "Words and Images," 18, 145–149

Sacco, Nicola. *See* Sacco-Vanzetti case
Sacco-Vanzetti case, 16, 103–112, 125
Sachs, Nelly, 267n1, 270
Sagarin, Edward, 113n1
Sandburg, Charles, 81n10, 204, 294
Sappho, 234, 305
Sarton, George, 257–258
Sarton, May, 236
Sartre, Jean-Paul, 15
Saturday Review of Literature (periodical), 13, 245, 251
Savage, Augusta, 17, 115n4
schizophrenia, 83n14
science, 21–22, 49, 70–71, 181n3, 182, 257, 281

Scottsboro Boys case, 9–10, 17, 111–126
Scottsboro Nine, 17, 112n33, 113n1, 125n8
Scripps College, 252nn1–2, 257n9
seeing. *See* sight
Seferis, George, 24
segregation, 17–19, 117, 159–166
Sexton, Anne, 27, 290–297
sexuality, 4, 230–231, 292–297, 304. *See also* queerness
sex work, 32, 114n2, 124–126, 197n42
Shakespeare, William, 91, 94–95, 166n20, 263
Sharif, Solmaz, 18
Shaw, George Bernard, 106n9
Sheridan, Richard Brinsley, 45
Sherwood, Robert, 173
sight, 22, 179–182
silence, 92; Dickinson and, 190, 192; Sacco-Vanzetti case and, 105
Sinclair, Upton, 106, 106n9
Singer, Isaac Bashevis, 272, 275–276
Sitwell, Edith, 225
Smith, Bessie, 196–198
Smith, Mamie, 196n37
Snow, C. P., 257n11
social justice, 8, 11–12, 21, 76. *See also* anti-racism; feminism; leftist politics
social transformation, 18
Sokolsky, George, 32, 33n7
Sontag, Susan, 18
Southern Agrarians, 81n10, 205n12
Spanish Civil War, 1, 10, 13, 17, 41, 85n15, 95n10, 127–144, 141n21, 157n3
Spender, Stephen, 208, 225
Stein, Gertrude, 66, 96n13, 238
Stern, James, 302
Stettheimer, Florine, 96n13
Stevens, Wallace, 79–80, 206, 251
Stoppard, Tom, 263n28
strikes. *See* labor
student activism, 9–10, 113–122
Student Review (periodical), 9, 17, 118n8
Supersight photography (Abbott), 22, 181nn1–2
surrealists, 63
Suzuki, D. T., 275
Swenson, May, 236

Taggard, Genevieve, 81n10, 225, 245
Tarkington, Booth, 224

Tate, Allen, 81n10, 206
Teasdale, Sara, 245
Tennyson, Alfred, 64
Thayer, Webster, 103, 105
theater, 12, 91–92, 94–95, 206n14, 247n3, 263n28; Greek theater, 230. *See also* plays
39 Steps, The (1935), 60–61
Thomas, Dylan, 24, 243–244
Thomson, Virgil, 96n13
Thoreau, Henry David, 11, 83n12, 277–289
Tiempo, El (newspaper, Mexico), 146–147
Tin Pan Alley, 197
Tischter, Ernest, 20n48, 157n3
Toller, Ernst, 95n13
Townshend, Petrie, 134n1
tradition, 45–46, 74–75, 77–78, 96–97, 99–100
transition (literary magazine), 206
translations, 267–276
Trent, Lucia, 109
troubadours, in Provence, 24, 197
truth, 281–282, 290; Dickinson and, 187; reality and, 179, 183; usable, 50–51, 74–76, 85, 99–100
Twain, Mark, 224

Untermeyer, Louis, 13, 214, 249–250, 254, 305

Valéry, Paul, 220–221
Vallejo, César, 274
van Paassen, Pierre, 33
Vanzetti, Bartolomeo. *See* Sacco-Vanzetti case
Vassar College, 9, 13–14, 203n1
Vassar Miscellany News (newspaper), 9, 26, 207
Vaughan, Henry, 236
Vietnam conflict, 11, 16–17, 167–171, 259n16, 268n2, 277n1, 285, 295n18
violence, 12, 91, 99, 110, 230; nonviolence and, 261, 284–285. *See also* lynching
visual arts, 180–182; war posters, 145–149. *See also* films; photography

Walker, Alice, 27
Walker, Margaret, 236
war, 17–18; air raids, 78n3, 96, 155; fear and, 43–47; poetry and, 24, 77–89, 150–151; powerlessness and, 259.

See also Spanish Civil War; Vietnam conflict; World War I; World War II
waste, 28, 47, 79, 237–238, 304
Watson, David Lindsay, 70–71
Weems, Charley. *See* Scottsboro Nine
Welch, Marie de Laveaga, 225, 236, 240, 285, 306
Welles, Orson, 95n10, 96
Wells, H. G., 106n9
Wheelwright, John (Jack), 245
White, Josh, 25, 198–199, 199nn48–49
Whitehead, Alfred North, 70n6
white supremacy, 11, 19, 73n13. *See also* racism and racial justice
Whitman, Walt, 47, 50, 238, 240, 278
wildness, 69, 229, 278–280, 288–297
Williams, Clarence, 196n38
Williams, Eugene. *See* Scottsboro Nine
Williams, Tennessee, 247
Williams, William Carlos, 3, 65n16, 206, 207n17, 224, 251, 259
Willkie, Wendell, 5, 64n14, 93n5
Wilson, Woodrow, 111
Wolfe, Thomas, 224
Wolfert, Helen, 236
Wolff, Helen, 303
Wolff, Kurt, 303
Woman Alone, The (1936), 61
women: as artists, 226; greatness and, 67; marginalization of women writers, 28; poets, 232–241, 304–307; Scottsboro case and, 123–126
women's colleges, 253. *See also* Scripps College; Vassar College
Wordsworth, Dorothy, 217n3, 218–219
Wordsworth, William, 64, 83, 297
Works Progress Administration, 22, 95n13
World of Translation, The (1971), 276
World Split Open, The (Berkinow, ed.), 27–28, 304–307, 304n1
World War I, 79, 150, 209n5, 301
World War II, 14–15, 43–47, 52–54, 83–87; air raids, 78n3; Moore and, 248n12, 249n15; US neutrality in, 100n24, 235n11; US propaganda posters, 145–149
Wovoka (Jack Wilson), 76n17. *See also* Ghost Dance movement
Wright, Ada, 123–124. *See also* Scottsboro Boys case
Wright, Andy. *See* Scottsboro Nine
Wright, C. D., 18

Wright, Frank Lloyd, 238
Wright, Roy. *See* Scottsboro Nine
Writers and Teachers Collaborative, 291
Wulf und Eadwacer (epic poem), 235
Wylie, Elinor, 81n10, 206, 245, 293

xenophobia, 111–112

Yeats, William Butler, 65n16, 215

Zaturenska, Marya, 27, 216–219, 236, 305–306, 306n10

Milton Keynes UK
Ingram Content Group UK Ltd.
UKHW012149111023
430419UK00005B/390